QOHELETH (ECCLESIASTES)

WISDOM COMMENTARY

Volume 24

Qoheleth (Ecclesiastes)

Lisa Michele Wolfe

Athalya Brenner-Idan
Volume Editor

Barbara E. Reid, OP
General Editor

A Michael Glazier Book

LITURGICAL PRESS

Collegeville, Minnesota

www.litpress.org

A Michael Glazier Book published by Liturgical Press

1   2   3   4   5   6   7   8   9

Library of Congress Cataloging-in-Publication Data

Names: Wolfe, Lisa M. (Lisa Michele), author. | Brenner-Idan, Athalya, editor, writer of foreword. | Reid, Barbara E., editor, writer of introduction.
Title: Qoheleth (Ecclesiastes) / Lisa Michele Wolfe ; Athalya Brenner-Idan, volume editor ; Barbara E. Reid, OP, general editor.
Description: Collegeville, Minnesota : Liturgical Press, [2020] | Series: Wisdom commentary ; volume 24 | "A Michael Glazier Book." | Includes bibliographical references and index. | Summary: "This commentary on Qoheleth (Ecclesiastes) provides a feminist interpretation of Scripture in serious, scholarly engagement with the whole text, not only those texts that explicitly mention women. It addresses not only issues of gender but also those of power, authority, ethnicity, racism, and classism" —Provided by publisher.
Identifiers: LCCN 2019029635 (print) | LCCN 2019029636 (ebook) | ISBN 9780814681237 (hardcover) | ISBN 9780814681480 (epub) | ISBN 9780814681480 (mobi) | ISBN 9780814681480 (pdf)
Subjects: LCSH: Bible. Ecclesiastes—Feminist criticism. | Bible. Ecclesiastes—Commentaries. | Women in the Bible.
Classification: LCC BS1475.52 .W65 2020 (print) | LCC BS1475.52 (ebook) | DDC 223/.806082—dc23
LC record available at https://lccn.loc.gov/2019029635
LC ebook record available at https://lccn.loc.gov/2019029636

Dedicated to Mom, the first one to teach me the power of feminism

Contents

Acknowledgments   ix

List of Abbreviations   xi

List of Contributors   xv

Foreword: *"Tell It on the Mountain"*—or, *"And You Shall Tell Your Daughter [as Well]"*   xvii
  Athalya Brenner-Idan

Editor's Introduction to Wisdom Commentary:
  "She Is a Breath of the Power of God" (Wis 7:25)   xxi
  Barbara E. Reid, OP

Author's Introduction: A Feminist Toolbox for Interpreting Qoheleth   xli

Qoheleth 1:1-18   Learning Qoheleth's Language   1

Qoheleth 2:1-26   A Test: Is Pleasure *Hevel*?   17

Qoheleth 3:1-22   What Time?   37

Qoheleth 4:1–5:20 [19]   From *Hevel* to *Carpe Diem* and Much in Between   63

Qoheleth 6:1–7:14   Good, Better, Wise   83

Qoheleth 7:15-29   On Wisdom and Women (or Woman Wisdom)   99

Qoheleth 8:1–9:6   From Wisdom to Death   127

Qoheleth 9:7-18   *Carpe Diem* and Related Imperatives   141

Qoheleth 10:1–12:14   Closing Advice and Epilogue   151

Afterword: Qoheleth as a Model for Feminist Hermeneutics   167

Works Cited   173

Index of Scripture References and Other Ancient Writings   185

Index of Subjects   197

Acknowledgments

Thanks to:

Harold Washington, my long-time colleague and friend, for all your conversations with me over the years about Qoheleth, often in front of a class. I am eternally grateful to you for getting me started on this project.

Fred Mischler, my dear husband, as it was no small thing to support me over the years on this project. Thank you especially for enduring the fact that I found Qoheleth-isms in absolutely everything. Thank you for helping me prioritize and for helping to clear writing time for me.

Bram and Phoebe, for your patience with me during summers and evenings and Saturdays when it seemed like I should not have had to be working.

Christina and Jerry Young, Katy Wolfe, Jonah and Amelia Zahn, and Beth Kloker, for all the extra "summer camps" you created for the kids while I was writing.

Kathleen R. Farmer, who got me started on this journey with Qoheleth back in 1995. Thanks more than twenty years later for reading part of my manuscript and providing helpful feedback.

The remarkable students, faculty, and staff of the Wimberly School of Religion at Oklahoma City University, for support, encouragement, collegiality, patience, and chocolate. I couldn't ask for a better community.

All the students who have discussed Qoheleth with me in undergraduate, seminary, temple, and church classrooms (and even a Sukkah); thank you for providing your insights and for listening to me teach about Qoheleth no matter what topic we were supposed to be learning.

Oklahoma City University, for giving me a sabbatical in fall 2015, a grant to fund my research assistants in 2018, and a quiet (in the summer) second-floor office with a view.

Saint Paul's Episcopal Cathedral in Oklahoma City, for giving me writing space in fall 2015; especially the Rev. Canon Mother Susan Colley Joplin and Cathy O'Connor and the Ignatian Retreat in Daily Life Group, for helping me stay grounded while I wrote that fall; thanks to Brian Speers and Gigi, for greeting me so warmly every morning.

Catie and Robbie Knight, for child care help and general moral support.

The Book Club, for encouragement and cheerleading.

Peyton Wagner and Jenny Johnson, for help with the Hebrew and the footnotes, and Blake Bulger, for help on the Scripture index.

Athalya Brenner-Idan, for including positive feedback and encouragement with your lists of edits. It was a true honor and privilege to work with you.

Barbara Reid, for your gentle and calm management of this project and for having the vison to start it in the first place.

LMW
From the Library overlooking the Cloister at Saint Paul's
Episcopal Cathedral, OKC,
Various coffee shops and libraries all over the country,
And the West Wing of the Gold Star Building
at Oklahoma City University
Oklahoma City, Oklahoma

Abbreviations

AB	Anchor Bible
ABD	*Anchor Bible Dictionary*
AOTC	Abingdon Old Testament Commentaries
BAR	*Biblical Archaeology Review*
BCE	Before the Common Era
BDB	*Brown Driver Briggs and Gesenius Hebrew-English Lexicon*
BH	Biblical Hebrew
BHS	*Biblia Hebraica Stuttgartensia*
BHQ	*Biblia Hebraica Quinta*
BibInt	Biblical Interpretation
BJS	Brown Judaic Studies
BLS	Bible and Literature Series
CE	Common Era
CEB	Common English Bible
CTR	*Criswell Theological Review*
DSS	Dead Sea Scrolls
ERV	English Revised Version (1885)
FCB	Feminist Companion to the Bible
GBS	Guides to Biblical Scholarship
HUCA	*Hebrew Union College Annual*

IBC	Interpretation: A Bible Commentary for Teaching and Preaching
IFT	Introductions in Feminist Theology
Int	*Interpretation*
ITC	International Theological Commentary
JBL	*Journal of Biblical Literature*
JFSR	*Journal of Feminist Studies in Religion*
JHebS	*Journal of Hebrew Scriptures*
JPS	Jewish Publication Society
JSOT	*Journal for the Study of the Old Testament*
JSOTSup	Journal for the Study of the Old Testament Supplement series
JTS	*Journal of Theological Studies*
KJV	King James Version
LXX	Septuagint
MH	*Mishnaic Hebrew*
MT	Masoretic Text
NASB	New American Standard Bible
NEA	*Near Eastern Archaeology* (formerly *Biblical Archaeologist*)
NET	New English Translation
NIB	*New Interpreter's Bible*
NICOT	New International Commentary on the Old Testament
NIDB	*New Interpreter's Dictionary of the Bible*
NIRV	New International Reader's Version
NISB	*New Interpreter's Study Bible*
NIV	New International Version
NJB	New Jerusalem Bible
NJPS	New Jewish Publication Society Translation
NLT	New Living Translation
NRSV	New Revised Standard Version
OBT	Overtures to Biblical Theology

OTL	Old Testament Library
OTM	Old Testament Message
RSV	Revised Standard Version
SBLDS	Society of Biblical Literature Dissertation Series
SymS	Symposium Series
TDOT	*Theological Dictionary of the Old Testament*. Edited by G. Johannes Botterweck and Helmer Ringgren. Translated by John T. Willis et al. 8 vols. Grand Rapids: Eerdmans, 1974–2006.
ThTo	*Theology Today*
TSAJ	Texte und Studien zum antiken Judentum
USQR	*Union Seminary Quarterly Review*
VT	*Vetus Testamentum*
WBC	Word Biblical Commentary
WTJ	*Westminster Theological Journal*
ZAW	*Zeitschrift für die alttestamentliche Wissenschaft*

Contributors

Mercedes L. García Bachmann has a PhD in Old Testament from the Lutheran School of Theology at Chicago (LSTC). She taught for almost twenty years at the ecumenical school of theology in Buenos Aires (Isedet). Currently she directs the Institute for Contextual Pastoral Studies for the United Evangelical Lutheran Church (Argentina-Uruguay) and teaches online for her alma mater and for other schools.

Dr. Athalya Brenner-Idan is professor emerita of the Hebrew Bible/Old Testament Chair, Universiteit van Amsterdam, The Netherlands, formerly at the Bible Department, Tel Aviv University, Israel; and now research associate at the Free State University, South Africa.

Ora Brison received her PhD from Tel Aviv University, department of Jewish Studies (2015). Her research interests include gender-critical readings of the Bible, contextual readings of biblical texts, and their reception in contemporary Israeli Jewish societies.

Laura Choate, a native American of the Choctaw people, was a founding board member of Herland Sister Resources and Oklahoma Institute for Child Advocacy. She was one of the eight named plaintiffs in the 1978 class action "Terry D lawsuit." She manages the Church of the Open Arms, UCC food pantry in Oklahoma City.

Funlola O. Olojede is a research fellow with the Gender Unit of the Faculty of Theology, Stellenbosch University, South Africa.

Marie Turner is an adjunct senior lecturer in biblical studies at Flinders University in South Australia, Australia.

Foreword

"Tell It on the Mountain"—or, "And You Shall Tell Your Daughter [as Well]"

Athalya Brenner-Idan

Universiteit van Amsterdam/Tel Aviv University

What can Wisdom Commentary do to help, and for whom? The commentary genre has always been privileged in biblical studies. Traditionally acclaimed commentary series, such as the International Critical Commentary, Old Testament and New Testament Library, Hermeneia, Anchor Bible, Eerdmans, and Word—to name but several— enjoy nearly automatic prestige, and the number of women authors who participate in those is relatively small by comparison to their growing number in the scholarly guild. There certainly are some volumes written by women in them, especially in recent decades. At this time, however, this does not reflect the situation on the ground. Further, size matters. In that sense, the sheer size of the Wisdom Commentary is essential. This also represents a considerable investment and the possibility of reaching a wider audience than those already "converted."

Expecting women scholars to deal especially or only with what are considered strictly "female" matters seems unwarranted. According to Audre Lorde, "The master's tools will never dismantle the master's house."[1] But this maxim is not relevant to our case. The point of this commentary is not to destroy but to attain greater participation in the interpretive dialogue about biblical texts. Women scholars may bring additional questions to the readerly agenda as well as fresh angles to existing issues. To assume that their questions are designed only to topple a certain male hegemony is not convincing.

At first I did ask myself: is this commentary series an addition to calm raw nerves, an embellishment to make upholding the old hierarchy palatable? Or is it indeed about becoming the Master? On second and third thoughts, however, I understood that becoming the Master is not what this is about. Knowledge is power. Since Foucault at the very least, this cannot be in dispute. Writing commentaries for biblical texts by feminist women and men for women and for men, of confessional as well as non-confessional convictions, will sabotage (hopefully) the established hierarchy but will not topple it. This is about an attempt to integrate more fully, to introduce another viewpoint, to become. What excites me about the Wisdom Commentary is that it is not offered as just an alternative supplanting or substituting for the dominant discourse.

These commentaries on biblical books will retain nonauthoritative, pluralistic viewpoints. And yes, once again, the weight of a dedicated series, to distinguish from collections of stand-alone volumes, will prove weightier.

That such an approach is especially important in the case of the Hebrew Bible/Old Testament is beyond doubt. Women of Judaism, Christianity, and also Islam have struggled to make it their own for centuries, even more than they have fought for the New Testament and the Qur'an. Every Hebrew Bible/Old Testament volume in this project is evidence that the day has arrived: it is now possible to read *all* the Jewish canonical books as a collection, for a collection they are, with guidance conceived of with the needs of women readers (not only men) as an integral inspiration and part thereof.

In my Jewish tradition, the main motivation for reciting the Haggadah, the ritual text recited yearly on Passover, the festival of liberation from

---

1. Audre Lorde, "The Master's Tools Will Never Dismantle the Master's House," in *Sister Outsider: Essays and Speeches* (Berkeley, CA: Crossing Press, 1984, 2007), 110–14. First delivered in the Second Sex Conference in New York, 1979.

bondage, is given as "And you shall tell your son" (from Exod 13:8). The knowledge and experience of past generations is thus transferred to the next, for constructing the present and the future. The ancient maxim is, literally, limited to a male audience. This series remolds the maxim into a new inclusive shape, which is of the utmost consequence: "And you shall tell your son" is extended to "And you shall tell your daughter [as well as your son]." Or, if you want, "Tell it on the mountain," for all to hear.

This is what it's all about.

Editor's Introduction to Wisdom Commentary

"She Is a Breath of the Power of God" (Wis 7:25)

Barbara E. Reid, OP

General Editor

Wisdom Commentary is the first series to offer detailed feminist interpretation of every book of the Bible. The fruit of collaborative work by an ecumenical and interreligious team of scholars, the volumes provide serious, scholarly engagement with the whole biblical text, not only those texts that explicitly mention women. The series is intended for clergy, teachers, ministers, and all serious students of the Bible. Designed to be both accessible and informed by the various approaches of biblical scholarship, it pays particular attention to the world in front of the text, that is, how the text is heard and appropriated. At the same time, this series aims to be faithful to the ancient text and its earliest audiences; thus the volumes also explicate the worlds behind the text and within it. While issues of gender are primary in this project, the volumes also address the intersecting issues of power, authority, ethnicity, race, class, and religious belief and practice. The fifty-eight volumes include the books regarded as canonical by Jews (i.e., the Tanakh); Protestants (the "Hebrew Bible" and the New Testament); and Roman Catholic, Anglican, and Eastern Orthodox

Communions (i.e., Tobit, Judith, 1 and 2 Maccabees, Wisdom of Solomon, Sirach/Ecclesiasticus, Baruch, including the Letter of Jeremiah, the additions to Esther, and Susanna and Bel and the Dragon in Daniel).

A Symphony of Diverse Voices

Included in the Wisdom Commentary series are voices from scholars of many different religious traditions, of diverse ages, differing sexual identities, and varying cultural, racial, ethnic, and social contexts. Some have been pioneers in feminist biblical interpretation; others are newer contributors from a younger generation. A further distinctive feature of this series is that each volume incorporates voices other than that of the lead author(s). These voices appear alongside the commentary of the lead author(s), in the grayscale inserts. At times, a contributor may offer an alternative interpretation or a critique of the position taken by the lead author(s). At other times, she or he may offer a complementary interpretation from a different cultural context or subject position. Occasionally, portions of previously published material bring in other views. The diverse voices are not intended to be contestants in a debate or a cacophony of discordant notes. The multiple voices reflect that there is no single definitive feminist interpretation of a text. In addition, they show the importance of subject position in the process of interpretation. In this regard, the Wisdom Commentary series takes inspiration from the Talmud and from *The Torah: A Women's Commentary* (ed. Tamara Cohn Eskenazi and Andrea L. Weiss; New York: Women of Reform Judaism, Federation of Temple Sisterhood, 2008), in which many voices, even conflicting ones, are included and not harmonized.

Contributors include biblical scholars, theologians, and readers of Scripture from outside the scholarly and religious guilds. At times, their comments pertain to a particular text. In some instances they address a theme or topic that arises from the text.

Another feature that highlights the collaborative nature of feminist biblical interpretation is that a number of the volumes have two lead authors who have worked in tandem from the inception of the project and whose voices interweave throughout the commentary.

Woman Wisdom

The title, Wisdom Commentary, reflects both the importance to feminists of the figure of Woman Wisdom in the Scriptures and the distinct wisdom that feminist women and men bring to the interpretive process. In the Scriptures, Woman Wisdom appears as "a breath of the power of God, and a pure emanation of the glory of the Almighty" (Wis 7:25), who was present and active in fashioning all that exists (Prov 8:22-31; Wis 8:6). She is a spirit who pervades and penetrates all things (Wis 7:22-23), and she provides guidance and nourishment at her all-inclusive table (Prov 9:1-5). In both postexilic biblical and nonbiblical Jewish sources, Woman Wisdom is often equated with Torah, e.g., Sirach 24:23-34; Baruch 3:9–4:4; 38:2; 46:4-5; 2 Baruch 48:33, 36; 4 Ezra 5:9-10; 13:55; 14:40; 1 Enoch 42.

The New Testament frequently portrays Jesus as Wisdom incarnate. He invites his followers, "take my yoke upon you and learn from me" (Matt 11:29), just as Ben Sira advises, "put your neck under her [Wisdom's] yoke and let your souls receive instruction" (Sir 51:26). Just as Wisdom experiences rejection (Prov 1:23-25; Sir 15:7-8; Wis 10:3; Bar 3:12), so too does Jesus (Mark 8:31; John 1:10-11). Only some accept his invitation to his all-inclusive banquet (Matt 22:1-14; Luke 14:15-24; compare Prov 1:20-21; 9:3-5). Yet, "wisdom is vindicated by her deeds" (Matt 11:19, speaking of Jesus and John the Baptist; in the Lucan parallel at 7:35 they are called "wisdom's children"). There are numerous parallels between what is said of Wisdom and of the *Logos* in the Prologue of the Fourth Gospel (John 1:1-18). These are only a few of many examples. This female embodiment of divine presence and power is an apt image to guide the work of this series.

Feminism

There are many different understandings of the term "feminism." The various meanings, aims, and methods have developed exponentially in recent decades. Feminism is a perspective and a movement that springs from a recognition of inequities toward women, and it advocates for changes in whatever structures prevent full flourishing of human beings and all creation. Three waves of feminism in the United States are commonly recognized. The first, arising in the mid-nineteenth century and lasting into the early twentieth, was sparked by women's efforts to be involved in the public sphere and to win the right to vote. In the 1960s and 1970s, the second wave focused on civil rights and equality for women. With the third wave, from the 1980s forward, came global feminism and the emphasis on the contextual nature of interpretation. Now a fourth wave may be emerging, with a stronger emphasis on the intersectionality of women's concerns with those of other marginalized groups and the increased use of the internet as a platform for discussion and activism.[1] As feminism has matured, it has recognized that inequities based on gender are interwoven with power imbalances based on race, class, ethnicity, religion, sexual identity, physical ability, and a host of other social markers.

Feminist Women and Men

Men who choose to identify with and partner with feminist women in the work of deconstructing systems of domination and building structures of equality are rightly regarded as feminists. Some men readily identify with experiences of women who are discriminated against on the basis of sex/gender, having themselves had comparable experiences; others who may not have faced direct discrimination or stereotyping recognize that inequity and problematic characterization still occur, and they seek correction. This series is pleased to include feminist men both as lead authors and as contributing voices.

Feminist Biblical Interpretation

Women interpreting the Bible from the lenses of their own experience is nothing new. Throughout the ages women have recounted the biblical stories, teaching them to their children and others, all the while interpreting them afresh for their time and circumstances.[2] Following is a very brief sketch of select foremothers who laid the groundwork for contemporary feminist biblical interpretation.

One of the earliest known Christian women who challenged patriarchal interpretations of Scripture was a consecrated virgin named Helie, who lived in the second century CE. When she refused to marry, her

1. See Martha Rampton, "Four Waves of Feminism" (October 25, 2015), at http://www.pacificu.edu/about-us/news-events/four-waves-feminism; and Ealasaid Munro, "Feminism: A Fourth Wave?," https://www.psa.ac.uk/insight-plus/feminism-fourth-wave.

2. For fuller treatments of this history, see chap. 7, "One Thousand Years of Feminist Bible Criticism," in Gerda Lerner, *Creation of Feminist Consciousness: From the Middle Ages to Eighteen-Seventy* (New York: Oxford University Press, 1993), 138–66; Susanne Scholz, "From the 'Woman's Bible' to the 'Women's Bible,' The History of Feminist Approaches to the Hebrew Bible," in *Introducing the Women's Hebrew Bible*, IFT 13 (New York: T&T Clark, 2007), 12–32; Marion Ann Taylor and Agnes Choi, eds., *Handbook of Women Biblical Interpreters: A Historical and Biographical Guide* (Grand Rapids: Baker Academic, 2012).

parents brought her before a judge, who quoted to her Paul's admonition, "It is better to marry than to be aflame with passion" (1 Cor 7:9). In response, Helie first acknowledges that this is what Scripture says, but then she retorts, "but not for everyone, that is, not for holy virgins."[3] She is one of the first to question the notion that a text has one meaning that is applicable in all situations.

A Jewish woman who also lived in the second century CE, Beruriah, is said to have had "profound knowledge of biblical exegesis and outstanding intelligence."[4] One story preserved in the Talmud (b. Berakot 10a) tells of how she challenged her husband, Rabbi Meir, when he prayed for the destruction of a sinner. Proffering an alternate interpretation, she argued that Psalm 104:35 advocated praying for the destruction of sin, not the sinner.

In medieval times the first written commentaries on Scripture from a critical feminist point of view emerge. While others may have been produced and passed on orally, they are for the most part lost to us now. Among the earliest preserved feminist writings are those of Hildegard of Bingen (1098–1179), German writer, mystic, and abbess of a Benedictine monastery. She reinterpreted the Genesis narratives in a way that presented women and men as complementary and interdependent. She frequently wrote about the Divine as feminine.[5] Along with other women mystics of the time, such as Julian of Norwich (1342–ca. 1416), she spoke authoritatively from her personal experiences of God's revelation in prayer.

In this era, women were also among the scribes who copied biblical manuscripts. Notable among them is Paula Dei Mansi of Verona, from a distinguished family of Jewish scribes. In 1288, she translated from Hebrew into Italian a collection of Bible commentaries written by her father and added her own explanations.[6]

Another pioneer, Christine de Pizan (1365–ca. 1430), was a French court writer and prolific poet. She used allegory and common sense

---

3. Madrid, Escorial MS, a II 9, f. 90 v., as cited in Lerner, *Feminist Consciousness*, 140.

4. See Judith R. Baskin, "Women and Post-Biblical Commentary," in *The Torah: A Women's Commentary*, ed. Tamara Cohn Eskenazi and Andrea L. Weiss (New York: Women of Reform Judaism, Federation of Temple Sisterhood, 2008), xlix–lv, at lii.

5. Hildegard of Bingen, *De Operatione Dei*, 1.4.100; PL 197:885bc, as cited in Lerner, *Feminist Consciousness*, 142–43. See also Barbara Newman, *Sister of Wisdom: St. Hildegard's Theology of the Feminine* (Berkeley: University of California Press, 1987).

6. Emily Taitz, Sondra Henry, Cheryl Tallan, eds., *JPS Guide to Jewish Women 600 B.C.E.–1900 C.E.* (Philadelphia: Jewish Publication Society of America, 2003), 110–11.

to subvert misogynist readings of Scripture and celebrated the accomplishments of female biblical figures to argue for women's active roles in building society.[7]

By the seventeenth century, there were women who asserted that the biblical text needs to be understood and interpreted in its historical context. For example, Rachel Speght (1597–ca. 1630), a Calvinist English poet, elaborates on the historical situation in first-century Corinth that prompted Paul to say, "It is well for a man not to touch a woman" (1 Cor 7:1). Her aim was to show that the biblical texts should not be applied in a literal fashion to all times and circumstances. Similarly, Margaret Fell (1614–1702), one of the founders of the Religious Society of Friends (Quakers) in Britain, addressed the Pauline prohibitions against women speaking in church by insisting that they do not have universal validity. Rather, they need to be understood in their historical context, as addressed to a local church in particular time-bound circumstances.[8]

Along with analyzing the historical context of the biblical writings, women in the eighteenth and nineteenth centuries began to attend to misogynistic interpretations based on faulty translations. One of the first to do so was British feminist Mary Astell (1666–1731).[9] In the United States, the Grimké sisters, Sarah (1792–1873) and Angelina (1805–1879), Quaker women from a slaveholding family in South Carolina, learned biblical Greek and Hebrew so that they could interpret the Bible for themselves. They were prompted to do so after men sought to silence them from speaking out against slavery and for women's rights by claiming that the Bible (e.g., 1 Cor 14:34) prevented women from speaking in public.[10] Another prominent abolitionist, Isabella Baumfree, who adopted the name Sojourner Truth (ca. 1797–1883), a former slave, quoted the Bible liberally in her speeches[11] and in so doing challenged cultural assumptions and biblical interpretations that undergird gender inequities.

7. See further Taylor and Choi, *Handbook of Women Biblical Interpreters,* 127–32.

8. Her major work, *Women's Speaking Justified, Proved and Allowed by the Scriptures,* published in London in 1667, gave a systematic feminist reading of all biblical texts pertaining to women.

9. Mary Astell, *Some Reflections upon Marriage* (New York: Source Book Press, 1970, reprint of the 1730 edition; earliest edition of this work is 1700), 103–4.

10. See further Sarah Grimké, *Letters on the Equality of the Sexes and the Condition of Woman* (Boston: Isaac Knapp, 1838).

11. See, for example, her most famous speech, "Ain't I a Woman?," delivered in 1851 at the Ohio Women's Rights Convention in Akron, OH; http://www.fordham.edu/halsall/mod/sojtruth-woman.asp.

Another monumental work that emerged in nineteenth-century England was that of Jewish theologian Grace Aguilar (1816–1847), *The Women of Israel*,[12] published in 1845. Aguilar's approach was to make connections between the biblical women and contemporary Jewish women's concerns. She aimed to counter the widespread notion that women were degraded in Jewish law and that only in Christianity were women's dignity and value upheld. Her intent was to help Jewish women find strength and encouragement by seeing the evidence of God's compassionate love in the history of every woman in the Bible. While not a full commentary on the Bible, Aguilar's work stands out for its comprehensive treatment of every female biblical character, including even the most obscure references.[13]

The first person to produce a full-blown feminist commentary on the Bible was Elizabeth Cady Stanton (1815–1902). A leading proponent in the United States for women's right to vote, she found that whenever women tried to make inroads into politics, education, or the work world, the Bible was quoted against them. Along with a team of like-minded women, she produced her own commentary on every text of the Bible that concerned women. Her pioneering two-volume project, *The Woman's Bible*, published in 1895 and 1898, urges women to recognize that texts that degrade women come from the men who wrote the texts, not from God, and to use their common sense to rethink what has been presented to them as sacred.

Nearly a century later, *The Women's Bible Commentary*, edited by Carol A. Newsom and Sharon H. Ringe (Louisville: Westminster John Knox, 1992), appeared. This one-volume commentary features North American feminist scholarship on each book of the Protestant canon. Like Cady Stanton's commentary, it does not contain comments on every section of the biblical text but only on those passages deemed relevant to women. It was revised and expanded in 1998 to include the Apocrypha/Deuterocanonical books, and the contributors to this new volume reflect the global face of contemporary feminist scholarship. The revisions made in the third edition, which appeared in 2012, represent the profound advances in feminist biblical scholarship and include newer voices. In both the second and third editions, *The* has been dropped from the title.

---

12. The full title is *The Women of Israel or Characters and Sketches from the Holy Scriptures and Jewish History Illustrative of the Past History, Present Duty, and Future Destiny of the Hebrew Females, as Based on the Word of God.*

13. See further Eskenazi and Weiss, *The Torah: A Women's Commentary*, xxxviii; Taylor and Choi, *Handbook of Women Biblical Interpreters*, 31–37.

Also appearing at the centennial of Cady Stanton's *The Woman's Bible* were two volumes edited by Elisabeth Schüssler Fiorenza with the assistance of Shelly Matthews. The first, *Searching the Scriptures: A Feminist Introduction* (New York: Crossroad, 1993), charts a comprehensive approach to feminist interpretation from ecumenical, interreligious, and multicultural perspectives. The second volume, published in 1994, provides critical feminist commentary on each book of the New Testament as well as on three books of Jewish Pseudepigrapha and eleven other early Christian writings.

In Europe, similar endeavors have been undertaken, such as the one-volume *Kompendium Feministische Bibelauslegung*, edited by Luise Schottroff and Marie-Theres Wacker (Gütersloh: Gütersloher Verlagshaus, 2007), featuring German feminist biblical interpretation of each book of the Bible, along with apocryphal books, and several extrabiblical writings. This work, now in its third edition, has recently been translated into English.[14] A multivolume project, *The Bible and Women: An Encylopaedia of Exegesis and Cultural History*, edited by Irmtraud Fischer, Adriana Valerio, Mercedes Navarro Puerto, and Christiana de Groot, is currently in production. This project presents a history of the reception of the Bible as embedded in Western cultural history and focuses particularly on gender-relevant biblical themes, biblical female characters, and women recipients of the Bible. The volumes are published in English, Spanish, Italian, and German.[15]

Another groundbreaking work is the collection The Feminist Companion to the Bible Series, edited by Athalya Brenner (Sheffield: Sheffield Academic, 1993–2015), which comprises twenty volumes of commentaries on the Old Testament. The parallel series, Feminist Companion

---

14. *Feminist Biblical Interpretation: A Compendium of Critical Commentary on the Books of the Bible and Related Literature*, trans. Lisa E. Dahill, Everett R. Kalin, Nancy Lukens, Linda M. Maloney, Barbara Rumscheidt, Martin Rumscheidt, and Tina Steiner (Grand Rapids: Eerdmans, 2012). Another notable collection is the three volumes edited by Susanne Scholz, *Feminist Interpretation of the Hebrew Bible in Retrospect*, Recent Research in Biblical Studies 7, 8, 9 (Sheffield: Sheffield Phoenix, 2013, 2014, 2016).

15. The first volume, on the Torah, appeared in Spanish in 2009, in German and Italian in 2010, and in English in 2011 (Atlanta: Society of Biblical Literature). Five more volumes are now available: *Feminist Biblical Studies in the Twentieth Century*, ed. Elisabeth Schüssler Fiorenza (2014); *The Writings and Later Wisdom Books*, ed. Christl M. Maier and Nuria Calduch-Benages (2014); *Gospels: Narrative and History*, ed. Mercedes Navarro Puerto and Marinella Perroni; English translation ed. Amy-Jill Levine (2015); *The High Middle Ages*, ed. Kari Elisabeth Børresen and Adriana Valerio (2015); and *Early Jewish Writings*, ed. Eileen Schuller and Marie-Theres Wacker (2017). For further information, see http://www.bibleandwomen.org.

to the New Testament and Early Christian Writings, edited by Amy-Jill Levine with Marianne Blickenstaff and Maria Mayo Robbins (Sheffield: Sheffield Academic, 2001–2009), contains thirteen volumes with one more planned. These two series are not full commentaries on the biblical books but comprise collected essays on discrete biblical texts.

Works by individual feminist biblical scholars in all parts of the world abound, and they are now too numerous to list in this introduction. Feminist biblical interpretation has reached a level of maturity that now makes possible a commentary series on every book of the Bible. In recent decades, women have had greater access to formal theological education, have been able to learn critical analytical tools, have put their own interpretations into writing, and have developed new methods of biblical interpretation. Until recent decades the work of feminist biblical interpreters was largely unknown, both to other women and to their brothers in the synagogue, church, and academy. Feminists now have taken their place in the professional world of biblical scholars, where they build on the work of their foremothers and connect with one another across the globe in ways not previously possible. In a few short decades, feminist biblical criticism has become an integral part of the academy.

Methodologies

Feminist biblical scholars use a variety of methods and often employ a number of them together.[16] In the Wisdom Commentary series, the authors will explain their understanding of feminism and the feminist reading strategies used in their commentary. Each volume treats the biblical text in blocks of material, not an analysis verse by verse. The entire text is considered, not only those passages that feature female characters or that speak specifically about women. When women are not apparent in the narrative, feminist lenses are used to analyze the dynamics in the text between male characters, the models of power, binary ways of thinking, and the dynamics of imperialism. Attention is given to how the whole text functions and how it was and is heard, both in its original context and today. Issues of particular concern to women—e.g., poverty, food, health, the environment, water—come to the fore.

---

16. See the seventeen essays in Caroline Vander Stichele and Todd Penner, eds., *Her Master's Tools? Feminist and Postcolonial Engagements of Historical-Critical Discourse* (Atlanta: Society of Biblical Literature, 2005), which show the complementarity of various approaches.

One of the approaches used by early feminists and still popular today is to lift up the overlooked and forgotten stories of women in the Bible. Studies of women in each of the Testaments have been done, and there are also studies on women in particular biblical books.[17] Feminists recognize that the examples of biblical characters can be both empowering and problematic. The point of the feminist enterprise is not to serve as an apologetic for women; it is rather, in part, to recover women's history and literary roles in all their complexity and to learn from that recovery.

Retrieving the submerged history of biblical women is a crucial step for constructing the story of the past so as to lead to liberative possibilities for the present and future. There are, however, some pitfalls to this approach. Sometimes depictions of biblical women have been naïve and romantic. Some commentators exalt the virtues of both biblical and contemporary women and paint women as superior to men. Such reverse discrimination inhibits movement toward equality for all. In addition, some feminists challenge the idea that one can "pluck positive images out of an admittedly androcentric text, separating literary characterizations from the androcentric interests they were created to serve."[18] Still other feminists find these images to have enormous value.

One other danger with seeking the submerged history of women is the tendency for Christian feminists to paint Jesus and even Paul as liberators of women in a way that demonizes Judaism.[19] Wisdom Commentary aims to enhance understanding of Jesus as well as Paul as Jews of their day and to forge solidarity among Jewish and Christian feminists.

---

17. See, e.g., Alice Bach, ed., *Women in the Hebrew Bible: A Reader* (New York: Routledge, 1998); Tikva Frymer-Kensky, *Reading the Women of the Bible* (New York: Schocken Books, 2002); Carol Meyers, Toni Craven, and Ross S. Kraemer, *Women in Scripture* (Grand Rapids: Eerdmans, 2000); Irene Nowell, *Women in the Old Testament* (Collegeville, MN: Liturgical Press, 1997); Katharine Doob Sakenfeld, *Just Wives? Stories of Power and Survival in the Old Testament and Today* (Louisville: Westminster John Knox, 2003); Mary Ann Getty-Sullivan, *Women in the New Testament* (Collegeville, MN: Liturgical Press, 2001); Bonnie Thurston, *Women in the New Testament: Questions and Commentary*, Companions to the New Testament (New York: Crossroad, 1998).

18. Cheryl Exum, "Second Thoughts about Secondary Characters: Women in Exodus 1.8–2.10," in *A Feminist Companion to Exodus to Deuteronomy*, FCB 6, ed. Athalya Brenner (Sheffield: Sheffield Academic, 1994), 75–97, at 76.

19. See Judith Plaskow, "Anti-Judaism in Feminist Christian Interpretation," in *Searching the Scriptures: A Feminist Introduction*, ed. Elisabeth Schüssler Fiorenza (New York: Crossroad, 1993), 1:117–29; Amy-Jill Levine, "The New Testament and Anti-Judaism," in *The Misunderstood Jew: The Church and the Scandal of the Jewish Jesus* (San Francisco: HarperSanFrancisco, 2006), 87–117.

Feminist scholars who use historical-critical methods analyze the world behind the text; they seek to understand the historical context from which the text emerged and the circumstances of the communities to whom it was addressed. In bringing feminist lenses to this approach, the aim is not to impose modern expectations on ancient cultures but to unmask the ways that ideologically problematic mind-sets that produced the ancient texts are still promulgated through the text. Feminist biblical scholars aim not only to deconstruct but also to reclaim and reconstruct biblical history as women's history, in which women were central and active agents in creating religious heritage.[20] A further step is to construct meaning for contemporary women and men in a liberative movement toward transformation of social, political, economic, and religious structures.[21] In recent years, some feminists have embraced new historicism, which accents the creative role of the interpreter in any construction of history and exposes the power struggles to which the text witnesses.[22]

Literary critics analyze the world of the text: its form, language patterns, and rhetorical function.[23] They do not attempt to separate layers of tradition and redaction but focus on the text holistically, as it is in

20. See, for example, Phyllis A. Bird, *Missing Persons and Mistaken Identities: Women and Gender in Ancient Israel* (Minneapolis: Fortress, 1997); Elisabeth Schüssler Fiorenza, *In Memory of Her: A Feminist Theological Reconstruction of Christian Origins* (New York: Crossroad, 1983); Ross Shepard Kraemer and Mary Rose D'Angelo, eds., *Women and Christian Origins* (New York: Oxford University Press, 1999).

21. See, e.g., Sandra M. Schneiders, *The Revelatory Text: Interpreting the New Testament as Sacred Scripture*, rev. ed. (Collegeville, MN: Liturgical Press, 1999), whose aim is to engage in biblical interpretation not only for intellectual enlightenment but, even more important, for personal and communal transformation. Elisabeth Schüssler Fiorenza (*Wisdom Ways: Introducing Feminist Biblical Interpretation* [Maryknoll, NY: Orbis Books, 2001]) envisions the work of feminist biblical interpretation as a dance of Wisdom that consists of seven steps that interweave in spiral movements toward liberation, the final one being transformative action for change.

22. See Gina Hens-Piazza, *The New Historicism*, GBS, Old Testament Series (Minneapolis: Fortress, 2002).

23. Phyllis Trible was among the first to employ this method with texts from Genesis and Ruth in her groundbreaking book *God and the Rhetoric of Sexuality*, OBT (Philadelphia: Fortress, 1978). Another pioneer in feminist literary criticism is Mieke Bal (*Lethal Love: Feminist Literary Readings of Biblical Love Stories* [Bloomington: Indiana University Press, 1987]). For surveys of recent developments in literary methods, see Terry Eagleton, *Literary Theory: An Introduction*, 3rd ed. (Minneapolis: University of Minnesota Press, 2008); Janice Capel Anderson and Stephen D. Moore, eds., *Mark and Method: New Approaches in Biblical Studies*, 2nd ed. (Minneapolis: Fortress, 2008).

its present form. They examine how meaning is created in the interaction between the text and its reader in multiple contexts. Within the arena of literary approaches are reader-oriented approaches, narrative, rhetorical, structuralist, post-structuralist, deconstructive, ideological, autobiographical, and performance criticism.[24] Narrative critics study the interrelation among author, text, and audience through investigation of settings, both spatial and temporal; characters; plot; and narrative techniques (e.g., irony, parody, intertextual allusions). Reader-response critics attend to the impact that the text has on the reader or hearer. They recognize that when a text is detrimental toward women there is the choice either to affirm the text or to read against the grain toward a liberative end. Rhetorical criticism analyzes the style of argumentation and attends to how the author is attempting to shape the thinking or actions of the hearer. Structuralist critics analyze the complex patterns of binary oppositions in the text to derive its meaning.[25] Post-structuralist approaches challenge the notion that there are fixed meanings to any biblical text or that there is one universal truth. They engage in close readings of the text and often engage in intertextual analysis.[26] Within this approach is deconstructionist criticism, which views the text as a site of conflict, with competing narratives. The interpreter aims to expose the fault lines and overturn and reconfigure binaries by elevating the underling of a pair and foregrounding it.[27] Feminists also use other postmodern approaches, such as ideological and autobiographical criticism. The former analyzes the system of ideas that underlies the power and

24. See, e.g., J. Cheryl Exum and David J. A. Clines, eds., *The New Literary Criticism and the Hebrew Bible* (Valley Forge, PA: Trinity Press International, 1993); Edgar V. McKnight and Elizabeth Struthers Malbon, eds., *The New Literary Criticism and the New Testament* (Valley Forge, PA: Trinity Press International, 1994).

25. See, e.g., David Jobling, *The Sense of Biblical Narrative: Three Structural Analyses in the Old Testament*, JSOTSup 7 (Sheffield: University of Sheffield, 1978).

26. See, e.g., Stephen D. Moore, *Poststructuralism and the New Testament: Derrida and Foucault at the Foot of the Cross* (Minneapolis: Fortress, 1994); *The Bible in Theory: Critical and Postcritical Essays* (Atlanta: Society of Biblical Literature, 2010); Yvonne Sherwood, *A Biblical Text and Its Afterlives: The Survival of Jonah in Western Culture* (Cambridge: Cambridge University Press, 2000).

27. David Penchansky, "Deconstruction," in *The Oxford Encyclopedia of Biblical Interpretation*, ed. Steven McKenzie (New York: Oxford University Press, 2013), 196–205. See, for example, Danna Nolan Fewell and David M. Gunn, *Gender, Power, and Promise: The Subject of the Bible's First Story* (Nashville: Abingdon, 1993); David Rutledge, *Reading Marginally: Feminism, Deconstruction and the Bible*, BibInt 21 (Leiden: Brill, 1996).

values concealed in the text as well as that of the interpreter.[28] The latter involves deliberate self-disclosure while reading the text as a critical exegete.[29] Performance criticism attends to how the text was passed on orally, usually in communal settings, and to the verbal and nonverbal interactions between the performer and the audience.[30]

From the beginning, feminists have understood that interpreting the Bible is an act of power. In recent decades, feminist biblical scholars have developed hermeneutical theories of the ethics and politics of biblical interpretation to challenge the claims to value neutrality of most academic biblical scholarship. Feminist biblical scholars have also turned their attention to how some biblical writings were shaped by the power of empire and how this still shapes readers' self-understandings today. They have developed hermeneutical approaches that reveal, critique, and evaluate the interactions depicted in the text against the context of empire, and they consider implications for contemporary contexts.[31] Feminists also analyze the dynamics of colonization and the mentalities of colonized peoples in the exercise of biblical interpretation. As Kwok Pui-lan explains, "A postcolonial feminist interpretation of the Bible needs to investigate the deployment of gender in the narration of identity, the negotiation of power differentials between the colonizers and the colonized, and the reinforcement of patriarchal control over spheres where these elites could exercise control."[32] Methods and models from sociology and cultural anthropology are used by feminists to investigate

---

28. See Tina Pippin, ed., *Ideological Criticism of Biblical Texts: Semeia* 59 (1992); Terry Eagleton, *Ideology: An Introduction* (London: Verso, 2007).

29. See, e.g., Ingrid Rosa Kitzberger, ed., *Autobiographical Biblical Interpretation: Between Text and Self* (Leiden: Deo, 2002); P. J. W. Schutte, "When *They, We,* and the Passive Become *I*—Introducing Autobiographical Biblical Criticism," *HTS Teologiese Studies / Theological Studies* 61 (2005): 401–16.

30. See, e.g., Holly Hearon and Philip Ruge-Jones, eds., *The Bible in Ancient and Modern Media: Story and Performance* (Eugene, OR: Cascade, 2009).

31. E.g., Gale Yee, ed., *Judges and Method: New Approaches in Biblical Studies* (Minneapolis: Fortress, 1995); Warren Carter, *The Gospel of Matthew in Its Roman Imperial Context* (London: T&T Clark, 2005); *The Roman Empire and the New Testament: An Essential Guide* (Nashville: Abingdon, 2006); Elisabeth Schüssler Fiorenza, *The Power of the Word: Scripture and the Rhetoric of Empire* (Minneapolis: Fortress, 2007); Judith E. McKinlay, *Reframing Her: Biblical Women in Postcolonial Focus* (Sheffield: Sheffield Phoenix, 2004).

32. Kwok Pui-lan, *Postcolonial Imagination and Feminist Theology* (Louisville: Westminster John Knox, 2005), 9. See also, Musa W. Dube, ed., *Postcolonial Feminist Interpretation of the Bible* (St. Louis: Chalice, 2000); Cristl M. Maier and Carolyn J. Sharp,

women's everyday lives, their experiences of marriage, childrearing, labor, money, illness, etc.[33]

As feminists have examined the construction of gender from varying cultural perspectives, they have become ever more cognizant that the way gender roles are defined within differing cultures varies radically. As Mary Ann Tolbert observes, "Attempts to isolate some universal role that cross-culturally defines 'woman' have run into contradictory evidence at every turn."[34] Some women have coined new terms to highlight the particularities of their socio-cultural context. Many African American feminists, for example, call themselves *womanists* to draw attention to the double oppression of racism and sexism they experience.[35] Similarly, many US Hispanic feminists speak of themselves as *mujeristas* (*mujer* is Spanish for "woman").[36] Others prefer to be called "Latina feminists."[37] Both groups emphasize that the context for their theologizing is *mestizaje* and *mulatez* (racial and cultural mixture), done *en conjunto* (in community), with *lo cotidiano* (everyday lived experience) of Hispanic women as starting points for theological reflection and the encounter with the divine. Intercultural analysis has become an indispensable tool for working toward justice for women at the global level.[38]

Prophecy and Power: Jeremiah in Feminist and Postcolonial Perspective (London: Bloomsbury, 2013).

33. See, for example, Carol Meyers, *Discovering Eve: Ancient Israelite Women in Context* (New York: Oxford University Press, 1991); Luise Schottroff, *Lydia's Impatient Sisters: A Feminist Social History of Early Christianity*, trans. Barbara and Martin Rumscheidt (Louisville: Westminster John Knox, 1995); Susan Niditch, *"My Brother Esau Is a Hairy Man": Hair and Identity in Ancient Israel* (Oxford: Oxford University Press, 2008).

34. Mary Ann Tolbert, "Social, Sociological, and Anthropological Methods," in *Searching the Scriptures*, 1:255–71, at 265.

35. Alice Walker coined the term (*In Search of Our Mothers' Gardens: Womanist Prose* [New York: Harcourt Brace Jovanovich, 1967, 1983]). See also Katie G. Cannon, "The Emergence of Black Feminist Consciousness," in *Feminist Interpretation of the Bible*, ed. Letty M. Russell (Philadelphia: Westminster, 1985), 30–40; Renita Weems, *Just a Sister Away: A Womanist Vision of Women's Relationships in the Bible* (San Diego: Lura Media, 1988); Nyasha Junior, *An Introduction to Womanist Biblical Interpretation* (Louisville: Westminster John Knox, 2015).

36. Ada María Isasi-Díaz (*Mujerista Theology: A Theology for the Twenty-First Century* [Maryknoll, NY: Orbis Books, 1996]) is credited with coining the term.

37. E.g., María Pilar Aquino, Daisy L. Machado, and Jeanette Rodríguez, eds., *A Reader in Latina Feminist Theology* (Austin: University of Texas Press, 2002).

38. See, e.g., María Pilar Aquino and María José Rosado-Nunes, eds., *Feminist Intercultural Theology: Latina Explorations for a Just World*, Studies in Latino/a Catholicism (Maryknoll, NY: Orbis Books, 2007).

Some feminists are among those who have developed lesbian, gay, bisexual, and transgender (LGBT) interpretation. This approach focuses on issues of sexual identity and uses various reading strategies. Some point out the ways in which categories that emerged in recent centuries are applied anachronistically to biblical texts to make modern-day judgments. Others show how the Bible is silent on contemporary issues about sexual identity. Still others examine same-sex relationships in the Bible by figures such as Ruth and Naomi or David and Jonathan. In recent years, queer theory has emerged; it emphasizes the blurriness of boundaries not just of sexual identity but also of gender roles. Queer critics often focus on texts in which figures transgress what is traditionally considered proper gender behavior.[39]

Feminists also recognize that the struggle for women's equality and dignity is intimately connected with the struggle for respect for Earth and for the whole of the cosmos. Ecofeminists interpret Scripture in ways that highlight the link between human domination of nature and male subjugation of women. They show how anthropocentric ways of interpreting the Bible have overlooked or dismissed Earth and Earth community. They invite readers to identify not only with human characters in the biblical narrative but also with other Earth creatures and domains of nature, especially those that are the object of injustice. Some use creative imagination to retrieve the interests of Earth implicit in the narrative and enable Earth to speak.[40]

Biblical Authority

By the late nineteenth century, some feminists, such as Elizabeth Cady Stanton, began to question openly whether the Bible could continue to be regarded as authoritative for women. They viewed the Bible itself as

---

39. See, e.g., Bernadette J. Brooten, *Love between Women: Early Christian Responses to Female Homoeroticism* (Chicago and London: University of Chicago Press, 1996); Mary Rose D'Angelo, "Women Partners in the New Testament," *JFSR* 6 (1990): 65–86; Deirdre J. Good, "Reading Strategies for Biblical Passages on Same-Sex Relations," *Theology and Sexuality* 7 (1997): 70–82; Deryn Guest, *When Deborah Met Jael: Lesbian Feminist Hermeneutics* (London: SCM, 2011); Teresa Hornsby and Ken Stone, eds., *Bible Trouble: Queer Readings at the Boundaries of Biblical Scholarship* (Atlanta: Society of Biblical Literature, 2011).

40. E.g., Norman C. Habel and Peter Trudinger, *Exploring Ecological Hermeneutics*, SymS 46 (Atlanta: Society of Biblical Literature, 2008); Mary Judith Ress, *Ecofeminism in Latin America*, Women from the Margins (Maryknoll, NY: Orbis Books, 2006).

the source of women's oppression, and some rejected its sacred origin and saving claims. Some decided that the Bible and the religious traditions that enshrine it are too thoroughly saturated with androcentrism and patriarchy to be redeemable.[41]

In the Wisdom Commentary series, questions such as these may be raised, but the aim of this series is not to lead readers to reject the authority of the biblical text. Rather, the aim is to promote better understanding of the contexts from which the text arose and of the rhetorical effects it has on women and men in contemporary contexts. Such understanding can lead to a deepening of faith, with the Bible serving as an aid to bring flourishing of life.

Language for God

Because of the ways in which the term "God" has been used to symbolize the divine in predominantly male, patriarchal, and monarchical modes, feminists have designed new ways of speaking of the divine. Some have called attention to the inadequacy of the term *God* by trying to visually destabilize our ways of thinking and speaking of the divine. Rosemary Radford Ruether proposed *God/ess*, as an unpronounceable term pointing to the unnameable understanding of the divine that transcends patriarchal limitations.[42] Some have followed traditional Jewish practice, writing *G-d*. Elisabeth Schüssler Fiorenza has adopted *G*d*.[43] Others draw on the biblical tradition to mine female and non-gender-specific metaphors and symbols.[44] In Wisdom Commentary, there is not one standard way of expressing the divine; each author will use her or his preferred ways. The one exception is that when the tetragrammaton, YHWH, the name revealed to Moses in Exodus 3:14, is used, it will be without vowels, respecting the Jewish custom of avoiding pronouncing the divine name out of reverence.

41. E.g., Mary Daly, *Beyond God the Father: A Philosophy of Women's Liberation* (Boston: Beacon, 1973).

42. Rosemary Radford Ruether, *Sexism and God-Talk: Toward a Feminist Theology* (Boston: Beacon, 1983).

43. Elisabeth Schüssler Fiorenza, *Jesus: Miriam's Child, Sophia's Prophet; Critical Issues in Feminist Christology* (New York: Continuum, 1994), 191 n. 3.

44. E.g., Sallie McFague, *Models of God: Theology for an Ecological, Nuclear Age* (Philadelphia: Fortress, 1987); Catherine LaCugna, *God for Us: The Trinity and Christian Life* (San Francisco: Harper Collins, 1991); Elizabeth A. Johnson, *She Who Is: The Mystery of God in Feminist Theological Discourse* (New York: Crossroad, 1992). See further Elizabeth A. Johnson, "God," in *Dictionary of Feminist Theologies*, 128–30.

Nomenclature for the Two Testaments

In recent decades, some biblical scholars have begun to call the two Testaments of the Bible by names other than the traditional nomenclature: Old and New Testament. Some regard "Old" as derogatory, implying that it is no longer relevant or that it has been superseded. Consequently, terms like Hebrew Bible, First Testament, and Jewish Scriptures and, correspondingly, Christian Scriptures or Second Testament have come into use. There are a number of difficulties with these designations. The term "Hebrew Bible" does not take into account that parts of the Old Testament are written not in Hebrew but in Aramaic.[45] Moreover, for Roman Catholics and Eastern Orthodox believers, the Old Testament includes books written in Greek—the Deuterocanonical books, considered Apocrypha by Protestants.[46] The term "Jewish Scriptures" is inadequate because these books are also sacred to Christians. Conversely, "Christian Scriptures" is not an accurate designation for the New Testament, since the Old Testament is also part of the Christian Scriptures. Using "First and Second Testament" also has difficulties, in that it can imply a hierarchy and a value judgment.[47] Jews generally use the term Tanakh, an acronym for Torah (Pentateuch), Nevi'im (Prophets), and Ketuvim (Writings).

In Wisdom Commentary, if authors choose to use a designation other than Tanakh, Old Testament, and New Testament, they will explain how they mean the term.

Translation

Modern feminist scholars recognize the complexities connected with biblical translation, as they have delved into questions about philosophy of language, how meanings are produced, and how they are culturally situated. Today it is evident that simply translating into gender-neutral formulations cannot address all the challenges presented by androcentric texts. Efforts at feminist translation must also deal with issues around authority and canonicity.[48]

---

45. Gen 31:47; Jer 10:11; Ezra 4:7–6:18; 7:12-26; Dan 2:4–7:28.

46. Representing the *via media* between Catholic and reformed, Anglicans generally consider the Apocrypha to be profitable, if not canonical, and utilize select Wisdom texts liturgically.

47. See Levine, *The Misunderstood Jew*, 193–99.

48. Elizabeth Castelli, "*Les Belles Infidèles*/Fidelity or Feminism? The Meanings of Feminist Biblical Translation," in *Searching the Scriptures*, 1:189–204, here 190.

Because of these complexities, the editors of the Wisdom Commentary series have chosen to use an existing translation, the New Revised Standard Version (NRSV), which is provided for easy reference at the top of each page of commentary. The NRSV was produced by a team of ecumenical and interreligious scholars, is a fairly literal translation, and uses inclusive language for human beings. Brief discussions about problematic translations appear in the inserts labeled "Translation Matters." When more detailed discussions are available, these will be indicated in footnotes. In the commentary, wherever Hebrew or Greek words are used, English translation is provided. In cases where a wordplay is involved, transliteration is provided to enable understanding.

Art and Poetry

Artistic expression in poetry, music, sculpture, painting, and various other modes is very important to feminist interpretation. Where possible, art and poetry are included in the print volumes of the series. In a number of instances, these are original works created for this project. Regrettably, copyright and production costs prohibit the inclusion of color photographs and other artistic work. It is our hope that the web version will allow a greater collection of such resources.

Glossary

Because there are a number of excellent readily available resources that provide definitions and concise explanations of terms used in feminist theological and biblical studies, this series will not include a glossary. We refer you to works such as *Dictionary of Feminist Theologies*, edited by Letty M. Russell with J. Shannon Clarkson (Louisville: Westminster John Knox, 1996), and volume 1 of *Searching the Scriptures*, edited by Elisabeth Schüssler Fiorenza with the assistance of Shelly Matthews (New York: Crossroad, 1992). Individual authors in the Wisdom Commentary series will define the way they are using terms that may be unfamiliar.

A Concluding Word

In just a few short decades, feminist biblical studies has grown exponentially, both in the methods that have been developed and in the number of scholars who have embraced it. We realize that this series is limited and will soon need to be revised and updated. It is our hope that Wisdom Commentary, by making the best of current feminist biblical scholarship available in an accessible format to ministers, preachers, teachers, scholars, and students, will aid all readers in their advancement toward God's vision of dignity, equality, and justice for all.

———————————

Acknowledgments

There are a great many people who have made this series possible: first, Peter Dwyer, director of Liturgical Press, and Hans Christoffersen, publisher of the academic market at Liturgical Press, who have believed in this project and have shepherded it since it was conceived in 2008. Editorial consultants Athalya Brenner-Idan and Elisabeth Schüssler Fiorenza have not only been an inspiration with their pioneering work but have encouraged us all along the way with their personal involvement. Volume editors Mary Ann Beavis, Carol J. Dempsey, Amy-Jill Levine, Linda M. Maloney, Ahida Pilarski, Sarah Tanzer, Lauress Wilkins Lawrence, and Gina Hens-Piazza have lent their extraordinary wisdom to the shaping of the series, have used their extensive networks of relationships to secure authors and contributors, and have worked tirelessly to guide their work to completion. Four others who have contributed greatly to the shaping of the project are: Linda M. Day, Mignon Jacobs, Seung Ai Yang, and Barbara E. Bowe of blessed memory (d. 2010). Editorial and research assistant Susan M. Hickman has provided invaluable support with administrative details and arrangements. I am grateful to Brian Eisenschenk and Christine Henderson who have assisted Susan Hickman with the Wiki. I am especially thankful to Lauren L. Murphy and Justin Howell for their work in copyediting; and to the staff at Liturgical Press, especially Colleen Stiller, production manager; Stephanie Lancour, production editor; Angie Steffens, production assistant; and Tara Durheim, associate publisher.

Author's Introduction

A Feminist Toolbox for Interpreting Qoheleth

For the master's tools will never dismantle the master's house. They may allow us to temporarily beat him at his own game, but they will never enable us to bring about genuine change. And this fact is only threatening to those women who still define the master's house as their only source of support.

—*Audre Lorde*[1]

Qoheleth has been dangerous—even deadly—for women. For some of us who are feminists, that would be enough reason to stop reading. Such a suggestion is not unheard of in our circles, from Mary Daly rejecting the Bible outright to Renita Weems acknowledging that resistant readings are our only way to survive.[2] Qoheleth easily morphs into a handy tool for misogyny, and misogynists have implemented it with ease. Furthermore, some parts of the book that are not

---

1. Audre Lorde, "The Master's Tools Will Never Dismantle the Master's House," in *Sister Outsider: Essays and Speeches by Audre Lorde* (Berkley: Crossing Press, 1984, 2007), 110–13.

2. Daly told *The Guardian*: "I hate the Bible. . . . I always did." Mel Steel, "Mary, Mary, Quite Contrary," *The Guardian* (August 25 1999); Renita J. Weems, *Battered Love: Marriage, Sex, and Violence in the Hebrew Prophets*, OBT (Minneapolis: Fortress, 1995), 103.

obviously misogynistic nonetheless glorify the patriarchal mind-set of empire-supporting hierarchy and wealth. Yet oddly enough, the questions raised in Qoheleth—the kinds of questions and our persistence in asking them—may also become tools for the feminist to undermine patriarchy, hierarchy, racism, homophobia, and classism. Qoheleth insistently questions doctrinal beliefs. This crucial practice in the hands of feminists has become our pickax against the walls of patriarchal theology and even against the so-called "stained-glass ceiling."[3] Qoheleth fosters and encourages a hermeneutic of suspicion toward much of ancient Israelite theology, an approach that has long been acknowledged as crucial for feminist biblicists and theologians. Indeed, use of Qoheleth for feminist aims involves subversive reading that must reject many of the Sage's basic assumptions if we are to start a revolution that will truly create something new. As Jennifer L. Koosed has aptly observed,

> In the end, Ecclesiastes may offer a word of advice to feminist activists. Espousing a revolutionary feminist agenda runs the risk of dismissal; working within sexist systems to reform these systems runs the risk of co-optation. Revolution and reform must work in tension and in tandem, often deliberately defying or subverting conventional notions of consistency, in order to transform the world.[4]

Similarly, Audre Lorde warns me that even though my feminist methodology drives me to ask who is fixing the feast for Qoheleth's *carpe diem*, my biblical analysis had better not overlook the women who care for my children and who clean my house.[5] Lorde is right that we may well be in trouble if we think the very tools of "the master" will solve our

---

3. The earliest citation of this term appears to have been from Ruth Fitzpatrick, the national coordinator of the Women's Ordination Conference. An April 1992 draft of a pastoral letter, addressed to American bishops for review, continued to exclude Roman Catholic women from ordination. In response, Fitzpatrick said that in the document the women only got "crumbs." "Some women will say, let's take these crumbs. . . . I say, we've got to stop licking up the floors and break the stained glass ceiling." Ari L. Goldman, "The Nation: Even for Ordained Women, Church Can Be a Cold Place," *New York Times* (April 9 1992), 18.

4. Jennifer L. Koosed, "Ecclesiastes," in *Women's Bible Commentary*, ed. Carol Ann Newsom, Sharon H. Ringe, and Jacqueline E. Lapsley, 3rd ed. (Louisville: Westminster John Knox, 2012), 246.

5. Lorde wrote, "If white american [sic] feminist theory need not deal with the differences between us, and the resulting difference in our oppressions, then how do you deal with the fact that the women who clean your houses and tend your children while you attend conferences on feminist theory are, for the most part, poor women and women of Color? What is the theory behind racist feminism?" ("The Master's Tools," 112).

problems. Our task is to create new tools, though who says we cannot use the old ones as raw material?

Date

Qoheleth's book is famously difficult to date. Traditionalist readings place the book in the time of the monarchy, due to the reference in 1:1, "son of David," and a reference to "the king" at the end of the "test of pleasure" in 2:1-12, which details luxuries that have much in common with what is elsewhere reported from King Solomon's reign (1 Kgs 4:20-34). Nonetheless, we have long known that just because a biblical book mentions a biblical figure, it does not mean we can date that book to the time of that figure—whether Moses, or Joseph, or Ruth. Probably the most promising method for dating Qoheleth is through linguistic analysis. Even beginning Hebrew students can tell that the grammar and vocabulary in this book are noticeably different from what they learned in their first semester. A number of scholars have identified Qoheleth's writing as late, pre-Mishnaic Hebrew and thus place it in the Hellenistic period.[6] Similarly, the Hellenistic philosophical ideas Qoheleth suggests help establish it in this era.[7] Qoheleth has struck most interpreters as post-Persian, and many locate it in the Ptolemaic era.[8] Choon-Leong Seow notably departs from this dating of the book; he makes the case that it hails from the Persian period, largely due to word usage.[9]

---

6. James L. Crenshaw, *Ecclesiastes: A Commentary*, OTL (Louisville: Westminster John Knox, 1987), 49; Michael V. Fox, *A Time to Tear Down and a Time to Build Up: A Rereading of Ecclesiastes* (Grand Rapids, MI: Eerdmans, 1999), 6 n. 10; Robert Gordis, *Koheleth: The Man and His World* (New York: Jewish Theological Seminary of America, 1951), 60; Antoon Schoors, *The Preacher Sought to Find Pleasing Words: A Study of the Language of Qoheleth* (Leuven: Peeters Press, 1992), 221; Antoon Schoors, *Ecclesiastes* (Leuven: Peeters, 2013), 2–7.

7. Robert Gordis, *Koheleth—The Man and His World* (New York: Bloch, 1962), 30–34, 54, 63–68; Martin Hengel, *Judaism and Hellenism: Studies in Their Encounter in Palestine During the Early Hellenistic Period*, trans. John Bowden (Philadelphia: Fortress, 1974), 115–30; Thomas Krüger, *Qoheleth: A Commentary*, ed. Klaus Baltzer, trans. O. C. Dean, Hermeneia (Minneapolis: Fortress, 2004), 21–22.

8. Krüger, *Qoheleth*, 19–21. See also Ora Brison's view on the canonicity and canonization of the book in chapter 1.

9. Seow argues that the book belongs "specifically between the second half of the fifth century and the first half of the fourth." Choon-Leong Seow, "Linguistic Evidence and the Dating of Qoheleth," *JBL* 115 (1996): 643–66. Also see Choon-Leong Seow, *Ecclesiastes: A New Translation with Introduction and Commentary*, AB 18C (New York: Doubleday, 1997), 11–21.

In the end, there is no real scholarly consensus on a date for this book. If one date is more prevalent than others, it is probably a vague 250 BCE, but any scholar worth her salt will readily admit that is little more than a good educated guess and that other scholars have made decent arguments that place the book in a different time period. At the very least, the book was written after the monarchy, since it includes mention of a king. At the very latest, the fragments of Qoheleth found at Qumran (4Q109Qoh[a] and 4Q110Qoh[b]) date to 175–150 and even to the first century BCE, providing a *terminus ad quem*.[10] Additionally, the book seems not to reflect the violent conflicts of the Maccabees prompted by the abuses of Antiochus IV Epiphanes in 167 BCE.

For the purposes of this commentary, what matters about Qoheleth's date has to do with how it may have affected women in its time. For instance, when Qoheleth discusses inheritance (2:18-19; 5:13-14 [12-13];[11] 7:11), to what extent did that relate to women, in terms of their ability to inherit land or other property? When Qoheleth invokes the *carpe diem*, some version of "eat, and drink, and enjoy your life" (2:24; 3:12-13, 22; 5:18-19 [17-18]; 8:15; 9:7-9; 11:8-9), who would have been preparing and serving the food and drink? Scholars have a limited ability to answer these questions, and the answers to these questions vary from one era and geographical setting to another. Nonetheless, feminist scholars in particular have produced volumes of research that can help us address these questions, and I will do my best to consult their research as appropriate. The key scholars I consult for these matters include: Phyllis Bird, Jennie Ebeling, Tamara Cohn Eskenazi, Rachel Hachlili, Tal Ilan, Carol Meyers, and Harold Washington.[12] Bird, Meyers, and Ebeling primarily

---

10. Krüger, *Qoheleth*, 19.

11. Throughout the Hebrew Bible, including in Qoheleth, there are places where verse numbering differs between the Hebrew MT and most English translations. (A notable exception to this is Jewish Publication Society English translations, which use the MT numbering.) Usually, the numbering is off by one. When verse numbers differ, this volume will first note the English verse number(s); the Hebrew number(s) will immediately follow in brackets.

12. Phyllis Ann Bird, *Missing Persons and Mistaken Identities: Women and Gender in Ancient Israel* (Philadelphia: Fortress, 1997); Jennie R. Ebeling, *Women's Lives in Biblical Times* (London: T & T Clark, 2010); Tamara Cohn Eskenazi, "Out from the Shadows: Biblical Women in the Postexilic Era," *JSOT* 17 (1992): 25–43; Rachel Hachlili, *Jewish Funerary Customs, Practices and Rites in the Second Temple Period*, Supplements to the Journal for the Study of Judaism 94 (Leiden: Brill, 2005); Tal Ilan, *Integrating Women into Second Temple History* (Peabody, MA: Hendrickson, 2001); Tal Ilan, *Jewish Women*

address women in the Iron I and II eras. In all likelihood, some of what we can learn about women from these periods would have held true for at least some women (and perhaps most) for many centuries beyond, depending on setting, socio-economic status, and related factors. For instance, the archaeological record shows that the process for grinding flour changed over the centuries, while the domed, three-foot-across clay bread ovens continued in use in Middle Eastern villages into the 1900s of the Common Era.[13] Hachlili, Eskenazi, Ilan, and Washington address Second Temple women, primarily the early Second Temple period, while Ilan also differentiates some of the factors that affected women into the Greco-Roman Period. Unfortunately, even if we had a definitive date for the book of Qoheleth, that would not necessarily tell us what social and gender mores to apply—from marriage practices, to life expectancy, to inheritance rights, to division of labor—because those varied from one community to the next even in the same time period, depending on factors such as geography, socio-economic status, and external cultural influences, to name just a few.

One argument about women's roles in biblical times suggests that women had more freedom, independence, and equality in the agrarian pre-monarchic settings than in urban ones during the time of the monarchy. Thus, during the time of the biblical ancestors and judges, women seem to have had a greater role in household leadership and decision making than would have been the case in the time of the monarchy; this may again have been true shortly after the exile, when a village-type setting was again the norm. Carol Meyers, however, helpfully provides nuance for this theory. She points out that, not only would the type of governance matter, but also the context in which a given woman was living. Thus a woman living within the city walls of Jerusalem during the time of the monarchy would have perhaps enjoyed less freedom or equality with her male counterparts than a woman living in a village some distance from the city, even during the same time period.[14]

---

in Greco-Roman Palestine (Peabody, MA: Hendrickson, 1996); Carol Meyers, *Rediscovering Eve: Ancient Israelite Women in Context* (New York: Oxford University Press, 2012); Harold Washington, "The Strange Woman (אשה זרה/נכריה) of Proverbs 1–9 and Post-Exilic Judaean Society," in *Second Temple Studies*, vol. 2: *Temple Community in the Persian Period* (Sheffield: JSOT Press, 1994), 217–42.

13. Meyers, *Rediscovering Eve*, 131.

14. Ibid., 117.

Gleaning historical knowledge from the biblical texts themselves is a tricky enterprise since the dating of biblical texts is often highly debated. Thus a description of women inheriting property in the Pentateuch may well reflect a historical situation from the Persian period rather than the ancestral period.[15] Furthermore, we cannot make the assumption that just because women were able to inherit in one time period, they were allowed to do so after that time. To the extent that the Pentateuch (even the Hexateuch and Deuteronomistic History) bear clear marks of postexilic editing or authorship, their relevance even to Iron I or II culture falls into question.

We must not succumb to the evolutionary trap of believing that each new era brought more equality for women. Each era, community, and location was potentially governed by different laws and mores about inheritance rights, household duties, and gender roles. Of course, we need only look around the world today to see the enduring truth of this.

In order to navigate this difficult situation, I will do my best below to provide the most applicable historical research for a given issue in Qoheleth. In some cases, I have consulted material on women in the Iron Age when it seems safe to assume that certain of those background gender roles would have remained throughout the vast time period of "the biblical era." In other cases, I cite historical research on the Persian era, the broad "Second Temple period," and even into Greco-Roman periods. My caveat here is a reminder that we cannot know for certain which historical material would have been most relevant to Qoheleth. Further complicating matters is the possibility that Qoheleth may have been writing as a "persona" and even raising issues that would have been most pressing for a time other than the one in which Qoheleth wrote. My goal is to be transparent enough in my writing so that readers can easily unpack my arguments or suggestions about historical matters and interact with those ideas accordingly. There is much to gain from asking these questions and searching out their answers, all the while juggling different time periods and cultural settings and the way they may have impinged on gender roles, among other things.

That said, my general conclusions about the dating of Qoheleth include a date of approximately 250 BCE, with heavy influence from Hellenistic thought, despite the lack of precise quotations from Greek philoso-

---

15. Harold Washington makes this very point in his article "The Strange Woman," 217–42.

phers. I assume that Qoheleth was familiar with the basic content of the Pentateuch and the Prophets (though not that these scrolls would have been directly available) and that Qoheleth operated within the tradition of the Sages. As such, I assume that Qoheleth had some knowledge of and particular interest in engaging the material in Proverbs and Job. Based on Qoheleth's "test of pleasure" in 2:1-11, an urban, royal setting seems to fit better than an agrarian one. Furthermore, passages throughout Qoheleth seem to suggest a fairly hierarchical culture (2:1-11; 4:1; 5:8 [7]; 7:19, 21-22; 8:9; 10:7, 16-17, 20). It seems likely that women in Qoheleth's setting would have been living in a more entrenched patriarchal milieu than what would have been the case in the ancestral period or even the early Second Temple period, where a more agrarian setting relied on everyone—regardless of gender—to contribute to the work of the household as much as possible. Indeed, Carol Meyers agrees that Jerusalem women in the Hellenistic-Roman period probably had less autonomy and power than when they ran entire households.[16] Yet this pioneer of historical-critical, anthropological feminist biblical scholarship would correct my language here, omitting "patriarchal" and "hierarchical" in favor of "the recognition that there were intersecting systems and multiple loci of power with women as well as men shaping society. The heterarchy model allows for a more nuanced and probably more accurate view of Iron Age Israel—a view that acknowledges significant domains of female agency and power."[17] Without taking on Meyers' whole argument, I will say that while I agree we must acknowledge the variations in power structures related to gender and socio-economic status, I also find it crucial to name the ways in which women's lives were restricted, suppressed, and erased. In certain contexts, "patriarchy" and "hierarchy" do a good job of describing what we can ascertain from a biblical text or even from an archaeological record, even though they may not be accurate universal labels. I will do my best to provide detail in order to welcome readers to critique my own use of these terms in those contexts.

A significant open question relates to the matter of inheritance, which is a topic of great interest to Qoheleth. We see women able to inherit

16. Meyers, *Rediscovering Eve*, 206. Additionally, Meyers details the negative comments that Philo wrote about women in the Greco-Roman era (he lived 20 BCE to 50 CE) and notes how these views were just the beginning of anachronistically misogynistic biblical interpretations (210). Also see page 201 for her discussion of the way later sexist views affected the way Bible readers understood Hebrew Bible texts.

17. Ibid., 198.

in Numbers 27:1-11 and 36:1-13—at least for the sake of keeping tribal land under tribal auspices—and that practice seems relevant to the early Second Temple period.[18] Eskenazi observes that, in the early postexilic period, "on the basis of the Elephantine documents . . . daughters could inherit even when there were sons."[19] Tal Ilan's work on women inheriting, as it related to Jewish women in the Greco-Roman period, shows variations and debate on the topic between the Pharisees and the Sadducees, and the Schools of Shammai and Hillel; Ilan explores evidence from influential Roman practices, *Ketubot*, the Babylonian Talmud, and the Mishnah.[20] In general, it seems that Jewish women in the Greco-Roman period were rather limited in their ability to inherit according to biblical law and various interpretations of it. In practice, however, *Ketubot* allowed for a certain amount of inheritance for women and certainly the observance of the provisions set forth in Numbers 27:8-11 and 36:9. Ilan concludes, "The laws and remedies . . . enabled a father or a husband to transfer to his daughters or wife as much of his property as he wanted, and also to rest assured that in the event of his death they will be able to maintain a respectable standard of living—and all this despite the quite specific biblical laws against inheritance and property ownership by women."[21] Roman practices, which allowed women greater inheritance rights, seem also to have affected certain Jewish communities or individuals.[22] In the end, we cannot know for certain Qoheleth's experience with or views on women's inheritance. The cultural contexts from the early Second Temple period of Persian rule through to the Greco-Roman period allowed for a wide range of practices. The best we can do in analyzing Qoheleth's views on inheritance as they might have applied to women of the time is to keep in mind this variation and consider the different possibilities for how Qoheleth's comments may have affected women in those settings.

One strategy that I have undertaken in this commentary is to compare certain aspects of Qoheleth to biblical women. For instance, in order to ascertain the possible relevance of the poem in 3:1-8 to ancient women, I researched each verb in the poem to see whether and how often it appeared

18. Washington, "The Strange Woman," 235–36; Eskenazi, "Out from the Shadows," 35, 40; Ruth 4:3.

19. Eskenazi, "Out from the Shadows," 40.

20. Ilan, *Jewish Women*, 167–69.

21. Ibid., 170.

22. Ibid., 170–71.

with a female subject elsewhere in the Hebrew Bible. This provides helpful context and allows for the possibility that women could have found points of reference in this largely androcentric book. The limits of this strategy, however, have to do with the differences between biblical women and Israelite women. On this point, Carol Meyers aptly notes, "Assuming that the countless women inhabiting the villages and hamlets of ancient Israel can be seen in the several exceptional biblical ones is to believe we can see an entire structure when only a fragment is visible."[23] Throughout this commentary, biblical women serve as touchstones in an attempt to understand how a female audience might potentially have interacted with the book of Qoheleth. It is only right for me to note that these connections to biblical women can also be misleading.

Perhaps, amid all of these unanswered questions about women's issues throughout antiquity, the best we can do is rule out inaccurate universal claims. For instance, "Women had no rights." "Women could not inherit." "Women were chattel." "Women mattered only for their ability to bear children." While all of these claims seem to have some truth in some ancient contexts, they are by no means correct as blanket statements. Carol Meyers reminds us that "the division of labor by gender in traditional societies is rarely absolute."[24] Even if we omit "traditional societies" from this statement, it remains an effective observation. If we do nothing more than to explore the exceptions to these inaccuracies, we provide nuance to our understanding of the ancient world as a whole, and we let women into the picture. Let us not overstate the case of ancient patriarchy such that women become more excluded than they actually were.

Hevel [הבל]

Qoheleth's theme word poses both the key to solving and the barrier to understanding the book. Because the word *hevel* appears so often in the book and is so difficult to translate, I will refer to it in transliterated form throughout this commentary: *hevel*. In the Masoretic Text, the root הבל appears eighty-six times; of that, it occurs thirty-eight times in Qoheleth, 52 percent of the occurrences.[25] In several places, it has quite concrete meanings, which are clear from the literary context: the proper

23. Meyers, *Rediscovering Eve*, 3.
24. Ibid., 127.
25. The word appears eighty-seven and thirty-nine times, respectively, depending on emending Qoh 9:2; see commentary on that verse below.

name "Abel" (Gen 4), "idol" (as in foreign god; particularly seen in Jer 8:19; 10:8; 14:22), and "breath" (as in Isa 57:13, where *hevel* is in parallel with רוּחַ, "spirit or wind"). The translation "breath" finds additional support because Qoheleth often pairs *hevel* with the phrase "and a striving after wind."[26] The elusive aspect of breath, which is the literal meaning of *hevel*, fits well with this phrase, which describes a similarly elusive task. An even larger number of meanings fit in various contexts, including "worthless" (Isa 30:7), "insubstantial" (Ps 78:33), "futile" (Jer 10:3), "fleeting" (Ps 39:5 [6]), "unreliable" (Jer 2:5), "in vain" (Zech 10:2), and "foolish" (Job 27:12). Psalm 39 includes a concentrated use of *hevel* in order to express its topic of the brevity of life and the uselessness of worry in the face of God's knowledge and control in verses 5, 6, and 11 [6, 7, 12].[27] In some places in the Hebrew Bible the best translation for a given occurrence of *hevel* cannot be easily established because the context is too ambiguous. A good example is Psalm 94:11, in which the Lord knows human thoughts, and they are *hevel*. This is much like Qoheleth's repeated conclusions: the meaning is vague. It could suggest that human thoughts are fleeting, irrelevant, futile, meaningless, or absurd. This ambiguity, perhaps by intention on the part of Qoheleth, underlies the puzzling nature of Qoheleth's book.

Translating this word poses a challenge for all translators and interpreters. Actual translations of *hevel* abound. Most verbal translations select one word to use for all thirty-eight references, effectively signaling to the English reader each appearance of *hevel* in the MT. KJV, RSV, and NRSV nearly exclusively use the translation "vanity" every time *hevel* appears in the Hebrew. This translation choice arose first with the Latin Vulgate (around 400 CE: *vanitas*). "Vanity" has little corresponding meaning in contemporary English to what Qoheleth was apparently trying to express; yet the very obscurity of "vanity" has some benefit, in that readers may determine what *hevel* meant without filling in a great deal of their own knowledge about this little-used English word. NIV, NJB, and CEB also consistently use one word (and its appropriate variations): "meaningless," "futile," and "pointless," respectively. Thus, English readers of the KJV, RSV, NRSV, NIV, NJB, and CEB can fairly precisely determine where Qoheleth used *hevel*. One strategy interpreters may employ is to provide a translation that fits each context. Through this

26. Qoh 1:14; 2:11, 17, 26; 4:4; 6:9. In 4:6 the phrase occurs without *hevel*.

27. See James L. Crenshaw, *Qoheleth: The Ironic Wink*, Studies on Personalities in the Old Testament (Columbia: University of South Carolina Press, 2013), 40–48, for analysis of the psalm and comparison with Qoheleth as well as other biblical passages.

method, English readers easily miss Qoheleth's strategy of repetition, although they receive more meaning-filled passages. Thus NASB enlists a mix of "vanity," "futility," "emptiness," and "fleeting," and while NJPS most often uses "futile/futility" (1:2 and in most other cases throughout), it also provides "nothing" (3:19), "illusory" (7:6), "brief" (7:15), and "frustration" (8:10). Finally, NET wins the award for most diverse translations of *hevel*: "meaningless," "futile," "profitless," "fleeting," "fruitless," "enigma," "useless," and "obscure."

Needless to say, *hevel* has a substantial range of meaning, particularly in the hands of Hebrew-English translators of Qoheleth. The benefit in choosing different words for *hevel* throughout the book is that the translator can convey as effectively as possible what the word means in a given verse, considering the context. On the other hand, this method prevents the English reader from seeing Qoheleth's frequent use of this word, which is surely a significant literary feature of the book. Another drawback of trying to choose one word for each use of *hevel* in Qoheleth is that any English word chosen will carry its own connotations, and those will affect the reader's understanding of the book as a whole. Since the book is so wide open to interpretation, this one translation choice may easily become a way for a translator to impose her or his understanding of the book on the reader. As Julie Duncan has pointed out, Qoheleth contains such ambiguity that in the end it becomes "a Rorschach test for the interpreter."[28] One's translation choice for *hevel* may be the key to that test. A good example here is Huang Wei's innovative and fully contextualized comparison of *hevel* to the Chinese character *kong*, as used in the *Heart Sūtra* for emptiness.[29] Kathleen A. Farmer offers a helpful suggestion, which is to choose a literal translation, such as "breathlike"; the word then takes on metaphorical meaning throughout the book, based only on its literary context.[30] Julie Duncan discusses *hevel* extensively through the metaphorical translation "vapor" and its various uses throughout the Hebrew Bible and in Qoheleth.[31] Eugene Peterson does something like this in using "smoke" for *hevel* in his translation in *The*

---

28. Personal communication.

29. Huang Wei, "*Hebel* and *Kong*: A Cross-Textual Reading between Qoheleth and the *Heart Sūtra*," in *The Five Scrolls*, Texts@Contexts 6, ed. Athalaya Brenner-Idan, Gale A. Yee, Archie C. C. Lee (London: Bloomsbury T&T Clark, 2018), 135–44, at 140–41.

30. Kathleen Anne Farmer, *Who Knows What Is Good? A Commentary on the Books of Proverbs and Ecclesiastes*, ITC (Grand Rapids, MI: Eerdmans, 1991), 146.

31. Julie Ann Duncan, *Ecclesiastes*, AOTC (Nashville: Abingdon, 2017), 3–9.

Message.[32] A similar idea is simply to use *hevel* untranslated within an English translation; this avoids any preexisting meaning that the literal meaning contains and allows for a reader to fully infuse the word with the meanings provided by its context.

If pressed, my preferred translation of *hevel* is "absurd" or "absurdity." This translation was articulated by Michael V. Fox as early as 1986 and popularized in his subsequent commentaries.[33] Fox bases this translation on Albert Camus' understanding of "absurd/absurdity," explaining:

> The essence of the absurd is a disparity between two terms that are supposed to be joined by a link of harmony or causality but are, in fact, disjunct. Absurdity is an affront to reason, in the broad sense of the human faculty that looks for order in the world about us. The quality of absurdity does not inhere in a being, act, or event in and of itself (though these may be called "absurd"), but rather in the tension between a certain reality and a framework of expectations.[34]

My read of Qoheleth's book finds this disjunction at the very core of what bothers Qoheleth most. It is the God-given desire to know what the "right time" is, paired with the utter inability to discover that time (3:11). It is the difference between what we should expect from divine justice (8:12-13) and what we see instead (8:14). As I have observed above, however, this English word, like any, carries its own connotations for the reader. It may in fact be overly negative, which perhaps betrays my own reading of the book, or—if Qoheleth is like a Rorschach test—it betrays my own view of life. Of course, to read a biblical book through the lens of Camus, as offered by Fox, risks anachronism at the very least. In the end, part of this commentary series has to do with offering readers more interpretive choices rather than fewer. For that reason, I have determined to keep the Hebrew word *hevel* in transliteration throughout and let each reader choose her or his own appropriate translation(s).

32. Eugene H. Peterson, *The Message: The Bible in Contemporary Language* (Colorado Springs: NavPress, 2002).

33. Michael V. Fox, "The Meaning of *Hebel* for Qohelet," *JBL* 105 (1986): 409–27; Michael V. Fox, *Qoheleth and His Contradictions*, BLS 18 (Sheffield: Almond, 1989); Fox, *A Time to Tear Down*.

34. Fox, "The Meaning of *Hebel*," 409. Interestingly, Wei finds Fox's choice and explanation of "absurdity" for *hevel* similar to the use of *kong* in the *Heart Sūtra*. Huang Wei, "*Hebel* and *Kong*," 142.

Carpe Diem

Repeated seven times throughout the book, Qoheleth's refrain to "eat, and drink, and enjoy" (or some variation of that) provides the primary salve for the Sage's starkly realistic observations about life, theology, and anthropology.[35] While more than one commentator has used these repeated admonitions to dub Qoheleth a "preacher of joy," others—myself included—have found the *carpe diem* more of a distraction from *hevel* than a true experience of "sucking the marrow out of life."[36] Each reader must choose, of course, how to take this, and that will surely relate to one's own experiences and demeanor. But for the purposes of this commentary, an apt question is this: If our best or only recourse to the *hevel* of life is to enjoy food and drink, who is preparing and serving it? As far as women are concerned, to what extent can we participate in such pleasure, as opposed to being objectified as the ones who would provide such delights? Given the historical limitations detailed above, I will explore this question as much as possible, from looking at how women appear on Qoheleth's list of luxury items (2:8) to considering ancient women as the makers of beer (11:1). Of course, these questions matter not only for the women in Qoheleth's time but for women readers of Qoheleth today as well. Can I seize the day if I had to fix the feast? Does finding joy in life rely on someone else's servitude?

"Better-Than" Sayings in Qoheleth

One of Qoheleth's favorite methods of reflection involves use of "better-than" sayings. The form of these proverbs is familiar from the book of Proverbs—notably, both books contain twenty-three of these sayings—yet Qoheleth often uses them for surprising purposes. The large number of better-than sayings in Qoheleth raises the possibility that the Sage was creating a collection of such sayings for the rhetorical purposes of this book. Presumably, the Sage took at least some of these from wisdom collections now lost to us. It also seems likely that some of these were uniquely Qoheleth's.

The chart below shows that Qoheleth's "better-than" sayings often emphasize particular points by surprising the reader with an unexpected

35. Qoheleth's *carpe diem* ("seize the day") appears in 2:24-25; 3:12-13, 22; 5:18-19 [17-18]; 8:15; 9:7-9; and 11:8-9.

36. Roger N. Whybray, "Qoheleth, Preacher of Joy," *JSOT* 7 (1982): 87–98. Jerome N. Douglas revisits this title in his book *A Polemical Preacher of Joy: An Anti-Apocalpytic Genre for Qoheleth's Message of Joy* (Eugene, OR: Wipf and Stock, 2014); Henry David Thoreau, *Walden* (Black and White Classics, 2014; originally published 1854), 51.

comparison. For instance, in five cases the "better" item has to do with death or never having been born (4:2-3; 6:3; 7:1, 2, 8). Qoheleth also enlists proverbs that start out fulfilling our expectations, such as the ones that privilege wisdom (4:13; 7:5; 9:16, 18). In fact, as unconventional as Qoheleth's proverbs can be, none of them uses wisdom as the lesser item. In the case of more predictable comparisons, Qoheleth often places those in contexts that undermine traditional wisdom, for instance, by following a "better-than" proverb with a *hevel* statement (6:9) or by starting with "wisdom" as the "better" item and following that with a statement that undermines the efficacy of wisdom (9:16). Sometimes when Qoheleth presents a "better-than" saying in unexpected order, the Sage follows that with a phrase that undoes the reversal, for instance, in 7:3: "Sorrow is better than laughter" challenges our assumptions, but the following phrase, "for by sadness of countenance the heart is made glad," essentially turns "sorrow" into "gladness," bringing us back to something expected. Qoheleth 4:2-3 and 7:2 similarly contain follow-up statements that undermine their surprising nature. It could seem that Qoheleth's comparative formula emphasizes some kind of moral hierarchy throughout the book, but the Sage's use of these proverbs is not so simple as to consistently privilege certain categories, other than the fourfold emphasis that "nothing" is better than some version of the *carpe diem* (2:24; 3:12, 22; 8:15).

Reference	Better item	Lesser item	Immediate context
2:24	*carpe diem*		
3:12	*carpe diem*		
3:22	*carpe diem*		
4:2-3	"the one who has not yet been" (v. 3)	"the dead" and "the living" (v. 2)	"[the one who has not yet been] has not seen the evil deeds that are done under the sun"
4:6	"handful with quiet"	"two handfuls with toil"	"and a chasing after wind"
4:9	"two"	"one"	"they have a good reward for their toil"
4:13	"poor but wise youth"	"old but foolish king, who will no longer take advice"	

5:1 [4:17]	"to draw near to listen"	"the sacrifice offered by fools"	"[fools] do not know how to keep from doing evil"
5:5 [4]	"not vow"	"vow and not fulfill it"	
6:3	"stillborn child"	"a man who beget[s] a hundred children, and live[s] many years; but . . . does not enjoy life's good things, or has no burial"	
6:9	"sight of the eyes"	"wandering of desire"	*hevel*
7:1	"good name"	"precious ointment"	
7:1	"day of death"	"day of birth"	
7:2	"to go to the house of mourning"	"to go to the house of feasting"	"for this is the end of everyone, and the living will lay it to heart"
7:3	"sorrow"	"laughter"	"for by sadness of countenance the heart is made glad"
7:5	"to hear the rebuke of the wise"	"to hear the song of fools"	
7:8	"the end of a thing"	"its beginning"	
7:8	"patient in spirit"	"proud in spirit"	
7:10	"former days"	"these"	"do not say why . . ."
8:15	*carpe diem*		
9:4	"living dog"	"dead lion"	"whoever is joined with all the living has hope"
9:16	"wisdom"	"might"	"yet the poor man's wisdom is despised, and his words are not heeded"
9:18	"wisdom"	"weapons of war"	"but one bungler destroys much good"

Gendered Language in Qoheleth[37]

Jennifer Koosed rightly points out that "the gender ideologies in the book of Ecclesiastes are more complex than they first appear."[38] This became increasingly apparent to me in the process of writing this commentary. Qoheleth takes us from "gender-bending" to gender ambiguity to what seems to be all-out misogyny. An early starting point for me was to determine how to most accurately translate איש (*'ish*), "man"; אשה (*'ishshah*), "woman"; and אדם (*'adam*), "human being," in Qoheleth. Since the publication of the NRSV in 1989, the convention of translating אדם as "human" has become the norm. This translation does not, however, always accurately convey the appropriate sense of the word according to its context. Given Qoheleth's mixed reputation as a misogynist (7:26, 28) and lover (9:9), it is worth assessing the use of אדם throughout the book, to discover whether "human" is an accurate translation of the word there. When does אדם mean "male," and when does it mean "humankind"? This difficulty persists even in twenty-first-century English, both on the evening news and in my students' papers, despite the explanatory inclusive language instructions I place in each of my syllabi. It is no surprise, then, that confusion about this abounds also in the book of Qoheleth. My goal as a feminist interpreter is to discover as best as possible Qoheleth's meaning behind the two Hebrew words that most commonly hide behind the English translations of "man," "men," "humans," "humanity," and "humankind." These Hebrew words are איש (with אנשים as its plural) and אדם. Thus, if all the contextual clues suggest that Qoheleth means "male" when using אדם, then I want to know that—even if it seems logical to have included women in a reference. In other words, if Qoheleth routinely ignored the fact that women were part of everyday life, and rather just attended to the experience of men, then I want to know that. It is not my goal to rescue Qoheleth from whatever gender bias affected this book or the culture out of which it arose.

Our contemporary context complicates this since those of us who are translators and interpreters, feminists and nonfeminists alike, have also been considering how to best understand references to mixed-sex groups, particularly when the original language uses a specifically male term.

---

37. Parts of this section were excerpted from Lisa Wolfe, "Man, Woman, or Human? *'Ish, 'Ishah,* and *'Adam* in Ecclesiastes," presented at the Annual Meeting of the Southwest Commission on Religious Studies (Dallas, 2015).

38. Koosed, "Ecclesiastes," 244.

This project has been attended to by the New Revised Standard Version, according to their "mandates given to the Committee in 1980 by the Division of Education and Ministry of the National Council of Churches of Christ." To quote from the NRSV's "To the Reader," by Bruce Metzger:

> During the almost half a century since the publication of the RSV, many in the churches have become sensitive to the danger of linguistic sexism arising from the inherent bias of the English language toward the masculine gender, a bias that in the case of the Bible has often restricted or obscured the meaning of the original text. The mandates from the Division specified that, in references to men and women, masculine-oriented language should be eliminated as far as this can be done without altering passages that reflect the historical situation of ancient patriarchal culture. As can be appreciated, more than once the Committee found that the several mandates stood in tension and even in conflict. The various concerns had to be balanced case by case in order to provide a faithful and acceptable rendering without using contrived English.[39]

I am absolutely sympathetic to this philosophy, particularly when the primary use of the translation is in liturgical or lay settings where the distinction between what it "meant" and what it "means" (to quote Krister Stendahl) is essentially collapsed.[40] For the sake of scholarship, however, it is all the more important to learn the most likely meaning of words in their own time, regardless of the gender bias they exude. To that end, the NRSV translation of הָאָדָם (with the definite article) as "humankind" in Genesis 1:27 and as "man" in Genesis 2:7 (neither with the definite article) has prompted debate among scholars and clergy alike.

In an effort to better understand whether Qoheleth has a gender bias— and if so to know what it is—I have examined all the occurrences of אדם, "human," and אִישׁ, "man," in the book. According to *The Brown-Driver-Briggs (BDB)*, the standard lexicon in the field, the word אִישׁ refers to "man"—that is, a male—in almost every one of its 339 occurrences in the Hebrew Bible. So, this word seems like an easy and logical starting point. The *BDB* does list occasions, however, when women are included in the

---

39. Bruce Metzger, for the Committee, "To the Reader," in Harold W. Attridge, ed., *The HarperCollins Study Bible: Fully Revised and Updated* (New York: HarperCollins, 2006), xxiii.

40. Krister Stendahl, "Biblical Theology, Contemporary," in *The Interpreter's Dictionary of the Bible Supplement*, ed. George Arthur Buttrick (New York: Abingdon, 1962), 418–32.

"distributive" use of this term, though those are, of course, debatable.[41] Furthermore, in at least one case, איש even refers to inanimate objects.[42] In Qoheleth, איש appears ten times. In four of those cases, the word clearly refers to a male person.[43] But in two of those places, it could arguably indicate a generic group of men *and* women. In the NRSV translation of 1:8, Qoheleth asserts that "all things are *hevel*, more than one [איש] can express." Presumably, Qoheleth's point is that *hevel*, or "absurdity," exceeds the ability of anyone—either man or woman—to articulate it. And if Qoheleth thinks that *hevel* is too much for a man to communicate, then it would likely rule out a woman as well. It is also possible, however, that Qoheleth would have scarcely considered the possibility of a woman speaking the phrase. Another place where Qoheleth possibly uses איש as a gender-neutral term is 7:5, in a proverb that states, "It is better to hear the rebuke of the wise than [for an איש] to hear the song of fools." Again, surely men and women alike are able to hear both wise rebuke and foolish song, but I wonder if Qoheleth would not have considered women as part of the audience here and so only איש would be necessary; Qoheleth may well have meant it precisely as "men." After all, in 11:9, Qoheleth gives a direct address to a "young man" (בחור). Less likely instances of איש that could refer to humanity are 4:4 and 9:14. In 4:4, Qoheleth refers to toil (עמל) that leads to envy, so that may well refer to male toilers. In 9:14, we get part of a wisdom parable about a "little city with few אנשים, *'anashim*, in it," which is under siege. While that could refer to the population as a whole—NRSV translates אנשים as "people"—the battle reference most likely indicates the inability of the city to defend itself, based on its specifically male population.

In four other cases, the use of איש (or the plural אנשים) in Qoheleth seems to specifically apply to males. The topics of "wealth, possessions, and honor" in 6:2 suggest that the two references to איש there indicate males, as we would not normally expect women to be associated with those things in the historical context. In the following verse, Qoheleth uses the *hiphil* of ילד with איש, meaning "beget" or "sire," thus unmistakably referring to a male. Qoheleth's point there seems to be that an איש with many offspring is better off dead without a good, long life and decent burial. As I mentioned earlier, 9:15 refers to the "poor wise איש" who saves the besieged city of אנשים, in which case the איש is most

---

41. For instance, Job 42:11; 1 Chr 16:3.
42. *BDB* 36a for Gen 15:10.
43. Qoh 6:2, 3; 9:15; 12:15.

certainly male—not because no female could save a besieged city (see Judg 9:53-54 and 2 Sam 11:21), but because it refers to a single individual, who through אִישׁ is gendered as male. Finally, in the closing poem of chapter 12, Qoheleth writes that "the strong אֲנָשִׁים are bent" (v. 3). That line parallels an odd line about "grinders," a feminine participle (and *hapax*); many interpreters take this word as a reference to old women, which would suggest the parallel אֲנָשִׁים as old men. Thus, Qoheleth uses אִישׁ and אֲנָשִׁים mostly to refer to males; in some cases, however, the Sage could conceivably be using the words for mixed-sex groups.

The *BDB* defines אָדָם more broadly as "man," or "mankind." While the first meaning *BDB* assigns to the word is "a man" (I would think that *could* mean "male"), yet it also says that "a man" equals (with an actual = as though we are doing math) "human being." And where is "woman" in this equation? I, for one, would like more clarity than that. Is אָדָם "male," or is it "human being"? *BDB* goes on to provide many more examples of the word's second definition, the collective "mankind" (as in "humankind," presumably). Indeed, NRSV often renders אָדָם as "humankind," including in Genesis 1:26-27, the *imago dei* passage. Since this is a feminist commentary on Qoheleth, at first it seemed like a foregone conclusion that I would use the so-called inclusive translation of אָדָם, but it did not take me long to realize that Qoheleth may not have had an inclusive intent when using this word—even if it is used within its reasonable semantic range!

Qoheleth enlists the word אָדָם forty-seven times. I attempted to sort the אָדָם references in Qoheleth between citations that apply either to a mixed-gender group or specifically to males. There are five cases in which אָדָם seems to specifically indicate a male: 2:8, 12, 18, 21; and 7:28. In 2:8, Qoheleth is reporting on the test of pleasure (2:1-11), and while the Hebrew of the verse is difficult, it seems likely that this part of the verse specifically indicates male sexual pleasures. The reference in 2:12 is about the אָדָם who will follow the king—surely a male. Verses 2:18, 21 are similar: both are about the results of a man's labors—in verse 18 they are Qoheleth's labors, and in verse 21 they are those of an אָדָם being passed on to another אָדָם. In each case, it is fair to assume that mainly males would have been bequeathing the fruits of their labors and then passing them on to other males. The most blatant example of Qoheleth using אָדָם for a male is 7:28, which places אָדָם over against אִשָּׁה, "woman."

In five different instances, Qoheleth's use of אָדָם could legitimately apply to all humans, though we cannot know whether the Sage had women in mind: In 7:2 and 12:5 Qoheleth concludes that everyone (הָאָדָם,

as a collective noun) dies. In 7:20 the point is that no one (אדם) never sins. In 9:15 Qoheleth writes a parable about a poor wise man (there Qoheleth uses איש) whom no one (אדם) remembered, and in 12:13 the epilogue chastises everyone (האדם) to observe the commandments. This final instance is debatable as a generic use, however, since in much of the Pentateuch the commandments are directed exclusively toward men, such as the admonition in Exodus 20:17 not to covet "your neighbor's wife." There are nineteen other places where we could make an argument to translate אדם as "human" in Qoheleth.[44] These are less certain than the previous five I just named; in these cases, it is somewhat plausible that Qoheleth may have had a mixed-sex group in mind, though the Sage may well have intended only males. In fourteen instances it seems less likely still that Qoheleth would have been referring to both men and women in the use of אדם or האדם.[45]

On a final note, in four of the seven *carpe diem* passages, Qoheleth uses the term אדם to recommend enjoyment of life and toil, for instance, in 2:24: "there is nothing better for an אדם but to eat, and drink, and show himself enjoyment in his toil" (also see 3:12-13, 22; 8:15). In two other instances (5:17-18 [16-17]; 9:7-9) Qoheleth does not refer to אדם or איש but instead uses the male pronoun inherent in the gender of the conjugated verbs. Since the final *carpe diem* in 11:9-10 contains בחור, "young man," and relates to האדם in the previous verse, it is a reasonable hypothesis that Qoheleth had males in mind for all of these sayings.

In sum, Qoheleth seems to use איש and אדם fairly interchangeably, with both איש and אדם referring both to males and to humans. This complicates the translator's job, making it impossible to choose just one English word for each Hebrew word and always be accurate. The closest thing to a bottom line here is that Qoheleth's use of either term to indicate "humans"—including women—is minimal, and based on this review it seems likely that Qoheleth sees no reason to differentiate between all-male or mixed-sex groups.

Furthermore, to translate איש or אדם as "human" in Qoheleth does not adequately take into account the cultural setting or mind-set, which may even have prevented Qoheleth from considering that a city includes women (9:15) or that the specter of death haunts women as much as

44. In the following verses from Qoheleth, it seems reasonable to translate אדם as "human": 2:3, 24, 26; 3:10, 11, 13, 18, 19, 21, 22; 7:14, 29, 8:11, 15, 17; 9:1, 3, 12; 10:14.

45. In 1:3, 13; 2:22; 5:19 [18]; 6:1, 7, 10, 11, 12; 8:1, 6, 8, 9; 11:8 it seems unlikely that Qoheleth was indicating "human(s)" in using אדם or האדם.

men (7:2; 12:5). On those few occasions when Qoheleth clearly indicates a female, the Sage uses אשה: 7:26, 28; 9:9. It may well be that those are the only times Qoheleth considers women in this book. Apparently, Qoheleth's default setting is male.

Thus the questions linger as we investigate Qoheleth: If pressed, would Qoheleth have advocated that women "eat, drink, and enjoy" or that they just serve the food (and if so, should they have enjoyed that toil)? Even in the places where Qoheleth may have had a mixed-sex group in mind, it is still quite feasible that Qoheleth truly only meant males and would not have included women even in the comments that we would readily apply to all humans, male and female alike.[46] Of course, we cannot know what was in Qoheleth's mind. That leaves us with the reader's burden of wondering what Qoheleth meant. But it also gives us—even women—the freedom to lament,

הבל הבלים הכל הבל, (Qoh 1:2)

whether Qoheleth ever imagined a woman uttering this mantra or not. Qoheleth surely lives on in these words, but we have the liberty to read, reinterpret, and reinscribe as we see fit, even if we conclude that Qoheleth and the worldview and language that permeate the book are *hevel*.

Qoheleth: Book, Person, Persona

In the Hebrew Bible and in Jewish tradition, the book as well as the person identified in 1:1 goes by the name Qoheleth. The title "Ecclesiastes" carries anachronistic Christian connotations. Though it arose first from the Septuagint (*Ekklesiastes*), later use of the Greek term, including in the New Testament, became centrally identified with the church. To attempt reading the book without those Christian connotations, I will adopt the Jewish convention and identify the book as "Qoheleth," or "the book of Qoheleth."

The third-person identification of the book's author as קהלת (*Qoheleth*) provides both fascinating and perplexing information about the book it introduces. The word קהלת appears seven times in the book (1:1, 2, 12; 7:27; 12:8, 9, 10), most often without the definite article, though twice the term includes the definite article (הקהלת), suggesting the possibility of a title rather

---

46. In these verses, it seems possible that Qoheleth was referring to a mixed-sex group: for איש, 1:8; 4:4; 7:5; 9:14; for אדם, 7:2, 20; 9:15; 12:5, 13.

than a name.[47] The grammatical form appears to be a feminine participle of the root קהל (*qhl*). The feminist speculation this invites appears below. This book tells us that, among other things, Qoheleth made declarations (1:2; 12:8), shared reflections (7:27), and was identified as one of David's sons and as "king over Israel in Jerusalem" (1:1, 12). The lengthiest third-person description of Qoheleth is from 12:9-10, which could be from a separate epoligist or frame-narrator but is nonetheless worth our consideration: "In addition, Qoheleth was wise, and taught knowledge to the people, and weighed and studied the straightness of many proverbs. Qoheleth sought to find pleasing words, and wrote upright and truthful words" (12:9-10).[48] This passage makes Qoheleth sound like a good, upstanding sage, fully in the tradition of those who wrote and assembled ancient Israel's aphorisms and who diligently taught them to all those who would listen. Yet much of the book prior to that point would make us puzzle at this description.

Debates persist about the etymology and meaning of the term "Qoheleth." The ambiguity of the word itself—from its root, to its stem, to its grammatical gender—serves as ongoing fodder for those deliberations. The meaning of the term likely has something to do with one who addresses an assembly. Thus we could consider Qoheleth as "the assembler of an assembly," "one who addresses a group," "the leader of a congregation," a collective reference to the voice of the group itself, or even "the arguer."[49] The NRSV's and NIV's translations "The Teacher" are surely apt. On the other hand, the KJV's and NASB's "The Preacher" has anachronistic Christian connotations; furthermore, the context of its earliest use by Martin Luther in the sixteenth century make that a decidedly male referent. The JPS's Tanakh leaves it at the transliteration "Koheleth," with or without the definite article, depending on the Hebrew. "The Philosopher" fits the likely Hellenistic context of the book as well as the outlier translation "the arguer." In the literary-historical context of the Hebrew Bible, "Sage" or "Wisdom Teacher" describes the likely role of

47. The definite article appears in the MT and LXX in 12:8; in 7:27 MT allows for its presence with an emendation supported by LXX. LXX also has the definite article in 1:2. See Y.A.P. Goldman, "Commentaries on the Critical Apparatus of Qoheleth" in Y. A. P. Goldman, *Biblia Hebraica Quinta, Fascicle 18: General Introduction and Megilloth* (Stuttgart: Deutsche Bibelgesellschaft, 2004), 64*.

48. Translations that depart from NRSV are my own unless otherwise indicated.

49. For a helpful summary of views, see Schoors, *Ecclesiastes*, 31–34. He points out that the meaning "assemble" applies specifically only to the *hiphil* of the root, not the *qal*. Since we do not have BH examples of the root in the *qal*, he highlights work such as Ullendorff's who uses Semitic cognates to arrive at "the arguer" (Schoors, *Ecclesiastes*, 34, citing E. Ullendorff, "The Meaning of קהלת," *VT* 12 [1962].

Qoheleth. I will refrain from selecting one translation of Qoheleth to retain the ambiguity of meaning as a possible interpretive key. Instead I will refer to this elusive figure (or compilation) as "[the] Qoheleth."

As soon as one concedes that Qoheleth is not King Solomon, we are in a position to ask who Qoheleth is—or was. Some author has taken on the persona of King Solomon (1:1, 12); perhaps it is the same voice who very occasionally narrates the book (1:1, 2; 7:27; 12:8-14). Michael V. Fox popularized the idea that the persona of that "frame-narrator" and the one who provides the other content of the book are one in the same.[50] Part of this consideration involves asking what purpose one would have for creating such a persona. As we will see, the book contains a good deal of material that could be construed as critical of that character. Who would want to critique King Solomon in those ways, and why? Given my historical assumptions about the book, an open question remains: Was Qoheleth reflecting on an urban, royal, hierarchical culture as an insider or as an outsider? I will return to these matters below.

For the purposes of this particular commentary, it is important to explore not only the idea and purpose of persona but especially the sex of a given persona and/or author. Thus the crucial question: what pronoun shall I use to identify [the] Qoheleth? "He," because the author of the book identifies Qoheleth as male by virtue of the masculine verb paired with this subject in 1:2 and throughout the book (except, maybe, 7:27; see below)? The designations בן־דוד,"son of David," מלך בירושלם, "King in Jerusalem" (1:1), and Qoheleth's self-identification as "King over Israel in Jerusalem" (1:12) suggest that the author (or persona) is male. Maybe we should assume Qoheleth is male just because the cultural context seems to suggest that few if any females would have been performing the role of sage or scribe. In one of the seminal feminist works on Qoheleth, Athalya Brenner and Fokkelien van Dijk-Hemmes propose methodology for determining "F" (feminine/female) versus "M" (masculine/male) voices in the text, while acknowledging that "many biblical texts are potentially dual-gendered."[51] Brenner offers a detailed argument based on 3:1-8, identifying Qoheleth as an "M" voice.[52] Furthermore, virtually

50. Fox, *Qohelet and His Contradictions*, 311–21.

51. Athalya Brenner and Fokkelien van Dijk-Hemmes, *On Gendering Texts: Female and Male Voices in the Hebrew Bible*, BibInt 1 (Leiden: Brill, 1993), 7–9. Note that "voice" does not necessarily equate with "author" (7).

52. Brenner, *On Gendering Texts*, 150–63. Also see Brenner-Idan's "Qoheleth 3:1-9—Structure and Sense with Verse 5 as a Key," below, which summarizes her earlier argument.

every published translation and publication of a commentary on this book thus far has referred to Qoheleth as "he."

But what about using "she" to refer to Qoheleth? The feminine aspect of the word plants the idea of feminine or female authorship.[53] Though the word Qoheleth is a feminine participle, as with any other gendered language, the gender identification of a noun does not reliably correlate that item with biological sex. Additionally, in other cases of biblical Hebrew, feminine participles have been assumed to form personal names for men, both with and without the definite article.[54] Tamara Eskenazi and Wil Gafney have asserted, however, that these titles refer to women; we should not assume they are male names.[55] The feminine pronoun in the consonantal text of 7:22 addresses a female audience, mixing up stereotypes about the gender of Qoheleth's conversation partner(s). Furthermore, the feminine verb אמרה ("she [grammatically feminine] said"), paired with "Qoheleth" in MT 7:27, seems to support the idea of calling Qoheleth "she." That instance of gender ambiguity has usually been "solved" by moving the letter /ה/ from the end of the third feminine singular verb, אמרה ("she said"), to the beginning of the following word, קהלת, adding the definite article to *qoheleth*, resulting in אמר הקהלת, "*haqoheleth* said" [grammatically masculine]).[56] That emendation finds

---

53. W. Sibley Towner observes: "True, the word *qōhelet* offers slight warrant for claiming that the author was a woman, because it has the form of a feminine singular participle of the Hebrew verbal root קהל (*qhl*, 'assemble')." Towner goes on to add the textual evidence for Qoheleth as male (male titles in this form, references to Qoheleth as "son," and masculine verb forms paired with the term "Qoheleth" in most places). Towner determines to call Qoheleth "him" ("The Book of Ecclesiastes," in *The New Interpreter's Bible*, ed. Leander E. Keck [Nashville: Abingdon, 1998], 5:268).

54. Neh 7:57 has ספרת; Ezra 2:57 and Neh 7:59 have פכרת ; Ezra 2:55 has הספרת, which notably includes the definite article. The translations all transliterate these as proper names, though the names could be translated into meaningful titles such as "the scribe" for הספרת. These, as well as references from MH and DSS have led some commentators to suggest the feminine participial form was one way of creating a proper name out of a title. Seow makes the comparison with the English title "Smith," which then became a surname; he also includes discussion of additional Semitic cognates that function similarly (*Ecclesiastes*, 96). Also see Fox, *A Time to Tear Down*, 160–61. Schoors discusses a number of options and is most persuaded that this is not a *qal* participle (since MT does not contain this verb in the *qal*) but a noun that indicates one's occupation (*Ecclesiastes*, 34–35).

55. Eskenazi, "Out from the Shadows," 36; Wilda Gafney, personal communication.

56. For instance, see Wilhelm Gesenius, *Gesenius' Hebrew Grammar* (Boston: Gould, Kendall, and Lincoln, 1839), §122r. On both of these issues, see commentary section below for additional explanation.

support from the *qere* (Masoretic notation of how to read the Hebrew text, even if written differently) and from the logic that says it makes more sense to have an additional instance of "The Qoheleth" (along with 12:8, and 1:2 in LXX) than to have a single instance of a feminine verb paired with "Qoheleth." Yet, that is not the only way to resolve this issue. T. A. Perry makes the point that we could just as easily see 12:8 as the problem and emend it by moving the letter /ה/ to *Qoheleth*, so that we get *'amrah Qoheleth*, "Qoheleth said," and argue that it and the masculine verb in 12:10 are "further instances of denying female authorship." Perry goes on to argue that, "at the very least, there seems to be as good reason to speak of a Lady Kohelet as of a 'Lady J' in the Pentateuch, as Harold Bloom (1990) proposed."[57]

Some commentators have attributed that feminine verb as well as the feminine form of Qoheleth's name to Qoheleth's identification with Woman Wisdom.[58] The idea of a wisdom teacher as female has a solid foundation in the personification of חכמה, "wisdom," as a woman in Proverbs 1:20-33; 4:5-9; 7:1-5; 8:1–9:6; and 14:1.[59] Jennifer Koosed observes that in 7:22 "the coherent male audience slips." Fast on the heels of that, in 7:27 "the gender of Qoheleth slips." She then makes a fascinating

---

57. T. Anthony Perry, *Dialogues with Kohelet: The Book of Ecclesiastes; Translation and Commentary* (University Park: Pennsylvania State University Press, 1993), 178. I must note, however, that Bloom's "Lady J" idea did not gain broad acceptance. I will discuss this further in the chapter on 7:15-29, below. Harold Bloom, *The Book of J*, trans. David Rosenberg (New York: Grove, 1990).

58. As long ago as 1860, Ernst Wilhelm Hengstenberg explained that in 7:27 "a contrast is drawn between the Koheleth and the stranger, the foreigner, i.e., philosophy and wanton seduction: and the evidently intentional construction of Koheleth with the feminine, can only be explained by its being descriptive of the wisdom which is from above." Ernst Wilhelm Hengstenberg, *Commentary on Ecclesiastes: With Other Treatises* (Philadelphia: Smith, English & Co.; New York: Sheldon, 1860), 41. Also see Schoors, *Ecclesiastes*, 34.

59. Towner ("Ecclesiastes," 268) notes this form "offers slight warrant for claiming that the author was a woman," though he agrees with other commentators that feminine participial forms of names occur for men elsewhere in the Hebrew Bible. Bartholomew agrees with Fox's assessment that the meaning of Qoheleth as "'teacher to the public' . . . rightly discerns parallels with the personification of wisdom as a woman in Prov. 1–9 in which she preaches in the public areas of the city." Craig G. Bartholomew, *Ecclesiastes* (Grand Rapids, MI: Baker Academic, 2009), 103; citing Michael V. Fox, *The JPS Bible Commentary: Ecclesiastes* (Philadelphia: Jewish Publication Society, 2004), 3. Fox reviews the uses of the feminine participle for occupation-related titles in *A Time to Tear Down*, 161. Nonetheless, most agree that the *"ben david"* designation settles the matter that the author (or his persona) is male.

lxvi   *Qoheleth (Ecclesiastes)*

association for Qoheleth: "Marjorie Garber names this type of unstable, boundary-crossing, category-confusing figure 'the transvestite.'"[60] How striking it is that beside the most apparently misogynistic statement of Qoheleth (7:26) we find gender ambiguity!

As a point of comparison, an illuminating example is the "gender-bending" liturgical *piyyut* (poem) *Yedid Nefesh* ("Soul Mate"; for the *Kabbalat Shabbat*), attributed by some to Elazar ben Moshe Azikri from Safed, in the sixteenth century, which includes feminine endings referring to God.[61] Perhaps this could help us imagine that an ancient author, or even one from the late Middle Ages, would use gendered endings more fluidly and with less intent than we might assume; maybe we are more concerned with grammatical gender consistency—or gender categories as a whole—than the authors of previous eras. Another point of reference here is Numbers 11:15, in which Moses uses a feminine pronoun in speaking to God. This actually makes some sense in the context, which implied feminine imagery for God in verse 12.[62]

Given the ambiguity of Qoheleth's gender, perhaps it would be best to adopt one set or another of the gender-neutral pronouns that are gaining in popularity among transgender and genderqueer individuals and allies since the 1990s: "*s/he* or *sie*—both pronounced 'sea' " or "*ze* ([pronounced] zee). The possessive gender-neutral pronoun coming into popular usage is *hir* (like in here and now)."[63] Or, perhaps I should use "they," which is gaining in use as a gender-neutral pronoun even for singular subjects, particularly in transgender-friendly circles.[64] "They" also allows for the

---

60. Jennifer Koosed's intriguing discussion on this adds a crucial chapter to feminist commentary on Qoheleth. Jennifer L. Koosed, *(Per)Mutations of Qohelet: Reading the Body in the Book*, T & T Clark Library of Biblical Studies (New York: Bloomsbury, 2006), 83–84. Marjorie Garber, *Vested Interests: Cross-Dressing and Cultural Anxiety* (New York; London: Routledge, 2011), 354.

61. I am grateful to Rabbis Abby Jacobsen and Juan Mejia who pointed out this beautiful prayer to me as a possible way to understand the apparently puzzling feminine ending in Qoh 7:27. The description "gender-bending" is theirs.

62. Thanks to Kathleen A. Farmer for bringing this to my attention.

63. Leslie Feinberg, *Trans Liberation: Beyond Pink or Blue* (Boston: Beacon, 1998), 71. "Transgender | Gender Neutral Pronoun Blog," https://genderneutralpronoun .wordpress.com/tag/transgender/.

64. The 2017 *Associated Press Style Book* includes use of "they/their" as an acceptable generic pronoun. Paula Froke et al., eds., *The Associated Press Stylebook 2017: And Briefing on Media Law* (New York: Basic Books, 2017), 274.

possibility of multiple authorship, which is at least worth acknowledging, though the idea has been out of vogue for several decades.[65]

The gender ambiguity about Qoheleth and the book's audience serves as an opening nod to considering feminine authorship even in a book that otherwise contains troubling and historically deadly passages for women (see excerpt from *Malleus Maleficarum* below). Thus with the name "Qoheleth," I will refrain from assigning one particular translation to it and simply use this capitalized transliteration to refer to the book's central figure and author. If any nongendered pronoun has gained consensus for use in contemporary English, it is "they," so in order to conduct a sustained exercise in at least considering that Qoheleth was not strictly male, I will use that, or repeat "Qoheleth" throughout the commentary.

Though I cannot decisively conclude the sex of the book's author, my assumptions about that affect my interpretation of the book. A male author carries a worldview different from that of a female author. On the one hand, Athalya Brenner makes a compelling argument about Qoheleth exhibiting an "M voice," particularly in 3:5.[66] On the other hand, the book provides intriguing echoes of an "F voice" in grammar and apparent text-critical problems and even verbal associations with women's work.[67] Thus it seems incumbent upon us to consider the possibilities of Qoheleth as "transvestite" (to use Koosed's proposed category), toying with both the audience's and Qoheleth's own gender; or Perry's "Lady Kohelet"; or that a satirical female ghostwriter is hiding behind the Qoheleth persona, betraying only a few hints of their presence. Is it possible that the apparent misogyny in the book is all a farce, an effort to make fun of and undermine the misogyny therein? Could we view Qoheleth as an impersonator? A caricature? A student of mine suggested comparing Qoheleth to a woman impersonating a man as parallel to political comedian Stephen Colbert doing a satirical impersonation.[68] If that angle has been lost on us, then the critique may not seem to matter much. As one reader pointed out—the book seems too antagonistic to women for it to be satire. If a woman had written it in order to make fun

65. Carl Siegfried, *Prediger und Hoheslied* (Göttingen: Vandenhoeck und Ruprecht, 1898).

66. In Brenner and van Dijk Hemmes, *On Gendering Texts*; see also Brenner-Idan's "Qoheleth 3:1-9—Structure and Sense with Verse 5 as a Key," below.

67. See my analysis of 3:1-8 below.

68. Colbert hosted *The Colbert Report* and *The Late Show* as platforms for his satire. Chanda Adams, Saint Paul School of Theology "Ecclesiastes" class, Spring 2016.

of a Solomon-like figure, she would likely not have gone so far in her negative comments about women.[69] My hope is that in leaving Qoheleth's gender out of my language in the commentary, we will be more able to honestly entertain these questions.

Feminist Method

When I teach "Methods of Scriptural Analysis" to my undergraduate religion students, my most basic definition of "method" is this: a category of questions that scholars bring to a text. Thus, historical criticism asks questions about history, form criticism inquires about genre, and so forth. In a basic way, then, feminist criticism explores questions about women. But at its roots, feminism has to do with more than women. Feminist biblical criticism challenges us to ask intensive questions of biblical texts about gender, sex, sexuality, gender roles, equality, freedom, race, relationships, choice, age, power, hierarchy, individuality, culture, violence, religion, and more. In its truest form, feminism looks well beyond women's rights to the rights of all humans, even extending to all creation. The history of the feminist movements shows that this truest form has rarely played out in reality, such that Susan B. Anthony and Elizabeth Cady Stanton pursued voting rights for white women rather than voting rights for all. In a more recent example, Audre Lorde's "An Open Letter to Mary Daly" pointedly protests the marginalization of women of color in Daly's *Gyn/Ecology*.[70] As a white woman, I would not be able to write a womanist, or "black feminist," commentary, though the questions that relate to women of color deserve to be posed to Qoheleth equally with my own questions.[71] Furthermore, as someone well-tutored in the "Master's" methodologies, I am condemned by Lorde's "Master's House" quote even as I choose it as an epigraph. I can only pledge to do my best to include all marginalized persons here, not only those who share my experience or skin tone. A few sidebars from diverse "Contributing Voices" makes a start at that inclusion, but since my privilege and my

69. Linda Matorin Sweenie, "Qoheleth in the Sukkah Women's Conversation," Temple B'nai Israel, Oklahoma City, OK, September 29, 2015.

70. Lorde, *Sister Outsider*, 66–71; Mary Daly, *Gyn/Ecology: The Metaethics of Radical Feminism* (Boston: Beacon, 1978).

71. Wilda Gafney offers the short definition "black feminist" for "womanist," as well as a longer one: Wilda Gafney, *Womanist Midrash: A Reintroduction to the Women of the Torah and the Throne* (Louisville: Westminster John Knox, 2017), 2. For Alice Walker's definitive articulation of "womanist" see *In Search of Our Mothers' Gardens* (Wilmington, MA: Mariner Books, 2003; original publication date, 1983), xi–xii.

whiteness will inevitably show, my hope is that the questions I ask will provide invitation for missing voices to always pose further questions.

Feminist biblical interpretation entails uncovering—and recovering— the missing, lost, and ignored voices from the text through persistent questions on behalf of those voices. Feminist biblical interpretation may mean asking how Bathsheba felt in an episode in which she was a key figure, though the author of that narrative gave her only one line of speech, which consists of two words in Hebrew (2 Sam 11:5). Feminist biblical interpretation may mean wondering how Ruth felt after her night on the threshing floor: used but at least having food, or in love (3:15)? In many cases feminist biblical criticism asks questions such as "Where are the women in this passage?" Often, they seem to be well behind the scenes. Another question I frequently entertained was "How might this have affected women from ancient times until now?" Much of Qoheleth's material seems relevant to anyone, regardless of gender, location, or time period. In those cases, I pushed myself to consider whether and how those passages would have truly applied to ancient women—or to contemporary ones. When the English translations provide gender-neutral terminology for what was androcentric in the Hebrew, I have pointed that out, working from the premise that we are no better off in thinking that the material was directed at women as well as men if the actual text specified only men. If women were excluded, I want to know.

The recovery of the text for feminist purposes can then become a later and crucial task. Admittedly, however, I mainly offer hints, suggestions, and possible direction for doing that work of reconstruction. If feminist method requires not only deconstruction but also reconstruction for the sake of revolution, then Qoheleth has more to offer on the front end of that hermeneutical circle. For reconstruction and revolution we must look elsewhere, and I leave the fullness of that task to the community.

There has been no dearth of women commentators on Qoheleth—no more so than women commentators on other books of the Bible. They include Dianne Bergant, Athalya Brenner-Idan, Ellen Davis, Katharine J. Dell, Julie A. Duncan, Kathleen A. Farmer, Carole Fontaine, Elizabeth Huwiler, Jennifer Koosed, Amy Plantinga Pauw, Elsa Tamez, Marie Turner, and others. The most sustained works that enlist an intentional feminist hermeneutic are by Brenner-Idan and Koosed.[72] As far as I know,

---

72. Dianne Bergant, *Israel's Wisdom Literature: A Liberation-Critical Reading* (Minneapolis: Fortress, 1997); Dianne Bergant, *Job, Ecclesiastes* OTM 18 (Wilmington, DE: Glazier, 1982); Athalya Brenner and Fokkelien van Dijk Hemmes, *On Gendering Texts*; Ellen Davis, *Proverbs, Ecclesiastes, and the Song of Songs*, WBC (Louisville: Westminster John Knox,

however, this volume will be the first work to provide a thoroughgoing feminist critique of the book.

While feminist questions will drive my work in this commentary, I will attempt not to neglect any relevant methodologies. As I discussed in the "Date" section of this introduction, historical questions permeate this commentary. How would Qoheleth's book have related to women in the likely time of the book's writing? Questions about historical context are equally important as making every effort to accurately translate the Hebrew. True, the postmodern critique rightly cautions us to be wary of our certainty about historical context, the idea of authorial intent, and even the reliability of the text. But I am convinced that accessing this information to the best of our ability, with caveats abounding, is worth it. We are better off having a vague idea of women's roles and rights in the various possible time periods of the book's authorship than in having no idea at all.

When a passage calls for it, I have enlisted text criticism, grammatical criticism, literary criticism, ethnographic criticism, and ideological criticism. Qoheleth is fertile for ideological readings because it contains so many gaps that beg to be filled in order to make sense of the book. This means that we commentators may insert more of our opinions than we might in other exegetical endeavors. Furthermore, those of us who use Qoheleth commentaries find ourselves drawn to those with which we share ideologies; in turn, we may find ourselves rejecting commentaries that insert what we view as egregious ideologies. (For instance, I have concerns about Craig Bartholomew's commentary, which pairs solid exegesis with heavy emphasis on Calvinist theology and even advocates a traditional—i.e., the past two hundred years in the West—view of

---

2000); Katharine J. Dell, *Interpreting Ecclesiastes: Readers Old and New*, Critical Studies in the Hebrew Bible 3 (Winona Lake, IN: Eisenbrauns, 2013); Julie A. Duncan, *Ecclesiastes*; Farmer, *Who Knows*; Carole R. Fontaine, " 'Many Devices' (Qoheleth 7.23–8.1): Qoheleth, Misogyny and the *Malleus Maleficarum*," in *A Feminist Companion to Reading the Bible: Approaches, Methods and Strategies*, ed. Athalya Brenner and Carole Fontaine, FCB 2d ser. 2 (Sheffield: Sheffield Academic, 1998), 137–68; Roland E. Murphy and Elizabeth Huwiler, *Proverbs, Ecclesiastes, Song of Songs*, Understanding the Bible Commentary Series (Grand Rapids, MI: Baker, 2012); Jennifer Koosed, *(Per)Mutations of Qohelet*; Amy Plantinga Pauw, *Proverbs and Ecclesiastes*, Belief: A Theological Commentary on the Bible (Louisville: Westminster John Knox, 2015); Elsa Tamez, *When the Horizons Close: Rereading Ecclesiastes* (Maryknoll, NY: Orbis Books, 2000); Marie Turner, *Ecclesiastes: An Earth Bible Commentary; Qoheleth's Eternal Earth* (New York: Bloomsbury T&T Clark, 2017).

Christian marriage, along with a concurrent jab at divorce and homo-sexuality.[73] While I found no relevance for these ideologies in a Qoheleth commentary, Bartholomew may well find no place for my argument to refrain from calling Qoheleth "he.") This is to say that, on the one hand, Qoheleth is a perfect book to address in a feminist commentary series, since the text is so wide open to various hermeneutical approaches. On the other hand, I face the constant danger—even more so than usual—of reading in Qoheleth only what I want to read and neglecting the primary exegetical task of taking the text on its own terms.

As for method, I find helpful both Audre Lorde's quote at the beginning of this section, and Claudia Camp's methodological essay at the beginning of her *Wisdom and the Feminine in the Book of Proverbs*:

> If the canon is to remain a living force today (and here again an engagement is assumed, namely my own experience with a living Word), it must do so as a conversation partner within our own historical, economic and political situations, not as a disembodied, a-historicized voice from beyond. One way it can do this is through our willingness to observe the sociological dynamics involved in the production and/or appropriation of different parts of the canonical literature (and, one might add, where possible, the disappropriation of contemporaneous non-canonical literature). We may in this way gain insight into the dynamics of the relationship of Scripture and community, both in its positive (life-affirming, liberating) and negative (oppressive, minority-silencing) forms. Last, and probably deservedly so, is the simple fact that I like to look at Scripture in all these different ways. It's fun. So there.[74]

I resonate greatly with Camp's concluding comments on method, which follow her discussions of the merits and drawbacks of the numerous types of criticism she would use in her monograph on Proverbs. While Lorde emboldens us to reject "the master's" tools, Camp's bold yet playful claim for using a diversity of methodologies invites those of us who came up through "the master's house" of male-dominated biblical scholarship to re-fashion those tools. In my case, however, I had the luxury of learning from and with women and men feminists who had come before me and had already begun that work of refashioning: Kathleen A. Farmer, Carolyn Stahl Bohler, Phyllis A. Bird, Julie A. Duncan, Ken Stone, and Harold Washington, among others. They, and

---

73. Bartholomew, *Ecclesiastes*, 174.

74. Claudia V. Camp, *Wisdom and the Feminine in the Book of Proverbs*, BLS 11 (Sheffield: Almond, 1985), 20.

many others whose work I studied pushed me to hear those missing, lost, and forgotten voices. Taking their lead, engaging my own initiative to include the disenfranchised, I launched into a field that was fertile for innovative method, combined with those standards of critical biblical scholarship. What follows is my effort to bring those refashioned tools to the work site at hand: Qoheleth.

Chapter 1

Learning Qoheleth's Language (1:1-18)

Superscription (1:1)

Qoheleth's introduction in this opening verse invites a list of questions that we will struggle with throughout the book: superscription or frame-narrative; persona or person; female/feminine or male/masculine; monarch or sage; assembler or philosopher. As I detailed in my introduction, I will entertain a variety of these possibilities below, leaving room for readers to make their own conclusions by refraining from gendering Qoheleth, providing historical context from more than one time period, and digging around for hints on all of these issues. Knowing Qoheleth, the answers are not likely in an either/or but somewhere unknowable in between.

Qoheleth: Canonicity and Canonization

Rav Judah son of R. Samuel b. Shilath said in Rab's name: The Sages wished to hide the Book of Qoheleth, because its words are self-contradictory; yet why did they not hide it? Because its beginning is religious teaching and its end is religious teaching. (b. Šhabb. 30b)

All the Holy Scriptures defile the hands. The Song of Songs and Qoheleth defile the hands. Rabbi Judah says: The Song of Songs defiles the hands, but there is a dispute about Qoheleth. (m. Yad. 3:5)

1

Qoh 1:1

1:1The words of the Teacher, the son of
David, king in Jerusalem.

In the Jewish Bible, the book of Qoheleth is included in the collection of the Five *Megilloth* (Scrolls) that has been traditionally associated with the annual Jewish holidays and is publicly read in synagogues on the feast of Tabernacles/Sukkot (a practice that probably began in the Middle Ages).

Qoheleth is also considered to be one of the biblical wisdom writings (together with Proverbs and Job), presenting philosophical/theological themes and questions regarding life's meaning, human suffering, and mortality, as well as God's sovereignty, divine justice, God's involvement in the world's order, and human behavior and destiny.[1] Nevertheless, Qoheleth is distinctly different from either Job or Proverbs and is considered to be a unique and unusual book within the Hebrew biblical canon. The book's tone as well as its content is as far removed from the usual biblical norms as can be. For example: Qoheleth 5:4-5 [3-4] criticizes the theological rationale of certain deuteronomistic laws (23:22-24) and reworks them.[2] The main theme of the Hebrew Bible, describing God's activity in history or his relationship with the people of Israel, is absent from the book, as is the Tetragrammaton (YHWH, God's name).[3] The book ignores almost completely the omnipresence of God, with which most of the biblical texts are suffused. Qoheleth projects an atmosphere of despondency and pessimism with the repeated refrain הבל. While the text verges on hopelessness on the one hand, there is at places a suggestion for possible individual contentment, but only through wisdom and

1. Jacob Klein, "The Book of Qoheleth: Introduction," in *Qoheleth, Olam Hatanach* [Hebrew] (Tel Aviv: Divrei Ha'yamim Publication, 1999), 162–68.

2. See Bernard M. Levinson, "Better That You Should Not Vow Than That You Vow and Not Fulfill: Qoheleth's Use of Textual Allusion and the Transformation of Deuteronomy's Law of Vows," in *Reading Ecclesiastes Intertextually*, ed. Katharine Dell and Will Kynes (London: Bloomsbury T&T Clark, 2015), 28–41.

3. See Michael J. Broyde, "Defilement of the Hands, Canonization of the Bible, and the Special Status of Esther, Ecclesiastes, and Song of Songs," *Judaism* 44 (1995): 65–79; Megan Fullerton Strollo, "Initiative and Agency: Towards a Theology of the Megilloth," in *Megiloth Studies*, ed. Brad Embry (Sheffield: Phoenix, 2016), 150–60.

morality. In the epilogue (chap. 12) Qoheleth seems to return to the biblical norms that the most important thing is to fear God and observe the commandments (12:13-14). These two verses stand out in contrast to the rest of the book.

It is therefore hardly surprising that Qoheleth was one of the three books (with Esther and the Song of Songs) whose status within the canon has been disputed and discussed in the Mishnah and the Babylonian Talmud (m. Nez. Adayoth 5:3; b. Meg. 7a; Šabb. 30b). The dispute of the Jewish Sages (of the first and early centuries CE) concerning the canonicity of Qoheleth is formulated in the context of the halachic discussion concerning the "defiling of the hands" (m. Yad. 3:5 and b. Meg. 7a). Sacred writings are considered as "defiling the hands," that is, making them unclean for dealing with profane tasks: touching sacred objects, including sacred canonical writings, requires the hands to be washed in order to return to profane, mundane activities. In contrast, dealing with profane writings does not make the hands "unclean" and does not require washing. (As paradoxical as this may sound to the modern mind, this was presumably decreed in order to minimize the handling of Holy Writings.)

As in many Talmudic debates, the issue of the reasons for Qoheleth's inclusion in the canon is left open. There are reasons for and against such inclusion. The fact of the matter is, clearly, that Qoheleth was indeed added to the canonized writings, probably because of its popularity at least in certain circles.

Another reason might have been the tradition of attributing the book's authorship to King Solomon, understanding literally the designation קהלת בן דוד מלך בירושלם ("Qoheleth son of David, king in Jerusalem") in the superscription of the book (1:1). For instance, the first *parasha* of Midrash *Shir Ha-Shirim Rabbah* contains several references attributing to King Solomon authorship of three biblical books, in this order: Song of Songs, Proverbs, and Qoheleth (1:6, 7, 8). Finally, in 1:10, two opinions are cited in the name of two Jewish scholars. One, that Solomon composed the Song of Songs while young, Proverbs while a mature man, and Qoheleth while an old man. And the second, that when in old age Solomon received divine inspiration (רוח הקדש, literally "sacred spirit"), he composed all three together. The discussion is concluded by the statement that nobody disputes the Solomonic authorship for all three books.

At any rate, early hesitation about Qoheleth's canonicity was later forgotten and full acceptance followed, as evidenced by the adopted custom of reading the scroll at the synagogue on an important annual festival (Sukkot).

The scarcity of fragments of this atypical biblical text among the Dead Sea Scrolls (Qumran) findings seems, however, to attest to its precarious standing in as much as the biblical canon was concerned. Only two fragments were discovered so far, both in Cave 4 of Qumran: 4Q109 Qohelet[a], dated between 175 and 150 BCE and containing Qoheleth 5:14-18 [13-17]; 6:1, 3-8, 12; 7:1-10, 19-20; and 4Q110 Qohelet[b], dated between 30 BCE and 68 CE and containing Qoheleth 1:10-14.

Ora Brison

Opening *hevel* (הבל) Statement (1:2)

This verse begins with a first-person quotation from Qoheleth reported by a third-person narrator, presumably the author of 1:1, though that could be a persona of Qoheleth.[4] The opening statement finds a fitting place just after the superscription, since it introduces a major focus of the book through a five-time repetition of the perplexing and elusive theme-word הבל, *hevel*, traditionally translated "vanity."

In a literal sense, *hevel* refers to a "breath" (Isa 57:13), which poses an interesting metaphor if one plugs it in for *hevel* throughout the book of Qoheleth. After all, a breath utterly sustains life, and the thought of being without it is enough to make any asthmatic break out in a cold sweat. Yet a breath also illustrates all that is insubstantial. A breath can scarcely be touched or seen or heard; it lasts only a moment and must be repeated continually to sustain life. A breath has its own life to the extent that it continues even in sleep and comatose states. Beyond the literal meaning "breath," *hevel* refers to that which is fleeting, whether the life of the biblical character who bears the term as his name (Heb. *hevel* = Abel, in Gen 4:2, 4, 8, 9, 25) or as a prophet's put-down to what he views as a useless idol (Jer 10:3).

The most convincing translation for *hevel* in Qoheleth that I have found is Michael V. Fox's "absurd/absurdity."[5] Fox describes absurdity in terms of Camus' explanation that it identifies the disjunction between what one expects and what actually occurs. This seems a remarkable match for what Qoheleth tries to describe throughout the book. Our best opportunity to understand what Qoheleth might mean through the repetition of

---

4. Michael V. Fox, "Frame-Narrative and Composition in the Book of Qohelet," *HUCA* 48 (1977): 83–106.

5. See discussion on this and other translations of *hevel* in the introduction to this volume.

Qoh 1:2

²Vanity of vanities, says the Teacher,
vanity of vanities! All is vanity.

hevel, however, is to leave the word in Hebrew, even for English readers, and let them fill in the meaning based on the context. It is analogous to replacing *hevel* with a nonword—even a number string—and then allowing the rest of Qoheleth's writing to determine the meaning. Benjamin Sommer, professor of Bible at Jewish Theological Seminary, has suggested that Qoheleth's use of *hevel* has much in common with the way e. e. cummings uses words and gives them new meanings throughout the course of a poem.[6]

Aside from the narrator's inserted "says Qoheleth," the only word in 1:2 that is not *hevel* (or its plural, or the definite article) is כל, "all" or "everything." Thus,

הבל הבלים אמר קהלת הבל הבלים הכל הבל,

and translated/transliterated, for the sake of illustrating the alliteration: "*havel havalim*, says Qoheleth, *havel havalim*, everything is *havel*." The grammatical construction ("vanity of vanities" in NRSV) indicates an absolute superlative. The same construction refers to the best poem in שיר השירים, "the Song of Songs," and to Canaan in Genesis 9:25 as an עבד עבדים, "slave of slaves, an abject slave."[7] The superlative communicates quality: "utter" *hevel*.[8] It does not necessarily express "a multitude of examples of *hevel*," although the repetition of the word both in this opening phrase and throughout the book effectively communicates quantity as well.

Qoheleth's addition of the word "everything" adds another level of emphasis to Qoheleth's already redundant use of *hevel* in 1:2. Qoheleth has crafted a phrase that accentuates what is already a superlative! Furthermore, this construction prepares us for Qoheleth's frequent use of *hevel* to evaluate myriad life situations: כל, or "everything," foreshadows Qoheleth's sweeping use of that term throughout the book in making broad generalizations about, of course, everything. The use of "everything" in this verse also serves as a fitting introduction for the rest of

6. Personal conversation, July 2002.
7. Bruce K. Waltke and Michael Patrick O'Connor, *Introduction to Biblical Hebrew Syntax* (Winona Lake, IN: Eisenbrauns, 1990), 267.
8. Ibid.

the book; W. Sibley Towner points out that כל, "everything," "occurs in 41 percent of the 222 verses in the book."[9] Thus it is indeed fitting that "everything" would stand alongside *hevel* in order to open the book.

As we will see, Qoheleth does not hesitate to criticize either individuals or groups, from women (7:26, 28) to royalty (4:13). But in 1:2 Qoheleth's proclamation does not devalue one particular group or situation over another; Qoheleth truly deems everything *hevel*, invoking this word (in the singular or the plural) a total of thirty-eight times. The five-time repetition of *hevel* in 1:2 is unprecedented elsewhere in the book, though 12:8 has it three times, and 8:14 and 9:9 contain the word twice. Because this second verse of the book consists of 63 percent *hevel*, and since the meaning of the word itself defies a single translation, it is as though the book opens with a riddle.

While verse 2 effectively introduces the book by stating this refrain, the verse does not obviously connect either to verse 1 or verse 3. Only the mention of Qoheleth, who was introduced in 1:1, recurs in 1:2, thus minimally linking verses 1 and 2. Nonetheless, 1:1 certainly stands alone as the superscription. In 1:3 the author launches into a poem that arguably illustrates the point of verse 2, though not blatantly. Thus 1:2 serves as a bridge between 1 and 3, with connections to both; yet it also uniquely announces the word-theme of the book.

Poem on Circularity (1:3-11)

Natural imagery dominates this poem. Verse 3 focuses on humanity and its concerns (אדם), which leads into "generation" (דור) at the beginning of verse 4. In verses 4-7 the emphasis is on the rest of the created

9. W. Sibley Towner, "Ecclesiastes," in *NIB* (Nashville: Abingdon, 1997), 5:278. Indeed, Eric Christianson cites John Jarick as saying that "the choice of placing הבל ['absurdity'] and הכל ['everything'] together may be purposefully to portray a visual word-play. They occur together only in Ecclesiastes and the only visual (and minimal) difference between them is a serif-mark." Eric S. Christianson, *A Time to Tell: Narrative Strategies in Ecclesiastes*, JSOTSup 280 (Sheffield: Sheffield Academic, 1998), 88 n. 39. While that theory would depend on the script in use in the first Qoheleth manuscript, according to Ada Yardeni the *bet* and *kaf* letters at stake in this proposal were formed similarly from the late third century BCE through mid first century BCE. Ada Yardeni, *The Book of Hebrew Script: History, Palaeography, Script Styles, Calligraphy and Design* (London; New Castle, DE: The British Library and Oak Knoll Press, 2002). Also see discussion of this in Huang Wei, "*Heḇel* and *Kong*: A Cross-Textual Reading between Qoheleth and the Heart Sūtra," in *The Five Scrolls*, Texts@Contexts 6, ed. Athalaya Brenner-Idan, Gale A. Yee, Archie C. C. Lee (London: Bloomsbury T & T Clark, 2018), 138.

Qoh 1:3-11

³What do people gain from all the toil
  at which they toil under the sun?
⁴A generation goes, and a generation
    comes,
  but the earth remains forever.
⁵The sun rises and the sun goes down,
  and hurries to the place where it
    rises.
⁶The wind blows to the south,
  and goes around to the north,
round and round goes the wind,
  and on its circuits the wind returns.
⁷All streams run to the sea,
  but the sea is not full;
to the place where the streams flow,
  there they continue to flow.
⁸All things are wearisome;

more than one can express;
the eye is not satisfied with seeing,
  or the ear filled with hearing.
⁹What has been is what will be,
  and what has been done is what
    will be done;
  there is nothing new under the sun.
¹⁰Is there a thing of which it is said,
  "See, this is new"?
It has already been,
  in the ages before us.
¹¹The people of long ago are not
    remembered,
  nor will there be any
    remembrance
of people yet to come
  by those who come after them.

order: "earth" (ארץ) in verse 4, "sun" (שמש) in verse 5, "wind" (or "spirit,"
רוח) in verse 6, and "streams" (נחלים) in verse 7.

While verses 2-3 worked together to set up two of Qoheleth's major themes—*hevel* and יתרון/עמל, "gain and toil"—the emphasis in verse 3 is on the unreliability of toil. At the same time, mention of "under the sun" (תחת השמש) in verse 3 helps connect it to verses 4-7 since "sun" reappears in verse 5. Verse 3 in the NRSV reads, "What do people gain from all the toil at which they toil under the sun?" In contrast, a wooden rendering of the Hebrew would be, "What advantage [יתרון] is there for a man [אדם] in his toil [עמל] in which he toils under the sun?" This translation better illustrates the emphasis on advantage and toil based on word order and repetition in the Hebrew; it also reveals that the NRSV translation has made the reading gender-inclusive where the Hebrew has masculine pronouns. The NRSV presents a possible but perhaps wishful reading of the verse. This translation should raise questions about the decision to translate Qoheleth's book as gender-inclusive.[10] This involves the tricky

10. For further discussion on this topic, see Phyllis A. Bird, "Translating Sexist Language as a Theological and Cultural Problem," *USQR* 42 (1988): 89–95; Wilda Gafney, *Womanist Midrash: A Reintroduction to the Women of the Torah and the Throne* (Louisville: Westminster John Knox, 2017), 281–89.

business of speculating about authorial intent. We can only hypothesize about that, based on Qoheleth's cultural context and the rest of the book.[11] The rest of the book suggests that Qoheleth objectifies women (7:26-29; 9:9) and otherwise mostly ignores them. Thus Qoheleth would not seem to have considered their "toil," even as they served him food and drink (2:24 and the other *carpe diem* passages) or labored as servants (2:7) or sexual playthings (2:8). In that sense, we would be most accurate to translate אדם as "man" (as in "male," not in the so-called generic sense) and to render the pronoun here male rather than making it plural (contra the NRSV's "they"). We cannot, however, be sure of this. It seems that Qoheleth must have acknowledged, at least to some extent, that women toiled along with the whole of creation whose repetitive cycles of work Qoheleth sketches in the following eleven verses.

In any case, for women who read this book, the toil Qoheleth points to in 1:3 is real, weighty, and of questionable gain. Thus, even if "Qoheleth" (whoever that is) did not "intend" (however we are to access that) women as toilers, we *are*, every bit as much as men, and when it comes to certain spheres such as childbearing, child care, and housework, even more so. Because of that, this book is relevant to women readers as well as to men; women may take it for what it means to us regardless of what Qoheleth may have intended or acknowledged. And we women need at least as much reflection and critique on the topic of toil and its outcomes as do men.

The repetitions of *hevel* and "all" in verse 2 fittingly introduce the repetitions that will follow in the poem of 1:3-11. Verses 5, 6, and 9 have two words that repeat: verse 5, זרח, "rise," and השמש, "the sun"; verse 6, the root סבב, "go around" (appears four times), and רוח, "wind"; verse 9, היה, "to be," and עשה, "to make" or "do." Verses 11 and 7 contain three words that repeat: verse 11, זכרון, "remembrance," אחרנים, "yet to come," and יהיה, "will be"; verse 7, נחל, "stream," ים, "sea," and the root הלך, "run, go, flow," which repeats three times. Verses 3, 4, and 8 contain at least one word that repeats (not including prepositions, pronouns, or particles): verse 3, עמל, "toil"; verse 4, דור, "generation"; verse 8, (ים)דבר, "thing(s)" and "speak." Furthermore, the verb הלך appears six times throughout the passage, with increasing frequency: once in verse 4, twice in verse 6, and three times in verse 7. While 1:10 does not contain its own repetition, it closely links to the previous verse as they both make the point

---

11. See the author's introduction to this volume.

that there is nothing new (חדש). The repetition of these words mimics and reinforces the point of the poem, which is that movement does not go anywhere other than back to where it began; there is no real progression, only stuttering.

Verse 4 arises from a biblical tradition that enlists the phrase לדור ודור, "from generation to generation." This indicates "a long time" or even "forever" in terms of human history, often referring to God's eternal care of the people of Israel, Israel's unending devotion to God (Ps 119:90, among others), or even to God's apparent abandonment of Israel (Ps 77:8 [9]).[12] In Judaism the *Kedusha* prayer of holiness (part of the Amidah or standing prayer) is also referred to as the *Le-dor va-ador* prayer, based on the incorporation of Psalm 146:10 in the prayer, which reads, "The Lord will reign forever, your God, O Zion, *from generation to generation* [דור ודור]. Praise the Lord!" With a probable nod to this Psalms passage, Qoheleth invokes a theology of omnipotence—or at least a strong sense of eternal divine care.

While verses 4-7 evoke a sense of longing for completion, their juxtaposition with verses 2-3 suggests that longing will be forever unfulfilled. Ironically, the repetition in verses 4-7 ultimately describes movement— ironic because it is movement that ends where it began and then begins again. Thus the passage may conjure, on the one hand, Sisyphus eking out his life's punishment from Zeus of pushing a massive boulder uphill, only to always have it roll back down where he has to start again.[13] On the other hand, it may call to mind a Zen-like oneness with the moon, tide, and life cycle, or finding joy in a never-ending task like tending a garden. Such openness to interpretation invites us to read into the book our own experiences in order to determine its tone. For instance, when the death of a beloved and quite elderly grandparent coincides with the welcome birth of a healthy child, one may hum Harry Chapin's "All My Life's a Circle" or "The Circle of Life" from *The Lion King* while weeping bittersweet tears.[14] If that same death coincides with the birth of an unplanned child for whom one has little capacity to support, while also

---

12. The phrase appears fourteen times in the Hebrew Bible (in both *plene* and *defectiva* forms), primarily in the Psalms.

13. Robert Graves, *The Greek Myths: Complete and Unabridged Edition in One Volume* (Mount Kisco, New York: Moyer Bell, 1988), 216–20.

14. Harry Chapin, *Sniper & Other Love Songs*, Audio CD (Wounded Bird Records, 1972). Elton John, *The Lion King / Soundtrack Version* (Walt Disney, 1994).

being saddled with an unpaid-for funeral and sudden lack of a help-ful grandparent, then Sisyphus comes to mind. Yet Qoheleth offers us more than our own experiences as interpretive cues here. While לְעוֹלָם, "forever" (v. 4, and in the plural in v. 10), may offer hope or devastation, toil without gain (v. 3) more likely leads to lethargy than joy. An unre-membered life provides depression rather than solace (v. 11). The cyclical movement that goes nowhere in verses 4-7 and Qoheleth's comments in verses 2-3 and 8 lend themselves more to Sisyphus than Zen. From the repetitions of *hevel* in verse 2 to the apparently unproductive work (עָמָל) in verse 3 to Qoheleth's summary statement—"all things are wearisome (יְגֵעִים)" in verse 8 (in Deut 25:18 and 2 Sam 17:2 this word refers to being exhausted)—Qoheleth would presumably add a "damn" before "circle" in Chapin's folk song title.

Notably, these "wearisome" cycles are not just any cycles but those of nature. Women embody those natural cycles in gestation, birth, feed-ing, and cleaning their babies for about the first year of their lives (more exclusively so in biblical times); women's typical roles as gardeners, gatherers, and food preparers underscores the linkage with creation in the poem. The cycles of women's bodies, whether that of pregnancy or menstruation—presumably the former was more common in the ancient world while the latter is more common in contemporary times—would be a fitting addition to this poem. Surely women vary as to whether they view such cycles as Sisyphean or Zen-like.

We might assume that for the ancient Israelites, the power for those cycles rested squarely with YHWH, but the evidence for ancient Israelite worship of other Gods and Goddesses, particularly those associated with creation and nature, complicate that picture.[15] In our own time, we might colloquially personify these cycles as "Mother Nature"; for Qoheleth's audience, perhaps this imagery evoked El Shaddai, the name for the nurturing—arguably feminine—"God of the breasts" in passages such as Genesis 28:3 and Ruth 1:21.[16] Yet Qoheleth does not mention God at all here. Qoheleth seems more interested in pressing the questions "Is there any gain?" (v. 3); "Is there anything new?" (v. 10); "Is there any remem-

---

15. Tikva Simone Frymer-Kensky, *In the Wake of the Goddesses: Women, Culture, and the Biblical Transformation of Pagan Myth* (New York: Free Press, 1992); Phyllis A Bird, "The Place of Women in the Israelite Cultus," in *Missing Persons and Mistaken Identities: Women and Gender in Ancient Israel* (Minneapolis: Fortress, 1997), 91–92, 102.

16. For the association of Shaddai with breasts, see Harriet Lutzky, "Shadday as Goddess Epithet," *VT* 48 (1998): 16.

brance?" (v. 11). While those questions surely had—and have—theological implications, Qoheleth leaves those to the audiences' own imaginations.

In verses 9-11 we find additional opportunities to understand the poetic images of verses 3-8. The sentiments of verse 9, "what has been is what will be," echo throughout history and even into contemporary popular culture, such as Doris Day's performance of "Que Será Será" ("and whatever will be, will be; the future's not ours to see") in Alfred Hitchcock's *The Man Who Knew too Much*, or U2's "Acrobat," "What are we going to do? / Now it's all been said / No new ideas in the house / And every book has been read."[17] Doris Day's playful vocals liltingly mock the dire tone of the film's circumstances, and Bono's lyrics transcend the Edge's wailing riffs with the resolution: "And I know that the tide is turning 'round / So don't let the bastards grind you down."[18] Qoheleth could have similarly undermined the Sisyphean effect of 1:3-11 by placing the *carpe diem* here, but we have to wait until 2:24 for the first "eat, and drink, and enjoy." Even there the admonition is to "enjoy your toil," which sounds like more of a challenge than a relief.

Qoheleth's use of עולם (NRSV translates "forever" and "the ages" in vv. 4 and 10, respectively) might once have provided a reassuring sense for the passage through the sustaining role of nature. Yet a contemporary ecofeminist perspective must assert that Qoheleth's idea, "the earth remains forever [עולם]," has been rendered dubious in light of human destruction of creation. Ironically, the idea that the earth would last forever may have contributed to human abuse and neglect of it. Similarly, the ongoing lack of remembrance (v. 11) engenders human disregard for creation, as well as other humans.[19] For Qoheleth, nature goes on while

17. Alfred Hitchcock et al., *The Man Who Knew Too Much* (The Criterion Collection, 2013); U2, *Achtung Baby*, Audio CD (Island, 1991), permission requested.

18. Robyn Brothers, "Time to Heal, 'Desire Time': The Cyberprophecy of U2's 'Zoo World Order,'" in *Reading Rock and Roll: Authenticity, Appropriation, Aesthetics*, ed. Kevin J. H. Dettmar and William Richey (New York: Columbia University Press, 1999), 237–67. On pp. 250–51 Brothers discusses Bono's (the lead singer of U2) stated association of the Zoo TV tour and the book of Qoheleth, and points to the song "Acrobat" as a clear statement of the "ennui" associated with technology that the tour critiqued. Brothers's discussion of irony in the *Achtung Baby* album also has much in common with the book of Qoheleth. Just as Qoheleth may be viewed as an ironic persona in order to mock culture, Bono's personae of the Zoo TV tour took on that very task. In both cases, the effect may well have been lost on the audience (243).

19. See Marie Turner, *Ecclesiastes: An Earth Bible Commentary; Qoheleth's Eternal Earth* (New York: Bloomsbury, 2017), 30.

humans come to a final end.[20] The dilemma of our time is that some people of faith believe humans do not even affect nature, a view that likely contributes to our very demise.

Overall Reflections on Finding Wisdom (or Not) (1:12-18)

This passage opens with a clear assertion of Qoheleth's royal autobiography mode.[21] The traditional association of Qoheleth with Solomon becomes clear in 1:12-13a, which identifies Qoheleth as "the king over Israel in Jerusalem" who sought out "wisdom" (חכמה) with his "heart" (לב; NRSV "mind," since in the Bible the heart is the seat of intellect, not emotion). In King Solomon's famous prayer of 1 Kings 3 he asks YHWH for a לב שמע, "hearing heart" (3:9; NRSV "understanding mind"), and YHWH in turn gives him a לב חכם, "wise heart" (3:12; NRSV "wise . . . mind").

By verse 13b Qoheleth has changed course from the fictive identity of Solomon and returns to the emphasis on work, which first appeared in 1:3 (NRSV has "toil" in 1:3 and "business" in 13). This time Qoheleth uses ענין, a word for "task" that we find only in Qoheleth's book (here and in 2:26; 3:10; 4:8; 5:3 [2]; and 8:16). Qoheleth harshly declares God's designated work for humans "bad" (רע; NRSV "unhappy"). Solomon's assessment of life's work differed greatly from this: the biblical narrator closely associates Solomon's wisdom (חכמה) with his wealth (1 Kgs 4:20-34). Notably, that same section on Solomon's divinely granted, wisdom-infused leadership opens with the *carpe diem* (1 Kgs 4:20), which we see repeated seven times throughout the book of Qoheleth, but not here.[22]

Starting from the evaluation of life's work as "evil" in 1:13, Qoheleth piles on the negative adjectives as the passage continues. In 1:14 Qoheleth deems all the "deeds" on earth *hevel* and "chasing after wind."[23] From there, the author moves to irreparability ("what is crooked cannot be made straight"; see 7:13, in which the responsibility for this brokenness is blamed squarely on God) and incomprehensibility ("what is lacking

20. James L. Crenshaw, *Qoheleth: The Ironic Wink*, Studies on Personalities in the Old Testament (Columbia: University of South Carolina Press, 2013), 81. He points out that Job and Ben Sira shared this view.

21. On royal and fictional autobiography see Craig G. Bartholomew, *Ecclesiastes* (Grand Rapids, MI: Baker Academic, 2009), 122–23; Antoon Schoors, *Ecclesiastes* (Leuven: Peeters, 2013), 99–106.

22. See introduction and the discussion of 2:24 below.

23. See the discussion in the introduction about how *hevel* and this phrase work together to express Qoheleth's views.

Qoh 1:12-18

¹²I, the Teacher, when king of Israel in Jerusalem, ¹³applied my mind to seek and to search out by wisdom all that is done under heaven; it is an unhappy business that God has given to human beings to be busy with. ¹⁴I saw all the deeds that are done under the sun; and see, all is vanity and a chasing after wind.

¹⁵What is crooked cannot be
made straight,
and what is lacking cannot be
counted.

¹⁶I said to myself, "I have acquired great wisdom, surpassing all who were over Jerusalem before me; and my mind has had great experience of wisdom and knowledge." ¹⁷And I applied my mind to know wisdom and to know madness and folly. I perceived that this also is a chasing after wind.

¹⁸For in much wisdom is much
vexation,
and those who increase
knowledge increase
sorrow.

cannot be counted"). Verses 16 and the first half of 17a move back—with renewed zeal—to the Solomonic fiction for the wisdom quest, but before completing 17a, Qoheleth again makes a surprise turn—this quest is not just for wisdom but also for הוללות ושכלות, "madness and folly" (also see 2:12, the conclusion of the "test of pleasure"). Whether satirical or pessimistic, "madness and folly" sully a commendable quest for "wisdom" in a truly disconcerting manner. It would be fair to ask whether one could possibly embark on a quest for wisdom with such an attitude.

Qoheleth 1:17b concludes by returning to the phrase of 1:14 (and a frequent theme in the book): this is "a chasing after wind." In the end (1:18), Qoheleth poetically eviscerates the concept of Solomonic wisdom: "in much wisdom is much anguish, and increasing knowledge increases distress." Qoheleth has turned Solomonic wisdom on its head. This is only the first time Qoheleth will make that point, and we are not yet out of the first chapter of the book. Qoheleth's radical rhetoric here invokes the "golden boy" and "golden age" of Solomon's early rule, only to turn around and persuade the audience of the view that the "business" of life and even "wisdom" is "unhappy" (v. 13), *hevel* (v. 14), irreversibly "crooked," utterly "lacking" (v. 15), worthy of pairing with "madness and folly," akin to "chasing wind" (v. 17); it is "anguish" and "distress" (v. 18), and all of this—given by God (v. 13). Qoheleth does not hold back for the sake of propriety, tact, or piety! This exaggerated challenge to tradition suggests the possibility of a satirical genre. Could Qoheleth be making fun of Solomon and his "golden age," or at least be ridiculing those who would retell the early monarchy in that way?

In this forthrightness that flies in the face of theological tradition, Qoheleth may serve as inspiration for feminist hermeneutics, which privileges experience over traditional doctrine: feminist readings rely on challenges to the (male-dictated) status quo. While the book of Qoheleth poses much difficulty for women (see the *Malleus Maleficarum* insert below), it also serves as a canonized model for reading suspiciously, a central tenet of feminist hermeneutics.[24] And perhaps this is a good time to turn Qoheleth's suspicion back on Qoheleth. Is it true that "What is crooked cannot be made straight, and what is lacking cannot be counted"? While it may seem that way, history does prove otherwise. Change can occur. Of all people, women have seen that even though certain situations have seemed Sisyphean—from women's suffrage to equal pay—the work toward change of those situations has not ultimately been fruitless. Yet if we take Qoheleth's proverb in 1:15 to heart, we might never try to effect change. The resignation to "what is crooked cannot be made straight" does not lend itself toward social change—certainly not to the kinds of social change that have created liberation and opportunities for women in the past century. Qoheleth's resignation may result in dangerous skepticism, immobilizing pessimism, the unwillingness to work toward change.

While, on the one hand, we must question and be willing to reject what Qoheleth says in this book, we must also consider the truth of Qoheleth's statements. If the quest for wisdom only shows us "unhappy business," *hevel*, crookedness, anguish, and distress; if the quest for wisdom is akin only to "chasing after wind"—why do it? Why does Qoheleth? Why do we? Could it merely be because it is the "unhappy business that God has given to human beings to be busy with" (1:13)? If that is the case, then we are Sisyphus, and God may as well be the Greek Judges of the Dead meting out our punishment. Surely, Qoheleth's critique of wisdom in 1:12-18 plays an important role in the book and more broadly. It may be an "unhappy business," but evaluating claims to truth and wisdom plays a crucial role in philosophical and theological reflection.

Evaluating the fruitfulness—or fruitlessness—of seeking wisdom has become ever-more relevant since the time Qoheleth wrote up till now. Phyllis Tickle has identified the late twentieth and early twenty-

---

24. See the author's introduction and afterword in this volume; also Lisa Michele Wolfe, "Seeing Gives Rise to Disbelieving: Experiences That Prompt a Hermeneutic of Suspicion in Ecclesiastes and Wendy Farley's Theodicy of Compassion" (PhD diss., Northwestern University, 2003), 158–95.

first centuries as "The Great Emergence," which has been significantly created by the rise of the internet. Tickle compares this period to "The Great Reformation" of the sixteenth century CE, propelled forward in part by the Enlightenment. One distinguishing feature of "The Great Emergence" consists of the enormous mass of information calling for our constant attention. The quantity and quality of this "wisdom" (if we can categorize this information glut in that way) beg for evaluation in terms of their effect on culture, religion, and our very psychology.[25] Furthermore, the genocides of the last century proved that even the wisest thinkers cannot solve the world's problems; education does not immunize us from committing atrocities. George Steiner laments the reality that neither great education nor the presence of high culture prevented the Holocaust: "Why did humanistic traditions and models of conduct prove so fragile a barrier, or is it more realistic to perceive in humanistic culture express solicitations of authoritarian rule and cruelty?"[26] The latter part of Steiner's crucial question aligns well with Qoheleth's final statement in chapter 1: "For in much wisdom is much anguish, and increasing knowledge increases distress."

25. Phyllis Tickle, *The Great Emergence: How Christianity Is Changing and Why* (Grand Rapids, MI: Baker, 2012), 103–7; Phyllis Tickle, *Emergence Christianity: What It Is, Where It Is Going, and Why It Matters* (Grand Rapids, MI: Baker, 2012), 151–56.

26. George Steiner, *In Bluebeard's Castle: Some Notes Towards the Redefinition of Culture* (New Haven: Yale University Press, 1974), 30 *et passim*, ch. 2, "A Season in Hell," 29–56.

Qoheleth 2:1-26

A Test: Is Pleasure Hevel?

The Test (2:1-11)

This section opens by reporting both the undertaking and the outcome of Qoheleth's "test of pleasure." The first verse alerts us to the spoiler that will suffuse the passage. What might otherwise sound like a party is instead *hevel* (2:1). Even "laughter" is "madness" (2:2). Qoheleth's up-front report of this produces neither suspense nor surprise as the following narration of this life-experiment ensues. Nonetheless, Qoheleth will explore—with wine and wisdom—both "folly" and what is "good . . . under heaven" (2:3). The structure of 2:1-11 opens with the spoiler introduction in 2:1-3. Verses 4-8 detail the "test of pleasure," with its title "great works" in 2:4a; 2:4b-6 lists those works; the possessions that Qoheleth accumulates appear in 2:7-8. Then 2:9-10 summarizes the greatness and pleasure Qoheleth amassed through this "test," even while "my wisdom remained with me." In the end (2:11), Qoheleth draws the same conclusion as in the beginning of this pericope (2:1), which is the same conclusion that opened the whole book (1:2): הכל הבל, "everything is *hevel*." This time, Qoheleth adds that all is *hevel* "under the sun." Yet, where else would Qoheleth's observations have taken place or apply? In 2:3 Qoheleth describes the location of this quest for "what was good" as taking place "under heaven," but this begs the question, what is the difference? Some take this as a hint that Qoheleth

2:1I said to myself, "Come now, I will make a test of pleasure; enjoy yourself." But again, this also was vanity. 2I said of laughter, "It is mad," and of pleasure, "What use is it?" 3I searched with my mind how to cheer my body with wine—my mind still guiding me with wisdom—and how to lay hold on folly, until I might see what was good for mortals to do under heaven during the few days of their life. 4I made great works; I built houses and planted vineyards for myself; 5I made myself gardens and parks, and planted in them all kinds of fruit trees. 6I made myself pools from which to water the forest of growing trees. 7I bought male and female slaves, and had slaves who were born in my house; I also had great possessions of herds and flocks,

was entertaining ideas of the afterlife.[1] If that is the case, the Sage does not seem to find much solace in the thought. Another possibility is that Qoheleth is contrasting the (*hevel*) experiences of humans (under the sun/under heaven) with those of God, who is in heaven above the sun. If so, this joins the list of passages in which Qoheleth does not hesitate to criticize the deity.

The structure of 2:1-10—in which Qoheleth begins with the conclusion to the "test," then reports the details, and returns to the conclusion—has a curious rhetorical effect. We, the audience, do not have a chance to make up our own minds about this "test" because Qoheleth tells us its outcome from the start. The order of the passage ensures that we will not be so foolish as to embark on such a test ourselves. Perhaps the opening to the passage persuades the audience so much that we scarcely pay attention to its details. Yet for those of us who are feminist readers, at least two features of the pericope invite questions. The first has to do with a

1. E.g., the Christian commentator John Edwards (1726) took for granted that Qoheleth indicated an afterlife in 11:9; Eric S. Christianson, *Ecclesiastes through the Centuries*, Blackwell Bible Commentaries (Malden, MA: Blackwell, 2007), 223–24; Kathleen Anne Farmer proposes that as a whole, "Qohelet and his audience share an interest in the question of the existence of some form of afterlife" (*Who Knows What Is Good? A Commentary on the Books of Proverbs and Ecclesiastes*, ITC [Grand Rapids, MI: Eerdmans, 1991], 203–6). Shannon Burkes states that "in the final centuries BCE older models for approaching religious questions in Israel such as death were breaking down, and . . . religious thinkers were confronting the new situation in a variety of ways. Qoheleth is one of the first, among those writings that have survived, to face the question" (*Death in Qoheleth and Egyptian Biographies of the Late Period* [Atlanta: Society of Biblical Literature, 1999], 89).

more than any who had been before me in Jerusalem. [8]I also gathered for myself silver and gold and the treasure of kings and of the provinces; I got singers, both men and women, and delights of the flesh, and many concubines.

[9]So I became great and surpassed all who were before me in Jerusalem; also my wisdom remained with me.

[10]Whatever my eyes desired I did not keep from them; I kept my heart from no pleasure, for my heart found pleasure in all my toil, and this was my reward for all my toil. [11]Then I considered all that my hands had done and the toil I had spent in doing it, and again, all was vanity and a chasing after wind, and there was nothing to be gained under the sun.

grammatical construction uniquely ubiquitous in Qoheleth's writing. That is, the frequent use of the first person; more specifically, the use of a first-person common singular verb along with a technically unnecessary independent first-person pronoun. This usage, as we will see, creates a self-centered focus on the wealthy, purportedly male sage, who marginalizes all others. The second issue of concern for feminist readers of this pericope relates to the first: 2:8 contains a possible reference to female sex slaves as objects in Qoheleth's test of pleasure.

Excursus: Qoheleth in and as First Person

Several commentators have reflected on the ubiquity of the first person in the book of Qoheleth, some at great length.[2] This usage appears first in 1:12 and 16, but the form becomes prominent in 2:1, where three words in a row include a first-person reference: "*I*-said/*I*/in-*my*-heart" (italics added to emphasize first-person use). In English this redundancy seems less prominent, as in 2:1 where the NRSV merely reads, "I said to myself." Throughout the book, readers of English translations may only notice the repetition of "myself" and "I," though Qoheleth's superfluous use of the first person in Hebrew persists. The technical term "pleonasm" identifies this unnecessary use of a personal pronoun

---

2. Eric S. Christianson, *A Time to Tell: Narrative Strategies in Ecclesiastes*, JSOTSup 280 (Sheffield: Sheffield Academic, 1998), 33–42, *et passim*; Daniel C. Fredericks, *Qoheleth's Language: Re-Evaluating Its Nature and Date* (Lewiston, NY: E. Mellen Press, 1988), 83; Gary D. Salyer, *Vain Rhetoric: Private Insight and Public Debate in Ecclesiastes*, JSOTSup 327 (Sheffield: Sheffield Academic, 2001), 172, 202, 299, 305.

following a conjugated verb that already contains the person number and gender.[3] Of the times Qoheleth uses first-person verbs, 27 percent include a pleonastic first-person independent pronoun, as opposed to the rest of the Hebrew Bible where this occurs with a first-person verb at a drastic fraction of the time: .07 percent.[4] Thus, Qoheleth pairs the first-person independent pronoun with the first common singular verb form excessively in comparison to the rest of the Hebrew Bible. For instance, the self-centeredness of 2:4 especially verges on the ridiculous: "I-made-great/my-works/I-built/for-myself/houses"; KJV renders this with a choppy English translation that effectively reflects the Hebrew: "I made me great works; I builded me houses." Each of the first four words in this sentence contains either the first-person pronoun as part of the verb's conjugation or the first-person possessive ending, creating a four-time repetition of the first person.

This grammatical usage even produces an aural poetic effect. In Hebrew both the independent first-person pronoun and its related possessive suffix and verbal suffix conjugation occur as word endings with a long "e" sound (though the vowel is classified and transliterated as "i"). In both 2:1 and 2:4 the first-person repetition thus creates assonance that literally calls out Qoheleth's self-centered perspective. In the opening line of the passage (2:1), the Hebrew reads אמרתי אני בלבי, *'amarti 'ani belibi*, "I-said/I/in-my-heart"; in 2:4 we find הגדלתי מעשי בניתי לי בתים, *higdalti ma'asay baniti li batim*, "I-made-great/my-works/I built/myself/houses" (with bold highlighting the assonance). This shrill-sounding repetition, as well as the meaning behind it, calls to mind a scene in the Disney film *Finding Nemo*, which features a father clownfish searching the ocean for his missing son. In one scene, a flock of hungry seagulls fight over a single crab, anthropomorphically screeching, "Miiiine! Miiiine! Miiiine!" sounding much like seagulls' cries.[5] Could Qoheleth's repetition of the first-person similarly employ sound and satire to express "it's all about me, me, me!" perhaps serving as hyperbole to lampoon an individual

---

3. Bruce K. Waltke and Michael Patrick O'Connor, *Introduction to Biblical Hebrew Syntax* (Winona Lake, IN: Eisenbrauns, 1990), 293.

4. Percentages calculated based on the numbers of Robert D Holmstedt, "'Anî Welibbî [אני בלבי]: The Syntactic Encoding of the Collaborative Nature of Qohelet's Experiment," *JHebS* 9 (2009): 4.

5. Andrew Stanton and Lee Unkrich, *Finding Nemo* (Disney Pixar, 2003). Memes of this scene and a similar one that follows later in the film are readily available online.

who would be so self-centered, or could some other purpose be driving this grammar?

The purpose of this usage remains open to conjecture. Robert Holmstedt suggests that Qoheleth uses the pleonastic first person, with the unique placement of the independent pronoun after the first common singular verb in order to distinguish the author's לב, "heart," as a "conversation partner."[6] This seems a likely possibility, and it points to the genre of the book as something like a journal.[7] Bruce Waltke and Michael O'Connor explain that this first-person redundancy can hardly be meaningless and thus is not true pleonasm. In other words, surely more lies behind this style than Qoheleth being a wordy writer. The construction commonly provides "emphasis," but Waltke and O'Connor note that this category needs clarification. They place Qoheleth's repeated pronoun use in their category "psychological focus" and describe 1:16 and 2:1 as illustrations of "profound meditation."[8] They refer to Takamitsu Muraoka, who writes of Qoheleth's frequent use of the first person: "The recurring 'I' is, as it were, an expression of the philosophical, speculative and introspective meditating ego of Qoheleth, as he observes and meditates upon the world around him and human life in it."[9]

The description of Qoheleth's self-referential style as a "meditating ego" sounds fairly complimentary. Instead, could we identify the redundant use of the personal pronoun as self-absorption or navel-gazing? The difference may be elusive and may rely, as is often the case, on preconceived determinations about Qoheleth as a positive or negative book.[10] Muraoka does entertain possibilities for the meaning of the pleonastic first person beyond his "philosophical meditating ego" description of Qoheleth. These include "various psychological factors" such as "emotional elevation, intensified self-consciousness, self-assertion, special interest or attention and the like" as well as "rebuke, indignation, penitence, narration of unusual experiences like strange dreams, supplication, boasting, response, conclusion of contract, promise, etc." While this seems a promising list of options for effectively describing Qoheleth's repeated use of the first-person pronoun, Muraoka does not

---

6. Holmstedt, "*'Anî Welibbî*," 14, 19, *et passim.*

7. With Farmer, *Who Knows What Is Good?*, 149.

8. Waltke and O'Connor, *An Introduction to Biblical Hebrew Syntax*, 293.

9. T. Muraoka, *Emphatic Words and Structures in Biblical Hebrew* (Leiden: Brill, 1985), 49.

10. Also see discussion in the author's introduction about the book of Qoheleth as a "Rorschach test for the interpreter."

actually apply the list to Qoheleth.[11] What if we were to apply some of these other categories to Qoheleth, in particular "intensified self-consciousness, self-assertion," and "boasting"?

Thus, we may rightly wonder if this language indicates something well beyond introspection: egotism, Muraoka's "boasting," or even solipsism, particularly insofar as Qoheleth seems oblivious to what anyone other than Qoheleth contributed to this grand "test of pleasure." Surely, we are not to believe that Qoheleth conducted this "test" single-handedly. That being the case, was it "pleasure" for the vintners (2:4), the gardeners (2:5), the slaves (2:7), the concubines (2:8) whose toil provided all the luxuries for the sake of Qoheleth's philosophical experiment?[12] The fact that other ancient Near Eastern royal inscriptions use similar first-person language underscores this point rather than detracting from it: Qoheleth is placed squarely in the role of the self-focused king.[13] Qoheleth's redundant first-person use conveys a level of forcefulness, bossiness, and authoritarianism. The grammar itself places everyone but Qoheleth in the category of "other." We might even identify it as "heterosexual" or "male" based on Teresa de Lauretis's discussion on "Eccentric Subjects."[14]

Notably, 45 percent of the pleonastic first-person uses in the Hebrew Bible feature the deity as the speaker. Could Qoheleth's use of the pleonastic first person further satire the author by subtly suggesting that Qoheleth had a God complex? If Qoheleth is the only speaker in the Hebrew Bible other than God who uses this form regularly, does that not imply that Qoheleth has some ego issues, at the very least? And even if Qoheleth does not in any way have divine aspirations, such self-centeredness could no doubt impair one from paying due homage to another entity. This could be an apt connection to the extent that Qoheleth identifies as a king here, and ancient Near Eastern royalty often aspired to divinity.

If the book of Qoheleth is a fantasy, or fiction, could this redundant use of "I" be an overdone signal designed to foster the illusion that Qoheleth is an "I," something along the lines of "The lady doth protest too much,

---

11. Muraoka, *Emphatic Words and Structures*, 58.

12. With Thomas Krüger, *Qoheleth: A Commentary*, ed. Klaus Baltzer, trans. O. C. Dean, Hermeneia (Minneapolis: Fortress, 2004), 66.

13. Choon-Leong Seow, *Ecclesiastes: A New Translation with Introduction and Commentary*, AB 18C (New York: Doubleday, 1997), 128.

14. Teresa de Lauretis, "Eccentric Subjects," in *Figures of Resistance: Essays in Feminist Theory* (Urbana: University of Illinois Press, 2010), 151–82.

methinks"?[15] If the book of Qoheleth is satire, this passage effectively ridicules the wealthy, powerful elite male who would claim the great building projects he oversaw as "mine!" while ignoring the reality of those who actually did the building. In the context of this particular passage—the "test of pleasure" and all it entails—the redundant first person arguably places Qoheleth in the role of oblivious oppressor. As satire, this passage caricatures a wealthy CEO who invites his staff, having recently received pay cuts, to fawn over the beautiful new furniture in his home. He is oblivious to their eye-rolling and sideward glances as they seethe with jealousy and anger at his insensitivity. After all, it was their devalued work that allowed him to have those things—things that are out of reach for them, except on the occasional visit as brief guests in his under-used home. Thus, hierarchy and the assumptions that uphold it provide the backdrop for this passage.

The burden lies with the interpreter to consider whether Qoheleth perpetuates or criticizes that hierarchical structure—or both. That interpretive task requires that we ask whether we even see the upper-class assumptions driving this rhetoric, or if we are so steeped in them ourselves that we miss them entirely. Again, the dilemma for the feminist interpreter of Qoheleth is whether the book reinforces the status quo or whether it effectively challenges the social class system through satire of it. If much of the book's readership through history has "missed" any critique inherent in the book, then it has been ineffective anyway.

The second significant issue in 2:1-11 for feminist interpreters arises in 2:7-8. In 2:7, Qoheleth names both "male slaves" (עבדים) and "female slaves" (שפחות) as part of the "test of pleasure." Qoheleth blithely lists these human commodities along with "cattle" (2:7) and "orchards" (2:5) as some of the many luxuries acquired in order to attain the good life. As that already troubling list continues, however, one crucial item additionally troubles feminists and perplexes translators. In 2:8b Qoheleth uses a difficult phrase, תענוגת בני האדם שדה ושדות. The translation options for this phrase range from Choon-Leong Seow's "humanity's treasures in chests" to Thomas Krüger's "the highest desire of men: women and more women."[16]

The first word in this phrase is the plural noun תענוגת, "pleasure" or "luxury"; the singular of this, תענוג, appears in Proverbs 19:10 and Micah

---

15. Queen Gertrude in Shakespeare, *Hamlet*, 3.2.228.
16. Seow, *Ecclesiastes*, 118; Krüger, *Qoheleth*, 56.

2:9 with a non-erotic meaning. In Song of Songs 7:6 [7], however, the context lends the word a decidedly sexualized tone, which may be relevant in this instance.[17] Furthermore, the translation of this first term relates to the understanding of the repeated *hapax legomena* at the end of the phrase: שדה ושדות, used first as a singular and then as a plural. Antoon Schoors provides a thorough review of the scholarship on this phrase, listing translation options including "coffers," "concubines," "female cup-bearers" (i.e., "waitresses"), and "breasts" (as a euphemism for a sexual partner). Even that exhaustive study does not lead Schoors to a definitive conclusion, but he finally translates the phrase as "the delights of humans, many waitresses/concubines."[18] Indeed, several contemporary translations read "concubines" here (NRSV, RSV, NASB).

Having now examined the words at the beginning and end of this phrase, we come finally to the middle, where the seemingly straightforward בני האדם, "sons of the *'adam*," becomes a key to the whole translation. As the (heteronormative) logic goes, if it is "luxuries of men," i.e., "males," then "concubines" seems a fitting object of this description; if it is "luxuries of humans," then something like "coffers" (NJPS) or "treasures in chests" might make more sense.[19] Thus in part, the translation of 2:8b relates to our overall understanding of the term אדם, *'adam*, as either "male" or "human." My broader analysis of the book suggests that Qoheleth means "male" unless "female" is specified, with possible exceptions in instances that refer broadly to the human condition.[20] Even in those cases, the larger context suggests that Qoheleth would only include "women" in the category "human" by default rather than by intention. This suggests the likelihood of the translation "luxuries of men, concubines and concubines."

Qoheleth's mind-set elsewhere in the book presents additional support for the idea that the Sage refers to "concubines" in 2:8b rather than "treasures." In 7:21, Qoheleth assumes that humans make appropriate chattel, whether male or female. Qoheleth 5:12 [11] romanticizes the sound sleep of the slave, which points to Qoheleth's overall trivialization of slavery, and in 10:7 the Sage seems incensed by reversals of hierarchy between slave and master. Furthermore, Qoheleth's overall "test of pleasure" has several items in common with the reported extravagances of King Solo-

---

17. Antoon Schoors, *Ecclesiastes* (Leuven: Peeters, 2013), 162–63.
18. Ibid., 162–65.
19. See Seow, *Qoheleth*, 130–31.
20. See author's introduction, "Gendered Language."

mon (1 Kgs 4:20-34). If Qoheleth includes commodified women as part of that list, it would coincide with what we read about King Solomon's thousand "princesses and . . . concubines" from all over the world (1 Kgs 11:1-3). Qoheleth elsewhere invokes a Solomonic fiction (1:1, 12; 2:12), so inclusion of a Solomon-style harem in Qoheleth's test of pleasure fits that scenario. For all these reasons, the translation we find in NRSV, "the delights of the flesh, and many concubines," and NIV, "a harem as well—the delights of the heart of man," fit soundly in the wider context of the book. Given this context, we are rightly left wondering if the proscription against a king having many wives in Deuteronomy 17:17 and the divine judgement against Solomon rendered in 1 Kings 11:2-13 may provide inner-biblical interpretive lenses of negative judgment on Qoheleth's "test."

Thus Qoheleth gives us ample reason to translate this list of commodities so as to include the sexual pleasures provided by concubines to a wealthy patriarch. What may at first have sounded like a lovely summer villa in 2:4-6 becomes a disturbing picture of domesticated oppression in 2:7-9, akin to Phyllis Trible's *Texts of Terror*.[21] The hierarchy and subjugation of the scenario in 2:4-9 are so embedded in the text—and perhaps into our consciousness—that we may miss its disturbing aspects. That a reader could look beyond the items "male and female slaves, . . . who were born in my house, . . . and many concubines" without concern or offense highlights the extent to which such human commodification has been overlooked in the biblical culture. Contemporary culture has similarly turned a blind eye to abuse; the #MeToo movement has highlighted this. As this movement has invited countless numbers of sexually abused, assaulted, and harassed women out of their silence, we have realized how profoundly we had overlooked their plight.

Since we cannot know for sure about Qoheleth's "original intent" for 2:7-8, it does make sense to also consider the reception history of the passage. The highly influential KJV of 1611 provided the cryptic, "and the delights of the sons of men, as musical instruments, and that of all sorts." As far back as the Geneva Bible (1599) the rendering was, "as a woman taken captiue, and women taken captiues [*sic*]." In 1917, JPS translated "women very many," while the NJPS revision in 1985 moved to "the luxuries of commoners—coffers and coffers of them." The ERV

---

21. Phyllis Trible, *Texts of Terror: Literary-Feminist Readings of Biblical Narratives*, OBT (Philadelphia: Fortress, 1984).

(1885), RSV (1952), NASB (1977), and NRSV (1989) all translate "many concubines" for שדה ושדות, the final two words of 2:8. Thus, the vast majority of English readers of this passage in the modern era have read that Qoheleth had "concubines" as part of the test of pleasure. In recent history, the word "concubines" has meant little to nothing to most English readers other than additional wives of a king. It is such a foreign concept to most contemporary readers that we may read "concubines" in English as seemingly innocuous, though foreign-sounding, yet without thinking through the reality that such individuals were essentially sex slaves with no rights to say yes or no to sex, and no freedom through divorce or other options. Thus we may read it without thinking of it as a text of terror; we may read it without being challenged to consider who in our world is a sexually commodified human being. Perhaps the ambiguity itself is the key to the passage—the difficulties surely compel us to spend more time wondering how to interpret and understand the verse than we would have otherwise.

Gregory of Nyssa (335–395 CE) wrote an early and outstanding critique of Qoheleth 2:7, appropriately shaming Qoheleth and all subsequent slaveholders throughout history for their callous and cruel commodification of human beings.

> For what is such a gross example of arrogance . . . as for a human being to think himself the master of his own kind? "I got me slaves and slave-girls," he says, and "homebred slaves were born for me." Do you notice the enormity of the boast? This kind of language is raised up as a challenge to God. . . . [W]hen someone turns the property of God into his own property and arrogates dominion to his own kind, so as to think himself the owner of men and women, what is he doing but overstepping his own nature through pride, regarding himself as something different from his subordinates?[22]

But this forceful rejection of slavery would not be the prevailing interpretive response to the passage over the centuries. It is embarrassingly easy for many privileged readers to agree that a life of pleasure and luxury will neither produce "gain" (2:11) nor eradicate *hevel* (2:1, 11) while ignoring human commodification—sexual or otherwise—as a way of testing those ideas. If we can read this passage without noticing it as a text of terror, that betrays much about our own social location and the

---

22. Gregory of Nyssa, quoted in Christianson, *Ecclesiastes through the Centuries*, 158. *Gregory of Nyssa: Homilies on Ecclesiastes*, ed. S. G. Hall (Berlin: de Gruyter, 1993), 73.

way that it allows us to turn a blind eye to the abuses and oppressions that structure our own privilege. Luxury rarely exists but at the expense of those who may not themselves enjoy it.

Is Qoheleth's response of *hevel* to these luxuries akin to the fabled comeback of Marie Antoinette, when told the peasants had no bread: "Let them eat cake"?[23] In other words, the test of pleasure assumes access to these luxuries when, in fact, most people would have no access to them and, in fact, suffer for the merest crumbs of such excess; so the description of these luxuries as *hevel* both taunts the poor and betrays the author or the persona of the author as an ivory-towered ingrate. Qoheleth is overburdened by what we would call first-world problems; it is an existential dilemma for those with too much rather than the dilemma of existence suffered by those truly trying to survive. In those ways, those of us who live amid excess—for instance most white upper-class North Americans and Western Europeans, particularly white men—can relate to Qoheleth all too well, and that too is the problem. If we can read about someone who would undertake such an experiment relying on such lavish commodities, including humans, someone who then proceeds to complain about it, without ourselves noticing the callous, even tyrannical, boasting involved, then we too must acknowledge that our sympathies lie with the privileged. Perhaps we would be best off to see Qoheleth as a caricatured idiotic wealthy man whom we would not want to emulate. And indeed, perhaps that is the point.

A reader who lives in poverty could respond not with indignation but rather with a sense of vindication—"See! Ha! You thought that wealth would bring you happiness; look how wrong you were!" On the other hand, this passage could cause someone who is unburdened by wealth to have pity for Qoheleth. For instance, one of the most joy-filled persons I ever knew was a woman who did not have her own place to live, by choice. She almost always found a bed or a couch or a pew on which to sleep, whether house-sitting for a friend or acquaintance, or in a church whose congregation she had befriended; if all else failed, she slept in her car. She was scarcely the recipient of charity, as she provided much love and care for those whom she met; she arranged flowers for churches with which she associated and taught others do so as well. She was adamant

23. Jean-Jacques Rousseau seems to have been the first to have published something like this in the eighteenth century, but it was "let them eat brioches," and it was attributed to "a great princess." Jean-Jacques Rousseau, *Confessions* (Oxford: Oxford University Press, 2000), 262.

that her life was perfect as it was, because she was utterly reliant on God rather than on wealth or conventional security. She was deeply connected to God and palpably shared God's love with all those whom she met. When this woman gave me a carefully selected present with her sparse funds, it was one of the most precious gifts I ever received. She would not have shaken her head at Qoheleth but would have prayed for someone who suffered under the weight of so many possessions and so much wealth. Somehow, this woman had learned well the lesson of *hevel* and had risen quite above the level of lamenting it.

But remember, Qoheleth told us from the beginning that this "test of pleasure" would be *hevel* (2:1). Qoheleth reiterates that front-loaded conclusion at the end of the passage (2:11), lest we miss it. Qoheleth's critique of the endeavor notably surrounds the entire passage, and as I have shown above, Qoheleth's redundant first-person grammar may also serve as an embedded satire of the gluttonous, oppressive, lascivious Solomonic figure Qoheleth supposedly embodies or perhaps ridicules. The text itself invites us to reject the male-dominant, hierarchy-reliant wealth that 2:1-11 describes, raising even further questions about the book and its apparent author. Shall we read this as the infuriating words of a wealthy, unfeeling patriarch, concerned only with his own pleasure, even though he has already said that quest is a failure? Could this be a farcical description of such a man in order to lambaste his excesses and debauchery—even one acted out by a woman? More pointedly, might this section, which lists items that seem specifically associated with King Solomon, act as a critique of his reign or of those who glorified that time as a golden era, perhaps in order to justify further abuses of hierarchy, gender, and wealth?

On Finding "Wisdom and Madness and Folly" (2:12-16)

The idea of Qoheleth's quest having to do with "wisdom" *and* "folly" and "madness" (NRSV) arose first in 1:17. It partially reappeared in 2:3 (only "wisdom" and "folly"), but we see it fully again in 2:12. We have already discussed the oddity of a sage searching for both wisdom and folly, but in 1:17 and 2:12, we find the addition of הוללות , a little-used version of what *TDOT* classifies as "הלל *hll* III."[24] The root appears in a smattering of places in the Prophets and Writings, with "undoubtedly

---

24. H. Cazelles, "הלל III," in *TDOT*, 3:411–13.

[12]So I turned to consider wisdom and madness and folly; for what can the one do who comes after the king? Only what has already been done. [13]Then I saw that wisdom excels folly as light excels darkness.

[14]The wise have eyes in their head, but fools walk in darkness.

Yet I perceived that the same fate befalls all of them. [15]Then I said to myself, "What happens to the fool will happen to me also; why then have I been so very wise?" And I said to myself that this also is vanity. [16]For there is no enduring remembrance of the wise or of fools, seeing that in the days to come all will have been long forgotten. How can the wise die just like fools?

pejorative" meaning, "refer[ring] to irrational behavior."[25] Its translations range from "deceive" to "worthless," depending on the form. The specific word הוללות occurs only in Qoheleth, and it does so five times: 1:17; 2:12; 7:25; 9:3; 10:13. In the first three of those cases, the term adjoins סכלות, "folly," as a "hendiadys," a literary device in which two terms work together to create a single concept.[26] At the very least, the word pair helps us better understand the meaning of "madness" here. It has more to do with foolishness or boastfulness than insanity; the connotation of mental illness is unfortunate and incorrect.[27] The use of this unusual word in the book of Qoheleth may yet again point to the idea of Qoheleth as an impersonator, a caricature-creator whose writing levels a critique against those who would have the nerve to pair such words as "foolishness" or "boastfulness" with "wisdom."

In 2:13, it first appears that Qoheleth is going to move on to a more traditional line of reasoning: "Then I saw that wisdom excels folly as light excels darkness" (2:13). But then Qoheleth resumes the ongoing critique of wisdom. The next three verses (2:14-16) assert that the wise have no advantage.[28] The closing rhetorical question of the pericope (v. 16) articulates one of Qoheleth's many laments about the injustice of death: How is it that death of the wise is just like that of the fool? The

25. Cazelles states in *TDOT* that the root occurs "19 (or 20)" times. (One occurrence is disputed.) 3:411.

26. See Abraham Even-Shoshan, *A New Concordance of the Hebrew Bible* (Tel-Aviv: Kiryat Sefer, 2018), 284; Y. A. P. Goldman, "Commentaries on the Critical Apparatus: Qoheleth," in *BHQ: Megilloth*, 68*; *BDB*, 2411.

27. Also see H. Cazelles in *TDOT* "הלל III," 3:413.

28. In these verses, however, Qoheleth does not specifically use the Hebrew term typical elsewhere in the book: יתרון (Qoh 1:3; 2:11, 13; 3:9; 5:9 [8], 16 [15]; 7:12; 10:10, 11).

motivation for this question arises several times in 2:14-16, the point being that wisdom does not ensure an advantageous outcome for the wise over against the foolish. Yet in this lament against the injustice of death, Qoheleth seems oblivious to the greater injustices that work to his advantage. We can imagine one of Qoheleth's laborers laughing at the wealthy sage's lament: "Poor Qoheleth! Yes, you'll die just like the rest of us! But here's another one for you: How can I work twice as long and hard as you and still have half as much to eat? How can you take all the credit for your 'test of pleasure' when I did all the work?" We can imagine a concubine laughing, "Poor Qoheleth! Yes, you'll die just like the rest of us! But here's another one for you: How does your anatomy privilege you with power over me even though I bear your children, at great physical risk?" These questions raise further questions for contemporary readers: Is this a book only for the privileged (or at least this passage and several similar ones)? What use of, or response to, this book do marginalized persons have? Is it as potentially insulting and offensive as it seems?[29] Qoheleth's lament calls to mind the irony-soaked Twitter feed #firstworldproblems, though Qoheleth does not seem self-aware enough to ironically tweet this paraphrase of 2:1-16: "Live a life of luxury and great wisdom; die anyway. Poor me." Or maybe this passage just becomes a great opportunity for the marginalized to laugh at those privileged ones who are miserable even while wallowing in their wealth.

Conclusion: The Senseless Pursuit of Toil (עָמָל) and the Distraction/Relief of the *Carpe Diem* (2:17-26)

Qoheleth 2:12-16 leads us into Qoheleth's offensive conclusion to the "test of pleasure" in 2:17-26. "I hated life" (2:17), as a response to the exercise in gluttony Qoheleth conducted in 2:4-8, would especially boggle the minds of those who eke out a survival existence. What a privilege to "hate life" when the living is so extravagant! On the other hand, perhaps someone who struggles just to get by would find Qoheleth's comments a relief, or even hilarious: so even someone who could afford to wallow in so much wealth could be miserable? As a whole, 2:17 articulates Qoheleth's most pessimistic views using caustic language as well as a vocabulary emblematic of the book as a whole: "hates," "under the

---

29. See below: Laura Choate, "The Test of Pleasure Endures; Compassion Is True Remembrance."

¹⁷So I hated life, because what is done under the sun was grievous to me; for all is vanity and a chasing after wind.

¹⁸I hated all my toil in which I had toiled under the sun, seeing that I must leave it to those who come after me ¹⁹—and who knows whether they will be wise or foolish? Yet they will be master of all for which I toiled and used my wisdom under the sun. This also is vanity. ²⁰So I turned and gave my heart up to despair concerning all the toil of my labors under the sun, ²¹because sometimes one who has toiled with wisdom and knowledge and skill must leave all to be enjoyed by another who did not toil for it. This also is vanity and a great evil. ²²What do mortals get from all the toil and strain with which they toil under the sun? ²³For all their days are full of pain, and their work is a vexation; even at night their minds do not rest. This is also vanity.

²⁴There is nothing better for mortals than to eat and drink, and find enjoyment in their toil. This also, I saw, is from the hand of God; ²⁵for apart from him who can eat or who can have enjoyment? ²⁶For to the one who pleases him God gives wisdom and knowledge and joy; but to the sinner he gives the work of gathering and heaping, only to give to one who pleases God. This also is vanity and a chasing after wind.

sun," "unhappy"; it is *hevel* and "chasing after wind" (see the author's introduction for discussion of these throughout the book).[30] Qoheleth continues this pitiful and strongly worded lament through 2:26; there, and in 2:23, the repetition of *hevel* draws us back to its use at the beginning of 2:17.

Meanwhile, throughout 2:17-23, Qoheleth laments about עמל, "toil," often with a possessive ending, twice each in verses 2:18-22. In 2:18 Qoheleth dramatically repeats the word שנא, "hate," which first appeared in 2:17, where Qoheleth "hated life." Now, Qoheleth also hates toil. In a reminder of the "turning" in 1:6, in 2:20 Qoheleth again "turns," but this time to despair (in Hebrew in a *piel* verb form from the root יאש, "to cause desperation"). This strong term, appropriately enough, is uttered by Job as well: "Do you think that you can reprove words, as if the speech of the desperate were wind?" (6:26, NRSV).

---

30. Qoheleth שנאתי, "hates," in 2:17, 18; 3:8; finds what is done תחת השמש, "under the sun," in 1:3, 9, 14; 2:11, 17, 18, 19, 20, 22; 3:16; 4:1, 3, 7, 15; 5:13 [12], 17; 6:1, 12; 8:9, 15, 17; 9:3, 6, 9, 11, 13; 10:5; and uses the term רע, "unhappy," in 1:13; 2:17; 4:3, 4, 8, 17; 5:14 [13]; 6:2; 7:3; 8:3, 5, 9, 11, 12; 9:3, 12; 10:13; 12:14.

While Qoheleth invoked the word רע, "evil, unhappy" in 2:17 to describe "all the deeds that are done under the sun," in 2:21 Qoheleth
amplifies that word (here in the feminine form, with the same meaning)
with the adjective "great," רעה רבה, and applies it to the perceived injustice
that "you can't take it with you"—some no-good lazybones may be the
recipient of your life's work. The pessimism in Qoheleth's view here
is striking, though. One possible response to the idea that "you can't
take it with you" would be generosity and enjoyment, such as we see
in the 1936 play and 1938 film of the same name, in which the historical
context of the Great Depression was significant.[31] While Qoheleth does
eventually get there with the *carpe diem* in 2:24 and elsewhere in the
book, the justification for the conclusions *hevel* and "great evil" in 2:21
relies on the assumption that the recipient of Qoheleth's wealth will not
have worked for it.

Ordinarily, this is precisely the reasoning that motivates people to
save, so that the wealth can go to one's children and spouse, who have
not worked for it but deserve it nonetheless. Qoheleth does not seem to
entertain this notion but, instead, detests the idea that one's hard-earned
wealth could go to someone undeserving of it. Does this again point to
Qoheleth's self-centeredness? Could it be a way for a persona to make fun
of a wealthy, egomaniacal, childless single male who has never stopped
to think about others? Could it have prevented readers throughout the
centuries from behaving charitably to those who survive them? How
might this affect women and children? Would Qoheleth or other sages
have viewed women and children as undeserving of inherited wealth?
Would the "toil" they contributed to the family matter to Qoheleth?

Qoheleth's strong negative language culminates in 2:23 with a chiastic
parallelism:

> For all his **days** are מכאבים distress
> And כעס anguish is his **task**

This verse uses the same vocabulary as 1:18 and certainly makes a similar
point; here there is just the more specific context of Qoheleth's "test of
pleasure." In light of the excesses of 2:1-10, this is offensive whining,
an insult to those who truly work hard in order to provide for their
families both during their lives and after their deaths, as opposed to
Qoheleth, who simply tried out those luxuries and found them wanting.

---

31. Moss Hart and George Simon Kaufman, *You Can't Take It with You: Comedy in
Three Acts* (Dramatists Play Service, Inc., 1937); Frank Capra, *You Can't Take It With
You* (Columbia Pictures Corp, 1938).

This statement trivializes those who worked in "pain" and "anguish" to accomplish the building projects for which Qoheleth took credit.

Aside from "toil," the repetitions in this passage include *hevel*, which appears four times in this passage.[32] The last three all contain the phrase גם־זה הבל, "this is also *hevel*," which additionally emphasizes the mere repetition of *hevel*. There is *hevel*, *hevel*, all around. Five times in this section Qoheleth describes the location of all this *hevel* and toil: "under the sun."[33] חכם, "wise, be wise," appears twice in 2:19, and again as a noun, חכמה, "wisdom," in 2:21; in all cases but the last, even this attribute ultimately leads to *hevel*, which seems quite an affront to the endeavors of a Sage. Qoheleth asks rhetorical questions in 2:19a, "who knows?" and 22a, "what becomes of a man?" These questions also result in negative answers. My translation of verse 22a betrays Qoheleth's androcentric focus on toil, hidden in the NRSV. Yet again, Qoheleth seems to utterly ignore any toil undertaken by women.

The tone definitely shifts in 2:24-26, and the vocabulary repetitions reflect this as they did in the preceding section. Starting in 2:24, the word טוב, "good," appears four times (twice in 2:24 and twice in 2:26). Thankfully, Qoheleth has something "good" to recommend after all the preceding harsh language expressing a negative outlook on life. In 2:24 we get relief from Qoheleth's negativity through the book's first passage of the so-called *carpe diem*—though we don't yet have "eat, drink, and be merry"; instead, it's "eat, drink and enjoy your toil."[34] It is a refreshingly different view of "toil" from what we read earlier in the chapter. But after all the "hate" (2:17, 18) and other strong language, would anyone want to "eat" and "drink" (2:24) with this person?

Qoheleth's self-obsession continues through this section, something that jumps out at the Hebrew reader through over-use of the first-person independent pronoun, first-person verbs, first-person pronoun endings, and first-person possessive endings.[35] These excessive first-person references continue what we saw in 2:19, in which Qoheleth apparently claims sole credit for the creations of the test of pleasure: כל עמלי שעמלתי, "all *my* toil for which *I* toiled"; "[with] *my* wisdom." That phrase relies

---

32. 2:17, 19, 21, 23.

33. 2:17, 18, 19, 20, 22.

34. Also see Isa 22:13, in which *carpe diem* is justified with a reference to death, a sentiment that Qoheleth would seemingly have resonated with well.

35. The first-person independent pronoun appears in 2:18 [twice], 20, 24; first-person verbs are in 2:17, 18, 19 [twice], 20 [twice], 24; first-person pronoun endings appear in 2:18; and first-person possessive endings are used in 2:18, 19, 20.

on the callousness of 2:4-8. Throughout the chapter, Qoheleth will not let us forget: "It's all about me."

Qoheleth frames the *carpe diem* in 2:24b-26 theologically, asserting that this enjoyment comes from God. Yet this compromises any relief the *carpe diem* may have offered, particularly when we get to 2:26, where God's benevolence occurs capriciously, depending on whether or not one "pleases" God. The questions from 2:19a and 22a multiply in this section, with two in verse 25, "who can eat; who can enjoy?" The caveat Qoheleth provides along with these rhetorical questions apparently emphasizes divine power: "apart from me." The word repetitions that began in 2:17-23 continue here, linking 2:17-23 and 2:24-26. In 2:26 Qoheleth returns to חכם, "wise/be wise," and חכמה, "wisdom" (2:19 [twice], 21), and the topic עמל, "toil," appears for an eleventh time since 2:17 in 2:24. Unsurprisingly, *hevel* closes the larger section in 2:26. To the extent that divine capriciousness amplifies *hevel* at the end of this section, it at least gives Qoheleth a taste of the exclusion that drove the test of pleasure at the beginning of chapter 2. While slaves and singers, gardeners, and diggers labored to construct the scenario that Qoheleth described as having personally created (note the pleonastic first person in vv. 4-8), not even this self-centered Sage has the assurance of divine approval.

The Test of Pleasure Endures; Compassion Is True Remembrance

What I gathered from this passage was: whoever wrote this was testing all he could gain for pleasure. He amassed land, houses, vineyards. For me, the gathering of slaves and concubines went too far, but in those times this was a sign of wealth. People still do this "gathering" in the stealth of our time. The 218 schoolgirls who were kidnapped in 2014 by the Boko Haram militant group in Nigeria are an example of this. The Boko Haram funded their cause in part by selling those girls, so we see human trafficking remains a problem in our own time.[36]

Qoheleth did not at first consider himself a fool: "Work hard and have anything you want" was his mind-set. The

36. For one report on girls being sold by Boko Haram, see Ofeibea Quist-Arcton, "The Lament of the Boko Haram 'Brides,'" *NPR: Weekend Edition Sunday* (August 27, 2017), https://www.npr.org/sections/goatsandsoda/2017/08/27/545912049/the-lament-of-the-boko-haram-brides.

writer felt he was owed this wealth for all his work; it was his, because he earned it. But it seems that he wanted wisdom most of all. He was amassing things to acquire wisdom. Upon realizing the wise and fools alike "will have been forgotten" (2:16), it was clear that none of that would matter in the end. His riches would be squandered. And he would be leaving all he had amassed for those who never worked for it, and he would not be appreciated for what he had done to acquire it. After going through this "test of pleasure," though, he realized he had been a fool.

I see this a lot in my work helping the working poor or the drug addicts. They see people with everything desirable and know they can never have that life. So they imitate the wealthy by purchasing the items they covet, even though they can't afford them. They seek pleasure in "items"; today it's electronics, and tomorrow it will be virtual realities. They rapidly give up in despair because there is not enough to leave their kids, so they spend all they have. They see no future, just day-to-day survival and paying bills. The idea of inheritance is gone.

I do not understand the author's use of the word "vanity" so much. I see people all the time with zero self-esteem; how can they be "vain"? The author speaks of God rewarding those that please him, and those that don't please him must work harder—how is this "vanity"? Does he mean their work is in vain? We all end up worm food and are all equally forgotten in time. I choose to help as many souls as I can while I am here, not to be remembered, but to remember those who helped me. They did not live in vain.

Laura Choate

Qoheleth 3:1-22

What Time?

"Time" Poem (3:1-8)

This poem is surely the most recognizable and familiar part of Qoheleth, both for those who read the Bible and for those who do not. It is one of the only parts of the book that appears in the New Revised Common Lectionary used by Christians, and it is sometimes read for funerals.[1] Aside from those liturgical uses, Pete Seeger's musical setting of the KJV of 3:1-8, "Turn, Turn, Turn," popularized by The Byrds in 1965, propelled the song into popular consciousness in a lasting way. Seeger's ever so slight alterations of the KJV, in which he omits "a time for war" (3:8b) and adds the phrase "I swear it's not too late" after "a time for peace," turned his biblical song into a famous peace anthem.

The poem has a compelling aesthetic, both visually and aurally. From verses 2 to 8, each verse contains two lines, each of which repeats עֵת, "time," paired with an infinitive construct (־לְ, "to" + infinitive form of a verb, except in the cases of 4b and 8b, which omit the ־לְ, "to," and in

---

1. Recommendations for 3:1-8 for use in funerals appear at https://www.swan boroughfunerals.com.au/funeral-scripture-ecclesiastes/; http://www.funeralhelper .org/bible-reading-ecclesiastes-3-short.html; https://urc.org.uk/images/Free-Ebooks /WB2_Funeral_Readings.pdf; https://www.funeralwise.com/plan/ceremony/read /scriptures/. The Revised Common Lectionary lists Qoheleth 3:1-13 as one of the texts for the New Year Service in all three years of the liturgical cycle.

3:1For everything there is a season, and a time for every matter under heaven:
²a time to be born, and a time to die;
a time to plant, and a time to pluck up what is planted;
³a time to kill, and a time to heal;
a time to break down, and a time to build up;
⁴a time to weep, and a time to laugh;
a time to mourn, and a time to dance;
⁵a time to throw stones, and a time to gather stones together;
a time to embrace, and a time to refrain from embracing;
⁶a time to seek, and a time to lose;
a time to keep, and a time to throw away;
⁷a time to tear, and a time to sew;
a time to keep silence, and a time to speak;
⁸a time to love, and a time to hate;
a time for war, and a time for peace.

8b the verbs are replaced by nouns). In each line the two infinitives state opposite sentiments. Thus the poet repeats "time" twenty-nine times, four each for verses 2-8, and once in verse 1. This arguably creates a series of "merisms," literary devices in which the named items not only identify an antithesis but also stake out the end points of a range that indicates a whole spectrum.

One of the most helpful and sustained feminist interpretations of any portion of Qoheleth is Athalya Brenner-Idan's analysis of this passage. Brenner-Idan's larger project with Fokkelien van Dijk-Hemmes involves identifying the "M (masculine/male)" and "F (feminine/female)" voices in the biblical text; looking for signals of a "gendered" text.[2] Brenner-Idan discovers an M voice in Qoheleth, particularly in 3:1-8. The notable verse that indicates the M voice here is 3:5; Brenner-Idan argues that the imagery here is sexual and that it assumes a male perspective.[3] If we accept this analysis, what does the passage do to a feminine/female reader? Does it distance us women from the poem, since then we are simply objects, the recipients of the "stones" and "embraces" of verse 5? Are we reduced to the unnamed bodies who would "give birth" in verse 2? Are women even further alienated by the M-oriented transla-

2. Athalya Brenner and Fokkelien van Dijk Hemmes, *On Gendering Texts: Female and Male Voices in the Hebrew Bible*, BibInt 1 (Leiden: Brill, 1993), 7–8.

3. See below, "Qoheleth 3:1-9—Structure and Sense with Verse 5 as a Key" by Athalya Brenner-Idan.

tion of verse 2, "a time to beget"? Perhaps for contemporary English readers, the alienation is not as bad as it might have been in an ancient context. The NRSV's "a time to be born" in 3:2 does not utterly exclude a woman's experience, since the inaccurate passive translation could include any human being. Similarly, casting and gathering stones sounds to contemporary English-speaking ears like warfare or perhaps building, activities from which many contemporary women would not assume we are excluded. And, though embracing or not may have a gendered and sexualized meaning even in translation, it need not necessarily carry that connotation. Many contemporary women arguably feel full autonomy in choosing when and with whom and with what gender of person we would embrace. Such is the dilemma of revealing or veiling the hidden patriarchy in the biblical text.

Thus the M voice that may well have composed 3:1-8 does not utterly alienate women from the experiences of this poem. A survey of the verbs (and nouns, in v. 8) contained in these well-known verses shows that, in nearly all cases, female actors have engaged in these actions within the literature of the Hebrew Bible. As with any biblical passage, I encourage contemporary readers of 3:1-8 to adopt the challenging but crucial exercise of trying to read this poem with new eyes and ears and understanding. For the purposes of this commentary specifically, the challenge is to read the poem through feminist eyes, asking how and whether the poem matters or mattered for women. The opening word, לכל, "for/to everything," suggests a universalism of experience that warrants our hermeneutic of suspicion but also invites us to consider how the poem may in fact include women's experiences, even from an ancient Near Eastern context, or, more specifically, that of women in the literature of the Hebrew Bible. Thus, I will proceed to investigate the verbs of 3:1-8 to discover the extent to which they appeared with female subjects in the Hebrew Bible.

This poem begins with a distinctly female verb: ללדת, "to bear," belongs exclusively to women, at least in the biological sense.[4] We see the word used that way clearly in Genesis 4:2, where Eve gives birth to Cain. Yet most translations have obscured this most gynocentric of the poem's infinitive pairs by translating in the passive, "a time to be born." The LXX supports the "give birth" translation, as does the rest of the poem,

---

4. In most cases, the *qal* formation of the verb produces the translation "bear," with a female subject. In the *hiphil* formation (הוליד), the root ילד has males for its subjects, usually translated in line with the KJV "beget." *BDB*, 408–9.

with active verbs throughout.[5] While the Hebrew can also indicate "to beget," as in "procreate" as opposed to specifically "give birth," *BDB* states that translation applies to the *qal* of this root "less often."[6] It seems likely that the KJV translation—"a time to be born"—created a paradigm or tradition that swayed most subsequent translators, regardless of what the Hebrew reads here. Thomas Krüger notes that the passive translation may have arisen from analyzing ללדת, "to bear," as a *hophal* or *niphal* stem (as in 7:1, הולדו).[7] This seems a generous assessment, since the word does not bear the marks of either of these forms. Another conclusion is that the mistaken translation arose from sexism, a suppression, perpetrated intentionally or otherwise, of what otherwise could have appeared as women's wisdom. Between the hegemony of the KJV and the additional ossification of that translation that arose from Seeger's song, reclaiming the gynocentric character of this poem will be no small task.

While death is obviously a universal experience, women would have related in gender-specific ways to the time "to die" in 3:2. Women had particular roles in mourning practices even into the Second Temple period, such as keening, as we see in Jeremiah 9:17-20 [16-19].[8] Later sources especially show women taking on special responsibilities in care for the dead, since corpse uncleanness would not matter for them the way it would have for men with obligations related to the feasts.[9] Additionally, infant and maternal mortality rates were so high even into the Hellenistic period that death would have been constantly looming, insofar as most

---

5. Thomas Krüger, *Qoheleth: A Commentary*, ed. Klaus Baltzer, trans. O. C. Dean, Hermeneia (Minneapolis: Fortress, 2004), 75.

6. *BDB* notes this as the second definition of ילד, used "less often" than "bear, bring forth" (408b). Antoon Schoors provides a helpful discussion of text-critical issues and translation options and reviews the varying scholarly views. He concludes, "Both interpretations are acceptable, but the parallelism with למות is closer in the passive meaning, and therefore lightly pleads in favour of the majority opinion." *Ecclesiastes* (Leuven: Peeters, 2013), 236–37. Of course "lightly . . . in favour" would be lost on most of those reading in translation.

7. Krüger, *Qoheleth*, 75.

8. Jennie R. Ebeling examines female-focused mourning practices in the Iron I period in ancient Near Eastern and Egyptian contexts: *Women's Lives in Biblical Times* (London: T & T Clark, 2010), 141. Also see Rachel Hachlili, *Jewish Funerary Customs, Practices and Rites in the Second Temple Period*, Supplements to the Journal for the Study of Judaism 94 (Leiden: Brill, 2005), 236–37. Also see Phyllis Ann Bird, *Missing Persons and Mistaken Identities: Women and Gender in Ancient Israel* (Philadelphia: Fortress, 1997), 117–18.

9. Hachlili, *Jewish Funerary Customs*, 236–37.

women's lives would have been consumed with pregnancy, childbirth, and the rearing of vulnerable infants.[10] L. Juliana M. Claassens adds significant theological gravitas to these activities in illustrating mourning as part of the character of the deity.[11] These issues will arise again in 3:4, with the specific mention of "a time to mourn."

Qoheleth 3:2 introduces the verb נטע, "plant" (in the *qal* stem), which finds a female connection in the אשת חיל, "Strong Woman," of Proverbs 31, who "plants" as one of her activities (v. 16; she is specifically planting a vineyard). The verb עקר "to pluck up" (again in the *qal*) completes that pair in 3:2b. Although numerous biblical texts evidence women's involvement in agricultural activities, this specific verb appears only here and in Zephaniah 2:4, where the word connotes destruction of a crop before its time.[12] Thus 3:2b does not seem to describe planting and harvest but rather planting and the malicious uprooting of what has been planted.

The killing and healing, tearing down and building up in 3:3 has a number of connections to women's work. We know from the stories of Rahab (Josh 2:1, 3; 6:17, 23, 25), Deborah and Jael (Judg 4–5), Esther (9:12), and Judith (8:32-34; 11:1–14:4) that women commanded troops and spied during wartime. The verb הרג (*qal*), "kill," is specifically associated with Esther's leadership, as well as with the activity of the Strange Woman of Proverbs 7:26.[13] The healing arts tend to be viewed as a stereotypical female activity, particularly in preindustrial societies, but we see only a few women healers reflected in biblical texts. רפא (*qal*), "heal," in the Bible overwhelmingly takes place as an activity of the deity, while human

---

10. Ebeling lists the following statistics: "In the eastern Mediterranean world during the Iron Age, only 1.9 children survived out of the average 4.1 births per females. The threat to women in the process of giving birth was also great, as most women before the nineteenth century CE died before reaching menopause, at about age 30 in the Iron Age. In ancient Israel, a woman had to become pregnant nearly twice for every child that survived to age five and women's lifespans were approximately ten years shorter than those of men, who are believed to have lived to age 40 on average" (*Women's Lives*, 101). Also see Tal Ilan, *Jewish Women in Greco-Roman Palestine* (Peabody, MA: Hendrickson Publishers, 1996), 116–19.

11. L. Juliana M. Claassens, *Mourner, Mother, Midwife: Reimagining God's Delivering Presence in the Old Testament* (Louisville: Westminster John Knox, 2012), chap. 2.

12. For women's involvement in agricultural activities, see Ruth 2; Prov 31:16; and Ebeling, *Women's Lives*, 35–36.

13. The verb הרג (*qal*), "kill," as associated with Esther's leadership appears in Esth 8:11; 9:6, 10, 12, 15, 16.

efforts toward healing are viewed with suspicion (2 Chr 16:12). An exception to this is 2 Kings 5:1-14, where we meet an Israelite girl who had been captured by the Arameans; that passage, however, does not include the specific Hebrew term רפא. This slave girl facilitated the healing of Na'aman by sending him to the prophet Elisha. Midwives appear in Genesis 35:17; 38:28; and Exodus 1:19. These few examples suggest the activity of healing as relevant to the work of women.[14]

The Hebrew root פרץ (*qal*), translated as "break down" in 3:3 (NRSV) has a distinctly female connotation in the first definition *BDB* provides for it, which is "*break* or *burst out*, from womb," as in Genesis 38:29, where it etiologically describes the birth of Perez (פרץ). Other reasonable translations exist for this term in the *qal*, which would not have a specifically feminine referent or context and which might make more sense as the opposite of "build up." For our purposes, however, it makes sense to consider that here the poem contains hints of yet another birth scenario. Furthermore, בנה, "build up," can also indicate birth, to the extent that it indicates increasing the number of children in a family; we see that related to biblical women in Ruth 4:11; Genesis 16:2; 30:3. We could think of these two terms as something of opposites if we understood פרץ as a child breaking out of the womb and בנה as conception for the sake of building (the contents of) the womb and, ultimately, building the family. In this paradigm, both would be women's work. If it seems repetitive to verse 2, that is nothing unique to this poem: we have several death-related references in verses 2, 4, and 6; why not, then, more than one birth reference?

The verb בכה (*qal*), "weep," links to many biblical women, including Hagar (Gen 21:16), Hannah (1 Sam 1:7, 8, 10), Jephthah's daughter (Judg 11:37), Ruth and Orpah (Ruth 1:9, 14), and Delilah (Judg 14:16-17). Furthermore, we find a legal code in Deuteronomy 21:13 about a foreign captive woman who is given time to "weep" for her parents before an Israelite man who desires her is allowed to have sex with her and make her "his woman." Finally, there is the infamous reference to women "weeping for the Tammuz," an "abomination" that God shows Ezekiel in an effort to illustrate the evils that would bring on divine wrath (Ezek 8:14).

---

14. Notably, Claassens links the work of a midwife to that of the deity. *Mourner, Mother, Midwife*, chap. 4.

In verse 4, צחק (*qal*, from the synonymous roots *sahak/tsahak*), "laugh," especially brings to mind Sarah in Genesis 18:12, 13, 15. Though her disbelief through laughter parallels that of her mate Abraham (Gen 17:17), Sarah's laughter has gained notoriety, perhaps because it seems to be the etiology for her son Isaac's name (יצחק, *yitshak*; Gen 21:6) or perhaps for sexist reasons. Very often *sahak/tsahak* indicates mocking more than fun (as in Ishmael of Isaac in Gen 21:9), though it can also indicate delight, as is notably the case in Proverbs 8:30, where God delights in Wisdom who משחקת, "plays" in front of God, and in the following verse, where she in turn delightfully plays in humanity. Finally, in Proverbs 31:25 the Strong Woman is so undaunted by the coming days that she "laughs" about the future![15]

The pairing "to mourn/to dance" in 3:4b again raises the issue of women's association with mourning and funerary rituals in the ancient Near East and into the Hellenistic context. In addition to the funerary rites and mourning rituals mentioned above, we see women ספד, "mourn," in 2 Samuel 11:26, where Bathsheba mourns over the death of Uriah; in Isaiah 32:12; Jeremiah 49:3; and Zechariah 12:12 women mourn over coming or current destruction. In Qoheleth, the type of dancing indicated in the Hebrew רקד (*qal*, "dance") usually relates to skipping or leaping and most often refers to animals or even mountains. In Psalm 30:11 [12], mourning is paired with dancing, similar to what we see in Qoheleth 3, though the Psalms reference does not use the same Hebrew word. The term for dancing in Psalm 30:11 [12], however—מחול—elsewhere refers to women's celebratory movement: women rejoicing upon the return of King Saul (1 Sam 18:6).

This study of the key words in the poem of 3:1-8 shows that, for the most part, it would not have excluded women's experiences. Indeed, biblical women have significant connections to many of the stichs in this poem. This analysis does not preclude the association of the poem with an M voice (see below). What it does show is that women readers, then and now, might have found a place for themselves in this classic philosophical reflection. As we will see, the questions that follow the poem open it for critique, thus inviting the audience to deconstruct it as well, whether from a gendered view or otherwise.

15. R. Bartelmus, צחק/שׂחק, *TDOT*, 14:66, 69.

Qoheleth 3:1-9
Structure and Sense
with Verse 5 as a Key[16]

Searching for the "original" literary setting/meaning of a poem (vv. 2-8) quoted in a text and framed by an introduction (v. 1) and an epilogue (v. 9) is a legitimate quest. It has intrinsic interest and, besides, may well affect the way we understand the poem's adaptation to the frame. The original meaning, be it known to the author and his (yes, in this case!) readers or not, necessarily becomes a component of any new meaning imposed by its frame. It remains to be seen to what extent a detailed analysis of the poem will uncover an intrinsic sense which has nothing or little to do with its frame.

The poem's structure is fairly rigid and its style epigrammatic. Each stich begins with the phrase עֵת, "a time." This is mostly succeeded by the preposition לְ, "to." Then comes a construct infinitive (apart from in the second half of v. 8). The contrasted parallelism dictates an identical structure in the second half of the line. The parallel stich is introduced by the appropriate conjunction וְ, *we-* (and). Every two stichs form a formal and thematic stanza (signified as a verse in many printed editions). Three stanzas/verses follow this pattern (vv. 2-4). Then, a departure from the fairly tight structure is introduced. Verse 5 has the same basic pattern of its predecessors, albeit with a difference—in three of its four stichs (5a, 5b, 5d) a complement succeeds the infinitive form (a nominal object in the first two, a verbal complement in the last stich). Given the poem's tight rhythmical and metrical structure so far and later, this deviation is quite conspicuous, even if the semantic deviation can be explained away as the outcome of gradual textual amplification. Thereafter the shorter pattern of verses 2-4 is resumed in verses 6-8, albeit with one additional departure. In the very last line (8c-d) the parallelism between the two pairs is inverted, so that the infinitives "to love" and "to hate" in the first stich are matched by the inverted nouns "war" and "peace" (not "peace" and "war," as expected) in the concluding phrase.

When we get to the poem's end we realize that the poem contains the conventional number of seven units and is distinctly if somewhat loosely chiastic. Accordingly, attention is, must be, drawn to the middle and central stanza—verse 5, whose content significance is accentuated by its departure from the otherwise fairly consistent stylistic/structural pattern. The final line also, quite evidently, carries a sting in its

---

16. This piece is based on "The Case of Qoheleth 3.1-9," 133–55, in *On Gendering Texts*.

tail, for after thirteen matched pairs, the final inversion cannot but be highly suggestive. In short, even if we maintain that a chiastic structure (at least of sorts) obtains throughout the poem, the key to understanding the poem resides less in the understanding of particular positive/negative contrasts and their inversions. Rather, the significance of the central stanza (v. 5)—together with the final inversion 8c-d, and the latter's interrelation with the opening (v. 2) and the central stanzas (v. 5)—should be marked as indicative for the poem's indigenous purpose.

The poem's structure indeed obliges us to expect that verse 5 will contain the key to, or express the essence of, the meaning of the poem. Whether deliberately or due to our modern (mis)understanding, however, both the contextual and connotative senses of verse 5 seem less than obvious. The wording of the first stich, a time for "casting stones" and for "gathering stones," is vague figuratively as well as metaphorically. What does the "casting" and "gathering" of stones, in whatever sense, mean in the poem's context? Some commentators insist that a literal sense is quite acceptable: there are times for casting stones, such as when a field is being cleared or in war, and there are other times for gathering them, for example, when clearing ground or for building. Personally I find this quasiliteral interpretation

unconvincing: the other verses in the series, be their connotations and/or denotations "desirable" or "undesirable," positive or negative, do not receive grammatical complements (apart from the last verb in v. 2). As a result, their stichs are much shorter than the three longer ones in verse 5.

Other verbs in the poem have a much clearer—if less specific—denotation than the idea of casting/gathering stones: one does not question the possible denotation of "plant" or "uproot," for instance (2c-d). In the case of verse 5a-b, though, defining a denotation is not enough. If one opts for the literal interpretation, connotations and further explanations demonstrate that literality here is not as transparent as it should be, by definition. In short, formal and semantic considerations cancel the acceptance of a "simple" reading for the "stones" and the activities linked with them.

Another approach is to turn to the next line. Could it be that an internal clue resides in the contrasting pair in the second half of verse 5: There is a time for "embracing" and for "refraining from embracing"? Now, in almost all the other strophes the two contrasting pairs are complementary (only in the case of v. 7 is this not obvious). On the primary reading level at least, verse 2 deals with the life cycle, verse 3 with creation and destruction, verse 4 with joy and sorrow, verse 6 with acquisition and loss, and verse 8 with conflict and harmony. Verses 2 and 8 (quality of life) are interlinked, in addition to the internal duplication within them of the strophe's topic.

In ancient Jewish sources the "casting" and "gathering" of stones is at times read as an oblique (metaphorical) reference to performing or abstaining from the sexual act and, it is worth noting, the reading is done from an obviously male perspective. What gave rise to the "sexual" interpretation in the Jewish sources? At first glance it seems so far-fetched as to be inconceivable unless anchored in solid information that, unfortunately, is not readily available to modern readers. Indeed, several scholars agree; they cite Jewish sources and biblical passages that link "stones" with matters sexual and reproductive (Exod 1:16; Jer 2:27; the obscure Matt 3:9) but do not successfully explain the connotative meaning of the metaphor—if a metaphor it is. In short, how can the "sexual" interpretation be substantiated by the context or by other biblical intertexts?

Let us deal with the immediate context first, that is, with the second half of verse 5. It can be pointed out that "embrace" (from the Hebrew Root חבק, *qal*

in the third stich and then in the *piel* in the fourth, both with the meaning of "embrace") does not always designate erotic or sexual behavior. This is indeed so, especially in the wisdom literature idiom חבק + "hands," "to be idle" (Qoh 4:5; Prov 6:10; 24:33). Two other occurrences are figurative, hence not instructive for the present passage (Job 24:8; Lam 4:5). The remaining—and majority—eight occurrences all designate physical intimacy: four with family kin[17] and four with a lover of either sex.[18] In view of this inventory, an "intimacy" denotation at least should be accredited to חבק, and it is a toss-up whether the specialized erotic signification is not as primary, in the sense that it perhaps was as often or even more widely used, as the general (intimate but nonmotivated by erotics) "embrace." "Take into one's arms" as an overt sign of affection is certainly the referent shared by both groups of occurrences. Verse 5a-b, as argued above, would be best understood when linked up parallelistically with 5c-d.

Where else in the Hebrew Bible do "stones" have a semantic link with sexuality and reproduction? A metonymic link of sense obtains in the use of "millstones" and "grinding" as an allusion to the sexual act and gender roles within it. Thus says Job in his final confession:

---

17. Gen 29:13; 33:4; 48:10; 2 Kgs 4:16.
18. Prov 4:8; 5:20; Song 2:6; 8:3.

If my heart was ravished by the
   wife of my neighbor,
And I lay in wait at his door,
May my wife grind for another,
May others kneel over her!
   (Job 31:9-10; NJPS)

The NEB has another translation
for verse 10, but with the same
sense:

May my wife be another
man's slave and may other
men enjoy her.

The latter is a remarkably free
translation, which operates on
the "grinding is a woman's
work" convention and, at
the same time, obscures the
image by delimiting instead of
clarifying it. The link between
the grinding with millstones
and sexuality is derived not
only from social convention but
also, perhaps primarily, from the
image of two millstones, one on
top of the other. The woman is
the user of the [lower] millstone
as well as, by contiguity, its
metaphorical referent. This
extra-linguistic image, when
transformed into the realm
of language, may become a
particularized metaphor. The
upper grinding stone—in
Hebrew רכב, "riding" stone—
becomes the "male stone."
When a woman throws an upper
millstone from the town's wall
and kills Abimelech (Judg 9:53;
cf. 2 Sam 11:21), he quickly
perceives the significance of her
action. The woman has become
the upper millstone; she is now
male. By force of symmetry,
Abimelech is now in danger
of becoming female. The only

antidote for this outrageous
reversal of gender role is for him,
a dying man, to ask his armor
bearer to kill him (Judg 9:54).
Sexual mockery intertwined
with social mockery is easily
discernible here. In Isaiah 47:1-3a
we read:

Come down and sit in the dust,
   virgin daughter Babylon!
Sit on the ground without a
   throne,
   daughter Chaldea!
For you shall no more be called
   tender and delicate.
Take the millstones and grind
   meal,
   remove your veil,
strip off your robe, uncover
   your legs,
   pass through the rivers.
Your nakedness shall be
   uncovered
and your shame shall be
   seen. (NRSV)

Here too sexual (and social)
mockery serves as a foil for
something else, this time for
political ridicule. Once more,
the metaphor acquires "sexual"
force through the imagery of the
woman using a millstone, *being* a
millstone (as well as, in this case,
through the allusions to Babylon,
the metaphorical woman, who
is described as stripping off
her clothes and exposing her
nakedness).

We learn from postbiblical
Hebrew that the upper stone's
spouse is the שכב, literally the
"lying down" lower stone (from
שכב, *qal*, "lie down," also with
a sexual sense; b. B. Bat. 2a,
t. B. Bat. 3a). By analogy, this

lower stone will be associated particularly with women (see the image in Job 31:10). And yet, the associative differentiation of "millstones" into gendered parts does not exclude the application of the whole to "women" in postbiblical Hebrew sources (and see below).

To return to the Hebrew Bible, another link between stones, reproduction, and women can be established through Exodus 1:16. The Egyptian king says to the midwives, "When you assist the Hebrew women in giving birth, *look* at the *two stones.* If it is a son, kill him; if a daughter, let her live" (my translation). Even though the "stones" in Exodus 1:16 are, literally, "two stones" (האבנים), as the Hebrew pointing prescribes, no "millstones" are specifically designated. Like in the case of the potter's "two stones," that is, the potter's wheel (Jer 18:3), the "stones" seem obscure but are nevertheless "stones" identified as birth aids. Like Qoheleth 3:5, the Exodus passage has "stones," not "millstones." Nonetheless, the affinities of the "stones" with "women" are obvious. Since the context of Qoheleth 3:5a-b is far from clear, only hinted at by the parallel 5c-d, the possibility—illustrated by the biblical intertexts cited— that "women" are metaphorized into stones in Qoheleth 3:5a-b should be entertained. Women, then, use (mill)stones for reproduction and therefore are (mill)stones, especially the lower stone, since the upper (mill)stone

is considered male. Furthermore, in postbiblical Hebrew a woman, specifically a wife, is likened to millstones around her husband's neck (b. Kidd. 29b): in the light of the passages just read, "she" is so defined not because of the weighty need to support her only; there is a joke involved in the metaphor. And the act of marrying, taking a wife, is denoted in postbiblical Hebrew by the technical term כנס (*qal*, "bring in")—a term that appears in our verse together with "stones."

So far links between "stones" and female sexuality have been observed. Another alternative is to explore associations of "stones" and male sexuality. In this regard, the euphemistic and metaphoric reference to testicles by "stones" is well known. This euphemistic usage seems to underlie the Rabbis' explication of 3:5a-b in Qoheleth Rab.

Where do these allusions lead us? The following possibilities now emerge. The "stone" metaphor is complex indeed and can be invested with polyvalent levels of meaning. Initially, the throwing of stones (v. 5a) might be a beneficial or a peacefully motivated act. Nevertheless, it would probably conjure up violent associations for most beholders and readers. The image evokes battle scenes (see below) as well as the biblical practice of stoning—of sinning individuals, especially of an adulterous woman—more than it recalls the clearing of a field, for instance. The verb

להשליך (from the root שלך, *hiphil*, "throw"), since it is much stronger in connotation than its regular synonym זרק *qal*, while כנס *qal* serves as its antonym, with the meaning "gathering stones" (v. 5a)—for building, for stoning, for waging war?— remains opaque for the moment. If, on the metaphorical level, which is mutually inclusive in relation to the literal level, "stones," like millstones, might represent women, a few questions emerge. What happens to women within the life described in the poem? Are the women cast away? Women being taken as wives, as spouses, as (mill)stones? When all these possibilities are viewed together, a certain mood is established. On the next level, perhaps a figurative one now, the idea of casting and afterward gathering what has been cast, coupled with violence of action and the gender/sex allusions of the other two levels of meaning, may also recall the sexual act on the male's side and from a male's viewpoint (as for instance in Qoheleth Rabb. and the associations with male sexuality there). The same mood is enhanced in verse 5c-d: "to embrace," as previously pointed out, is not always "sexual" but does signify intimacy. It therefore appears that a "sexual" interpretation for the whole of verse 5 is indeed plausible, albeit not altogether transparent. Birth and death (v. 2a), love and hate (v. 8a) frame a poem for which verse 5 serves as a center; this enhances the plausibility of such a suggestion.

In the light of this discussion, verse 5 advances the following message. There is a (correct? proper? set? opportune?) time for indulging in the sexual act, or for getting rid of a woman, as for refraining from sex or, conversely, for taking a woman for a wife; just so, there is a time to embrace and a time to abstain from embracing. If this interpretation is entertained, and since verse 5 is central (in both senses) to the poem, we are obliged to reconsider the meaning of the whole poem in its light. The whole of verse 2a-b should be seen only as a prelude to these actions, which constitute the interchangeable bipolarity of human events and experience. Is it surprising that central to these actions are sexual and gender relations, sometimes suitable to an occasion and at others not so?

In what way, however, are sexual/gender relations so central that the entire poem is constructed around them? Does this merely imply that these are the most important things in life? Or does the emphatic structural place accorded to them suggest that the whole poem is to be read, at least on one readerly level, as a *double entendre*, as alluding to gender relations and sexual activity, to their causes and complexities and consequences, more so than any to other facets of human life? What is proposed here is a reading of the poem's careful structure as suggesting an overall, overarching meaning in addition to a simple sequence of contrasts. The poem has a code; once it is recognized, everything falls into place. The code resides in verse 5 and its meaning; once acknowledged, the result is clear: this is a piece about human sexual behavior, at the very least in its framed form.

And I suspect that consumers of this poem (hearers, readers) closer in time and place to its composition would have been immediately aware of what to us, contemporary readers, seems to be a riddle or an allusion that requires decipherment.

Athalya Brenner-Idan

Qoheleth 3:5 immediately stands out in this poem because it contains direct objects for its infinitive verbs, unlike all previous and following stiches other than 3:2b. While Brenner-Idan has argued for "stones" as euphemistic of sexual activity, marking the author here as male (or at least as an "M" voice), it is fair to at least examine the verbs of 3:5 for their applicability to women's work. The first verb in the verse, השליך, "cast, throw," occurs in the Hebrew Bible frequently enough that we find it paired with nearly every potential subject/actor, from men to women to the deity. For our purposes, it is worth noting that the first canonical use of this verb occurs with a woman actor, Hagar (Gen 21:15). Facing death of thirst and starvation in the wilderness, she makes what she expects to be her last act, that of "casting" her son Ishmael into some bushes. In a decidedly different scenario, a woman from Thebez "casts" an "upper millstone"—no small feat of strength—from the city tower, killing Abimelech from the invading army (Judg 9:53, with a reference in 2 Sam 11:21). Such a mark of dishonor would have befallen Abimelech had he been left to die from this millstone attack that he implored his servant to impale him rather than be remembered as a warrior who was killed by a woman (Judg 9:54).

On the other hand, the verb כנס, "gather," in 3:5 never appears in a specifically female context. As Brenner-Idan notes, the root even gains use as a term for a man's taking a woman as a wife in postbiblical Hebrew.[19] The second half of 3:5, about embracing (or not), invokes the lesser-used verb חבק. This term for "clasp, embrace" occurs in contexts ranging from intimate (Song 2:6, 8:3) to negative (Lam 4:5). In the majority of cases,

19. See Brenner-Idan, "Qoheleth 3:1-9—Structure and Sense with Verse 5 as a Key," above.

the verb has a male or a group as its subject, but in one case the verb specifically names the predicted action of a woman: the Shunnamite whose "embrace" of a child Elisha foretold (2 Kgs 4:16). Similarly, the citations in the Song of Songs involve the woman calling on her lover to "embrace me."

While the verbs in verse 6 appear often enough to have little distinction as particularly gender-specific, their uses with notable female biblical characters are worth highlighting for the sake of this exercise. "Seek" in 3:6 (בקשׁ, *piel*) is used when the woman who is the central character in the Song of Songs "seeks" her lover (3:1, 2; 5:6); her friends, the "Daughters of Jerusalem," join her in this quest in 6:1. Naomi "seeks" security for Ruth in Ruth 3:1, and Esther "seeks" the king's favor in Esther 4:8. Notably, "seek" will reappear as a theme in Qoheleth 7 (see below), where Qoheleth appears to be searching for Wisdom—and is unable to find her.

The term translated as "lose" in NRSV 3:6 is אבד in the *piel* form, which has the force of "destroy" or even "kill." This is not just about misplacing something. A fitting illustration of a woman as the subject of the verb in this form is its use to describe Queen Athaliah "killing" remaining potential inheritors of the throne in order to retain her own rule (2 Kgs 11:1). Furthermore, Esther repeats this verb in recounting Haman's villainous efforts to "destroy" the Jews (Esth 7:4; 8:5).

Beginning the next stich of 3:6 is from שׁמר (*qal*), "keep," a favorite word of the Deuteronomist, who admonishes all Israelites repeatedly to "keep" the statutes and commandments. Whether or not "all Israelites" would have specifically included the women in the community remains a matter of some debate, though certainly statutes that relate to childbirth and menstruation seem to indicate that the females in the community had legal obligations to "keep" certain ordinances even if their responsibilities were not the same as those of the men of Israel.[20] Aside from those communal instructions to "keep" commandments, only twice does שׁמר specifically have a female subject: in Judges 13:4, 13, 14, in which the angel of the Lord instructs the wife of Manoah to "keep" the rules of the Nazirite vow while pregnant with Samson; and in Proverbs 4:6, which provides instructions by which Wisdom will "keep" you. Finally in 3:6, the root שׁלך, "throw," repeats from "throw away stones" in the beginning of the previous verse, though this time at the end of the verse and

---

20. Carolyn Pressler, "Deuteronomy" in *Women's Bible Commentary*, ed. Carol Ann Newsom, Sharon H. Ringe, and Jacqueline E. Lapsley, 3rd ed. (Louisville: Westminster John Knox Press, 2012), 90.

without an object, as is more typical of the poem as a whole. This time the meaning has to do with "casting" as opposed to "keeping," in the more general terms that we see in verses 2-4 and 6-8.

Verse 7a introduces what sounds like the end of grief and its beginning, to the extent that tearing or repairing garments could correlate with ancient mourning practices. Since women had a prominent role in grief rituals, we might expect them to be frequently associated with this verb, but קרע, "tear," arises specifically with female subjects on only three occasions, two of which have to do with a situation of grief: Tamar "tears" her clothes as a grief-filled response to being raped by her half-brother Amnon (2 Sam 13:19); and Athaliah does the same in response to discovering that her rule has been usurped (2 Kgs 11:14//2 Chr 23:13). The final reference stretches the literal meaning of the term: In Jeremiah 4:30 the prophet criticizes women for the way they "tear" their eyes with kohl; some translations view this as a description of a ruined face (KJV); others as a way to make the eyes look bigger with makeup (NRSV, NJPS, NASB). The verb תפר, "sew," appears only four times in the Hebrew Bible, though it does have some association with women, particularly in Ezekiel 13:18, where women create garments in an unintelligible act of prophecy (v. 17), which Ezekiel condemns. In Genesis 3:7, both the first woman and the first man "sew" in order to cover their newly realized nakedness. Women are never specifically asked or said to "keep silence" with the term used in Qoheleth 3:7b, לחשות (from חשה *qal*). Indeed, in Isaiah 42:14, the Lord is said to curtail a period of self-silencing with sounds like a woman in childbirth.

Such a frequently used verb as דבר, *Pi'el* for "speak," the final verb in 3:7, would surely apply to women in numerous cases, but since women speak rather infrequently in the Hebrew Bible, it does require some searching to find the verb associated with female subjects. Even a search on the third-person feminine perfect form of the verb can be misleading, since the same form also functions as the second-person masculine perfect form. Nonetheless, we do find a number of Hebrew Bible women "speaking": from Potiphar's wife who "speaks" to her husband, alleging that Joseph has molested her (Gen 39:17), to Esther speaking with the king about Haman's genocidal plot (Esth 8:3). Other women who speak, דבר, include Delilah (Judg 16:10, 13), Abigail (1 Sam 25:24), the Queen of Sheba (1 Kgs 10:2//2 Chr 9:1), Jezebel (1 Kgs 21:5), the prostitutes who go to Solomon for judgment about their disputed baby (1 Kgs 3:22), and Athaliah (2 Chr 22:10). Perhaps the most significant instance in which "speak" appears with a female subject is Numbers 12:1, which notably uses the feminine singular form וַתְּדַבֵּר, "and she spoke," even though the verse says both Miriam and Aaron are the speaking subjects. In 1 Samuel 1:13, Hannah is מְדַבֶּרֶת אֶל־לִבָּהּ, "speaking in her heart" (or "to herself"), and in 1 Kings 1:22, Bathsheba is speaking with the king on behalf of herself and her son Solomon as successor to the throne.

The poem culminates with two weighty verbs, אהב, "love," and, שנא "hate," and, oddly, the final stich enlists two nouns instead of verbs: מִלְחָמָה, "war," and שָׁלוֹם, "peace." One biblical woman is especially known for "love," the woman in the Song of Songs (1:7; 3:1-4, "him whom my soul loves"; and the women in 1:3 "love"). In Ruth 4:15, the women of Bethlehem make a proclamation about Ruth, who "loves" Naomi. First Samuel 18:20 reports that Michal loved David; Wisdom says "I love those who love me" in Proverbs 8:17. "Hate" (שנא) in the passive participle form is sometimes translated as "unloved" or indicates "non-love" and perhaps relates to barrenness (Leah feels "unloved," Gen 29:31, 33) as well as to casuistic legal passages in which a woman is the object of disdain (Deut 21:15-17; 22:13, 16; 24:3). In Judges 14:16, Samson's wife speaks of his "hate" of her.

No Hebrew Bible passage specifically uses the Hebrew noun מִלְחָמָה, "war," with a female agent/actor. In Judges 4:1-16, however, Deborah leads a divinely sanctioned war; in the Apocrypha, the warrior-widow Judith calls for help from the Lord "who crushes wars" (9:7), and her hymn makes clear that the Lord's war against the Assyrians was carried out through Judith, who led the Lord's army (16:2, 5, 12). Finally, we find several instances in which "a time for peace"—or at least speaking "peace"—has direct association with Hebrew Bible women. In 1 Kings 2:13 Bathsheba asks Adonijah if he comes in "peace." The Shunnamite woman uses the one word שָׁלוֹם, "peace," to tell her husband all would be well, without specifying why she goes to visit the prophet Elisha (2 Kgs 4:23). She notably repeats this monosyllabic answer to Elisha himself; her proclamation "peace" in the face of her son's death may well have indicated a hope-filled plea more than a description of her emotional state (4:26).[21] Or perhaps it was ironic and defiant? Queen Jezebel ironically inquired about the "peace" of Zimri, when they both knew her demise was imminent (2 Kgs 9:31). In Song of Songs 8:10, the female lover uses "peace" to sing of her availability to her lover.

21. Claude F. Mariottini, "2 Kings," in *The New Interpreter's Study Bible: New Revised Standard Version with the Apocrypha*, ed. Walter J. Harrelson (Nashville: Abingdon, 2003), 530–31.

This analysis of the poem in 3:1-8 shows that even if Qoheleth did not intend to include women's experiences in this poem (or the book as a whole), and even if it exhibits an "M" voice, the language of the poem does not utterly alienate women, either now or in biblical times. Indeed, most of the verbs in the poem (nineteen out of twenty-six) specifically relate to women's activities elsewhere in the Hebrew Bible; six of the remaining seven have some kind of association with women.[22] A female reader who wanted—or who wants—to identify with this poetry could most certainly do so.

While it is clear that the activities of 3:1-8 could easily apply to women, a theological analysis also warrants consideration here. In researching the verbs in this poem, it would appear that often God is the actor paired with these verbs in the Hebrew Bible. This observation makes sense in light of Qoheleth's response to the poem in 3:9-22, in which the sage brings a theological critique to the poem. As we will see, Qoheleth's powerful theological analysis brings emphatic questions to the idea that divine activity fits into a framework that creates justice. Though the heavily structured poem lures its reader into envisioning divine activity as logical and ordered, the frequent trope of the Hebrew Bible, "justice and righteousness" (מִשְׁפָּט וּצְדָקָה), is notably absent from 3:1-8.

A potential risk in this passage for contemporary women is the way in which it may support complacency. If there is a "time for everything," including killing, breaking down, losing, throwing away, tearing, hating, and war, then what's to stop the hierarchy or patriarchy from using the logic "this is the time!" to justify abusive, oppressive, authoritarian, even genocidal plans? Yet this logic can also be turned on its head; the poem can similarly invite women and other oppressed groups to question the logic of hegemony. Thus, when governments have asserted that it is a "time for war," throughout history women's groups like Code Pink (an antiwar and pro–human rights organization led by women) and Women in Black (an international women's group that opposes war and militarism) have literally stood witness to the violence against humanity and asserted that instead it should be "a time for peace."[23] We might even look to Rizpah as a biblical woman model for these movements. In 2 Samuel 21:1-14 Rizpah's lengthy vigil over her executed sons' corpses draws at-

---

22. The number twenty-six includes the two nouns at the end, and accounts for the double use of "cast away/throw away" in vv. 3:5 and 6, and "embrace/refrain from embracing" in v. 5.

23. womeninblack.org/about-women-in-black; www.codepink.org/about.

tention to the injustice committed by King David. For centuries, women have fought for the right to safely determine when it is their time to be pregnant—and when it is definitely not that time.

Truly, the philosophical dilemma inherent in this poem is the struggle to understand which of these activities cannot be significantly affected by human control (such as the best times for planting and harvesting, the times of death and mourning) and those that can involve human control (such as tearing, sewing, keeping silence, and speaking). In those times when humans do have some control, then what is the right course of action, and when? In cultures that have traditionally suppressed female volition, these questions have dire import. When, if ever, does a woman leave her abusive husband? When is it time for an abortion? When has labor gone on long enough or caused enough distress to warrant a C-section, or is one even available? What of our torment when we simply cannot understand whether, or how, something is in the "right time"? The crux of the Serenity Prayer gets at this:

> God, grant me the serenity to accept the things I cannot change,
> The courage to change the things I can,
> And the wisdom to know the difference.[24]

Some of life's most infuriating ambiguities reside in "the difference." An ancient sage would likely focus on wisdom in this prayer: Wisdom must help answer these questions. For Qoheleth, in the remainder of chapter 3 and later in chapter 7, this does not necessarily help.

Reflections on the Poem (3:9-22)

Qoheleth's alternation between ראיתי, "I saw," in 3:10, and ידעתי, "I know," in 3:12, 14 and אמרתי אני בלבי, "I said in my heart," in 3:17, 18 provides an interpretive clue for this section. Qoheleth's beliefs—or at least doctrinal assertions—find voice in 3:12, 14, 17, and 18 with "I know" and "I said in my heart." In contrast, what Qoheleth "saw" continually challenges or undoes this internal confidence in 3:10, 16, and 22. The *carpe diem* surrounds this internal dialogue, perhaps offering ample comfort

---

24. Usually attributed to Reinhold Neibuhr, though some questions have been raised about authorship. Fred R. Shapiro, "Who Wrote the Serenity Prayer?," *Yale Alumni Magazine* (July/August 2008), http://archives.yalealumnimagazine.com /issues/2008_07/serenity.html.

Qoh 3:9-22

⁹What gain have the workers from their toil? ¹⁰I have seen the business that God has given to everyone to be busy with. ¹¹He has made everything suitable for its time; moreover he has put a sense of past and future into their minds, yet they cannot find out what God has done from the beginning to the end. ¹²I know that there is nothing better for them than to be happy and enjoy themselves as long as they live; ¹³more-over, it is God's gift that all should eat and drink and take pleasure in all their toil. ¹⁴I know that whatever God does endures forever; nothing can be added to it, nor anything taken from it; God has done this, so that all shall stand in awe before him. ¹⁵That which is, already has been; that which is to be, already is; and God seeks out what has gone by.

¹⁶Moreover I saw under the sun that in the place of justice, wicked-

in the face of uncertainty with a double dose of *carpe diem* in 3:12-13 and consolation in the face of death in 3:22.

Qoheleth's language and use of examples link the book's persistent questions to personal experience. Qoheleth's focus on experience is evidenced in frequent use of the *qal* verb ראה, "to see." Roland Murphy reports that this verb appears forty-six times in Qoheleth, twenty-one of those in the first person.[25] This privileging of experience for the sake of theological reflection directs Qoheleth to apply a hermeneutic of suspicion to religious tradition. The Sage is unwilling to ignore the dissonance of a religious belief such as retributive justice that does not coincide with lived experience. Qoheleth does not outright reject tradi-tional views but undoubtedly questions them by placing those views in stark contrast with observable reality. Qoheleth articulates this clearly in Qoheleth 3:16-17:

> ¹⁶Again I saw under the sun,
>> In the place of judgment—There!—was wickedness,
>> And in the place of righteousness—There!—was wickedness.
> ¹⁷I said in my heart,
>> "The righteous and the wicked, God will judge,
>> For he has appointed a time for every matter, and concerning
>>> every act.

---

25. Roland E. Murphy, *Ecclesiastes*, WBC 23A (Nashville: Thomas Nelson, 2018), xxx. Qoheleth's use of examples is evident in 3:16; 7:15; and 8:10.

ness was there, and in the place of righteousness, wickedness was there as well. ¹⁷I said in my heart, God will judge the righteous and the wicked, for he has appointed a time for every matter, and for every work. ¹⁸I said in my heart with regard to human beings that God is testing them to show that they are but animals. ¹⁹For the fate of humans and the fate of animals is the same; as one dies, so dies the other. They all have the same breath, and humans have no advantage over the animals; for all is vanity. ²⁰All go to one place; all are from the dust, and all turn to dust again. ²¹Who knows whether the human spirit goes upward and the spirit of animals goes downward to the earth? ²²So I saw that there is nothing better than that all should enjoy their work, for that is their lot; who can bring them to see what will be after them?

The Sage will not let the contradiction between what tradition teaches ("I said in my heart," v. 17) and what has been seen ("Again I saw under the sun," v. 16) go unnoticed.²⁶

In 3:19 we must surely hope that Qoheleth had "humans" in mind rather than just males in using the Hebrew אדם, *'adam*, "human." The NRSV translates,

> For the fate of humans and the fate of animals is the same; as one dies, so dies the other. They all have the same breath, and humans have no advantage over the animals; for all is vanity.

The KJV, in contrast, translates בני האדם as "sons of men" and האדם as "men":

> For that which befalleth the sons of men befalleth beasts; even one thing befalleth them: as the one dieth, so dieth the other; yea, they have all one breath; so that a man hath no preeminence above a beast: for all is vanity.

Here a female reader feels the full force of gendered language for a presumably gender-neutral intent. While, yes, the audiences of both the MT and the KJV would have known that this must include both men and women, the extent to which the language excludes women

---

26. Qoheleth also contrasts experience (marked by ראיתי, "I saw") with tradition in 3:22 / 3:20; 4:1-4 / 4:5-6; 4:7-8, 15-16 / 4:9-14; 8:10 / 12; and 9:13-15 / 9:16, respectively. In other instances, Qoheleth lifts up experience (also marked by "I saw") in such a way that it simply implies a contrasting tradition, as in 6:1-2; 8:9; 10:5-7.

even from a broadly human experience—death—proves alienating for today's readers.

Jennifer L. Koosed adds a level of feminist critique to this in her treatment of 3:19 in the *Women's Bible Commentary*, using it as an opportunity to question stereotypical gender differences and norms. She writes: "If the differences and distinctions between human and animal can be questioned because both die equally, cannot we also question the differences and distinctions between men and women? They are as ephemeral as the wind."[27] As usual, even amid Qoheleth's sexist assumptions and androcentric views, the Sage nonetheless may offer us ideas for how to undermine those very views.

The matter of complacency discussed above becomes all the more problematic in this section. If we "cannot find out" (3:11), if God is unpredictable yet worthy of awe (3:11-21), then should we ever struggle against cruelty and injustice? If "wickedness" prevails—particularly where we would expect a synonymous parallelism instead of a repetition of "wickedness" (3:16)—yet somehow God will judge (3:17), then where is the motivation to work for justice? What good is compassion?

As in chapter 2, we should note the privilege inherent in advising "that all should enjoy their work" (3:22) as recourse for existential pain. Qoheleth's own privilege eludes the Sage in recommending this upper-class remedy for the theological dilemmas of a well-reflected life. We could level a similar critique at the advice to enjoy one's עָמָל, "toil," in 3:13. Does this not assume a certain amount of choice in the toil one undertakes and in the ability to cease the toil for the sake of a little eating and drinking? And what about those who are unemployed or so underemployed that by the time the rent is paid, no money remains for food?[28]

While this theological conundrum at least has the *carpe diem* for recourse in 3:12 and 22, it offers very little in the way of hope or mercy.

27. Jennifer L. Koosed, "Ecclesiastes," in Newsom, Ringe, and Lapsley, *Women's Bible Commentary*, 244.

28. Jione Havea notes how the emphasis on toil in 3:13 and 22 loops back to the question in 3:9 about whether there is any gain from toil and provides a pointed Marxist critique. "The question [3:9] is in the interest of the workers, but Qoheleth's answer is in the interest of the masters, who have much to gain when their workers and slaves enjoy their toil. And the clearest sign that workers enjoy their toil is when they are obedient and silent. Qoheleth's answer would make Marx turn in his grave." Jione Havea, "'What Gain Have the Workers from their Toil?' (Con)texting Ecclesiastes 3:9-13 in Pasifika," in *The Five Scrolls*, ed. Athalya Brenner-Idan, Gale A. Yee, Archie C. C. Lee, Texts@Contexts 6 (London: Bloomsbury, 2018), 128.

Anne Lamott points out that even when we do have such apparent assurance, the ultimate sticking point remains the question that Qoheleth repeatedly asks about time: "Horribly, [mercy] does not issue printed schedules. When Julian of Norwich wrote that all will be well—and all will be well—she meant that things will be well at some point, in the infuriating fullness of time, when sick bodies dissolve back into light and spirit, or when God restores much of what the locusts have eaten, someday down the road. But what about this lifetime? What about sub-Saharan Africa, and the severely depressed teenager in my family? What about poor old Earth? What about me?"[29] Qoheleth scarcely asserts anything as hopeful as "all will be well"—3:17 might be the closest cynical version—but the Sage surely echoes Lamott's frustration with wondering when this might occur and even railing at a deity who would keep this from us (3:11-15). If Qoheleth's repetition of "under the sun" hints at hope for an afterlife, the Sage does not make that obvious or give us the sense of assurance it might offer to contemporary believers.[30]

When I push students to struggle with this pericope, they commonly express their discomfort that the descriptions of God as a powerful yet capricious judge do not coincide with their own theologies. This apparently troubling aspect of the text strikes me as an opportunity to grapple with one's view of biblical authority. Too often, particularly in contemporary Christianity, persons have been led to believe (or have been blatantly instructed) that the Bible tells us what to believe with no exception or nuance. Yet the Bible presents too many different theologies for this to work. Instead, the Bible illustrates the diversity of theologies within ancient Israel; this in turn explains and gives rise to the diverse faith communities we know today.[31]

The issue of biblical authority has been central to feminist theology, providing the opportunity to critique and then accept or reject biblical theologies according to various criteria, including that of women's experience, which has been excluded from theological conversations throughout most of Judeo-Christian history (see the author's introduction). Thus the ability to notice that a passage in the Bible challenges

29. From Anne Lamott, *Hallelujah Anyway: Rediscovering Mercy* (New York: Penguin Random House, 2017), 126.

30. "Under the sun" appears in 1:3, 9, 14; 2:11, 17, 18, 19, 20, 22; 3:16; 4:1, 3, 7, 15; 5:13 [12], 18 [17]; 6:1, 12; 8:9, 15, 17; 9:3, 6, 9, 11, 13; 10:5.

31. Benjamin D. Sommer, "The Source Critic and the Religious Interpreter," *Int* 60 (2006): 9–20.

one's own theology helps us to see that, of course, we do not all agree with every bit of the Bible in every situation and to realize that this is acceptable—even crucial—for the healthy life of faith (and of Bible study). Qoheleth, the questioner of tradition and of God, equips us with the tools that every questioning person of faith must use to build a long-term faith. Undoubtedly, women have received a legacy that means these questioner's tools may be the key to living the life of faith.[32]

Eternal Earth?

To the modern ecological reader, faced with the certain knowledge that Earth as we know it is under dire threat, there is an apparent reassurance in Qoheleth's claim that "A generation goes, and a generation comes, but the earth remains forever [עולם, *'olam*]" (Qoh 1:4). Qoheleth's worldview is of a stable, unchanging Earth in which endless cycles of generations move and have life. Human beings are able to have a sense of this eternity, this עולם, yet it remains always a mystery (3:11), appropriate only to God and Earth.

As I gaze on the Outback skies of my homeland, South Australia, I can believe in the poetic truth of Qoheleth's words when he claims that the works of God last forever (3:14). These southern skies, observed from a region that is among the most unpopulated on Earth, are unrivalled, except by the mirror-image skies of the Atacama Desert in Chile where the constellation known

32. Helpful feminist discussions of biblical authority include Phyllis A. Bird, *Faith, Feminism, and the Forum of Scripture: Essays on Biblical Theology and Hermeneutics* (Eugene, OR: Wipf and Stock Publishers, 2015); Athalya Brenner and Carole Fontaine, *A Feminist Companion to Reading the Bible: Approaches, Methods and Strategies* (Sheffield: Routledge, 2013); Tikva Frymer-Kensky, *Studies in Bible and Feminist Criticism*, JPS Scholar of Distinction Series (Philadelphia: Jewish Publication Society, 2010); Wilda Gafney, *Womanist Midrash: A Reintroduction to the Women of the Torah and the Throne* (Louisville: Westminster John Knox, 2017); Phyllis Trible, "Authority of the Bible," in Harrelson, *NISB*, 2248–53; Sharon H. Ringe, "When Women Interpret the Bible," in Newsom, Ringe, and Lapsley, *Women's Bible Commentary*, 1–9; Elisabeth Schüssler Fiorenza, Shelly Matthews, and Ann Graham Brock, *Searching the Scriptures*, vol. 1: *A Feminist Introduction* (New York: Crossroad, 1993); Renita J. Weems, *Battered Love: Marriage, Sex, and Violence in the Hebrew Prophets* (Philadelphia: Fortress, 1995); Letty M. Russell, *Feminist Interpretation of the Bible* (Louisville: Westminster John Knox, 1985).

as the Southern Cross is also visible. A nighttime visit I made to an astronomical site in the Atacama found me pondering the immensity of the night sky. Our guide was an astronomer-philosopher, and one gem of his philosophizing found deep resonance with me. It was the simple and true observation that "the Earth will not last forever." In that ethereal setting, the words carried the full import of what he was saying. And while paradoxical, I find no authentic contradiction in his observation and the concept of Eternal Earth. Viewed within the bounds of astronomical science, where we talk of light years and infinite space, of the Big Bang and the expansion and implosion of the universe, Eternal Earth still holds meaning in the unknowns of time and space. Seen in this light, Qoheleth's Eternal Earth is not such a far-fetched concept.

When Eternal Sophia (Prov 8:23) was alongside the Creator as agent and witness when Earth was first appearing, she was most likely gazing on my own Australian "bits of soil" and skies. Australia was possibly the first land of Earth to have emerged from

the sea. The first Australians are among the earliest settled peoples, inhabiting this country continuously with natural ecological awareness for at least forty thousand years. Truly Australia is עולם, *'olam*!

עולם, eternal, in the biblical sense does not simply mean ancient. It connotes time that stretches from the beginning and into the infinite future. It would indeed be unrealistic to believe that this Australian Earth, with its ancient fossils and its incomparable skies, is infinite. Nevertheless, a determination on the part of Australians to stand alongside Eternal Sophia and Earth עולם as ecologically responsible partners, will go some way toward realizing Qoheleth's vision of the enduring works of God (Qoh 3:11). This same sense of awe that Qoheleth experienced, that Sophia enabled, and that an Atacaman astronomer and an Australian stargazer shared will drive the ecological endeavor and ensure that this Earth will remain to be wondered at by inestimable, if not infinite, generations to come.

Marie Turner

Qoheleth 4:1–5:20 [19]

From Hevel *to* Carpe Diem *and Much in Between*

Reflections on Oppression, Death, Toil, *Hevel*, Companionship, Wisdom/Folly (4:1-16)

Chapter 4 opens with ושבתי אני, "and I turned/I," using the pleonastic first person, which the NRSV translates "again." Perhaps this is a way of Qoheleth saying, "I'm starting a new topic," or, "Here's one more bit of experience that contributed to my existential crisis—this time, oppression." To get the full force of the Hebrew in English we would need something like "And I myself turned, and I saw . . ." The opening verb שוב (*qal*), "turn," more likely indicates something new than something similar, in contrast with what the NRSV's "Again I saw" suggests.

And indeed the view Qoheleth expresses is new in the scheme of the book so far. After all of Qoheleth's solipsistic whining about the luxuries that did not solve life's existential dilemmas (2:1-11), suddenly Qoheleth exudes sympathy for the oppressed. Qoheleth truly seems to understand the solitary suffering of the least and lost in 4:1, as signaled by the repeated phrase "with no one to comfort them." Qoheleth presents a power analysis in 4:1, recognizing that the hierarchical structure leaves the lower classes without "comfort." Yet Qoheleth does not go into depth with this critique.

4:1Again I saw all the oppressions that are practiced under the sun. Look, the tears of the oppressed—with no one to comfort them! On the side of their oppressors there was power—with no one to comfort them. 2And I thought the dead, who have already died, more fortunate than the living, who are still alive; 3but better than both is the one who has not yet been, and has not seen the evil deeds that are done under the sun.

4Then I saw that all toil and all skill in work come from one person's envy of another. This also is vanity and a chasing after wind.

5Fools fold their hands
   and consume their own flesh.
6Better is a handful with quiet
   than two handfuls with toil,
   and a chasing after wind.
7Again, I saw vanity under the sun: 8the case of solitary individuals, without sons or brothers; yet there is no end to all their toil, and their eyes are never satisfied with riches. "For whom am I toiling," they ask, "and depriving

The following verse does not necessarily belong with 4:1, so what could have been an insightful commentary on the hierarchy remains an undeveloped, off-hand comment. The topical isolation of 4:1 may suggest it is a quote that Qoheleth enlists in order to "best" it with the following verses 4:2-3, in which death or the prospect of having never been conceived is preferable to life.

Thus Qoheleth effectively undermines the critique of hierarchy and insight about the oppressed that 4:1 contains by moving on to what Qoheleth arrogantly sees as a worse evil: life itself. For a wealthy, powerful individual to blithely and briefly criticize the lives of the oppressed and then move on to complain that everyone would be better off dead trivializes the lives of those who suffer; it undermines any joy they experience despite their suffering. We can imagine the oppressed responding to Qoheleth: "Maybe you wish *you* were dead, but you don't really know *my* pain or happiness, so speak for yourself!" This rhetorical reading of 4:1-3 again provides a caricature of Qoheleth as a wealthy person, so self-absorbed in a personal existential crisis that the actual suffering of the better part of humanity apparently has little effect on Qoheleth's worldview. On the other hand, perhaps Qoheleth indeed sympathizes with those who feel so ground down that death seems preferable.

The NRSV translation of 4:2, like 4:1, does not give the full force of the Hebrew. Better would be, "And I myself praised the dead." While one can certainly read this in an abstract, philosophical manner, it also raises concerns about the author's mental health. The next verse, 4:3, myself of pleasure?" This also is vanity and an unhappy business.

⁹Two are better than one, because they have a good reward for their toil. ¹⁰For if they fall, one will lift up the other; but woe to one who is alone and falls and does not have another to help. ¹¹Again, if two lie together, they keep warm; but how can one keep warm alone? ¹²And though one might prevail against another, two will withstand one. A threefold cord is not quickly broken.

¹³Better is a poor but wise youth than an old but foolish king, who will no longer take advice. ¹⁴One can indeed come out of prison to reign, even though born poor in the kingdom. ¹⁵I saw all the living who, moving about under the sun, follow that youth who replaced the king; ¹⁶there was no end to all those people whom he led. Yet those who come later will not rejoice in him. Surely this also is vanity and a chasing after wind.

amplifies this despondency. Qoheleth opens with the despairing comparison "better than both [the dead and the living] is one who has not yet been" and completes it with the justification "who has not seen the evil deeds that are done under the sun." This gives us a sense of what truly nags at Qoheleth: the problem of evil. Perhaps both oppression and death contribute to or illustrate the problem of evil and thus make sense of 4:1 and 4:2-3 in their current placement.

Yet, while the problem of evil is universal and well worth our intellectual agony, if our attention to it distracts us from rectifying the solvable evils in our midst, then our energies have been misplaced. This again illustrates how Qoheleth's apparent sympathies for the oppressed seem to be fleeting or disingenuous. If we are all better off dead, then why help anyone? And what is the difference between musing on "better off dead" with a full or empty belly? How would this "better off dead" sentiment sound to a pregnant woman in ancient times, who is hoping to deliver a live and healthy baby and to survive the labor herself? Perhaps Qoheleth's privilege is exposed here, since such existential abstractions suggest that the Sage has never fully experienced the terrifying reality of impending death that most women would have known in that time.[1] Nor, apparently, does Qoheleth seem to know the drive to persist in living, even in the face of death.

---

1. See discussion on 3:2, above.

Qoheleth's point in 4:4-6 is fairly opaque, particularly in English translation. While 4:4 makes a fair amount of sense—envy drives the motivation for toil, and that is *hevel*—4:5 and 6 are more perplexing. Folding one's hands? Consuming one's flesh? A handful of what? Commentators generally agree that in 4:5 Qoheleth quotes or composes a proverb against laziness. Maybe "twiddling one's thumbs" would translate better as a contemporary colloquialism for "folding [one's] hands." In 4:6 Qoheleth offers one of many internal contradictions, suggesting with another proverb that a modest existence with some respite ("a handful with quiet") is better than a life of luxury gained by running the "rat race" ("two handfuls with toil"). This loosely follows the form "A with B is better than C with D," which Farmer explains in regard to Proverbs 17:1 "is concerned with the hidden costs involved in making choices."[2] Taken in combination, 4:4-6 advocate moderation, though the inclusion of *hevel* and "chasing after wind" add cynicism to these proverbs. In this way, these verses have something in common with 7:15-18, in which Qoheleth also advises moderation.

Finding נחת, "quiet, rest" (4:6), is something Qoheleth reflects on more than once, such as that attributed to the "stillborn child" whom Qoheleth counts as better rested (6:5, also נחת) and entirely "better off" (6:3) than a man who has neither enjoyment of life nor a burial at his death (6:1-5). Qoheleth also advises that "the words of the wise" are most effectively spoken in "quiet" (9:17). But when your gender dictates that child rearing is one of your jobs, "quiet" is a little-known commodity.

How might we read 4:4-6 with a feminist hermeneutic? If, as the adage goes, "a woman's work is never done," then the admonition in 4:6 to moderate one's toil could sound either liberating or absurd to female audiences then and now. This verse relies on the assumption that one has the option to choose moderation of work, which has rarely been a reality for women, particularly not for women—or men—of lower classes. Yet verse 4 could apply to upper-class women who work without ceasing in order to pursue wealth or other external markers of success (see Prov 31:10-31). Here again we may see the text betraying Qoheleth's privileged social location. The passage recalls the difficult exegetical and homiletical history of Luke 10:38-42, in which Jesus apparently condemns Martha for being "distracted" by her work, while praising Mary for

---

2. Kathleen Anne Farmer, *Who Knows What Is Good? A Commentary on the Books of Proverbs and Ecclesiastes*, ITC (Grand Rapids, MI: Eerdmans, 1991), 72.

having "chosen the better part" (10:40-42).[3] Countless sermons, retreats, and Bible studies—often, but not always led by men—have chastised women to take this to heart as a parable applicable to contemporary life, where we juggle jobs, children, housework, and more, sometimes out of choice, and sometimes out of necessity. To work without ceasing and barely make ends meet for oneself and one's family, only to be admonished by someone who benefits from your work to do a better job of resting, rankles, to say the least. Extolling the virtues of "quiet" to someone who cares for small children and animals may elicit similar irritation. Unfortunately, many oppressed persons and especially women have suffered from well-meaning advice by individuals who can afford to recommend the luxuries of quiet, rest, and reflection. Even worse are those who have not been deemed worthy of the advice to slow down but have only ever been pushed to do more.

Another relevant gender analysis asks whether the point here is specifically "skilled work," in which case Qoheleth's point may have excluded women's work altogether. Women would be not only *de facto* excluded from Qoheleth's proverbs in 4:5-6 by virtue of having so little opportunity to find quiet but also entirely excluded since their work may not have even counted in what Qoheleth deemed "toil."[4]

Qoheleth 4:8 is a fascinating addition to the mix of what we have seen so far in the book of Qoheleth. The grammar of the verse is rather odd, and KJV stays closest to the Hebrew in 8a: "There is one alone, and there is not a second." To continue in a very wooden translation, "son and brother there are none to *him*." Until the masculine possessive, we could imagine Qoheleth describing a widow, since the prior words contain no gender distinction. The rest of the verse, however, brings us back to the scenario of the character in the "test of pleasure," who in 2:21 complains that his toil will go to someone who did not work for it.

---

3. See *Malleus Maleficarum*, part 1, question 4, p. 1, which uses Martha as an example of typical female jealousy. Barbara E. Reid explains that the Greek in this passage points to the gospel's emphasis on women being in public ministry (*Wisdom's Feast: An Invitation to Feminist Interpretation of the Scriptures* [Grand Rapids, MI: Eerdmans, 2016], 106–8). See also the discussion on this passage in Jane D. Schaberg and Sharon H. Ringe, "Gospel of Luke," in *Women's Bible Commentary*, ed. Carol A. Newsom, Sharon H. Ringe, and Jacqueline E. Lapsley, 3rd ed. (Louisville: Westminster John Knox, 2012), 507–8.

4. See Antoon Schoors, *Ecclesiastes* (Leuven: Peeters, 2013), 334.

Thus 4:8 seems to point to someone who has no legitimate heirs to inherit his wealth: incidentally, this was the complaint of Abram in Genesis 15:2. Yet Qoheleth's imagined complainer does not find the theophanic covenant encounter that Abram did later in Genesis 15. Furthermore, Qoheleth describes someone who sees and wants ever more "riches." (If Abram were that way, the description never made it into the text.) As a rhetorical question, the relevant point of 4:8 would seem to be that the questioner has no heir anyway, so why lose out on the fun of life by toiling so much? But what of Qoheleth's point about this person having such an unquenchable appetite for riches? That detail seems to be lost, unless Qoheleth mentioned it only in order to ridicule this "one" who would complain about something that is his own fault: toil at the expense of joy, driven by his insatiable appetite for riches when he has no heirs anyway.

Qoheleth's focus on the "one" when "there is not a second" (KJV) apparently continues in the converse in 4:9-12. Many a greeting card and framed calligraphy has cited these verses to extol the virtues of love and friendship, but Qoheleth's interest in companionship has purely practical motives: you get better pay with a partner (4:9); another person can provide physical assistance (4:10), body heat (4:11), and defense against enemies (4:12). If we go back to 4:8, we could include the "service" that one's family provides by being heir or even trustee of one's property. Aside from the issue of an heir, these matters would seem quite relevant to women, who at the time would have required family partnership for the sake of economic security (4:9), certain kinds of labor (4:10), and security and protection (4:12), and indeed they would have benefitted from keeping warm at night (4:11).[5]

While 4:9-12 do not come right out and use אדם, *'adam*, or איש, *'ish*, they use masculine pronoun endings, which likely rule out the possibility that Qoheleth was referring also to women. The plural endings in 4:9 could arguably include women, but that would be less likely the case with the singular endings in 4:10-12. Thus Qoheleth apparently assumes that a male would make the most fitting companion for these pragmatic settings of cooperation, prompting Jennifer Koosed to suggest that "there is even a hint of the homoerotic as the two male companions

5. Tal Ilan discusses the ways in which women were included and excluded from inheritance rights: Tal Ilan, *Jewish Women in Greco-Roman Palestine* (Peabody, MA: Hendrickson Publishers, 1996), 167–72.

huddle together throughout the night to produce heat."[6] This provides an important insight into the biblical text, which too often is read with an exclusively heteronormative hermeneutic. Nonetheless, there is additional benefit in considering a female companion here. There are plenty of instances in the Hebrew Bible where women provided a good deal more than warmth on a cold night: Sarai, who traveled halfway around the world (as far as they were concerned) with Abram (Gen 12:1-9); Deborah, who led Barak and the Israelite army to victory against the Canaanites (Judg 4:1-10; cf. Qoh 4:12); Ruth and Naomi, who provided help to one another as well as to Boaz; Esther, who helped her cousin Mordecai save her people from Haman's villainous plot, among others. Notably, another list of biblical women nobly acted alone, in some cases having been abandoned by the men whose help they could have used: Hagar, who bore Abram's first promised son and who met God in the wilderness (Gen 16:6-16); Rizpah, who stood as a witness for justice with the bodies of her (and Saul's) sons (2 Sam 21:8-14). Qoheleth either does not consider those examples or does not see fit to mention them—or even include them in the pronouns.

The other remarkable issue with 4:7-12 is that the statements rely on the assumption that living outside of community is an option. That would not have been—and still is not—the case for most women, and, frankly, for most men. Could it be that Qoheleth was trying to convince themself of the benefits of relationships, which for some reason seemed oppressive? Regardless of Qoheleth's elusive intentions about—or exclusion of—women in these verses, they do have relevance for women. We are just as likely as men to sing "You can't live with 'em; you can't live without 'em," for all of Qoheleth's pragmatic reasons and more.[7]

In 4:13-16, Qoheleth again sets us up for what seems like a good solid wisdom parable, in which, of course, wisdom triumphs over foolishness and goes on to prove more important than even power, wealth, royal office, or social standing. There is enough ambiguity in this section, however, that scholars dispute whether the characters introduced in 4:13 (the poor, a wise youth, an old but/and foolish king) can be directly connected to the one mentioned in 4:14 (a prisoner who becomes a king,

---

6. Jennifer L. Koosed, "Ecclesiastes," in Newsom, Ringe, and Lapsley, *Women's Bible Commentary*, 245.

7. Lyric from Paul Williams and Kenny Ascher, performed by Frank Oz, "I Hope that Something Better Comes Along," *The Muppet Movie Soundtrack* (Atlantic Records, 1979).

who either began poor [NRSV] or becomes poor [NJPS]). The ambiguity continues into verses 15 and 16, where again we cannot be sure if the youth (v. 15) or the leader (v. 16) indicate either the youth or the king in verses 13 or 14 or both—or neither![8] This leaves us with a parable obscure in meaning. The final scenario unsurprisingly receives Qoheleth's signature evaluation, "*hevel* and a striving after wind," and that has something to do with a leader who did not gain a long-term positive reputation. But whether that leader was poor and wise, or previously or eventually imprisoned, or old and foolish remains unclear. My minimal takeaway from this difficult passage arises mainly from 4:16 and the larger context of the book: we cannot rely on what seems to be better-than. Instead, what we see (4:15) is *hevel* (4:16).

We should ask about the emphasis on age in this parable. Despite the ambiguities about who's who and who's doing what when, in 4:13 Qoheleth emphasizes youth, counterintuitively paired with wisdom and poverty, over against age, paired with foolishness and the wealth of the king. In 4:14, however, the reversal apparently has more to do with economic and social standing than age. Whether or not Qoheleth has issues with ageism remains unclear.

Watch What You Do and Say (5:1-7 [4:17–5:6])

At the beginning of chapter 5, we continue to see a decisive shift away from Qoheleth's first-person obsession, which began in 4:5. The tone now sounds more like Proverbs 10–30, with imperative aphorisms and less of the self-absorbed reflections that dominated the early part of the book. As we will see, the vocabulary in 5:1-7 [4:17–5:6] makes clear its cultic focus, something unique so far in Qoheleth. Despite the fact that cultic matters usually fall strictly within the male purview, a comparison with Hannah's story in 1 Samuel 1–2 shows that this passage may apply to women as well, whether or not Qoheleth intended that. Qoheleth even includes a Torah verse: 5:4 [3] seems to quote Deuteronomy 23:21a [22a]. For another unique feature in Qoheleth so far, the setting of the passage is בית האלהים, "the house of God."

From the outset, Qoheleth admonishes the reader: In God's house, שמע (*qal*), "to listen," bests זבח, "sacrifice," albeit that of "fools" (5:1 [4:17]).

---

8. For a discussion of the options, see Schoors, *Ecclesiastes*, 317, 364–68; Choon-Leong Seow, *Ecclesiastes: A New Translation with Introduction and Commentary*, AB 18C (New York: Doubleday, 1997), 190–92.

⁵:¹Guard your steps when you go to the house of God; to draw near to listen is better than the sacrifice offered by fools; for they do not know how to keep from doing evil. ²Never be rash with your mouth, nor let your heart be quick to utter a word before God, for God is in heaven, and you upon earth; therefore let your words be few.

³For dreams come with many cares, and a fool's voice with many words.

⁴When you make a vow to God, do not delay fulfilling it; for he has no pleasure in fools. Fulfill what you vow. ⁵It is better that you should not vow than that you should vow and not fulfill it. ⁶Do not let your mouth lead you into sin, and do not say before the messenger that it was a mistake; why should God be angry at your words, and destroy the work of your hands?

⁷With many dreams come vanities and a multitude of words; but fear God.

The advice that anything might be better than sacrifice may seem odd in the context of the Torah, but it has clear precedent in the prophetic literature, such as Amos 5:21-24; Isaiah 1:10-17; and Hosea 6:6, where the prophets rail against empty ritual in the face of injustice. Qoheleth's comment about sacrifice similarly critiques the practice. The other cultic topic Qoheleth broaches in this passage is "vows," using the specific term נדר and the Deuteronomy citation in 5:4 [3] and again in 5:5 [4]; Qoheleth raises related matters about "rash" speech in 5:2 [1] and addresses the wisdom of taking great care with one's words—mostly by limiting them throughout 5:2-7 [1-6].

This passage calls to mind several notable biblical characters who may or may not have occurred to Qoheleth in the writing of this book. In 1 Samuel 1:11 Hannah makes a נדר, "vow," at the "house of the Lord" to devote her son as a Nazirite to the temple. Hannah and her husband Elkanah fulfill that vow in 1 Samuel 1:23-24. Lillian R. Klein points out in her entry on Hannah in *Women in Scripture* that this passage illustrates that a vow a woman made to God was expected to be observed by her husband as well.[9] Indeed, Elkanah apparently supported Hannah's vow, and the text gives no indication that it was out of the ordinary for him to have done so.

9. Lillian R. Klein, "Hannah," in *Women in Scripture: A Dictionary of Named and Unnamed Women in the Bible, the Apocryphal/Deuterocanonical Books, and the New Testament*, ed. Carol Meyers, Toni Craven, and Ross Shepard Kraemer (Grand Rapids, MI: Eerdmans, 2001), 90.

Hannah's silent prayer in 1 Samuel 1:12-13 raises some interesting points of comparison with Qoheleth's admonition to be careful with one's words in 5:2 [1]. What if those words are never fully uttered? Other points of connection between Hannah and Qoheleth's words in 5:1-7 [4:17–5:6] further link these passages. Sacrifices play a prominent role in Hannah's story. "Sacrifice" (זבח) appears in 1 Samuel 1:3, 4, and 21 and is referred to in 1:24-25. Hannah in particular has a significant role in the presentation of the sacrifice. Thus the Hannah text makes clear that, in the wider context of the Tanakh, Qoheleth's words in 5:1-7 [4:17–5:6] could just as easily apply to a female audience as male. Though the grammatical gender of the verbs in the Qoheleth passage is masculine, the same is true in the Torah prescriptions for cultic practice, and that clearly did not stop Hannah, or presumably other women in her time or afterward, from participating in cultic activities.

The emphases on not being "rash with your mouth" (5:2 [1]) and "not let[ting] your mouth lead you into sin" (5:6 [5]), paired with the admonition to fulfill whatever vow is made, recalls the story of Jephthah, whose infamous rash vow that "whoever comes out of the doors of my house to meet me, when I return victorious from the Ammonites, shall be the Lord's, to be offered up by me as a burnt offering" (Judg 11:31) had horrific unforeseen consequences for his daughter. In Judges 11:30 Jephthah "vowed a vow" in a bargain with God to ensure military victory and, more important, Jephthah's power and prestige among his people. In 11:39 "he did to her his vow that he had vowed"; the Hebrew emphasizes Jephthah's culpability in having made the vow.

The Jephthah passage, in conversation with Qoheleth's proverbs about vows, complicates matters for what might otherwise seem like straightforward wisdom sayings. Qoheleth advises against making a "rash" vow and contextualizes that advice in a strictly theological manner: "Never be rash with your mouth, nor let your heart be quick to utter a word before God, for God is in heaven, and you upon earth; therefore let your words be few" (5:2 [5:1]). The theological implication seems to be that humans should not be so arrogant as to think they can say the right thing or keep a promise to God. Yet in the Jephthah passage, God actually seems responsible for the Judge's foolish vow, since "the spirit of the Lord came upon Jephthah" (Judg 11:29) just prior to the vow.

The emphasis on fulfilling vows in Qoheleth 5:5 [4] becomes tragic if we apply it to Judges 11:35, in which Jephthah asserts that the vow must be fulfilled even though his daughter greeted him upon his return from battle (rather than a goat or some other more suitable burnt offering), and 11:39, in which he fulfills the gruesome promise. This raises the question that many a reader of Jephthah's story, but particularly feminist readers, have wondered about divine anger in regard to Jephthah, and Qoheleth's comment in 5:6 [5] makes this plain. Where was God's anger—and intervention based on such—before, during, and after Jephthah's vow? In all likelihood, both texts rely on a mind-set that assumes vows worked in a very mechanical fashion, with a vow once made being binding. The presence of God's spirit with Jephthah just prior to his vow, however, remains troubling. Qoheleth 5:6 [5] suggests that perhaps we could have expected God to intervene and allow Jephthah to lose the battle in order to thwart his foolish vow.

These comparisons with Hannah's story and the passage about the daughter of Jephthah show the potential relevance of Qoheleth's proverbs to biblical women, even though those connections may be rather hidden. This portion of Qoheleth's work ends with a reminder of *hevel*, paired again with the emphasis on "many words" (5:7a [6a]). Ultimately Qoheleth closes this passage in 5:7b [6b] with the oft-repeated admonition to "fear God." When we hold this up to the passages above, about Hannah and the daughter of Jephthah, we will rightly have some theological questions about Hannah giving up her firstborn (even though she had more later, 1 Sam 2:21) as well as Jephthah and his daughter. Did the daughter die due to fear of God or lack of the fear of God? Either way, her story is rightly troubling for those who would consider the weight, significance, and permanence of vows. Qoheleth's proverbs about vows, which generally recommend limiting them, provide an invitation to struggle with these issues but do not offer resolution.

Reflections on Oppression, Wealth, Toil, *Carpe Diem* (5:8-20 [7-19])

The sentiment Qoheleth expresses in 5:8 [7] has some commonality with what we saw in 4:1, which sympathizes with the oppressed. Both verses employ the same root, עשׁק, "to oppress, oppression," and they both rely on a certain amount of resignation to the realities of hierarchy. That apathy is more apparent in Qoheleth's admonition אל תתמה, "do not be astonished," at oppression or even at "the suppression of justice and right." One would expect something like astonishment at this situation, given the heavy emphasis on "justice and righteousness" throughout the Hebrew Bible.[10]

---

10. The phrase משפט וצדקה, "justice and righteousness," appears twenty-two times in the HB; twice we see the slightly different phrase Qoheleth uses here: משפט וצדק.

Qoh 5:8-20 [7-19]

[8]If you see in a province the oppression of the poor and the violation of justice and right, do not be amazed at the matter; for the high official is watched by a higher, and there are yet higher ones over them. [9]But all things considered, this is an advantage for a land: a king for a plowed field.

[10]The lover of money will not be satisfied with money; nor the lover of wealth, with gain. This is also vanity.

[11]When goods increase, those who eat them increase; and what gain has their owner but to see them with his eyes?

[12]Sweet is the sleep of laborers, whether they eat little or much; but the surfeit of the rich will not let them sleep.

[13]There is a grievous ill that I have seen under the sun: riches were kept by their owners to their hurt, [14]and those riches were lost in a bad venture; though they are parents of children, they have nothing in their hands. [15]As they came from their mother's womb, so they shall go again, naked

Indeed, the absence of justice and righteousness could even be viewed as a theological condemnation, since these attributes are closely associated with God.[11] Qoheleth goes on to explain this oppression as arising from structural hierarchy: three levels of "high above high," גבה מעל גבה, rulers ensure this fracturing of the way things should be. Like in 4:1, where the problem was כח, "power," Qoheleth has remarkable, albeit brief and sporadic, insight about the origins and outcomes of oppression but no solutions for it. The term Qoheleth uses in 5:8 [7], רש for "poor," is more specifically translated "poor man."[12] Here, as on so many occasions in the book of Qoheleth as well as the wider Hebrew Bible, poor women are essentially invisible in the passage, even though poor women (and their children) were among the most vulnerable in the ancient world. In this case, the NRSV's inclusive translation effectively creates a mixed-sex group of "the poor" in the imaginations of contemporary readers, while the original language does not at all make that clear.[13] Thomas Krüger links this scenario to the

---

11. James Crenshaw, "Popular Questioning of the Justice of God in Ancient Israel," *ZAW* 82 (1970): 384; Klaus Koch, "Is There a Doctrine of Retribution in the Old Testament?," in *Theodicy in the Old Testament*, ed. James L. Crenshaw, trans. Thomas H. Trapp (Philadelphia: Fortress, 1983), 57–87, esp. 57; Moshe Weinfeld, *Social Justice in Ancient Israel and in the Ancient Near East* (Minneapolis: Fortress; Jerusalem: Magnes, 1995), 7 *et passim*.

12. *BDB*, 930.

13. See Phyllis A. Bird, "Poor Man or Poor Woman," in *Missing Persons and Mistaken Identities: Women and Gender in Ancient Israel* (Philadelphia: Fortress, 1997), 67–78.

as they came; they shall take nothing for their toil, which they may carry away with their hands. ¹⁶This also is a grievous ill: just as they came, so shall they go; and what gain do they have from toiling for the wind? ¹⁷Besides, all their days they eat in darkness, in much vexation and sickness and resentment.

¹⁸This is what I have seen to be good: it is fitting to eat and drink and find enjoyment in all the toil with which one toils under the sun the few days of the life God gives us; for this is our lot. ¹⁹Likewise all to whom God gives wealth and possessions and whom he enables to enjoy them, and to accept their lot and find enjoyment in their toil—this is the gift of God. ²⁰For they will scarcely brood over the days of their lives, because God keeps them occupied with the joy of their hearts.

Ptolemaic multilevel taxation system, in which the lowest-rung individuals had little to gain other than the fact that their ability to pay taxes kept them from all-out slavery.[14]

Qoheleth 5:9 [8] is an exemplar of Hebrew obscurity, but the topics it seems to address include whatever makes for an advantage to a land and a king who somehow cares for the fields. It is within reason to think that this relates to the previous verse, insofar as a king who attends to justice and righteousness (rather than imposing oppression) will be one who ensures care for the fields so as to feed his people.[15] Nonetheless, most commentators agree only on the elusiveness of meaning. The remainder of the chapter focuses on wealth, toil, and, eventually, one version of the *carpe diem*. The vocabulary repetitions throughout the section point to these areas of concern for Qoheleth: כסף, "money"; המון, "wealth"; הטובה, "goods"; שבע, "surfeit"; עשיר, "rich/riches"; and עמל, "toil/toiling/toils."[16]

In 5:10 [9] Qoheleth hones in on "one who loves [אהב] money/silver" and, later in the verse, "wealth." The subject in both cases is "one who loves," a participle created out of the verb אהב (*qal*), "love." The language is strong and should get our attention. "Love" usually applies to God or to a particular and usually special individual; on some occasions, though,

14. Thomas Krüger, *Qoheleth: A Commentary*, ed. Klaus Baltzer, trans. O. C. Dean, Hermeneia (Minneapolis: Fortress, 2004), 20–21.

15. Schoors, *Ecclesiastes*, 414–16; see his citation of Eaton, 101–2.

16. כסף, "money," appears in 5:10 [9], twice; המון, "wealth," in 5:10 [9]; הטובה, "goods," in 5:11 [10] and שבע, "surfeit," in 5:12 [11]; עשיר, "rich/riches," appears in 5:12 [11], 13 [12], 14 [13], 19 [18]; עמל, "toil/toiling/toils," in 5:15 [14], 16 [15], 18 [17], 19 [18].

the word does call out misplaced affections. If there were some "advantage" to be had in 5:9 [8], the following verses point to lack of advantage. Specifically, wealth provides no advantage but only results in *hevel* (5:10 [9]); one with many possessions receives only the "reward" of watching others "eat" those hard-earned and abundant items (5:11 [10]). Qoheleth harps on these points throughout the book; we encountered it as early as chapter 2. Most people would agree that excess wealth creates all kinds of trouble and that you can't take it with you (5:10-11 [9-10]; cf. 2:21).

The point is well-taken that wealth often creates sleep-disturbing stress (5:12 [11]). Qoheleth, however, allows that view to slide into a problematic romanticization of the poor. The NASB translation of 5:12 [11] spells out the matter more explicitly than the Hebrew: "The sleep of the working man is pleasant, whether he eats little or much. But the full stomach of the rich man does not allow him to sleep." While "full stomach" is a rather interpretive translation of שבע, *sava'*, which as a noun means "abundance" or "plenty," it provides a useful contrast with the point in 5:12 [11] about workers who sleep well whether or not they have eaten. Over the years in teaching Qoheleth to undergraduates and seminary students, I have heard many students react to this verse with some version of "Easy for Qoheleth to say, he's rich! Why should any rich person get to assume anything about how a laborer sleeps? Does Qoheleth think you sleep well if you're not sure whether you'll have work the next day? Does Qoheleth think you sleep well if you have an empty belly or aching muscles from hard labor?" Given the lowly status of many women during much of antiquity, these questions could also particularly apply to women in that time. Indeed, sadly, the same could be said for many societies still today.

The common translations "laborers" (NRSV, in the plural for the Hebrew singular) or "working man" (NASB) for העבד in 5:12 [11] significantly tone down the plain meaning of "servant" or "slave" here. Indeed, LXX has δουλος, "slave," and there is no reason to avoid that translation.[17] Here again we see that the text betrays Qoheleth's point of view as a wealthy patriarch who has the distance and gall to imagine that life as a slave would afford one better sleep. An important question to reflect on here is where women would have fallen into the category of Qoheleth's "laborer"? In all likelihood, there would have been quite a bit of vari-

---

17. See Schoors, *Ecclesiastes*, 426–27. The MT term העבד is punctuated to read "laborer" (*ha-'oved*), with a slight vowel change from "slave" (*ha-'eved*).

ation in this. Thus there is probably no single answer to where women as a category—rich, poor, and/or slaves, married, widowed—would have fallen into the scheme of Qoheleth's musings. Some women in the Hellenistic-Roman period would have been wives who oversaw other "laborers," both male and female. It may well be that women in Qoheleth's time were more often "laborers" than in the ancestral and early postexilic period, as the economy shifted to a system of wage labor rather than household self-sufficiency.[18] In light of Qoheleth's comments about "male and female slaves" in 2:7, in which Qoheleth uses עבדים for "male slaves," from the same root as in 5:12 [11], this verse seems more trivializing and objectifying than sympathetic. The verse is all the more problematic for women slaves/workers/servants/laborers, whom Qoheleth does not even mention. Qoheleth's commentary on wealth in this section also fails to notice that in some parts of ancient Israel's history, women were considered part of a man's wealth. We saw that in Qoheleth 2:7; other biblical examples include Exodus 20:17 and 1 Kings 10:14–11:8.[19] Qoheleth's point speaks to the wealthy, not to the poor, and makes sense only if the "slave" to whom Qoheleth refers has a relatively stable life, assuming the provision of all basic needs—food, shelter, clothing, and basic security. At the same time, Qoheleth's critique of excess wealth in 5:10 [9] serves to undermine the traditional retributive idea of wealth as reward.[20] Qoheleth's comment on wealth may helpfully undermine its allure, perhaps functioning like Jesus' statement "blessed are the poor" (Luke 6:20) or his spiritual guidance to the rich man (Matt 19:16-24).

In 5:13 [12], we see a shift back to first-person narrative and apparently a discussion of one man through 5:16 [15]. The focus on that one man, an example for Qoheleth's point about the absurdity of amassing and losing wealth, could even continue through the end of the chapter, with the exception of 5:19 [18], where Qoheleth inserts "every man [אדם]" to generalize the previous points—at least among males. That focus on one particular man is lost in NRSV, which translates "their hurt" for "his hurt" (that of the hoarding rich man) and "their/they" instead of "his/he" throughout these verses in order to create a more inclusive scenario. Thus the NRSV's inclusive translation here invites women

18. Carol Meyers, *Rediscovering Eve: Ancient Israelite Women in Context* (New York: Oxford University Press, 2012), 206–9.

19. Jennie R. Ebeling, *Women's Lives in Biblical Times* (London: T & T Clark, 2010), 83.

20. Schoors, *Ecclesiastes*, 422 cites R. N. Whybray, *Ecclesiastes*, New Century Bible Commentary (Grand Rapids, MI: Eerdmans, 1989), 99.

to identify with a vignette that was originally written about a man. A more helpful translation to consult in chapter 5, at least for the sake of gendered pronouns and possessives, is NJPS (note it uses the Hebrew numbering). While the topics of excess wealth and hoarding relate to all people for all time, the Hebrew text gives us no reason to think that Qoheleth was talking about or to women in this passage. As is often the case in this book, women's experiences here are excluded and objectified rather than implicitly included.

The interjection ראיתי, "I have seen," in 5:13 [12] draws us into Qoheleth's experience and compels us to move our reflections from excess wealth (5:10-12 [9-11]) to hoarding (5:13 [12]), culminating again in the point that "you can't take it with you" (5:14-17 [13-16]; cf. 2:21). Yet Qoheleth evaluates this situation with the *inclusio* created with רעה חולה, "grievous ill," in 5:13 [12] and 16 [15]. The difficulty is in ascertaining whether Qoheleth is evaluating addiction to wealth or the fact of its impermanence. In other words, should we understand "grievous ill" as an "evil illness" or "a tragic reality"? Is it an admonition to not work too hard because wealth is impermanent or a lament that hard work has no lasting value? How would these matters affect ancient Israelite women, whose work may have produced little to no monetary gain in any case and was utterly repetitive? While addiction to wealth has contemporary applications for women and men alike, in ancient times that may well have affected men much more than women, since women had compromised or nonexistent earning power. And indeed, the subjects of Qoheleth's vignettes here as well as the verb forms make clear that the comments all relate to the male experience.

The NRSV reference to "parents of children" in 5:14 [13] has been made inclusive by the translators; the Hebrew reads "the one who begets a son." The verb form is masculine (הוליד, from ילד *hiphil*) so in all likelihood "a man who begets a son" would be indicated here. Inheritance would have passed almost exclusively from father to son so, for that reason as well, the patriarchal translation stands. The tragedy appears to be that, due to the loss of wealth experienced by the father, there is nothing to pass on to the son; the fact that there once had been great riches heightens the sense of misfortune. In this scenario we should note the absence of mother, who obviously was "the one who bore" no matter the sex of the offspring, and daughter(s), whose needs were usually expected to be cared for by her eventual husband and his family. The high and low of the man's wealth would surely have affected the mother or daughter(s) related to this family, though that aspect of the scenario remains hidden.

Daughters do play a role in inheritance in two notable biblical passages: the case that Mahlah, Noah, Hoglah, Milcah, and Tirzah bring to Moses about inheriting from their deceased father Zelophehad (Num 27:1-11; 36:1-12); and Jemimah, Keziah, and Keren-happuch, who inherited from their father "along with their brothers" (Job 42:14-15).[21]

In 5:15 [14] we find a stark example of how women's contributions were taken for granted while simultaneously ignored. For almost every time we read "they" or "their" in the NRSV, the Hebrew behind it indicates the masculine pronoun or possessive "he" or "his," which is the case six times in 5:15 [14]. Yet "the one who bore," who was notably absent in the last verse, here receives more specific mention—or at least her בטן, "womb," does. The generic "mother" of the universalized man in this verse interestingly receives mention, although in passing as the owner of her "womb." We might wonder the reason for explicitly including "mother's womb" in this verse, as the same sentiment could just as easily have been expressed with a more peripheral mention of mother and her body by using the verb ילד (*qal*), "bear/beget" (with "woman" as a subject).

The answer probably lies in the fact that this naked baby/naked corpse sentiment also appears in Job 1:21. While the grammatical structure of the two verses does not perfectly align, the vocabulary and meaning are similar enough that it seems Qoheleth and the author of Job had either a similar written or oral source or one copied from the other. This proverb about nakedness at birth and death helps Qoheleth again make the point that toil produces impermanent results: do not invest too much in the toil, as it will not ultimately pay off. Regardless of Qoheleth's source or influence for this material, we must attend to the way in which the hidden woman in this verse is objectified for her procreative function.

Qoheleth 5:17-18 [16-17] create one of Qoheleth's more notable contradictions—or perhaps it is a paradox or an intentional contrast? Does eating have negative (v. 17 [16]) or positive (v. 18 [17]) associations for Qoheleth? Is Qoheleth speaking of one man or of all humans? In verse 17 [16] a man (perhaps the one from the previous verses) eats in "darkness," with three negative adjectives describing the occasion. In the next

---

21. Tal Ilan confirms that these passages from Numbers only made it more difficult for women to inherit, except in the exact situation described here, of a family lacking male heirs. Tal Ilan, *Integrating Women into Second Temple History* (Peabody, MA: Hendrickson Publishers, 2001), 72–73. Naomi appears to have had an inheritance (Ruth 4:3-9), though it apparently did not provide for her like that of Judith (8:7). Lisa M. Wolfe, *Ruth, Esther, Song of Songs, and Judith* (Eugene, OR: Wipf and Stock, 2011), 220.

verse, Qoheleth broadens the admonition from this one man as example to a saying that is—at first—more universally applicable: "it is fitting to eat and drink and find enjoyment." Now eating, drinking, and finding enjoyment are טוב, "good." Some kind of shift has occurred here, perhaps a move from a vignette (5:13-17 [12-16]) to observations that somehow relate, perhaps as critique.

This contrast between 5:17 and 18 [16 and 17] is one of many occasions in which the interpreter must determine whether the contradictory views come from one voice or two, or from one individual speaking out of both sides of his—or her or their—mouth. Indeed, 5:18 [17] provides the same kind of relief that we find in most of the other *carpe diem* passages. The rhetorical movement of the passage leads us to identify with the despondent man in 5:17 [16], who finds "darkness . . . anguish and sickness and resentment" in his eating and drinking; the following verse brings the resolution that the same acts of eating and drinking and even עמל, "toil," can instead be טוב, "good." If we took 5:18-20 [17-19] out of context, the sentiment would seemingly coincide with the attitude of the wacky but joy-filled Sycamore/Vanderhof/Carmichael family in the 1938 film *You Can't Take It with You*—they are much more invested in loving life than in acquiring or succeeding.[22]

As the saying in verse 18 [17] finishes, the Hebrew again betrays Qoheleth's exclusive focus on male enjoyment of food, drink, and toil: "in all *his* toil with which *he* toils under the sun the few days of his life that God gave him." If Qoheleth considers the female experience, that remains unmentioned; perhaps unconsidered. In all likelihood, women prepared and served the food and drink, so their toil appears here, though veiled. Hence, the crucial women's work is taken for granted and ignored. It is important to note, however, that mainly lower-class women would have had this role, while there probably were some upper-class women who themselves could enjoy the feast without having to prepare or serve the food.[23]

As for theology, the final verses of this passage (5:18-20 [17-19]) assert that God-given wealth does—or at least may—come with joy, if God so determines. Qoheleth couches this sentiment in terms of האדם, *ha-'adam*, which could refer back to the "man" in the vignette of 5:13-17

---

22. Moss Hart and George Simon Kaufman, *You Can't Take It with You: Comedy in Three Acts* (Dramatists Play Service, Inc., 1937); Frank Capra, *You Can't Take It with You* (Columbia Pictures Corp, 1938).

23. Meyers, *Rediscovering Eve*, 206–8.

[12-16], or it could indicate an "everyman" indicating all males or even all humanity. The text does nothing to specifically include women in Qoheleth's audience, and most likely "wealth" and "possessions" in 5:19 [18] would exclude at least most women as the audience since they would not usually have been the owners of such, at least not in large portions and probably not for long periods of time.[24] Instead, it is more likely that women would have been considered one of many commodities that contributed to a man's affluence.

Though it is feasible to imagine that Qoheleth's useful admonitions about wealth could apply across gender lines, Qoheleth's writing here specifically calls on men as the audience. At least in this chapter, women appear only insofar as their wombs create a metaphor in Qoheleth's reflections. Qoheleth's ongoing critique of עמל, "toil" (vv. 15 [14], 16 [15], 18 [17], 19 [18]), as providing no long-term "advantage" (5:16 [15])—other than insofar as it is enjoyed (5:18-19 [17-18])—might be an overly obvious message for women, at least those in the ancient world. Typical women's work consists of tasks that must be continually repeated and for which excessive stockpiling would be neither possible nor effective. The washing, the cleaning, the gardening, the baking, the brewing, the weaving, the child care, and most other female-specific tasks would be ongoing, unending work in which one could easily either feel like Sisyphus or find deep joy in the repetition of those crucial tasks, which very specifically entail eating and drinking. Most likely, ancient women and contemporary women alike would find some combination of absurdity and joy in these tasks. Carol Meyers points out that in referring to the housework that contemporary Westerners might be tempted to trivialize, gender archaeologists have adopted the term "maintenance activities." She notes that this designation "draws attention to and valorizes women's contributions to household life."[25]

As for the man in Qoheleth's vignette of 5:13-17 [12-16], the concluding verse and the echoed evaluation "grievous ill" in 5:13 [12] and 5:16 [15] illustrate a decidedly Sisyphean view of such toil. This recalls the scenario described by Betty Smith in *A Tree Grows in Brooklyn*, in which she spent days working at a paper flower factory, doing the same task repeatedly. She connects this experience to the life of a wife in her culture.[26] The

24. Ilan, *Integrating Women*, 47–48; *Jewish Women*, 167–72.
25. Meyers, *Rediscovering Eve*, 126.
26. Betty Smith, *A Tree Grows in Brooklyn* (New York: Harper and Brothers, 1943), 276–77.

Rev. Mary Gadreau Hughes, a participant in the "Qoheleth in the Suk-kah" women's conversation, responded to Qoheleth's sentiments with the following proverb describing women's work: "(Best delivered with sigh and eyes rolling) 'Cleaning the house while children are growing is like sweeping the walk while it's still snowing.' "[27] Women who work low-wage jobs like cleaning houses, with no health insurance and little job security, surely feel the pain of this description in a less humorous way. When you work as much as you can and you still cannot support yourself, why try? What makes a survival existence worth it? This raises the question of whether Qoheleth and/or a specifically androcentric viewpoint inherently devalue ongoing, repetitive work as opposed to work that has an end goal and final product. If so, does that devaluation have to do with the work being women's work or does the logic move in reverse order?

27. Rev. Mary Gadreau Hughes, "Qoheleth in the Sukkah Women's Conversation," Temple B'nai Israel, Oklahoma City, OK, September 29, 2015.

Qoheleth 6:1–7:14

Good, Better, Wise

From Evil to Good and Much of What's in Between (6:1-12)

Qoheleth's reflections on wealth continue in 6:1-8 with another vignette, in which the androcentrism from the Hebrew text has been obscured by the NRSV's inclusive translation.[1] In 6:2-6 Qoheleth tells about two men. The opening word in 6:2 is אִישׁ, "man," the recipient of God's abundance: a rich man.[2] In 6:3 the desires of the first man's נפשׁ (the NRSV does not really translate this word) lack nothing; yet in 6:2 "God does not empower him to eat it [his riches]; instead a stranger will eat it" (NJPS: "God does not permit him to enjoy it; instead, a stranger will enjoy it"; NRSV: "God does not enable them to enjoy these things, but a stranger enjoys them"). The repeated verb אכל (*qal*), "eat," in 6:2 suggests the universal tone of the *carpe diem*, but here some "strange man" is the only one who might fulfill that, while the first man's efforts at the *carpe diem* will go divinely unfulfilled. The second man, in the latter part of the verse, is an אִישׁ נכרי, "stranger," literally "strange man," who enjoys the wealth of the first man.[3]

---

1. See the NRSV to the passage from 5:12-16 [11-15].

2. This man is the converse of 5:19 [18], in which God grants some individuals/ men joy out of their wealth. Antoon Schoors, *Ecclesiastes* (Leuven: Peeters, 2013), 419.

3. Most translations simply render this נכרי "stranger": KJV, NIV, NJPS. William Brown reflects on the "stranger" in Qoh 6:2 in connection to the "Strange" (זרה but

6:1There is an evil that I have seen under the sun, and it lies heavy upon humankind: 2those to whom God gives wealth, possessions, and honor, so that they lack nothing of all that they desire, yet God does not enable them to enjoy these things, but a stranger enjoys them. This is vanity; it is a grievous ill. 3A man may beget a hundred children, and live many years; but however many are the days of his years, if he does not enjoy life's good things, or has no burial, I saw that a stillborn child is better off than he. 4For it comes into vanity and goes into darkness, and in darkness its name is covered; 5moreover it has not seen the sun or known anything; yet it finds rest rather

In verse 3, the Hebrew opens with "If a man יוליד ['begets'] a hundred . . . ." The phrase contains neither an object (NRSV adds "children") nor mention of any mothers to bear and care for those children. The verse ends with a rather shocking first-person comparison, apparently made by Qoheleth, of this long-lived father of many to a "stillbirth" or "stillborn child" (NRSV). The Hebrew word order delivers that shock effectively by making "stillbirth" the final word in the verse: "If a man begets a hundred [offspring], and lives many years, however many may the days of his years be, but his נפש ['inner-self'] is not sated from the good, and also he does not have a burial—I say, better than him is a stillborn child (נפל)!" The word נפל, "miscarried [fetus]," occurs in only two other instances, and then in similar metaphorical uses.4

---

also נכריה) Woman in Proverbs (2:16; 5:3; 6:24; 7:5), whose presence acts as a foil over against Woman Wisdom. He writes, "The conflict embodied by these two mythic figures [Wisdom and the 'Strange' Woman] in Proverbs 1–9 reflects a pattern of social conflict in postexilic Israel. During this period, Palestine was filled with both indigenous and immigrant populations, the 'people of the land' and the returning exiles or *gōlâ* (see, e.g., Ezra 3:3; 4:1; 6:16; 9:1-2; Neh 9:24, 30; 10:30-31). It was a time when land and family were issues of great contention. Consequently, one's family roots played a decisive role in reclaiming land that was once lost in exile, not unlike the situation in Palestine today." William P. Brown, *Ecclesiastes*, IBC (Louisville: Westminster John Knox, 2011), 64–65. Harold Washington also links the use of נכרי in 6:2 to the postexilic era: "The Strange Woman (אשה זרה/נכריה) of Proverbs 1–9 and Post-Exilic Judaean Society," in *Second Temple Studies*, vol. 2: *Temple Community in the Persian Period* (Sheffield: JSOT, 1994), 229–30. See also my discussion in the section below on 7:15-29, regarding the female figures in Proverbs.

4. See Job 3:16 and Ps 58:8 [9]. The Hebrew root נפל means "to fall" in the *qal* stem. In the trial of a supposedly disloyal wife, the cursed water will cause "her thigh to fall and her stomach to distend" (Num 5:21 and similarly v. 22). The possible "falling"

than he. [6]Even though he should live a thousand years twice over, yet enjoy no good—do not all go to one place?

[7]All human toil is for the mouth, yet the appetite is not satisfied. [8]For what advantage have the wise over fools? And what do the poor have who know how to conduct themselves before the living? [9]Better is the sight of the eyes than the wandering of desire; this also is vanity and a chasing after wind.

[10]Whatever has come to be has already been named, and it is known what human beings are, and that they are not able to dispute with those who are stronger. [11]The more words, the more vanity, so how is one the better? [12]For who knows what is good for mortals while they live the few days of their vain life, which they pass like a shadow? For who can tell them what will be after them under the sun?

Stillbirths and miscarriages in ancient Judaism were often viewed as punishment for some sin of the father; that may actually heighten Qoheleth's point about this man, whose life is worse than a child born dead.[5] In all likelihood, a woman, then or now, would be less likely than a man to appreciate "stillborn child" as a metaphor for the sake of a philosophical reflection—particularly a woman who has delivered a stillborn child. This should give pause to all who would preach this text, using the verse as a philosophical exercise. For the sake of the persons in the congregation who have suffered a stillbirth, take care! One must explicate this passage as descriptive rather than prescriptive, a difficult task since many persons of faith are mistakenly under the impression that the whole canon is prescriptive. Similarly, Qoheleth's retributive morality in 6:3 ignores the mother who experienced the stillbirth, whose loss would have been most palpable. The "hundred children" at the beginning of 6:3 and the "stillborn child" at the end of the verse both conceal the role of the individual women who coupled with the man in question and who bore these children, whether alive or dead. This trivialization—this rendering of women invisible—is so common in the biblical text as well as in contemporary society as to be almost unnoticeable. For instance, in 2 Samuel 12:24 Bathsheba gets one word of consolation from King David after their child dies, and we the readers get

---

of the "thigh" (euphemism for vagina here), from the same root נפל, clearly indicates a miscarriage if she has been disloyal, hence became pregnant.

5. Tal Ilan, *Jewish Women in Greco-Roman Palestine* (Peabody, MA: Hendrickson, 1996), 114.

none of her own expression of grief. Before the verse even ends, David impregnates Bathsheba again and she bears another son, still with no words of her own. Furthermore, what about the children in Qoheleth 6:3 and in 2 Samuel 12:18 whose deaths and lives the text (and many a commentator) overlooks? A childist hermeneutic invites us to ask about the child whose life was the expense of David's transgressions. Similarly, what voice can we give to the stillborn child who was the object of Qoheleth's proverb, or indeed to the completely obscured (in the Hebrew) "hundred" whom this hypothetical "man" in 6:3 "begat"?[6] Qoheleth unnervingly carries on about the stillborn child in 6:4-5, personifying it without repeating the term נפל; rather, Qoheleth uses third-person masculine singular verb forms and suffix pronouns to refer to the unlived life of a stillborn child. Qoheleth's extended reflections on this stillbirth stand in glaring contrast to the "hundreds" that "a man begat" in verse 3, whose potential joy in life Qoheleth overlooks.

The goal that Qoheleth apparently seeks is something mentioned earlier in the book in 4:6: נחת "quiet, rest" in 6:5 will arise again in 9:17. Maybe this is what Qoheleth was also getting at in reflecting on the sleep of laborers in 5:12 [11]. The point seems to be that constancy of *hevel* and eternal rest—including darkness thrice-over and utter ignorance—seem preferable to an apparently rich but unenjoyed and uncelebrated life.[7] Qoheleth clarifies this with a strange but vivid phrase that envelopes the section in verses 3 and 7: "his inner-self [נפש] is not sated" (NRSV: "he does not enjoy"/"the appetite is not satisfied"). Qoheleth set the stage in 6:2 for these descriptions of the unsatisfied inner-self by introducing a man whose inner-self has everything it wants yet who still cannot be satisfied (cannot אכל, "eat," what he has).[8]

Having many riches, children, and years of life applies across the gender spectrum, though more so in today's world than in ancient times. Indeed, certain features in the framing of the passage lend themselves to

---

6. Julie Faith Parker defines and practices "childism" in her biblical interpretation, with the stated goal "to identify and appreciate the influence and importance of promising, compelling young biblical characters." Julie Faith Parker, *Valuable and Vulnerable: Children in the Hebrew Bible, Especially the Elisha Cycle*, BJS 355 (Providence, RI: Brown Judaic Studies, 2013), 18.

7. The three occurrences of darkness include חשך, "darkness," which appears twice in v. 4, and שמש לא־ראה, "has not seen the sun," in v. 5. Qoheleth articulates the concept of utter ignorance through the phrase לא ידע, "does not know," in v. 5.

8. See the above discussion on 6:2.

a universalized reading. The whole passage (6:2-8) speaks to the fact that life produces no gain, particularly life without enjoyment of the good. Both 6:1 and 6:7 contain the more generic term for "human," אדם, rather than איש, "man," perhaps suggesting that Qoheleth's message should apply to a wider audience than the one man in the story. Verse 8 seems to use broad rather than specific descriptions: חכם, "the wise"; כסיל, "the fool"; עני, "the poor"; החיים, "the living." Yet these categories all appear in masculine forms; but, indeed, broadening the field of Qoheleth's musings here to include women might well be going too far.[9] The vignette itself concerns male players participating in male-oriented activities. One reasonable interpretation is that the section critically refers to Solomon and his riches[10] or perhaps satirizes the collective Israelite longing for and glorification of that time. While Qoheleth's sentiments in this verse theoretically relate to women as well as to men, Qoheleth did nothing to specifically include women's experiences here.

Qoheleth provides final rhetorical questions in 6:8 about יותר, "advantage," that provisionally conclude verses 2-8 and also hark back to the opening complaint of the book in 1:3: מה-יתרון לאדם, "What does one gain?" Because, in Qoheleth's assessment, people gain nothing unless they have the God-given gift of enjoying their possessions or the good (6:2, 3, 6), because when a man's life-spirit is not sated, the answer is that there is no advantage, not even for "the wise" (6:8). This jab at wisdom may well contribute to a larger critique of wisdom that culminates in Qoheleth's famously misogynistic remarks in 7:26-28. As we will see, if 7:26-28 functions to reject the "Strange" Woman of Proverbs, then those Proverbs passages create a more widely meaningful scenario when paired with Qoheleth's remarks lamenting the inaccessibility of (woman) wisdom (see discussion of 7:15-29). The נפש, inner-life or life-spirit, that was un-sated in 6:3, 7 now "wanders" in 6:9 (the NRSV translates מהלך נפש as "wandering of desire"). Whether unsated or wandering, the passage undoubtedly describes a man with a desolate life-spirit. In 6:10 Qoheleth echoes the sentiments of 1:9, "what will be will be," and reinscribes Qoheleth's point about the intractable power of hierarchy ("him who is stronger," 10b). And this raises the questions: What about a woman's life-spirit? Does she have any greater or lesser access to wisdom?

9. See section in the introduction on איש vs. אדם in Qoheleth.

10. As described in 1 Kgs 5:2-8 and in chap. 10 thereof, especially vv. 14-22; see also 2 Chr 1:14-16; 9:13-26.

How are we to understand Qoheleth's emphasis on *hevel* (6:2, 9, 11, 12) and "grievous ill" (6:2, a carryover from 5:16 [15]) throughout this section? It perplexingly stands over against Qoheleth's advocacy to enjoy life (6:2, 3, 6). The Sage goes on longer about what happens if one does not enjoy life than if one does! Three of the four final verses in the chapter repeat *hevel* (9, 11, 12), and we find a particularly dire pronouncement in 6:12, in which לאדם, "for the man," his *hevel* life passes "like a shadow."[11] Would a woman's life pass similarly, or seem more or less *hevel* or shadowy? Based on the life expectancy of an ancient Near Eastern woman, which was shorter than a man's, it seems that Qoheleth's dim view could indeed apply to women, though that does not assume Qoheleth would have been thinking of them.[12] In antiquity, this would be all the more the case for children, who had the shortest life expectancy of all.[13] The beginning of 6:12, מי-יודע מה-טוב, "who knows what is good," essentially undermines the most positive sentiments of the preceding pericope, in which at least a man who could enjoy the טוב, "good" (6:3, 6), apparently would have some hope in this life. How can you enjoy the good if you cannot know what is good? The admonition to eat, drink, and enjoy is notably absent in this section, though most readers could probably use a drink by the end of this chapter!

Wisdom Sayings and Theological Reflections (7:1-14)

Ever intriguing, Qoheleth goes from asking, "Who knows what is good?" (6:12)—and implying the answer is "no one"—to reciting or composing proverbs precisely about what is good! Yet these statements stand as some of the most perplexing in Qoheleth's book, apparently privileging death over life, despair over joy. The first three verses of chapter 7 contain better-than sayings; Hebrew composes "better than"

---

11. Qoheleth also uses this metaphor of transparent ephemerality later, in 8:13.

12. Jennie R. Ebeling, *Women's Lives in Biblical Times* (London; New York: T & T Clark, 2010), 101; Ilan, *Jewish Women*, 116–19; Tal Ilan, *Integrating Women into Second Temple History*, TSAJ 76 (Peabody, MA: Hendrickson, 2001), 207.

13. Julie Faith Parker cites Martin Eng's research to differentiate between "life expectancy, or average age of a person at death," and "life span, which is the age one could expect to reach without interference from war, disease, death in childbirth, etc. He estimates that the life expectancy in ancient Israel was probably in the mid-thirties, whereas the typical life span (barring calamities) would be between forty and fifty." She consults Lawrence Stager's work, in which he "estimates that approximately two of six children would live to become adults." Parker, *Valuable and Vulnerable*, 9 n. 31.

Qoh 7:1-14

⁷:¹A good name is better than
   precious ointment,
   and the day of death, than the day
      of birth.
²It is better to go to the house of
   mourning
   than to go to the house of feasting;
for this is the end of everyone,
   and the living will lay it to heart.
³Sorrow is better than laughter,
   for by sadness of countenance
      the heart is made glad.
⁴The heart of the wise is in the house
   of mourning;

but the heart of fools is in the
   house of mirth.
⁵It is better to hear the rebuke of the
   wise
   than to hear the song of fools.
⁶For like the crackling of thorns under
   a pot,
   so is the laughter of fools;
   this also is vanity.
⁷Surely oppression makes the wise
   foolish,
   and a bribe corrupts the heart.
⁸Better is the end of a thing than its
   beginning;

by opening with טוב, *tov*, "good," and then using the comparative article מ־ for "than." Qoheleth drives home the theme of טוב, *tov*, "good," by repeating this root eleven times in these fourteen verses.[14] Due to the significant range of meaning of this word—from ethical goodness, to appropriateness, to beauty—I will refer to it in transliteration here. The varying uses of *tov* also prevent it from being completely apparent in English translation. The *tov* repetitions in Qoheleth 7:1-14 can function as a structuring device because the word opens seven verses; those could easily be understood as seven sections, as the content coheres in what follows each opening.[15] While the significance of *tov* in this section cannot be denied, there is no consensus on whether it imposes a specific pattern on this section.[16]

Qoheleth 7:1 repeats "good" twice because it is a better-than saying about a שם טוב, "good name." Despite the focus on "good," the content of these sayings has much in common with the improbable definition

---

14. 7:1 (2x), 2, 3, 5, 8 (2x), 10, 11, 14 (2x).

15. 7:1, 2, 3, 5, 8, 11, 14. Vv. 11 and 14 present some variation, as they open with טובה not טוב. Each section other than the first contains a saying and commentary on the saying.

16. Schoors, *Ecclesiastes*, 499, 518; Ellen F. Davis sees "six sayings grouped in three pairs" in 7:1-6 (*Proverbs, Ecclesiastes, and the Song of Songs*, Westminster Bible Companion [Louisville: Westminster John Knox, 2000], 199).

Qoh 7:1-14 (cont.)

the patient in spirit are better than the proud in spirit.
⁹Do not be quick to anger, for anger lodges in the bosom of fools.
¹⁰Do not say, "Why were the former days better than these?" For it is not from wisdom that you ask this.
¹¹Wisdom is as good as an inheritance, an advantage to those who see the sun.

¹²For the protection of wisdom is like the protection of money, and the advantage of knowledge is that wisdom gives life to the one who possesses it.
¹³Consider the work of God; who can make straight what he has made crooked?
¹⁴In the day of prosperity be joyful, and in the day of adversity consider; God has made the one as well as the other, so that mortals may not find out anything that will come after them.

of "good" in the previous chapter. There, Qoheleth found the nonlife of a stillborn child "better than" the wealthy father of many (6:2-3); here, Qoheleth favors "the day of death" over against "the day of birth" (v. 1), "the house of mourning" to "the house of feasting" (v. 2), "sadness" to "laughter" (v. 3), and "rebuke" rather than "song" (v. 5), and "the end of the thing" is better than its "beginning" (v. 8). What Qoheleth finds "good" is not what most people would think of as good; this makes the passage at least provocative, if not repelling.[17] These sayings have a similar effect as Jesus' sayings in the Sermon on the Plain (Luke 6:17-38) or the Sermon on the Mount (Matt 5:1-12). Those sayings rely on "reversal," such as the opening line in each: "Blessed are you who are poor" or "Blessed are the poor in spirit," respectively (Luke 6:20; Matt 5:3). For Qoheleth, however, the point seems to be more of a philosophical reflection on life than a critique of the ruling power.[18]

Qoheleth's praise of "a good name" as "better than good oil" may well refer to the opposite of the scenario in 6:2-3: a man who apparently had everything but who was prevented by God from enjoying it and who furthermore had "no burial." That would *not* be a man with a "good name," as we see in 6:4. This sentiment expresses much the same thing as Ben Sira (Sirach) 41:11, "The days of a good life are numbered, but a good name lasts forever," and Proverbs 22:1a, "Better chosen is a good

17. See also the chart of better-than sayings in the introduction.
18. Warren Carter, *Matthew and the Margins* (New York: T & T Clark, 2005), 130–32.

name than great riches." A number of other biblical references focus on a man's good name too.[19] Could a woman have aspired to have a "good name"—the kind of reputation that lives on beyond one's death? Only Judith 14:7 fully indicates the renown of a woman's name. Although it is suggested (Ruth 4:10-11) that Ruth the Moabite woman participated in the ongoing commemoration of Elimelech's family, a strict translation of the peoples' blessing at the end of her story diminishes her figure. "That you may proclaim a name in Bethlehem" (Ruth 4:11) indicates that the "you," second-person masculine form, and the appropriate Hebrew verb attached to it is directed primarily at Boaz, who is in fact addressed by the blessing. Nonetheless, we should not overlook Ruth's contributions to this tribute.

Oil has multiple uses throughout the Hebrew Bible, notably including anointing of the priests (Exod 29:7; Ps 133:2) and the king (1 Sam 10:1; 16:13; 1 Kgs 1:39). If one purpose of Qoheleth were to critique the view of the monarchy as having been "golden days," that could inhere in the reference to "oil," such that even an anointed monarch loses value if not remembered well.[20] In other biblical contexts oil could also refer to a generic healing agent (Isa 1:6), a beauty treatment (Ps 104:15; Song 1:3), or part of an offering (Lev 2:1; Mic 6:7). Apropos "the day of death," which is preferable to "the day of birth" in the latter part of the verse, oil was also known for use as an unguent for a corpse as well as for an offering at the time of a burial, and women would likely have used it for these purposes.[21] Amid these various uses of "oil" in the Hebrew Bible, its significance here likely has to do with its value—akin to "wealth" in 2 Kings 20:13. Readers familiar with the New Testament might find that this verse recalls the passage in which an unnamed woman from Bethany anoints Jesus with costly perfume (which, most commonly in the ancient worlds, was oil-based); she receives Jesus' praise in the face of ire from his male disciples (Mark 14:1-9). Qoheleth's point most likely has to do with the inherent value in one's reputation in life and after death, over against any kind of luxuries during one's life, all of which will be lost.

19. Those include 2 Sam 14:7; 18:18; Isa 56:5; and Sir 15:6; 37:26; 39:9, 11; 40:19; 41:11-13.

20. See discussions of 1:12-18 and 2:1-11 above for additional suggestions of this critique.

21. Rachel Hachlili, *Jewish Funerary Customs, Practices and Rites in the Second Temple Period*, Supplements to the Journal for the Study of Judaism 94 (Leiden: Brill, 2005), 376, 379, 382.

The second half of 7:1 holds particular implications for ancient women, for whom "the day of birth"—more specifically a day on which she gave birth—would have been a milestone, to say the least. Those were days in which women faced their own mortality and sometimes that of their newborn.[22] At the same time, a woman who bore a healthy child accomplished a central cultural task in making a "good name" for herself, which brings us back to the first saying of 7:1. While there are multiple connections to women in 7:1, the extent to which the closing phrase undermines "the day of birth" potentially has negative implications for the role and validity of women. Additionally, to the extent that "good name" refers to one's reputation, particularly one's sexual reputation, this especially applies to women, then and now. The sexualized references to the figure the "Strange" Woman of Proverbs 1–9 help illustrate this,[23] as does the aftermath of the rape suffered by Dinah, in which her vindictive brothers seem mostly interested in her reputation (and theirs, by association) and not so much in her basic well-being (Gen 34).

Qoheleth's emphasis on death intensifies in verses 2-4, where Qoheleth twice refers to בית-אבל, "the house of mourning" (vv. 2 and 4). Nowhere else in the Hebrew Bible do we find this phrase, though mourners and mourning receive frequent mention. Rachel Hachlili notes that in the Second Temple period women "were not under religious obligation to attend the 'house of mourning' but were allowed to attend funerals," but women would have likely participated in other religious activities associated with mourning.[24] We find a woman wearing בגדי אבל, "clothes of mourning," in 2 Samuel 14:2 and women performing mourning, אבל (Jer 6:26), or recovering from it (Jer 31:13). We also find female mourners in Jeremiah 9:17-20 [16-19], though the passage does not specifically use the root אבל to describe them; these lamenting women are identified as מקוננות ("mourning women") and חכמות ("skilled, wise women"), which also intersects in a fascinating way with Qoheleth 7:4, though in Qoheleth the masculine plural suggests a male group of "wise ones" (חכמים) in "the house of mourning" (בית אבל). In these ways, we can see that women could have found themselves in many of the images in 7:1-4, whether or not Qoheleth had them in mind.

22. Ilan, *Jewish Women*, 116–19.

23. In Prov 2:16-17; 5:8-17, 20; 6:23-33; 7:10-23; and see the discussion below, in the next chapter of this volume.

24. Hachlili, *Jewish Funerary Customs*, 326.

Over against "the house of mourning," Qoheleth places בית משתה, "house of banqueting" (literally "house of drink," 7:2). The Hebrew word for "banqueting" is constructed around the root for "drink" (שתה), giving an ethos of revelry to the description. This word appears ten times in the book of Esther, in which drinking parties—and all that they en-tail—play a central role.[25] If Qoheleth meant to reject this kind of excess, that seems more understandable than to rule out all celebrations in favor of funerals. Yet in 7:4 the concept widens to ridiculing בית שמחה, "house of joy," as where the "heart of fools" resides. Our best solution in the struggle to understand this preference for grief over joy probably lies in the opening lines of verse 1, which places more stock in one's legacy than in the vast uncertainty that the future holds.

Sandwiched between the two references to the "house of mourning" (vv. 2 and 4) we have a saying in verse 3 that privileges negative emo-tions. The NRSV translation misleads us into thinking that the verse focuses on "sadness" ("Sorrow is better than laughter, for by sadness of countenance the heart is made glad"). The Hebrew, however, employs two different words; the first, כעס, has a wide range of meaning that relates to grief, anger, and frustration. The Sage ranks that higher than laughter. The second half of the verse pairs two standard body parts with two standard descriptors: face and heart, "evil" (as a noun) and "good" (as a verb). Thus, "a sad face makes for a happy heart." The reference to "heart," the last word in verse 3, links to the opening word of verse 4, again reiterating Qoheleth's association of both a "happy" (v. 3) and "wise" (v. 4) heart with grief.

All this emphasis on death and grief—and, in fact, a preference for it—presents us with a tricky interpretive task. Does Qoheleth have some sort of death obsession, struggle with suicidal tendencies, or harbor profound cynicism about life? While we can imagine someone suffering from a chronic illness looking forward to death as a way of relieving their pain, for anyone with the capability to enjoy life and one's relation-ships, Qoheleth's admonitions reek of disillusionment. These apparent

---

25. Lisa M. Wolfe, *Ruth, Esther, Song of Songs, and Judith* (Eugene, OR: Wipf and Stock, 2011), 72. Notably, Jer 16:8 mentions the "house of banqueting" in the context of mourning, suggesting that sharing food and drink with mourners held a part in assuaging their grief—something that certainly occurs still in funerary contexts. Qoheleth's association of "mourning" with the "wise," in contrast to "banqueting" as something "fools" do, however, indicates that in Qoh 7:2, 4 the context is probably more like what we read in Esther than in Jeremiah.

preferences for death threaten to overshadow the *carpe diem* passages elsewhere in the book even though, as far as we know, Qoheleth was still physically able to enjoy life. Our best explanation probably lies in Qoheleth's emphasis on the lack of reliable outcome in life (6:9-12; we will see this again in 7:15-18), which makes death seem preferable. Death at least relieves the angst of wondering how to live.[26] The more pressing point is probably that a life well lived, reflected on, and remembered provides more satisfaction at the time of death than the looming uncertainty of what lies ahead.

Although Qoheleth may not have meant to praise women and women's roles in death and mourning through these proverbs, the sayings nonetheless implicitly elevate that gynocentric practice, which was so central to the community. L. Juliana M. Claassens has written a wonderful discussion about the positive role of mourning, in which God is the initial wailer. Claassens suggests that divine grief embraces human grief, contrary to the views of retribution theology. She brings our attention to Jeremiah 31:15-17, where Rachel weeps, and to Jeremiah 8:21–9:1 [8:23], in which God mourns.[27] While this view seems foreign to Qoheleth, the frequent mentions of mourning, grieving, and death stand as an implicit reminder of the women who historically participated in those processes, and Claassens's analysis may provide a way for us to feel less alienated from Qoheleth's death sayings in 7:1-4.

Qoheleth 7:5-14 similarly reflects on death, or at least the אחרית, "end" (7:8), but, simultaneously, a focus on חכם, "wise," and חכמה, "wisdom," that began in 7:4 reappears six more times.[28] This, importantly, leads into the following section, which may be a sort of lament at Qoheleth's inability to attain (woman) wisdom (see below). "Wise" invites a potentially generic usage (as in 7:5, 7). "The heart of the wise," חכמים, in 7:4 carries the connotation of "wise men," though it could feasibly include women too, but in 7:5 Qoheleth specifies the object of the proverb as "a man." Like a good Sage, Qoheleth weighs כסילים, "fools" (7:4, 5, 6, 9), over against "the wise" and "wisdom" throughout this passage in the same verses. Qoheleth associates fools with שמחה, "joy" (v. 4); שיר, "song" (v. 5); שחק,

---

26. See Julie Duncan's helpful discussion on this passage. Julie Ann Duncan, *Ecclesiastes*, AOTC (Nashville: Abingdon, 2017), 94–95.

27. L. Juliana M. Claassens, *Mourner, Mother, Midwife: Reimagining God's Delivering Presence in the Old Testament* (Louisville: Westminster John Knox, 2012), 26–27, 30–40.

28. Vv. 5 and 7 have חכם, "wise," as a singular or plural noun. Vv. 10, 11, and 12 [2x] have חכמה, "wisdom."

"laughter" (v. 6); and כעס, "anger" (v. 9), an intriguing list that ranges so widely as to render the comparisons almost meaningless.

In verses 11 and 12, Qoheleth names some of wisdom's complements: נחלה, "inheritance" (v. 11); כסף, "money" (v. 12); and יתרון דעת, "advantage of knowledge," all life-giving (v. 12). If we have been paying attention, these are confusing statements, because Qoheleth has made critical statements about inheritance, money, and life elsewhere in the book.[29] The Sage even invokes the word יתרון, "advantage" (vv. 11, 12), so that it briefly seems wisdom can actually help one get ahead, as opposed to what we saw elsewhere, where everything was of questionable advantage (1:3; 2:11).

But as soon as we thought we had the key to getting ahead—in relying on wisdom—Qoheleth takes a theological turn in 7:13-14. In 1:15, Qoheleth had stated in the passive "that which is crooked cannot be made straight"; in 7:13, Qoheleth makes the subject explicit: God is the one who created this crookedness. From Qoheleth's perspective, the joy, suffering, and damned uncertainty that makes death seem preferable to life all have divine origin. This theological view conflicts with a key belief that many persons of faith hold about God: omnibenevolence. Many believers take for granted the view that God is all good and hold this in tension with their assertions of omnipotence and the existence of evil through the free-will theory or some similar systematic theology. This Sage, and perhaps the theological community that produced this Sage, was not so intent on believing that the deity was all good. Instead, we see more of the theology that Job attacked: whatever is happening, no matter how good, bad, or indifferent, comes from God.[30] What Qoheleth lacks is the surety of retribution theology that coheres in the words of Job's interlocutors. Qoheleth, in contrast, does not assert that anyone gets what they deserve.

Qoheleth makes some important points with the apparent death obsession in 7:1-14: nothing is certain other than the past; laughter, song, and feasting are the stuff of fools. The benefit of this is in using Qoheleth as an "astringent."[31] We cannot escape this Scroll with our lives or eventual deaths unexamined. Yet most of us, instead, embrace a wisdom that asserts these views alone will not suffice. The material in 7:1-14 calls for some theological resistance. While Qoheleth can help inspire us to resist a death-oriented life—especially through the repeated *carpe diem*

---

29. In Qoh 2:8, 11, 18-19; 5:10 [9]; 6:3, 6.
30. For example, see Job 5–6; 18–21.
31. Harold Washington, personal conversation, July 21, 2018.

passages[32]—it still seems wise to be dissatisfied with Qoheleth's words. Perhaps our dissatisfaction can be a call to consider life's other attributes, aside from its injustices and uncertainties and inevitable ending: relationships, hope, joy, surprise, persistence, compassion, cooperation, and transformation all carry us through, and many of us would claim those as "better than the day of death" or "the house of mourning."

For the purposes of feminist interpretation, the question "who knows what is *tov*?" from 6:12, along with the repetition of *tov* ten times throughout 7:1-14, beckons us to consider Genesis 1–3 as a conversation partner for this part of Qoheleth.[33] In the creation material of Genesis 1, *tov* serves as a theme-word, repeated as divine affirmation throughout the seven-day cycle.[34] The culminating *tov* in that creation narrative receives emphasis with טוב מאד, "very *tov*" (1:31). This evaluates the apex of creation that was described in Genesis 1:27: "So God created humankind [אדם] in his image, in the image of God he created them; male and female." While we ought not to overgeneralize this statement as the Bible's final word on gender equality, at the very least, this verse guards against denying women the same full humanity as men. In Phyllis Bird's words, "Distinctions of roles, responsibilities, or social status on the basis of sex—or other characteristics—are not excluded by this statement. But where such distinctions have the effect of denying to an individual or group the full and essential status of humanity in the image of God, they contradict the word of creation."[35] The "very *tov*" creation encompasses male and female humans alike.

The conversation between Qoheleth and Genesis becomes even more intriguing when we look at *tov* in Genesis 2–3, where the word relates to divine wisdom—both withheld and illicitly accessed—and has been a focal point for sexist and feminist interpretation alike. In Genesis 2:9, the narrator introduces the "tree of the knowledge of טוב ורע [*tov we-ra'*; traditionally translated as 'good and evil']."[36] In 2:17, that tree is pro-

---

32. Qoh 2:24; 3:12-13, 22; 5:18-19 [17-18]; 8:15; 9:7-9; and 11:8-9.

33. Indeed, some commentators see Genesis 1–3 as much more than a conversation partner for Qoheleth. For instance, see Matthew Seufert, "The Presence of Genesis in Ecclesiastes," *WTJ* 78 (2016): 75–92.

34. Elohim deems some part of creation *tov* on days 1, 3, 4, 5, and 6 of creation in Gen 1:4, 10, 12, 18, 21, 25, 31.

35. Phyllis Bird, *Missing Persons and Mistaken Identities: Women and Gender in Ancient Israel* (Minneapolis: Fortress, 1997), 153–54.

36. רע in Hebrew has a wide range. It may mean "bad," "disagreeable," "uncomely," "causing unhappiness." By extension, it has often been understood in this passage and elsewhere as ethically and theologically "evil" (see, for instance, *BDB*, 948). This is the sense in which the translation "evil" is used in this discussion.

hibited; notably, the אשה, "woman," has not yet been created. In 3:5, a serpent interprets the Lord's concern to the woman: "God knows that when you eat of it your eyes will be opened, and you will be like God, knowing good [*tov*] and evil." And indeed, in the following verse, the woman "knows" that the fruit is *tov*. In the end, because the humans ate from the tree of knowledge of *tov* and evil, they must be expelled from the Garden (3:22). Meanwhile, *tov* has also marked the deity's reasoning for ultimately creating the woman in 2:18: "It is not *tov* that the man [האדם, *ha-'adam*] should be alone; I will make him a helper as his partner." Thus, the interplay between Genesis 2–3 and Qoheleth 7:1-14 (and beyond) lies in their shared vocabulary of *tov*, "know," ידע (and "knowledge"), and "die/death" מות, as well as in the similar questions the passages raise: Who knows what is *tov*? Is knowledge *tov* or not? Is knowledge of the *tov* (and evil) dangerous? Does female knowledge have different consequences than male knowledge? While Qoheleth agonizes about *tov* and knowledge and death, all under the auspices of wisdom, we are right to wonder where it all leaves the first woman, later named Eve, or "life." Her apparent desire for *tov* and knowledge (and perhaps in those, wisdom) led to expulsion from the Garden and eventually death and was ultimately transformed by Christian interpreters into personified sin of doctrinal proportions. It is Christian interpretation of the Garden that insisted on the translation of רע as "evil" rather than "bad," with dire consequences for women. Genesis 2 and 3 do not exegetically provide the basis for Eve's label as temptress, responsible for the persistent sinfulness of all creation. Eve and many women following her suffered a disproportionate and ongoing death rooted in the misinterpretation of this text. As we will see, Qoheleth will not help rehabilitate our reputations.

Qoheleth 7:15-29

On Wisdom and Women (or Woman Wisdom)

Wisdom, Women, and Woman Wisdom (7:15-29)

This section opens with a pointed question about theodicy in 7:15, which is unsurprisingly prefaced with *hevel*. In ancient words, Qoheleth here articulates the same dilemma as did Rabbi Harold Kushner in a popular book title thousands of years later: *When Bad Things Happen to Good People*.[1] The observation is Qoheleth's own, in the first person, and indeed it goes well beyond bad things happening to good people. Here, Qoheleth also points out that good things happen to bad people! Yet again, and by no means for the last time, things are not as they should be. Maybe that mutilation of the expected theodicy was driving the Sage's prior reflections on death. The NRSV universalizes the language in this verse so that what in Hebrew is "there is a righteous one perishing in his righteousness" becomes "there are righteous people who perish in their righteousness." Not only does this change have gender implications, making it appear that Qoheleth intended women as part of his audience when the Hebrew makes that less clear, but the NRSV

---

1. Harold S. Kushner, *When Bad Things Happen to Good People* (New York: Schocken Books, 1981).

Qoh 7:15-29

[15]In my vain life I have seen everything; there are righteous people who perish in their righteousness, and there are wicked people who prolong their life in their evildoing. [16]Do not be too righteous, and do not act too wise; why should you destroy yourself? [17]Do not be too wicked, and do not be a fool; why should you die before your time? [18]It is good that you should take hold of the one, without letting go of the other; for the one who fears God shall succeed with both.

[19]Wisdom gives strength to the wise more than ten rulers that are in a city.

[20]Surely there is no one on earth so righteous as to do good without ever sinning.

[21]Do not give heed to everything that people say, or you may hear your servant cursing you; [22]your heart knows that many times you have yourself cursed others.

[23]All this I have tested by wisdom; I said, "I will be wise," but it was

version may make this injustice seem more pervasive since it creates a plural rather than a singular subject.

Qoheleth's stark observation in verse 15 notably challenges the traditional view of retribution theology found elsewhere in the Hebrew Bible. Though Job also poses experiential challenges to a divinely run retributive justice (9:20-24; 10:15-16), Qoheleth arguably uses this aspect of experience to develop what we would now call a "hermeneutic of suspicion." In other words, Qoheleth uses experience to challenge traditional theology: 3:16-22; 7:15-18; and 8:10-15 are good examples of this. Qoheleth's theological observations are rooted in an experience-based methodology that prompts rigorous questioning of traditional views. As I have described elsewhere, for Qoheleth, "seeing gives rise to disbelieving."[2] This rigorous questioning of experience over against cultural "norms" creates an ongoing struggle to which many women can relate because religion, Scripture, and culture have systematically excluded women. Ironically, the same methodology that women have devised in order to authentically inhabit a world infected by patriarchy similarly marks the work of the arguably misogynistic Qoheleth.[3]

2. Lisa Michele Wolfe, "Seeing Gives Rise to Disbelieving: Experiences That Prompt a Hermeneutic of Suspicion in Ecclesiastes and Wendy Farley's Theodicy of Compassion" (PhD diss., Northwestern University, 2003).

3. Ibid., 187–88; also see afterword in this volume: "Qoheleth as a Model for Feminist Hermeneutics."

far from me. [24]That which is, is far off, and deep, very deep; who can find it out? [25]I turned my mind to know and to search out and to seek wisdom and the sum of things, and to know that wickedness is folly and that foolishness is madness. [26]I found more bitter than death the woman who is a trap, whose heart is snares and nets, whose hands are fetters; one who pleases God escapes her, but the sinner is taken by her. [27]See, this is what I found, says the Teacher, adding one thing to another to find the sum, [28]which my mind has sought repeatedly, but I have not found. One man among a thousand I found, but a woman among all these I have not found. [29]See, this alone I found, that God made human beings straightforward, but they have devised many schemes.

Following Qoheleth's suspicious antithetical parallelism of צדיק, "righteous," and רשע, "wicked," in verse 15, the Sage links those terms directly to a pair of strange imperative commands on the same topics. "Do not be too righteous" in verse 16 seems a rather shocking instruction coming from any sage. Qoheleth pairs that admonition with "Do not be too wicked," which also seems an odd thing for a sage to say—we would expect a no-holds-barred "Do not be wicked!" Indeed, in verse 16, Qoheleth mocks the traditional view of wisdom and righteousness, identifying neither righteousness nor wisdom as reliable for producing either negative or positive results. Furthermore, as Qoheleth makes clear in 7:16b, excessive efforts to attain righteousness and wisdom may be fruitless. Precisely because Qoheleth cannot "see" wisdom and righteousness (or wickedness and foolishness) as means to certain ends, the Sage ultimately recommends that people grapple with the traditional view of retribution theology (vv. 16-18a) and in turn that they fear the God who is responsible for this unpredictable life (v. 18b). We cannot know the outcomes of any of our behaviors, we cannot produce them, we cannot rely on God for them, so we must not make "great" effort in any direction.

"Not too much of this; not too much of that"—the general gist of verses 16-17—sounds like a call to moderation, but philosophers and theologians would exclude "not too wicked" (v. 17) from the moderate zone of their morality spectrum. This should not count as Aristotle's "golden mean" because, as Michael V. Fox argues, in that "peripatetic ideal . . . wisdom is not one of the extremes to be avoided. Wisdom is the midpoint between two extremes, which are too much and too little of any quality, while folly is defined as either extreme."[4] Furthermore, Aristotle explains that "not every action nor every passion admits of a mean." He uses the examples of "unjust, cowardly, and self-indulgent action . . . for at that rate there would be a mean of excess and of deficiency, and excess of excess, and a deficiency of deficiency."[5] So Qoheleth departs here not only from the biblical wisdom tradition but also from Greek philosophy. Qoheleth has again crafted provocative words, challenging traditional theology and the very God who prompts such speculation. As for who Qoheleth intends as the audience for these admonitions, the pronoun suffixes are second-person masculine singular. While that does not necessarily exclude women from Qoheleth's audience, it does not necessarily include us either.

In 7:18, a poetic puzzle draws in the readers. The surface structure of the parallelism contradicts its deep structure, making us carefully consider the meaning.[6] We readily visualize the imperatives "take hold" and "letting go" as antithetical on the surface level, yet a closer reading exposes the double-negative "without letting go" in the parallel phrase. The parallelism therefore holds a synonymous meaning on the deep level. Further confusing the verse, the actual object of each phrase— תאחז בזה וגם־מזה, "hold this and also that" (NRSV has "the one" and "the other")—offers no specificity whatsoever. So "you" (masculine, singular), says Qoheleth emphatically, should grasp "both" if you "fear God." This ending presents a vague conclusion to this subsection (7:15-18): to what do "this" and "that" refer? Assuming that "both" at the end of verse 18 refers to "this" and "that" from the beginning of the verse only reiterates our question. The usual reading assumes that the "both" indicates Qoheleth's advice in the two preceding verses to avoid the excesses of righteousness and wisdom.[7] Alongside this perfectly logical interpreta-

---

4. Michael V. Fox notes that his view is "contra Delitzsch, Hertzberg, Gordis." *A Time to Tear Down and a Time to Build Up: A Rereading of Ecclesiastes* (Grand Rapids, MI: Eerdmans, 1999), 260. Fox's view has support from C. C. W. Taylor, "Doctrine of the Mean," in *Oxford Companion to Philosophy*, ed. Ted Honderich (New York: Oxford University Press, 1995), 540. Aristotle writes in *Eth. Nic.* 1106b:36–1107a:1, "Excellence, then, is a state concerned with choice, lying in a mean relative to us, this being determined by reason and in the way in which the man of practical wisdom would determine it."

5. *Eth. Nic.* 1107a:9–23.

6. On surface and deep structure, see Adele Berlin, "Introduction to Hebrew Poetry," *NIB* 4:306.

7. Tremper Longman, *The Book of Ecclesiastes*, NICOT (Grand Rapids, MI: Eerdmans, 1998), 197. James L. Crenshaw, *Ecclesiastes: A Commentary*, OTL (Louisville:

tion, I would propose that the vagueness of the whole subsection underscores Qoheleth's overall cynicism about any kind of link between human behavior and divine action.

Qoheleth 7:19 opens with החכמה, literally "the wisdom." This attribute continues the theme of wisdom that runs throughout the chapter[8] and notably envelops verses 20-22. Similarly, as we will see at the end of the chapter, this theme may be a helpful interpretive lens for understanding Qoheleth's most notoriously misogynistic claims in 7:26-28. As for Qoheleth's references to the "ten rulers" in verse 19, we might think that the verse undermines hierarchy, or even government, in comparison to wisdom. Julie Duncan provides nuance for understanding this point by virtue of a "minor emendation," which renders the translation: "Wisdom gives strength to the wise more than the *wealth of the* rulers who are in the city." As she points out, this places the verse in the wider context of other passages that deem wisdom superior to wealth.[9] Truly, taking the comparison beyond simply wisdom and rulers to wisdom and wealthy rulers ups the ante in a comment that could be taken to critique both political and economic hierarchies.

Verse 20 opens with כי אדם אין, "indeed there is no אדם ['*adam*, 'man' or 'human']," raising the question of gender applicability for this proverb about the limits of righteousness and the ubiquity of sin. Yet again, we must return to the conundrum I explored in the introduction, which is to wonder whether this proverb originally applied to both women and men, and thus translate אדם as "human," or whether this proverb originally applied only to men, and thus translate אדם as "men." Certainly, the proverb has relevance for all humans. Based on Qoheleth's discourse in general, however, we can safely surmise that the Sage here only had men "in mind." After all, at the end of chapter 7, Qoheleth shows us that women are more to be objectified as examples in the Sage's proverbs than to be preached to as part of the Sage's audience.

Westminster John Knox, 1987), 142, and Roland E. Murphy, *Ecclesiastes*, WBC 23A (Nashville: Thomas Nelson, 2018), 70, provide similar interpretations. Whybray states, "Qoheleth's advice is positive: 'Do not sin in either of these two ways [vv. 16-17].'" Roger N. Whybray, "Qoheleth the Immoralist (Qoh 7:16-17)," in *Israelite Wisdom: Theological and Literary Essays in Honor of Samuel Terrien*, ed. John G. Gammie (Missoula, MT: Scholars Press, 1978), 201.

8. Vv. 4, 5, 7, 10, 11, 12 [2x], 16, 19 [2x], 23 [2x], and 25.

9. Julie Ann Duncan, *Ecclesiastes*, AOTC (Nashville: Abingdon, 2017), 107–9; italics hers. The passages she provides as that wider context are "Prov 3:13-15, 16:16; cf. Job 28:15-19."

In a homiletical article on 7:1-19, Rev. Susan R. Andrews interprets the passage broadly as advocating "authenticity," which "assumes imperfection, sinfulness, failure—for 'surely there is no one on earth so righteous as to do good without ever sinning.' (7:20)." Andrews concludes: "According to Qoheleth perfectionism is the opposite of wisdom."[10] True enough, this could be construed as one of Qoheleth's points, though we must note that Qoheleth says quite a bit more about the opposites of wisdom, including celebration (7:4) and oppression (7:7). Nonetheless, Andrews's observation that Qoheleth undermines perfectionism is worth some feminist reflection. In our own culture, perfectionism has been deemed a *bona fide* women's issue in the psychological literature. While this may not have been the case in Qoheleth's time, perfectionism in contemporary women has been researched in relation to the following areas: "academic; romance; competition; appearance; and (self) silencing."[11] Margo Maine and Joe Kelly observe that "few Western women can escape 21st-century media and marketing's promotion of myths about the body and perfection. Every day, this culture-as-family tells us that the most important and valuable thing about a woman is her external appearance."[12] One study discovered that "women who feel pressure to present as perfect to others are especially likely to experience distress and silence their voices in relationships."[13] In an impeccably well-researched memoir entitled *Wonder Women: Sex, Power, and the Quest for Perfection*, Debora L. Spar offers the critique that "insofar as [feminism] told women to pursue their dreams, so, too, did it lure them into the perpetual pursuit of perfection."[14] Similarly, Schrick et al. have observed that "the attempt to appear perfect is a central aspect of doing gender for women in Western cultures."[15] In light of this, perhaps 7:20, "no אדם can be so righteous on earth that they can only do good and not sin," offers support for women who have been inundated with perfectionistic ideals in our culture. This is more so in the NRSV and NIV translations of the verse, in which "no one" can be perfect, leaving the gender of the audience open, in contrast to the more androcentric Hebrew. Here is

10. Susan R. Andrews, "Ecclesiastes 7:1-19," *Int* 55 (2001): 300.

11. Brittney Schrick et al., "Never Let Them See You Sweat: Silencing and Striving to Appear Perfect among U.S. College Women," *Sex Roles* 67 (2012): 591–604.

12. Margo Maine and Joe Kelly, *Pursuing Perfection: Eating Disorders, Body Myths, and Women at Midlife and Beyond* (New York; London: Routledge, 2016), 121.

13. Schrick et al., "Never Let Them See You Sweat," 599.

14. Debora L. Spar, *Wonder Women: Sex, Power, and the Quest for Perfection* (New York: Farrar, Straus and Giroux, 2013), 99.

15. Schrick et al., "Never Let Them See You Sweat," 602.

another case in which an inclusive translation and a feminist interpretation can provide a liberative reading for women, despite the misogynistic statements that arise in 7:26-29. If we follow Andrews's interpretation, it is possible to ironically enlist 7:20 as an antiperfectionism adage for the purpose of liberating women to speak out rather than self-silence, and to reject rather than internalize appearance and relationship norms.

In some ways, 7:21 and 22 continue this theme of antiperfectionism, yet they add the issue of מְקַלֶּלְךָ, "[is] cursing you," and the way in which that might be problematically overheard. Verses 21-22 may stand alone as aphorisms against careless cursing, yet being sandwiched between the wisdom-laden verses 19 and 23 gives them a more sagacious overtone, something like "advice for the wise about cursing." Qoheleth notably attends to both sides of this scenario, so that it is not only the curses of others that one might overhear (7:21) but additionally being condemned by one's own curses (7:22). These verses suggest a social hierarchy through the idea of being cursed by one's servant. A proverb that assumes its audience could relate to having a servant suggests a privileged group. Furthermore, is there not some added sting to being cursed behind one's back, not only by just anyone, but by one's servant? Nonetheless, the following verse's note that "you have yourself cursed others" undermines that hierarchy somewhat, by suggesting that the admonition is more about cursing overall than it is about some added shame in being cursed by one's underlings.

We should wonder what might be entailed in the cursing Qoheleth discusses in 7:21-22. The verbal root קלל, which is here translated as "cursing/cursed," appears often in the Hebrew Bible. In the *piel*, as it appears here, the meaning ranges from "dishonor, disparage" (as in Exod 21:17; Lev 20:9) to "belittle" (1 Sam 17:43, Judg 9:27-28) and back to "disparage" here in Qoheleth 7:21-22.[16] Cursing, in the form of gossip, has female associations in our culture, similar to what we saw with perfectionism. A study by Frank McAndrew concludes that "the current evidence about sex differences in gossip . . . indicates that preconceptions about females being more likely to use gossip in an aggressive fashion are more than just anecdotal and more than just a stereotype." He goes on to note that in comparison to men, "women choose indirect relational aggression over physical aggression."[17] Getting back to Qoheleth's larger point about hierarchy, Sally Farley, Diane Timme, and Jason Hart conclude that, "for women, gossip can become an agency of control, allowing

16. J. Scharbert, "קלל *qll*," *TDOT*, 13:39.

17. Francis T. McAndrew, "The 'Sword of a Woman': Gossip and Female Aggression," *Aggression and Violent Behavior* 19 (2014): 196–99.

them to reaffirm their own power within the organization."[18] The anxiety
Qoheleth expresses about being cursed by a servant also betrays the
power that such speech can carry in a hierarchy. While our own culture
regularly deems "gossip"—particularly that of women—as uncouth at
minimum or immoral at worst, both the psychological research and the
Sage's own ancient words indicate its effectiveness as a method for the
powerless to gain traction in a hierarchical structure.

Reading an English translation, we would assume that Qoheleth's
vignette of 7:21-22 may have been directed at women as well as men, due
to the English second-person generic pronouns "you" in these verses.
Intriguingly, the Hebrew does not definitively clarify the gender of that
second-person pronoun. The *ketiv* in verse 22 reads את ("you," feminine),
while the *qere* and pointing have אתה ("you," masculine).[19] It seems fair
enough to assume that the *ketiv* is simply a defective spelling of the
second-person masculine pronoun אתה (the *qere*).[20] Indeed, the Masoretic
marginal notes identify this as the *qere*. Nonetheless, a feminist commentator would be remiss to overlook the feminine pronoun את "hiding" in the unpointed *ketiv*. The gender ambiguity here becomes all the
more intriguing in the context of the upcoming 7:27, which contains yet
another gender ambiguity raised by the MT.[21]

---

18. Sally D. Farley, Diane R. Timme, and Jason W. Hart, "On Coffee Talk and Break-
Room Chatter: Perceptions of Women Who Gossip in the Workplace," *Journal of Social
Psychology* 150 (2010): 365.

19. *Ketiv* means "[is] written" and refers to what appears in the body of the MT.
Qere, "[is] read," indicates a rabbinic tradition about how the word or phrase should
be read and understood. Both terms are from the Aramaic. The *qere* readings represent over a thousand years of rabbinic reading tradition; they currently appear in
the marginal notes of *BHS* and *BHQ* and are noted in various ways in other Hebrew
editions. While traditional interpretations have viewed *qere* as authoritative, *ketiv/qere*
contrasts invite interpretive interest in both readings. Indeed, part of the point of the
qere notations was to prevent scribal changes in the received *ketiv*. Dispute remains
about whether these two readings represent grammatical and spelling changes, varying traditions, or corrections of errors, among other speculated reasons. See William
S. Morrow, "Kethib and Qere" *ABD* 4:24–30.

20. This is also found in 1 Sam 24:18 [19]; Ps 6:3 [4]; Job 1:10; and Neh 9:6. See
BDB, 61b.

21. See additional discussion of this in the introduction, and, in particular, Jennifer
Koosed's analysis on v. 22 in tandem with v. 27 in *(Per)Mutations of Qohelet: Reading
the Body in the Book*, T & T Clark Library of Biblical Studies (New York: Bloomsbury,
2006), 83–84. Athalya Brenner-Idan notes that את appears in Mishnaic Hebrew as a
masculine pronoun (personal correspondence).

As we have seen, chapter 7 as a whole illustrates that Qoheleth is well situated in the thought world of traditional wisdom.[22] The chapter began in the spirit of Proverbs, with a series of better-than sayings (7:1-3). Further on, Qoheleth continues to explore the contrasting traits of the wise and the fool (7:4-12, 17, 19, 25), using language well established in the wisdom corpus: חכם, "wise"; כסיל, "fool"; רשע, "wicked, wickedness." In 7:23, Qoheleth seems to announce a "test of wisdom" akin to that of chapter 2. Qoheleth goes about this "test" with some zeal, using the verb חכם, "to be wise," in the first common (grammatically nongendered) singular: אחכמה, "I will be wise." Christianson notes that this is the only time that verb relates reflexively to the speaker.[23] Yet it seems that in this test of wisdom, Qoheleth is the one found wanting. The Sage concludes in verse 23 that Wisdom (היא, "she," in the feminine) is רחוקה ממני, "far from me." Qoheleth then poetically repeats "far from me" at the beginning of 7:24, "far off is what it is," reiterating this sentiment of distance and thus highlighting the fruitless search for wisdom that began in verse 23. We find an intriguing point of comparison with "far from me" in relation to Wisdom in Proverbs 31:10. That verse asks rhetorically, "Who can find an אשת חיל [a 'mighty woman']?" (which could refer to Woman Wisdom in Prov 1–9). The reference explains that "she" is רחוקה, "distant," though in an opposite manner from what we find in Qoheleth 7:23-24. In Proverbs 31:10, the mighty woman is distant from the value of "jewels," by far exceeding it; here she is distant from Qoheleth. Whether this linguistic connection provides significant insight into our interpretation of Qoheleth 7 has yet to be seen, but an accrual of similar vocabulary between Proverbs' references to Woman Wisdom and some of Qoheleth's more misogynistic passages in verses 25-29 prove at least notable.

Consistent with other parts of Qoheleth, 7:26 provokes widely divergent conclusions from commentators, particularly those concerned with women's issues. The verse reads:

> But I found more bitter than death the woman who is a trap.
> A net is her heart; ropes are her hands.
> One who is good before God will escape from her,
> but the sinner will be captured by her.

---

22. Parts of this analysis are from Lisa M. Wolfe, "Does Qoheleth Hate Women, a Woman, or Woman Folly?," paper presented at the annual meeting of the Southwest Commission on Religious Studies (Dallas, TX, 2013).

23. Eric S. Christianson, *Ecclesiastes through the Centuries*, Blackwell Bible Commentaries (Malden, MA: Blackwell, 2007), 195.

This, in combination with 7:28, has prompted more than one commentator—including myself—to suggest that Qoheleth was a misogynist.[24] Some have suggested that the woman in 7:26 referred to by Qoheleth is Eve;[25] others, that "she" represents "all of womankind."[26] As points of contextual comparison, Thomas Krüger notes that Ben Sira (Sirach) 25:24 and 42:13-14 are similarly "misogynistic," and Antoon Schoors provides a shocking list of similar statements from the likes of Euripides and Diogenes, among others who hail from the Hellenistic period.[27] A comment in the Talmud suggests that the passage refers to Qoheleth's mother,[28] and Mishnah Qoheleth Rabbah views this as a virtual personification of death, citing passages from Proverbs and Ben Sira.[29] Elizabeth Cady Stanton wrote that "Solomon must have had a sad experience in

24. "Qoheleth remains a misogynist." Michael V. Fox, *Qoheleth and His Contradictions*, BLS 18 (Sheffield: Almond, 1989), 238. Others who refer to Qoheleth in this way include Lisa Wolfe in Hea Sun Kim, Mary Lou Blakeman, and Lisa M. Wolfe, *Ecclesiastes: The Meaning of Your Life* (New York: Women's Division General Board of Global Ministries the United Methodist Church, 1995), 41; Carole R. Fontaine, "Ecclesiastes" in *Women's Bible Commentary*, ed. Carol Ann Newsom and Sharon H. Ringe, exp. ed. (Louisville: Westminster John Knox Press, 1998), 162. Eric Christianson lists Christian D. Ginsburg, Robert Gordis, K. Baltzer, Michael V. Fox, and Athalya Brenner as those who see Qoheleth's misogyny for what it is. "Qoheleth the 'Old Boy' and Qoheleth the 'New Man': Misogynism, the Womb and a Paradox in Ecclesiastes," in *A Feminist Companion to Wisdom and Psalms*, FCB, 2nd ser., no. 2, ed. Athalya Brenner-Idan and Carole Fontaine (Sheffield: Sheffield Academic, 1998), 117–26.

25. Duane A Garrett, "Ecclesiastes 7:25-29 and the Feminist Hermeneutic," *CTR* 2 (1988): 315. Also William P. Brown, *Ecclesiastes*, IBC (Louisville: Westminster John Knox, 2011), 84.

26. Delitzsch cited in Johan Yeong-Sik Pahk, "A Syntactical and Contextual Consideration of '*šh* in Qoh. Ix 9," *VT* 51 (2001): 373 n. 18. Michael V. Fox, *The JPS Bible Commentary: Ecclesiastes* (Philadelphia: Jewish Publication Society, 2004), 52, states regarding v. 26, "What Koheleth fears about women is that they 'trap' men by arousing their lust." He compares v. 26b to Prov 18:22.

27. Thomas Krüger, *Qoheleth: A Commentary*, ed. Klaus Baltzer, trans. O. C. Dean, Hermeneia (Minneapolis: Fortress, 2004), 145. Antoon Schoors, *Ecclesiastes* (Leuven: Peeters, 2013), 578–79 also cites the following utterly offensive example: "When [Diogenes] saw women hanged from a tree, he said: 'Oh, if all trees could bear such fruit'" (Diogenes Laertius 6.61).

28. Christianson, *Ecclesiastes through the Centuries*, 198, summarizes the Talmudic reference "our verse is deemed an adequate descriptor of a bad-tempered woman."

29. Ibid., 198. "Midrash Qoheleth associates the woman with death itself." It cites the story of Eve in Gen 3, and Sir 25:24; 26:22.

his relations with women."[30] Some of my Honors Introduction to Biblical Literature students similarly assumed this passage was based on a personal experience. One young woman's response to the passage was, "It seems like he was just talking to a group and then his 'ex' walked in" (referring to v. 26).[31] Another young woman quipped, "Who does he think is going to have his babies?!"[32] And a young man in my class said it sounded like poor Qoheleth got left at the altar.[33] Dominic Rudman links the "trap," "net," and "ropes" of the woman in 7:26 to divine actions elsewhere in the canon and concludes that the woman in this verse acts—with all women—as a "divine agent." He writes, "In a sense, Qoheleth's worldview is one in which Eve has ganged up with God against Adam."[34] I find some merit in the proposals that Qoheleth's rant in verse 26 arises from personal experience. After all, that is where this Sage roots most reflections. Since Qoheleth's experience is so difficult for us to access, though, I want to pursue the possibility that 7:26 here has more to do with wisdom thought than with bad personal relationships.

Reading Qoheleth 7 with Female Figures in Proverbs (Especially Proverbs 1–9)

Proverbs 1–9, and beyond, presents opposing personifications: חכמה, or Woman Wisdom, and her literary foil, whom I will identify as the "Strange" Woman. This personified nemesis of Woman Wisdom has a shape-shifting identity, apparently an attempt to cover the bases of all threats to budding sages, couched in the metaphor of certain kinds of women, cobbled together alternately using a variety of words: זרה,

30. Elizabeth Cady Stanton, *The Woman's Bible* (1895; repr., Boston: Northeastern University Press, 1993), 99. Similarly, Ellen Davis writes on vv. 25-26 that "the highly personal character of this statement distinguishes it from misogyny. It does not purport to be objective reflection on 'how women are.' Rather, it is an honest statement of disappointment, which Koheleth still feels keenly." Ellen F. Davis, *Proverbs, Ecclesiastes, and the Song of Songs* (Louisville: Westminster John Knox, 2000), 205.

31. Jacilyn Kennedy, Honors Introduction to Biblical Literature, OCU Spring 2013, March 5, 2013. This is comparable to Dominic Rudman's comment on v. 26 as a *non sequitur*; see "Woman as Divine Agent in Ecclesiastes," *JBL* 116 (1997): 414 n. 26.

32. Alex Johnson, Honors Introduction to Biblical Literature, OCU Spring 2013, March 5, 2013.

33. Alexander Knight, Honors Introduction to Biblical Literature, OCU Spring 2013, March 5, 2013.

34. Rudman, "Woman as Divine Agent in Qoheleth," 421.

"stranger";[35] נכריה, "foreign";[36], זונה "be or act as a harlot";[37] כסילות, "foolish" (9:13); אולת, "folly" (14:1; "foolish" in the NRSV); אשה מנאפת, "woman
of adultery" (30:20; NRSV has "adulteress"); finally, אשת רע, "wicked
woman" or "evil woman" (6:24; though NRSV provides "another
[woman]"). In the end, Proverbs seems to conflate "those women" as
a unified whole of all that foils wisdom.[38] This rhetoric was likely an
effective way for wisdom teachers to instruct their young male pupils
to choose the way of wisdom and avoid the way of foolishness. They
painted a persuasive picture with these metaphors: "Go to the heroic
Wise Woman who beckons you to a sumptuous meal of food and drink
set out by her servant girls" (a loose summary of Prov 9:1-6). And in
contrast, "Stay away from the foreign, strange, *'other'* woman, who trans-
gresses the boundaries of her home to wander the streets and force her
whore's-mouth onto yours like a bear-trap of seductive words and kisses
that will ultimately lure you like a caught animal into her lover's nest
while her husband is out of town" (a loose summary of Prov 7:5-23).
Both women call, "Hey you, naïve young man, turn in here!" (9:4//9:16).
Certainly, this rhetoric of two opposing women—one whom the male
students were supposed to *choose*, and the other whom they were to *reject*—would have grabbed the imaginations of the young male wisdom
students.

The search for Wisdom in Proverbs, and the simultaneous rejection
of the "Strange" Woman, provides relevant context for Qoheleth 7:23-
29, in which the word-theme מצא, "find," appears eight times in those
seven verses (vv. 26, 27 [2x], 28 [3x], 29), directing us to what Qoheleth
seeks: חכמה, "wisdom," and חשבון, "explanation, sum, scheme, reason"
(repeated in 25, 27, and 29). Complementing the repetitions of "find,"
Qoheleth uses בקש, "seek," three times in the pericope (vv. 25, 28, and
29); in verse 25 it appears as "I turned my mind to know and to search
and to seek wisdom" with a similar intentionality as "I will be wise" in
verse 23. Could the repeated uses of these words indicate Qoheleth's

35. Prov 2:16; 5:3; 5:20; 7:5; 22:14; NRSV translates "loose" in all but 5:20, for which
it provides "another (woman)."

36. Prov 2:16; 5:20; 6:24; 7:5; 23:27; NRSV translates "adulteress" in all of these
instances.

37. Prov 6:26; 7:10; 23:27; NRSV translates "prostitute."

38. For a thorough discussion of this, see Phyllis A. Bird, " 'To Play the Harlot': An
Inquiry into an Old Testament Metaphor," in *Missing Persons and Mistaken Identities:
Women and Gender in Ancient Israel* (Philadelphia: Fortress, 1997), 219–36.

own efforts to seek and find Woman Wisdom? If so, it seems Qoheleth
has been able to find only the "Strange" Woman, but Woman Wisdom
remains elusive. Qoheleth "knows" enough to reject "wickedness" and
"foolishness" (7:25) as any sage would. Qoheleth's discoveries in verses
26-29, however, illustrate the complexity of the problem. We see a similar
process of searching in Proverbs, where the "simple ones" (1:22) look for
Woman Wisdom, but "she" says, "they will not find me" (1:28). Thus,
is 7:23-29, with the theme of unfulfilled seeking, a self-condemnation of
Qoheleth as "simple" or a "fool"? Perhaps even Qoheleth is caught in the
"trap" that is the "Strange" Woman of Proverbs, while Woman Wisdom
stays hidden. It is no surprise to see Qoheleth critiquing the enterprise
of wisdom or, to use the metaphor, to read Qoheleth lamenting the very
elusive nature of Wisdom herself. In fact, it seems fitting for Qoheleth
to boldly take on tradition right on the heels of the antiwisdom saying
in 7:16-17. Along with the repetitions of "find" and "seek" in this passage, the repetition of "far from me" in 7:23-24 corroborates the theme
of Wisdom's distance in 7:23-29 as a whole.

Having examined Qoheleth's rhetoric in this section, and particularly the
connections between the language in chapter 7 and that relating to Woman
Wisdom in Proverbs 1–9, it seems likely that these words arose primarily
out of the Sage's context as an ancient Israelite wisdom teacher rather than
strictly arising out of personal experience or cultural misogynistic ideology.
My hypothesis is that in 7:25-29 Qoheleth was drawing on the imagery of
Proverbs' "Strange" Woman and led up to it with background discussion
of Woman Wisdom, who persistently could not be found in 7:23-24.[39] I find
further support for a connection between Proverbs' "Strange" Woman in
Qoheleth 7:25-29 (arguably the most misogynistic part of the pericope),
where there is a good deal of verbiage linking Qoheleth's description
with the "Strange" Woman of Proverbs, or at least with the book of Proverbs more broadly. In 7:25 Qoheleth rejects רשע, "wickedness," as "folly,"
one conclusion in the search for both wisdom and folly. Similarly, "wickedness" appears throughout Proverbs, notably in 8:7, where it is תועבות,
"abomination," to the mouth of Woman Wisdom. In 7:26, Qoheleth does
not have words for "womankind," as the word "woman" appears with
the definite article: האשה, "the woman." There is little reason to think this
verse applies to women as a whole. It is either about a particular woman
or a particular category of women, though the latter seems less likely

---

39. See also my discussion of this in the author's introduction.

based on the following verses.[40] Qoheleth applies the adjective מַר, "bitter," to the woman they condemn; the same word appears in Proverbs 5:4,
where it applies directly to the "Strange" Woman. Qoheleth's reference
to "bitter" has a comparative purpose—the woman to whom he refers
is said to be "more bitter than death." The word מוּת, "death," appears
also in Proverbs 5:5—the verse following the "bitter" reference—where
"death" is the destination of the "Strange" Woman. So, while Qoheleth
did not lift the exact phrase "more bitter than death" from Proverbs, both
"bitter" and "death" appear in reference to the "Strange" Woman and in
consecutive verses. Furthermore, Proverbs mentions death in the context
of the "Strange" Woman in the similar verses 2:18 and 7:27 (in both cases
her house descends to death) and in 8:36, which asserts that all who hate
Woman Wisdom love death. The מְצוֹדִים, "trap," of Qoheleth 7:26 does
not appear specifically in reference to the "Strange" Woman in Proverbs,
but it does refer to a tool of the "wicked" in Proverbs 12:12. And in 7:26,
Qoheleth uses the verb לכד יִלָּכֵד (לכד) in the *niphal* masculine singular imper-
fect, "[the sinner] is/will be captured [by her]") to describe the woman's
power; the same root in Proverbs describes the fate of those who speak
or act wickedly or carelessly (Prov 5:22; 6:2; 11:6).

I am by no means the first commentator to suggest a link between
Qoheleth's remarks in 7:23-29 and the "Strange" Woman of Proverbs,
or even to propose that the pericope indicates Qoheleth's inability to
find Woman Wisdom, though this latter view is less common.[41] Thomas
Krüger, among others, suggests that 7:26 may refer not to the "Strange"
Woman but instead to Woman Wisdom, based on how she is described
in Ben Sira 6:24-31. There, these restraining attributes of the woman are
disciplinary rather than strictly antagonistic.[42] The view in Ben Sira is

40. With Krüger, *Qoheleth*, 574.
41. Kathleen Anne Farmer, *Who Knows What Is Good? A Commentary on the Books
of Proverbs and Ecclesiastes*, ITC (Grand Rapids, MI: Eerdmans, 1991), 179; Krüger,
Qoheleth, 147; and Duncan, *Ecclesiastes*, 110, all see at least a possible link in 7:26 to
the Strange Woman in Proverbs 1–9. Brown calls the woman of 7:26 "the 'strange
woman' or 'foolish woman' portrayed in the book of Proverbs." He concludes this
based on the definite article on *'ishah* in v. 26, which he says "suggests that the following clause is syntactically restrictive" (Brown, *Ecclesiastes*, 83). Schoors, *Ecclesiastes*,
572–75, includes a helpful summary of views along these lines. Duncan agrees that
"Wisdom, the sage contends, is anything but accessible" (*Ecclesiastes*, 110).
42. Krüger includes his own translation of the Sirach passage, in which he highlights the vocabulary similarities to Qoh 7:26 (*Qoheleth*, 147). Duncan, *Ecclesiastes*, also
argues for this possibility (110–14).

that one should intentionally become confined by the woman's "fetters" (6:24), "net" (v. 29), "bonds" (v. 29), and "cords" (v. 30) because those restrictions would transform into positive—even royal—features such as "rest" and "joy" (6:28) and a "robe" (vv. 29, 31). The passage even mentions "purple" and "gold," heightening the royal aesthetic.[43] Thus Krüger argues that the woman with the negative features in Qoheleth 7:26a may be Qoheleth's description of Woman Wisdom, rather than the "Strange" Woman: "If 'wisdom' is a 'woman' who is as seductive and dangerous as the 'strange woman' against whom Proverbs 1–9 repeatedly warns, then she is 'more bitter than death' (v. 26a)."[44]

Julie Duncan also makes a good case that Qoheleth's harsh language is actually about the elusive Woman Wisdom. Duncan's point is that Qoheleth has had a single-minded focus in this section: Wisdom. Thus, "the sudden appearance of Woman Folly at this moment [would be] abrupt and unintegrated."[45] I find this proposal fascinating because the language of 7:25-29, otherwise applied to the "Strange" Woman, here would be turned toward Woman Wisdom herself. That would indeed be yet another radical move for Qoheleth, essentially collapsing Proverbs' dichotomy between the "Strange" Woman and Woman Wisdom, providing yet another challenge to the wisdom tradition and further muddying our ability to make sense of this section.

Claudia Camp's innovative work, *Wise, Strange, and Holy: The Strange Woman and the Making of the Bible*, potentially unites the seemingly opposite identifications of "the woman" in 7:26 as either Wisdom or "Strange" by describing their relationship as more "paradox" than "polarity." She views these figures as being "in dialectical tension with one another."[46] Thus we would not have to choose whether Qoheleth 7:26 is about Woman Wisdom or the "Strange" Woman; it could be about both—and more. Camp's argument goes on to add historical nuance and relevance to these metaphorical figures, linking them not only to the "strange" foreign women that concerned Ezra and Nehemiah in the reconstruction

---

43. From Krüger's translation of Sirach (*Qoheleth*, 147). Krüger also provides insightful comparisons to Song 4.4; 6.10; 7.5-6 [6-7] and Papyrus Harris 500, all of which additionally illustrate how the confining imagery about the woman in Qoh 7:26a can be viewed in more positive terms (147 n. 20).

44. Ibid., 147.

45. Duncan, *Ecclesiastes*, 111.

46. Claudia V. Camp, *Wise, Strange, and Holy: The Strange Woman and the Making of the Bible*, JSOTSup 320 (Sheffield: Sheffield Academic, 2000), 38.

period but also to a representation of strangeness for priestly concerns. Qoheleth's rhetoric about "strange" women, through Camp's lens, could be not only about personified folly *or* wisdom but "a cipher for deviant (=foreign) worship."[47]

These explanations help make sense of the cultural, historical, and theological frames Qoheleth places on one's interaction with "the woman" of verse 26. In the end, whether we read 7:26 through the lens of the "Strange" Woman, Woman Wisdom, or a complex interrelation of the two, it cannot alleviate the many misogynist readings of the passage that have prevailed over the centuries, something I will discuss in more depth below.

Moving on to Qoheleth 7:27-29, the challenge becomes simply trying to understand Qoheleth's meaning. My wooden translation here illustrates the difficulty:

> [27]See, this I found, said Qoheleth:
> One after another to find an explanation,
> [28]For again I myself sought but I did not find;
> One human in a thousand I found,
> But a woman in all these I did not find.
> [29]See, this alone I found:
> That God made the אדם upright,
> But they sought many explanations.

Commentators have understandably produced numerous interpretations of these vague verses. We find a fascinating gender complication in 7:27, in which the verb paired with the noun "Qoheleth" seems to be grammatically feminine. The standard solution for this "problem" has been to make the slightest emendation, moving the final letter of the verb (the feminine ending ה-) to the beginning of the following word, Qoheleth. There, it would function as the definite article ה-, for "the Qoheleth" (coinciding with what we find in MT 12:8 and 1:2 LXX), rendering Qoheleth's verb masculine once again so that we have אמר הקהלת, "the Qoheleth said." Yet why not the opposite proposal, in which we would emend 12:8 to move the definite article from Qoheleth (after all, this title appears most often with no article) to the verb, making it feminine? This proposal has received little, but notable, support. T. Anthony Perry suggests "postulating that our verse and 12:10 [which appears with a masculine verb and Qoheleth has no definite article] are further

47. Ibid., 61.

instances of denying female authorship. At the very least, there seems to be as good a reason to speak of a Lady Kohelet as of a 'Lady J' in the Pentateuch, as Harold Bloom (1990) has proposed."[48] Perry alternately argued the possibility that Qoheleth "feminizes his name" for the sake of "self-diminution."[49] Jennifer Koosed views this instance and 7:22's feminine pronoun as a way to see that "the gender ideologies in the text deconstruct themselves."[50] Truly, this may be a more helpful interpretive approach than to try to pin down Qoheleth's views on women.

Verse 28 raises another set of challenges for the interpreter; consequently, varying views of it abound. Krüger cites Diethelm Michel's paraphrase of verse 28b thus: "One finds one person among a thousand [sc. as true friend], but for this, a woman is out of the question."[51] Yet Krüger goes on to describe his own different view of the verse, in which "he found not a single woman who is 'more bitter than death' or exhibits the other characteristics named there, but at most some men who fit this description."[52] Furthermore, Krüger suggests an arguably feminist reading in proposing that the verse describes the wholly androcentric circle of sages, in which there is not a woman to be found.[53] Michael V. Fox compares the reference to "a thousand" in 7:28 to Solomon's thousand wives, who were described as his downfall in both 1 Kings 11:1-11 and Nehemiah 13:25-26.[54] Yet he concludes that "7:28 shows that Koheleth is denouncing all of womankind, not just the wicked among them, for he cannot find even one (satisfactory) woman in a thousand." Indeed, as Fox points out, Qoheleth is not even as optimistic as the author of Proverbs 31:10-31, who extols the "rare"—but existent—gem of a perfect wife.

---

48. Harold Bloom, *The Book of J*, trans. David Rosenberg (New York: Grove, 1990), quoted in T. Anthony Perry, *Dialogues with Kohelet: The Book of Ecclesiastes; Translation and Commentary* (University Park: Pennsylvania State University Press, 1993), 178. See also my discussion, "Qoheleth: Book, Person, Persona," in the author's introduction.

49. Perry, *Dialogues with Kohelet*, 132. Schoors rejects this proposal firmly. "If קהלת is a feminine character that has been replaced by a masculine, why has one instance escaped this patriarchal operation[?] It is by far more probable that the phrase in 7:27 is the result of a mechanical error, which has not been emended by the Masoretes out of respect for the text" (Schoors, *Ecclesiastes*, 30).

50. Jennifer Koosed, "Ecclesiastes," in *Women's Bible Commentary*, ed. Carol Ann Newsom, Sharon H. Ringe, and Jacqueline E. Lapsley, 3rd ed. (Louisville: Westminster John Knox, 2012), 245.

51. Krüger, *Qoheleth*, 148.

52. Ibid., 148.

53. Ibid.

54. Fox, *Ecclesiastes*, 52.

Instead, the negative comments about specific types of women in Proverbs 22:14 and 23:27 serve as a model: "Koheleth, however, here asserts that *all* women are like that."[55] My own view of 7:28 has to do with my reading of the larger pericope and the wisdom context to which it relates. Clearly, determining meaning in 7:28 requires a certain amount of filling in the gaps based on reading the wider context—always a tricky business.

Verse 29 returns to Qoheleth's word-theme of מצא, "find." But again, Qoheleth is unclear about what is found or how this relates to the preceding verses. The statement begins with an intriguing echo of "see, this I found" from verse 27, supplemented with לבד, "only" or "alone," and continues with a theological assertion that seems positive, "God made 'the human' [אדם] upright," followed by an anthropological assertion that seems negative, "But they sought many explanations." At least the sexist remarks seem to have ended with this verse, yet perhaps this verse relates closely to the "human" in 28b, who stands over against the one unfound woman there. Qoheleth is apparently weighing the foibles of humanity—and especially women, in verse 28—against the nature of God, a topic the Sage also took up in 7:13. Humans seem to be the ones lacking, at least in this particular passage. Additionally, Qoheleth may view women, or a woman, or Woman Wisdom, or the "Strange" Woman, as more culpable than men. In light of this analysis, I conclude that verses 27-29 describe Qoheleth's inability to find Woman Wisdom, in contrast to the entrapment of the "Strange Woman" in verse 26. This proposal furthermore relies on my analysis, starting back in 7:23, that the word-theme "find" in the passage illustrates that Qoheleth cannot find Wisdom.[56]

And what of the accusation of Qoheleth as a misogynist in 7:26-29? It seems possible to argue that if Qoheleth is talking about the personifications of Woman Wisdom and the "Strange" Woman rather than about actual women, that might really get the Sage "off the hook," as it were, as a woman-hater. But an effective metaphor has to be grounded in the audience's shared assumptions about the imagery it uses. Thus the Proverbs-based "good-versus-evil-woman" rhetoric situates Qoheleth in the androcentric, patriarchal, even misogynistic context of ancient Israelite sages. Going back to Proverbs 7:4-5, we read Woman Wisdom's pleas to stay away from the "Strange" Woman. Amid that rhetoric, the sages

---

55. Ibid., 51, italics his.
56. With Rudman, "Woman as Divine Agent in Ecclesiastes," 412–13.

include a parallelism that connects זרה, "strange" (NRSV "loose"), and
נכריה, "foreign" (NRSV "adulteress"). Thus the worldview of Proverbs
is itself rooted in arguably misogynistic, even xenophobic, assumptions;
it draws on the belief that women—especially women who are not of
our people—are not only antithetical to Wisdom's ideals but ultimately
dangerous as well. These negative stereotypes of women in the context
of ancient Israel's sages are what made the "Woman Wisdom versus
Strange Woman" metaphors effective. Based on the fact that even one
of the most progressive, academic, recent Bible translations picks up
on these assumptions with its translations (NRSV with "loose" and
"adulteress"), our contemporary context continues to assist in making
these metaphors effective. In that way, Qoheleth does not get "off the
hook" for using these comments just because they are personifications
or metaphors. Qoheleth's poetry and prose exude the misogynistic aura
of the culture in which they were composed.

If we scan to the other end of the meaning horizon, we find plenty to
lament in the reception history of this passage. The late fifteenth-century
guide to inquisitions against witches, the *Malleus Maleficarum, The Hammer against Witches*, invokes Qoheleth 7:26 (just one of many Bible verses
enlisted) to make its case for the violent and lethal prosecution of women
accused as witches.[57] Such a publication might seem insignificant, but
its sales were "second only to the Bible" up to the time of the *Pilgrim's
Progress* (1678).[58] This handbook was used alongside other similar publications to aid in the centuries-long "great witch-hunt" in Europe from
the sixteenth to the eighteenth centuries CE, resulting in the trials of
up to ninety thousand persons and the deaths (usually by burning)
of up to forty-five thousand. In most locations, 75 percent or more of

57. See the excerpt of the *Malleus* at the end of this chapter.
58. "*Malleus Maleficarum* (The Witch Hammer)," in *The Encyclopedia of Witches,
Witchcraft and Wicca*, by Rosemary Ellen Guiley, 3rd ed. (New York: Checkmark
Books, 2008), 223. Also see the thorough treatment of the *Malleus* and its relationship
to Qoheleth in Carole R. Fontaine, " 'Many Devices' (Qoheleth 7.23–8.1): Qoheleth,
Misogyny and the *Malleus Maleficarum*," in *Wisdom and Psalms: A Feminist Companion
to the Bible*, FCB 2nd ser. no. 2, ed. Athalya Brenner and Carole Fontaine (Sheffield:
Sheffield Academic Press, 1998), 137–68, at 161 *et passim*. The following essay in that
volume shows that the wisdom literature was not a major pillar of support for those
who persecuted women but rather places those parts of Scripture into a wider context
of materials used for the purposes of misogyny. Brian B. Noonan, "Wisdom Literature among the Witchmongers," in Brenner and Fontaine, *A Feminist Companion to
Wisdom and Psalms*, 169–74.

these individuals were women.[59] Carole R. Fontaine's discussion of the *Malleus* and Qoheleth 7 provides a thorough discussion of the various factors contributing to the witch hunt in Europe, from pre-Reformation religious animosity to the burgeoning number of widows created by illness.[60] In New England from 1620 to 1725, witchcraft accusations were leveled against "at least 344 persons," 78 percent of whom were female; of those, thirty-five were executed, 80 percent of whom were female.[61] The sentiments openly expressed in the *Malleus Maleficarum* help explain the "submerged assumptions" driving the New England witch hunts.[62] One short passage of the witch-hunters' manual repeats the phrase "more bitter than death" (Qoh 7:26a) four times, concluding: "More bitter than death, again, because bodily death is an open and terrible enemy, but woman is a wheedling and secret enemy."[63]

The excerpt at the end of this chapter from the *Malleus Maleficarum* enlists Qoheleth to further validate its condemnation of witchcraft in the fifteenth century. I have highlighted the portions that directly quote from Qoheleth. The phrase "more bitter than death" appears not only in the full quote of the verse but four additional times as a refrain that departs from the purported main topic of the *Malleus*—the detection and elimination of witches—to rail against women in general. "More bitter than death" here relates to "the sin of Eve" who "tempted" Adam, consequently bringing "death to our soul and body"; "more bitter than death" indicates that woman removes "grace" and leaves the body in "sin." Finally, the authors reason, woman is "more bitter than death" because her evil is deceptive and hidden, while that of death itself is clear for all to see. The *Malleus* authors further explicate 7:26 in order to substantiate their views on witches and women, especially by repeating certain words. These include "snare," which can be created by a woman's tears and works through women's hearts for the sake of the devil; "net," which is associated with female hatred; and "hands are

59. Brian P. Levack, *The Witch-Hunt in Early Modern Europe*, 3rd ed. (New York: Routledge, 2006), 23, 141.

60. Fontaine also provides a detailed analysis of the rhetoric in the *Malleus*. Fontaine, "Many Devices," 158–59.

61. Carol F. Karlsen, *The Devil in the Shape of a Woman: Witchcraft in Colonial New England* (New York: W. W. Norton & Company, 1998), 47–49.

62. Ibid., 159.

63. Quoted in Elizabeth A. Clark and Herbert Richardson, eds., *Women and Religion: The Original Sourcebook of Women in Christian Thought* (New York: Harper Collins, 1996), 128–29.

as bands for binding," which happens in cooperation with the devil. From the beginning of the *Malleus* we find the argument that the main problem with witches was not their own power but that they worked in partnership with the devil, for instance, laying hands on humans and animals in order to place the devil into them.[64] On this point, and that of its underlying wholesale misogyny, the authors fashion Qoheleth 7:27 into a readily helpful prop for articulating the point they already intend to make. By the end of the passage, it is clear that since women were not fortunate enough to have had their sex physically represented by Jesus, they are not saved by Jesus, either. Thus we see that *The Hammer against Witches* served ultimately as a hammer against women.

It seems remarkable that Western civilization has even remotely re-covered from this horrific, three-hundred-year period of institutional-ized misogyny, which resulted in the execution of tens of thousands of women or even more, depending on the researcher.[65] Elizabeth A. Clark and Herbert Richardson highlight "as particularly egregious examples, in 1585 two German villages were left with only one female inhabitant each."[66] The use of Qoheleth to fuel this gynocide to some extent sul-lies the text, no matter the author's original intent. Thus contemporary women may desire to reject Qoheleth due to the text's complicity (albeit unintentional) in one of history's deadliest chapters for the women and girls whom we may call mothers and sisters. Indeed, some self-identified pagan communities view this women's holocaust as worthy of special homage and memorial.[67]

---

64. Part 1, question 2, *et passim*. Also see part 3, Third Head, question 19, p. 3, regarding heresy and a witch's methods.

65. The numbers are somewhat disputed. Clark and Richardson state in *Women and Religion*, "From 1450 to 1750 tens (and perhaps hundreds) of thousands were accused and executed for witchcraft" (119). Brian Levack makes a nearly identical statement in *The Witch-Hunt in Early Modern Europe*, 1; he discusses the varying totals of those executed and prosecuted and concludes, "The total number of Europeans who were prosecuted for witchcraft probably did not exceed 90,000" (21). Furthermore, he as-serts, "We might reasonably conclude that European courts executed about 45,000 witches during the early modern period" (23).

66. Clark and Richardson, *Women and Religion*, 120; citing Hugh R. Trevor-Roper, *The European Witch-Craze of the 16th and 17th Centuries* (London: Penguin, 1990), 76.

67. For instance, this web page discusses witch hunts and information about their death toll: http://www.summerlands.com/crossroads/remembrance/burning.htm. It appears as part of "The Hall of Remembrance" on summerlands.com, which is described as "a Cyber Community, existing within an Other-worldly time and space . . . a safe haven for Druids and Witches and Pagans (oh my!)." Also see

Is it fair to blame Qoheleth for unintended consequences of these ancient words? Perhaps not. But it is surely fair and even responsible to consider the effects they have had throughout history. The evil-temptress-home-wrecker-seductive-foreign woman we meet in Proverbs persists in popular as well as religious consciousness. Carol Newsom makes a strong and intriguing case for this in her article "Woman and the Discourse of Patriarchal Wisdom," in which she highlights the seductive, crafty, and ultimately terrifying femme fatale Alex, played by Glenn Close in the 1987 film *Fatal Attraction*.[68] Skipping ahead to 2003, one prominent femme fatale to trap unsuspecting men with her nets and ropes (and to inspire young women that this is a great way to get noticed) was Britney Spears. This "best-selling teenaged artist of all time" turned out singles with titles including "Toxic" and "S&M."[69] Notably, the lingerie-like outfits on Britney and her dancers and backup singers from the *Femme Fatale* tour not only called to mind traps, nets, and ropes (as in Qoh 7:26) but also were eerily reminiscent of the prime femme fatale of my generation, Madonna, reminding us of the recurrence of these archetypes.[70] These are only more recent examples of the trope "dangerous woman who entraps men"—which in turn can make all women suspect of behaving in that manner. A related question has to do with women who voluntarily portray themselves this way, rather than being objectified in this way by men—does that subvert the misogyny or just make it self-loathing?

Usually in a metaphor the better-known item, the vehicle, explains the lesser-known item, the tenor. In this case, a "Strange" or Wise Woman personifies foolishness or wisdom, respectively. Often, the stated logic of a metaphor slips or reverses. This occurs here, in the case of Qoheleth's use of "Strange" Woman imagery: the reversed metaphor asserts that the general category "women" equates with strange, foreign, other, terrifying seductresses to avoid and, presumably, to be controlled—for safety's sake. Given that, the metaphor itself is and was misogynistic, rooted in

---

http://www.witchway.net/times/times.html; http://www.sacred-texts.com/bos/bos256.htm; seventeenth-century Norwegian witch executions have even prompted a memorial in Vardø, http://www.dezeen.com/2012/01/03/steilneset-memorial-by-peter-zumthor-and-louise-bourgeois/.

68. In Peggy Lynne Day, *Gender and Difference in Ancient Israel* (Minneapolis: Fortress, 1989), 142–60.

69. Melissa Ruggieri, "Music Notes," *Richmond Times-Dispatch* (December 19, 2000), D.13. Britney Spears, *In the Zone* (Jive Records, 2003).

70. Madonna, *Like a Virgin* (song and album of the same name) (Sire Records, 1984).

misogynistic assumptions that arose from a misogynistic culture. Thus, even if Qoheleth were rightly rejecting the personified, metaphorical Strange Woman rather than "women," the association of women with strangeness, adultery, and folly is and has been problematic (to say the least) for real women.

To that point, way back in 1861, C. D. Ginsburg made the understated observation that "men making women the embodiment of wickedness 'in all ages' has been 'to the detriment of themselves, the female sex, and society at large.'"[71] Similarly, the contemporary novelist Louise Erdrich writes:

> These words have stood through time in thought, no doubt been spoken from pulpits, used to punish uppity and opinionated women, been cited as God's actual credo on the female subject. These are words that have done historical harm, and yet they were probably written in the same short-sighted spirit that any gender uses in complaining about the other. That barstool spleen taken as divine revelation casts a sick pall upon the acquired wisdom of Koheleth.

Erdrich clearly admires this Sage. She observes, "I've never developed an attitude of mature acceptance, of heightened pleasantness, of genteel correctness about our uncertain lot, so I read Koheleth."[72] Erdrich's key here is in raising the issue of biblical authority through her phrase "taken as divine revelation." Were it not for the fact that these ambiguous or misogynistic statements appear in the sacred text, they would surely not have caused women so much trouble throughout history.

In sum, the likelihood that Qoheleth is referring to the "Strange" Woman of Proverbs in the scathing comments of 7:26-28 does not necessarily preclude misogyny. It may only spread the blame somewhat to the cohort of sages who were Qoheleth's community, to the wider culture of Qoheleth's time, and even perhaps to those who eventually determined to include Qoheleth in the canon. Furthermore, Qoheleth's apparently woman-friendly comment in Qoheleth 9:9 does not undo these earlier slurs. There, Qoheleth surprisingly enough commends the (apparently male) audience to "Enjoy life with the woman/wife that you

---

71. Paraphrased by Christianson, *Ecclesiastes through the Centuries*, 200; C. D. Ginsburg, *Coheleth (Commonly Called the Book of Ecclesiastes)* (1861; repr., New York: KTAV, 1970), 387.

72. Louise Erdrich, "The Preacher," in *Out of the Garden: Women Writers on the Bible*, ed. Christina Büchmann and Celina Spiegel (New York: Fawcett Columbine, 1995), 237, 236.

love." Given the above considerations, this should cause us to wonder how much that woman would have enjoyed her life!

The issue for women since Qoheleth's time and up to the present day is that we cannot seem to get out of the line of fire, given Qoheleth's enduring statements. The ambiguity—in which 7:26 might refer to the "Strange" Woman or to Woman Wisdom or to some random adulterous woman (whose crime remains vague) or to all women, or that 7:28 just might say something positive about women or it might say something negative about women—leaves women, as usual, vulnerable to the whims of cultural interpretations and co-optations. Qoheleth, as much as it might provide resources for women's own rebellious theology-making, just seems dangerous for us.[73] But that itself can be a valuable aspect of the Bible. A difficult text, like Qoheleth 7:15-29, gives women Bible interpreters the opportunity to make the courageous theological move akin to that of Howard Thurman's grandmother in Renita Weems's classic essay, "African American Women and the Bible."[74] Thurman would read the Bible to his grandmother, a former slave. But she persistently refused to hear anything from Paul's writings other than 1 Corinthians 13, the so-called Love Chapter. The pro-slavery parts of the Pauline Epistles (which most scholars would now refer to as pseudo-Pauline or disputed Pauline Epistles) had been used so often to keep her in her place as a slave that she in turn rejected the biblical authority of the Epistles as a whole. Will and should women similarly reject Qoheleth 7 as a hopelessly violence-inducing, historically tainted chapter? Or all of Qoheleth? Or do these troubling passages, amid challenges to traditional doctrine, offer us solidarity in an utterly complex existence? While Thurman's grandmother may have missed the freedom-inspiring Galatians 3:28 through her rejection of Paul's letters, we too could lose Qoheleth's repeated and crucial challenges to simplistic theology, such as in 8:14-15, and the ongoing calls to "seize the day" as a salve to an incoherent life. Or perhaps, with Thurman's grandmother, in avoiding the pro-slavery texts in the Epistles and the misogyny in Qoheleth, we are better off.

If Qoheleth 7 indeed relies on the Woman Wisdom/"Strange" Woman dialectic of Proverbs, then we should go on to consider questions that scholars—feminists and otherwise—have asked about the possibility of

73. See author's introduction.

74. Renita Weems, "Reading *Her Way* through the Bible: African American Women and the Bible," in *Stony the Road We Trod: African American Biblical Interpretation*, ed. Cain Hope Felder (Minneapolis: Fortress, 1991), 61–62.

suppressed goddess imagery in those personifications.[75] In her ground-breaking work *In the Wake of the Goddesses: Women, Culture and the Biblical Transformation of Pagan Myth*, Tikva Frymer-Kensky argues that the reason goddesses were associated with women has to do with the caregiving and teaching roles that women in the ancient Near East held. Frymer-Kensky notes that two powerful female figures open and close Proverbs, one "cosmic" (in Prov 8) and the other "the very prototype of the wise woman" (Prov 31:10-30).[76] If ancient Near Eastern goddesses lie behind the dialectic in Proverbs, then we could consider these deities at least vestigial in Qoheleth 7.

Qoheleth's Disinterest in Women and African Women's Disinterest in Qoheleth

"One man among a thousand I found, But a woman among all these I have not found." (Qoh 7:28)

Qoheleth 7:28 is said to point to unflattering and misogynist attitudes toward women that are common in ancient literature, and it reinforces negative statements about women in general. Although Qoheleth makes the statement in his search for virtue and in reference to men who might escape from the snare of a dangerous woman, the statement may well apply to instances in which men (or even women) stand out. It presupposes that in many situations in which one would find a rare man in a thousand, it is possible not to find a single woman among them. In other words, one has to look beyond a thousand men to find a rare woman. It is not surprising, however, that the last part of the verse is easily overlooked, perhaps because in the Old Testament world one would truly have to look beyond a thousand men to find an outstanding woman. It also appears that Qoheleth has not much to say about women or to women—they do not matter very much in his worldview, hence only six clear references to women occur in his reflections (2:7, 8; 5:15 [14]; 7:26, 28; 9:9) compared to approximately a hundred references to men besides the numerous references to kings, princes, sons, servants, brothers, etc.

---

75. Bernhard Lang's research in his *Wisdom and the Book of Proverbs: A Hebrew Goddess Redefined* (Cleveland: Pilgrim Press, 1986) initiated the conversation that Frymer-Kensky continued and nuanced with *In the Wake of the Goddesses: Women, Culture, and the Biblical Transformation of Pagan Myth* (Glencoe, IL: Free Press, 1992).

76. Frymer-Kensky, *In the Wake of the Goddesses*, 180.

The wisdom and philosophy of Qoheleth, which he presumably centers on men and addresses to a male audience, contrasts sharply with the book of Proverbs, which, in a sense, is regarded as "female friendly" because it is characterized by strong feminine imagery. Thus Proverbs, with its depiction of wisdom as a woman figure, shows that wisdom is not the exclusive preserve of males, as Qoheleth (c)overtly suggests. In the context of studies of wisdom literature in Africa the book of Qoheleth—unlike Proverbs—has received rather minimal attention, and of the few studies or notes that are available on the book, it is hard to find one by a woman. Female scholars, in particular African female biblical scholars, seem to be as disinterested in Qoheleth as much as he is in them! But there is a need for more (African) female scholars to brace up and demystify the androcentric wisdom of Qoheleth, if only to show the "meaninglessness" of a wisdom that ignores and denounces women or that at best places them at the disposal of men (9:9). An outstanding woman in the world of the Preacher could be a literary rarity; it is not necessarily a theological or sociological reality![77]

Funlola Olojede

Extract from **The Malleus Maleficarum (The Hammer Against Witches)** *of Heinrich Kramer and James Sprenger*

If we inquire, we find that nearly all the kingdoms of the world have been overthrown by women. Troy, which was a prosperous kingdom, was, for the rape of one woman, Helen, destroyed, and many thousands of Greeks slain. The kingdom of the Jews suffered much misfortune and destruction through the accursed Jezebel, and her daughter Athaliah, queen of Judah, who caused her son's sons to be killed, that on their death she might reign herself; yet each of them was slain. The kingdom of the Romans endured much evil through Cleopatra, Queen of Egypt, that worst of women. And so with others. Therefore it is no wonder if the world now suffers through the malice of women.

---

77. References: Fox, *Ecclesiastes*, xii, 48; Krüger, *Qoheleth*, 145–48; Jamal-Dominic Hopkins, "Qoheleth," in *The Africana Bible: Reading Israel's Scriptures from Africa and the African Diaspora*, ed. R. Hugh and Randall C. Bailey (Minneapolis: Fortress, 2009), 260–65.

And now let us examine the carnal desires of the body itself, whence has arisen unconscionable harm to human life. Justly we may say with Cato of Utica: If the world could be rid of women, we should not be without God in our intercourse. For truly, without the wickedness of women, to say nothing of witchcraft, the world would still remain proof against innumerable dangers. Hear what Valerius said to Rufinus: You do not know that woman is the Chimaera, but it is good that you should know it; for that monster was of three forms; its face was that of a radiant and noble lion, it had the filthy belly of a goat, and it was armed with the virulent tail of a viper. And he means that a woman is beautiful to look upon, contaminating to the touch, and deadly to keep.

Let us consider another property of hers, the voice. For as she is a liar by nature, so in her speech she stings while she delights us. Wherefore her voice is like the song of the Sirens, who with their sweet melody entice the passers-by and kill them. For they kill them by emptying their purses, consuming their strength, and causing them to forsake God. Again Valerius says to Rufinus: When she speaks it is a delight which flavours the sin; the flower of love is a rose, because under its blossom there are hidden many thorns. See Proverbs v, 3-4: Her mouth is smoother than oil; that is, her speech is afterwards as bitter as absinthium. [Her throat is smoother than oil. But her end is as bitter as wormwood.]

Let us consider also her gait, posture, and habit, in which is *vanity of vanities*. There is no man in the world who studies so hard to please the good God as even an ordinary woman studies by her vanities to please men. An example of this is to be found in the life of Pelagia, a worldly woman who was wont to go about Antioch tired and adorned most extravagantly. A holy father, named Nonnus, saw her and began to weep, saying to his companions, that never in all his life had he used such diligence to please God; and much more he added to this effect, which is preserved in his orations.

It is this which is lamented in *Ecclesiastes* vii, and which the Church even now laments on account of the great multitude of witches. *And I have found a woman more bitter than death, who is the hunter's snare, and her heart is a net, and her hands are bands. He that pleaseth God shall escape from her; but he that is a sinner shall be caught by her.* More *bitter than death*, that is, than the devil: Apocalypse vi, 8, His name was Death. For though the devil tempted Eve to sin, yet Eve seduced Adam. And as the sin of Eve would not have brought death to our soul and body unless the sin had afterwards passed on to Adam, to which he was tempted by Eve, not by the devil, therefore she is *more bitter than death*.

More bitter than death, again, because that is natural and destroys only the body; but the sin which arose from woman destroys the soul by depriving it of grace, and delivers the body up to the punishment of sin.

More bitter than death, again, because bodily death is an open and terrible enemy, but woman is a wheedling and secret enemy.

And that she is *more perilous than a snare* does not speak of the snare of hunters, but of devils. For men are caught not only through their carnal desires, when they see and hear women: for S. Bernard says: Their face is a burning wind, and their voice the hissing of serpents: but they also cast wicked spells on countless men and animals. And when it is said that her *heart is a net*, it speaks of the inscrutable malice which reigns in their hearts. And her *hands are as bands for binding*; for when they place their hands on a creature to bewitch it, then with the help of the devil, they perform their design.

To conclude. All witchcraft comes from carnal lust, which is in women insatiable. See Proverbs [30:15]: There are three things that are never satisfied, yea, a fourth thing which says not, It is enough; that is, the mouth of the womb. Wherefore for the sake of fulfilling their lusts they consort even with devils. More such reasons could be brought forward, but to the understanding it is sufficiently clear that it is no matter for wonder that there are more women than men found infected with the heresy of witchcraft. And in consequence of this, it is better called the heresy of witches than of wizards, since the name is taken from the more powerful party. And blessed be the Highest Who has so far preserved the male sex from so great a crime: for since He was willing to be born and to suffer for us, therefore He has granted to men the privilege.[78]

---

78. Excerpt from Part I, Question 6 (pp. 1–2), as published by Rev. Montague Summers in 1928; from the online edition "The Malleus Maleficarum" was transcribed by Wicasta Lovelace and Christie Rice; http://www.malleusmaleficarum.org/shop/the-malleus-maleficarum-pdf/ (Windhaven Network, Inc., 1998–2000). Emphasis added.

Qoheleth 8:1–9:6

From Wisdom to Death

Wisdom, Obedience, Power, Oppression (8:1-9)

C hapter 8 combines a number of typical-sounding proverbs with some classic Qoheleth musings (8:1-9), strung through with *hevel* (8:10-15). As usual, Qoheleth's comments serve to illuminate and often question the more classical views of ancient Israelites. Furthermore, we will see a focus on power in this section: that of a monarch in 8:2-4 and the things over which we lack power in verse 8. For our purposes, a question threads throughout the chapter, one that has relevance for all "generic" language in the biblical texts, whether proverbial or legal: Does this material apply to everyone or only to males? Did it then? Does it now? How can we know or decide? To explore this question, it is somewhat helpful to track the Hebrew for clues; in other cases, we are left to educated guesses and reflections.

This chapter opens with a rhetorical question about "wisdom" in 8:1a, which was also a central focus in the previous section. The concise two-word combination in the Hebrew of 8:1a, מי כהחכם, becomes less elegant in English: "Who is like a wise man?" While my feminist sensibilities make me want to translate "wise person," the Hebrew is clearly masculine. Though the beginning of 8:1 asks about a wise man, the second half of that verse uses the term "wisdom," musing more broadly about the topic and its effects on one's appearance, whether that be literal or symbolic.

8:1Who is like the wise man? And who knows the interpretation of a thing? Wisdom makes one's face shine, and the hardness of one's countenance is changed. 2Keep the king's command because of your sacred oath. 3Do not be terrified; go from his presence, do not delay when the matter is unpleasant, for he does whatever he pleases. 4For the word of the king is powerful, and who can say to him, "What are you doing?" 5Whoever obeys a command will meet no harm, and the wise mind will know the time and way. 6For every matter has its time and way, although the troubles of mortals lie heavy upon them. 7Indeed, they do not know what is to be, for who can tell them how it will be? 8No one has power over the wind to restrain the wind, or power over the day of death; there is no discharge from the battle, nor does wickedness deliver those who practice it. 9All this I observed, applying my mind to all that is done under the sun, while one person exercises authority over another to the other's hurt.

Verses 8:2-4 relate to an unnamed king. The statements read like axioms, but we must wonder whether the author had a specific instance in mind. While we might assume that these reflections on obedience and the fear invoked by a king would apply mainly to a male audience, they do recall the scene in Esther 4, where Queen Esther is terrified to go to the king and question the decree he unwittingly signed. Her three-time efforts to avoid explaining the situation of her people to King Ahasuerus could potentially fit the description of the powerful, terrifying king beyond reproach in Qoheleth 8:2-4. We cannot be sure whether a particular king inspired 8:2-4 or not; the comments are more likely applicable in a general sense, as is evident since we find similar sentiments in Proverbs 24:21; 25:6 and the *Proverbs of Ahiqar*.[1] The effect of verses 2-4 does not seem so much about loyalty to a monarch as it is a subtle critique of a ruler who is beyond reproach (vv. 3b and 4b).

Verse 5 essentially summarizes the previous three verses, again invoking the "wise man." It also draws a line all the way back to chapter 3, with reference to "time and judgment," since עת, "time," repeats four times each in verses 3:2-8. (Though, as I noted above in the section on 3:1-8, any version of "judgment" or "justice" is notably absent from that

---

1. Proverbs cited in Roland E. Murphy, *Ecclesiastes*, WBC 23A (Nashville: Thomas Nelson, 2018), 83; *Proverbs of Ahiqar* in Choon-Leong Seow, *Ecclesiastes: A New Translation with Introduction and Commentary*, AB 18C (New York: Doubleday, 1997), 280.

passage.) Qoheleth 8:6 thickens the line drawn back to Qoheleth 3, again mentioning "time and judgment" but also חפץ, "matter," a distinctive word from the opening line of the poem in 3:1. In 8:6b and throughout the rest of the chapter, the effect is similar to what we saw following 3:1-8: an enthusiastic questioning of the poem's apparent ethos, which would suggest one might be able to find the right "matter," "time," or "judgment." Instead, in verse 7, we get a definitive "he does not know"; in verse 8, "no אדם has power," and in verse 9, power relates to "hurt" or, in the most basic sense of רע, "evil." As a whole, verses 5-9 continue the emphasis on acceding to authority (v. 5, 9) even while (or perhaps because) uncertainty truly reigns (vv. 7 and 8).

Several aspects of this section suggest theological questions. Wind and death cannot be controlled by humans; the traditional assumption would be that God controls the day of death, as well as the רוח, "wind" (v. 8). The latter could even be an allusion to the deity, since it elsewhere in the Hebrew Bible refers to the divine spirit.[2] In addition, the lack of power in verse 8 is analogous to the descriptions of God later in this section, as something over which one has no power (8:12-13, 17). Similarly, Choon-Leong Seow suggests that the king figure may have implications for God.[3] Perhaps God, like the king, wields power that is best heeded without too many questions.[4] Likewise, 8:6 may allude to divine power, in its assertion that "for every matter there is a time and judgment." All of these images help anticipate Qoheleth's implicit questions about God's power in 8:10-15.

The cumulative effect of the rhetorical questions in 8:1 and 7 is the unknowability of meaning (8:1) and of future events (8:7). The statement in 8:7, "he does not know what will be," specifically works against 8:5, in which "the heart of the wise will know." This stands out as one of Qoheleth's definitive dilemmas, the point of which remains up for debate. Maybe such a contradiction is the bedrock of Qoheleth's philosophical rhetoric, as argued by Michael V. Fox.[5] Or does Qoheleth lay out these

---

2. A sampling of these instances includes: Gen 1:2; 6:3; 41:38; Exod 15:8; 31:3; 35:31; Num 16:22; 24:2; 27:16; Judg 3:10; 6:34; 13:25; 14:6; 15:14; Ps 33:6; 51:11 [13]; Neh 9:20, 30. Qoheleth notably uses רוח, "wind," most commonly to refer to the wind that humans tend to absurdly chase (metaphorically) (1:14; 2:11, 17, 26; 4:4, 6; 6:9), except in 11:4-5 and 12:7, in which it relates to the utterly mysterious life-breath.

3. Seow, *Ecclesiastes*, 290.

4. 8:2 suggests the comparison of God and king, since the NRSV's "sacred oath" arises from שבועת אלהים, "oath of God."

5. Michael V. Fox, *Qoheleth and His Contradictions*, BLS 18 (Sheffield: Almond, 1989).

options only to explore various possibilities? In either case, this inherent skepticism gives credence to the skeptical treatment of both theology and biblical studies that have been standard in feminist approaches.

As we will see, this questioning intensifies as chapter 8 progresses. How women fare amid Qoheleth's musings here again remains open to speculation. The Sage's masculine language would not seem to necessarily exclude females, but we cannot be certain of our inclusion here, either. The section closes in verse 9 with reference to Qoheleth's experience using the frequently repeated phrase השמש, ש.מ.ש השמים, "under the sun"; here it again gestures toward a critique of hierarchy, making a similar point as what we saw in the short passage about the king in 8:2-4. Like Qoheleth's suspicious approach in general, this undermining of authority lends itself to feminist interpretation, despite whatever intent the Sage may have had.

There Is No Justice, Only Death (8:10–9:6)

The topics of wisdom and uncertainty continue in this section, but here they are viewed particularly through the lens of death, the great leveler. While death obviously affects everyone in the end, regardless of sex, Qoheleth's generic language in this section has a masculine tone due to the usual androcentric verb forms. As I suggested in regard to the death-related references elsewhere in the book (3:2; 7:2-4), however, women in the ancient Near East bore the burdens of death inordinately, from care of corpses to burial and mourning practices. Furthermore, due to high maternal and infant mortality rates, often death would have personally affected women earlier than their male counterparts.

Verses 10-15 contain some of the most theologically weighty reflections in Qoheleth. This short pericope includes three repetitions of *hevel* and an assertion of the *carpe diem*, and it questions the justice—or injustice—of death throughout. "Who knows?" (8:1), the repeated theme of Qoheleth chapters 7–12, provides the background setting and tone for 8:10-15.[6] In this pericope and the section immediately surrounding it, Qoheleth addresses the topics not only of knowledge but also of power. The topic shifts in 8:10-15 to divine justice. Indeed, throughout the chapter, the three topics interact with one another. Qoheleth crafts this portion of

---

6. Kathleen Anne Farmer, *Who Knows What Is Good? A Commentary on the Books of Proverbs and Ecclesiastes*, ITC (Grand Rapids, MI: Eerdmans, 1991), 151. Also, see the introduction above.

¹⁰Then I saw the wicked buried; they used to go in and out of the holy place, and were praised in the city where they had done such things. This also is vanity. ¹¹Because sentence against an evil deed is not executed speedily the human heart is fully set to do evil. ¹²Though sinners do evil a hundred times and prolong their lives, yet I know that it will be well with those who fear God, because they stand in fear before him, ¹³but it will not be well with the wicked, neither will they prolong their days like a shadow, because they do not stand in fear before God.

¹⁴There is a vanity that takes place on earth, that there are righteous people who are treated according to the conduct of the wicked, and there are wicked people who are treated according to the conduct of the righteous. I said that this also is vanity. ¹⁵So I commend enjoyment, for there is nothing better for people under the sun than to eat, and drink, and enjoy themselves, for this will go with them in their toil through the days of life that God gives them under the sun.

¹⁶When I applied my mind to know wisdom, and to see the business that is done on earth, how one's eyes see sleep neither day nor night, ¹⁷then I saw all the work of God, that no one can find out what is happening under the

text such that the reader is left wondering "who knows" whether divine justice exists at all. The pericope contains traditional views about God's just responses to humans alongside contrasting illustrations of injustices that Qoheleth has seen. While such challenges to tradition are not at all new for Qoheleth, the rhetoric on this topic is more compelling here than anywhere else in Qoheleth. In 8:10-15, Qoheleth makes painfully clear the gap between what should be and what is, guiding the reader to Qoheleth's usual escape, the *carpe diem*, articulated here in verse 15.

Qoheleth's rhetorical question from 8:1, מי יודע, "who knows?" and subsequent answers, איננו ידע, "he does not know" (8:7), and לא ימצא, "he [ha-'adam] cannot find out" (8:17), act as an overarching critique of 8:10-14; these questions specifically contradict the statement embedded within the pericope, "I know" (8:12b). Thus the Sage heckles the reader with experiential evidence (8:10-12a, 14) to show that even in the face of knowing (8:12b-13), we truly do not know. Having effectively established the "absurdity" (*hevel*) of life (8:10, 14 [2x]), we will ultimately arrive at Qoheleth's oft-repeated diversion from absurdity, the *carpe diem* in 15a. This *carpe diem* contributes to the thematic unity of the book.

Having set the stage with questions about knowledge and power, in 8:10-15 we read about the tension Qoheleth sees with respect to divine sun. However much they may toil in seeking, they will not find it out; even though those who are wise claim to know, they cannot find it out.

⁹:¹All this I laid to heart, examining it all, how the righteous and the wise and their deeds are in the hand of God; whether it is love or hate one does not know. Everything that confronts them ²is vanity, since the same fate comes to all, to the righteous and the wicked, to the good and the evil, to the clean and the unclean, to those who sacrifice and those who do not sacrifice. As are the good, so are the sinners; those who swear are like those who shun an oath. ³This is an evil in all that happens under the sun, that the same fate comes to everyone. Moreover, the hearts of all are full of evil; madness is in their hearts while they live, and after that they go to the dead. ⁴But whoever is joined with all the living has hope, for a living dog is better than a dead lion. ⁵The living know that they will die, but the dead know nothing; they have no more reward, and even the memory of them is lost. ⁶Their love and their hate and their envy have already perished; never again will they have any share in all that happens under the sun.

justice. The wicked receive laudatory funerals (v. 10), evil festers without timely consequence (v. 11), and the righteous and the wicked receive treatment that should appropriately be accorded to the other (v. 14). At the same time, Qoheleth implies that those who fear God will prosper and live long lives, and the wicked will suffer (vv. 12b-13). These two views present a significant conflict, which is integral to the passage. Qoheleth uses this tension—between the view that divine justice works and that it does not—to draw the reader toward the only escape Qoheleth has found, the *carpe diem* in verse 15.

Qoheleth 8:10-15 teems with word and phrase repetitions that work together to underscore its topic of divine justice: טוב, "good" (8:12, 13, 15); רע, "evil/evil act" (8:11 [2x], 12); רשע/רשעים, "wicked one(s)" (8:10, 13, 14 [2x]); צדיקים, "righteous ones" (8:14 [2x]); ירא, "fearful [of God]" (8:12 [2x], 8:13); ארך (*hiphil*), "prolong [life]" (8:12, 13); and *hevel* (8:10, 14 [2x]). These recurring words bind the conflicting verses together and emphasize certain aspects of Qoheleth's struggle regarding divine justice. Furthermore, the eight-time repetition of the root עשה as "do/deed/doer"[7] places a focus on behavior (and lack thereof), both of humans and of God.[8]

---

7. 8:10, 11 [3x], 12, 14 [3x].

8. Of humans, 8:10, 11a, 11b, 12, 14 (2nd and 3rd references) of God, 8:11a, 14 (1st reference).

With the first verb in the pericope, רָאִיתִי, "I saw" (8:10a), the Sage begins a carefully crafted section that pits Qoheleth's experience over against Qoheleth's knowledge of tradition, which is marked here by יוֹדֵעַ אָנִי, "I know" (12b). The object of Qoheleth's gaze in 8:10 ("wicked ones," though in the masculine form, it would literally be "wicked men") helps set up the problem of justice that looms over this pericope. In 8:10a, it seems that some "wicked ones" are being buried. Several textual questions arise, however, regarding this burial scene. The problems with this verse are so considerable that I will concede from the outset that my hypothetical conclusions are drawn from my overall reading of the pericope and, indeed, the book as a whole.[9] In my opinion, the MT has suffered corruption, and the LXX has the preferable reading here:

> Then I saw wicked ones who were being brought to graves. They proceeded from a holy place.

In this case, "they" refers to those who are part of the processional. Thus "proceeded" describes the setting I explain below, in which a funeral procession leaves from a temple or local worship center. Reading with most commentators "from a holy place" expresses a minor emendation.[10] In the first half of verse 10a, Qoheleth has created an intentionally surprising scene in which people proceed from a holy place to a graveyard in a show of mourning for the wicked.[11] This translation presumes a contrast between the wicked people who are recognized in religious funerals (the first half of 10a) and the parallel line, the second half of 8:10a, where "ones who act justly are forgotten in the city."[12] The point of the

---

9. Crenshaw notes that "interpretations of this verse have one thing in common: tentativeness." James L. Crenshaw, *Ecclesiastes: A Commentary*, OTL (Louisville: Westminster John Knox, 1987), 154. In Longman's opinion, verse 10 "vies for the most difficult in the book." Tremper Longman, *The Book of Ecclesiastes*, NICOT (Grand Rapids, MI: Eerdmans, 1998), 218. See Antoon Schoors, *Ecclesiastes* (Leuven: Peeters, 2013), 622–26 for a summary of the text-critical issues.

10. F. Horst in *BHS* cites Codex Hillel (and multiple others) for this emendation of the construct to the absolute form. With Murphy, *Ecclesiastes*, 81, and Seow, *Ecclesiastes*, 284–85; also see Fox, *Qoheleth and His Contradictions*, 250.

11. There is some agreement that וּמִמְּקוֹם קָדוֹשׁ refers to a synagogue rather than the temple. Seow, *Ecclesiastes*, 285; Michael V. Fox, *A Time to Tear Down and a Time to Build Up: A Rereading of Ecclesiastes* (Grand Rapids, MI: Eerdmans, 1999), 284–85; Robert Gordis, *Koheleth: The Man and His World; A Study of Ecclesiastes*, rev. ed. (New York: Schocken, 1987), 286; Lee I. Levine, "The Nature and Origin of the Palestinian Synagogue Reconsidered," *JBL* 115 (1996): 438, 432.

12. The translation of the second half of v. 10a "forgotten" follows MT. See Michael V. Fox, *The JPS Bible Commentary: Ecclesiastes* (Philadelphia: Jewish Publication Society,

verse in this view is to contrast the wicked, who receive some kind of religious procession for their burial (first half of 10a), with the just, who are simply ignored (second half of 10a). Despite two possible translations of the second half of verse 10a, both describe the world as it should not be and warrant the conclusion: *hevel*.[13] The translation of the second half of 10a, which presents a contrast in the treatment of the righteous and the wicked at death, commends itself because the wicked and the righteous have each received treatment appropriate to the other, precisely as Qoheleth describes in 8:14. This rendering of verse 10a thus stands as an experiential illustration, introduced by "I saw," and helps build the tension that Qoheleth will so clearly articulate in 8:14. Verse 10a thus begins to describe and lead to Qoheleth's proclamation, "absurdity" (*hevel*), the conclusion of this verse—and ultimately of the whole passage (8:14b). What could be more absurd than undeserved treatment of both the wicked and the righteous even after their deaths?[14] Qoheleth 8:10b, "This also is absurdity," relates both to what precedes (v. 10a) and to what follows (vv. 11-12a); it lends wholeness to the pericope, since we find it repeated in verse 14b. Here again we should be reminded to envision the women mourners in this scene, keening in the background.[15]

In 8:11, Qoheleth suggests that the lack of appropriate retribution illustrated in 8:10 actually contributes to the persistence of evil. Whether this expected retribution should be assumed as divine or human remains ambiguous. The only other use of the word פתגם, "edict, command, word," in the Hebrew Bible is in the context of a human "decree" in Esther 1:20. It is thus difficult to know if it refers here to a divine command, especially since the preceding section (8:1-10) may allude to God. The following section, however, to which verse 11 is integrally connected, undoubtedly has divine justice as its topic.[16] Thus I find ample reason to consider that

---

2004), 249, and Seow, *Ecclesiastes*, 276. Seow also argues for the rendering of כן as "justly" (*Ecclesiastes*, 285; cf. *BDB*, 467a), with Murphy, *Ecclesiastes*, 79; Fox, *A Time to Tear Down and a Time to Build Up*, 284.

13. Other translations, relying on LXX, continue the topic of the wicked receiving unearned treatment in v. 10a and state that the wicked are "celebrated." Longman, *The Book of Ecclesiastes*, 216, 219; Gordis, *Koheleth*, 174, 286.

14. With Gordis, *Koheleth*, 294, who finds similar sentiments in Job 21:32-33 and Qoh 6:3.

15. See commentary on 3:2 and 7:2-4.

16. Crenshaw states that "the negligent officials may be civil authorities, or Qoheleth may have God in mind." In addition, Crenshaw concludes that "this blanket statement about human perversity shifts responsibility away from sinners to those

verse 11a indicates a decree that should have—but does not—come from God. Here we see Qoheleth's theological questioning intensifying.

In light of 8:10-11, Qoheleth's following comment, that evildoers live long lives (v. 12a), stands as yet another observation of unjust reality as protest against a system that does not work correctly. The following "fear God" statements (vv. 12b, 13b) actually support this interpretation: the way the system *should* work is that, for those who fear God, "it will be well" (v. 12b); verse 13 contains the converse. Nonetheless, the wicked live long lives that end with extravagant funerals (v. 10). Qoheleth is setting up the dilemma: retribution should work (vv. 11-12a), but as far as Qoheleth can "see" (v. 10a), it does not. Qoheleth deems this situation *hevel* (v. 10b).

Through repetition, verses 12a and 13a draw attention to opposing sentiments, which produce a dissonance of classic Qoheleth style. In verse 12a people are evil yet מַאֲרִיךְ, "live long," but in verse 13a God will *not* prolong (לֹא-יַאֲרִיךְ, using the same Hebrew root in the same stem) the days of the wicked one. Indeed, according to Qoheleth's rhetoric in 13a, God will not even prolong the days of the wicked one "like a shadow." While a shadow lengthens the object that is its source, it is an illusory, temporary, breathy, fleeting—one might say a *hevel* ("absurd")—kind of elongation.[17] Perhaps this comment may be considered sarcastic in the context. "Like a shadow" exaggerates how unlikely it *should* be for a wicked person to live for extended days. Though Qoheleth sees rewards for the wicked, Qoheleth also seems to question the ultimate significance of such long years.

Qoheleth 8:12 and 13 produce a dilemma for the reader. Qoheleth articulates that doing evil results in a long life (8:12a), that fearing God is beneficial (v. 12b), and that "wicked ones" will not be rewarded with many years (v. 13). The underlying sentiment of verse 12a is that divine retribution does not work, while in verses 12b-13 the idea is that it does work. Which does Qoheleth believe is the case? Does Qoheleth present one idea only to refute it with the other? Proverbs 11:30-31 illustrates that 8:12b-13 is rooted in tradition. Michael V. Fox explains that 8:12-13

---

entrusted with punishing them. People are guilty of evil but God must take some blame, since a breakdown has occurred in the scheme of reward and punishment" (*Ecclesiastes*, 154–55).

17. Seow (*Ecclesiastes*, 288) provides a whole list of other references in which "shadow" is an illustration for the fleeting nature of life: Pss 102:11 [12]; 109:23; 144:4; Job 8:9; 14:2; 17:7; 1 Chr 29:15, as well as Qoheleth's own prior use of this image in 6:12.

is one of those instances in which Qoheleth, as a believer in traditional wisdom, holds up a description of retribution theology alongside the reality that it does not always "work." It is one of Qoheleth's classic "contradictions." I disagree with commentators who read verses 12b-13 as a traditional statement of retribution (that ones who fear God will prosper, while those who do not fear God will suffer), which Qoheleth states only in order to reject on the basis of experience.[18] I concur here with Fox's view that Qoheleth is presenting and critiquing tradition, though ultimately not rejecting it. We have seen that the Sage continues to raise the topic of retribution for reflection, rather than refuting it and moving on. In this way, Qoheleth expresses internal and existential dissonance about tradition rather than a firm conclusion to abandon it. Qoheleth's use of יודע אני, "I know" (12b), to express traditional belief, in contrast with ראיתי, "I saw" (10a), to illustrate experience, supports this interpretation. These are two ways of knowing, but both kinds of knowledge belong to Qoheleth.

In the end, despite the contradictions and difficulties in 8:11-13, Qoheleth has woven the three verses together through similarities in vocabulary and the topic of retribution. Here is one more reason to suspect that the antithetical statements are part of Qoheleth's rhetorical intent to convince the reader that even Qoheleth's own traditional beliefs about retribution are in reality elusive at best, as Qoheleth will express again in the next verse. Ultimately, we are moving toward the only real advice Qoheleth has to give in light of this absurd predicament: the *carpe diem* in 8:15.

Finally, in 8:14 we read about Qoheleth's view of reality even more vividly than in the preceding verses. It is *hevel* that the wicked and the righteous receive the opposite treatment from what they deserve according to their מעשה, "act, deed." The *hevel* that is נעשה, "done," in 14a may well be something that Qoheleth blames on God's inaction. Perhaps "is done" here mirrors an earlier implicit accusation of God in 8:11a, in which אין־נעשה, "a decree is not made." The passive form of עשה (*niphal*), "done," creates the lack of clarity about who or what causes this inappropriate treatment. This reflects the overall ambiguity in this passage about whose responsibility it is to ensure retribution. Further, this ambiguity resumes the questions of power that began in 8:4, and it specifically calls into question divine power, since, according to deuteronomistic tradition, such "treatment" was God's job.

---

18. Fox cites Gordis as the contrary view. Fox, *Ecclesiastes*, 252–53.

Given its context and structure, 8:14 is a poetically compelling and perfectly balanced description of the imbalance of justice. Qoheleth has mentioned "righteous ones" and "wicked ones" twice in 8:14; furthermore, Qoheleth's discussion of these topics is enveloped with "absurdity." Furthermore, *hevel* and descriptions of injustice in 8:14a and 10a reverse in order, producing a chiastic parallel between the two verses. The two middle stichs in verse 14 use exactly the same vocabulary and virtually identical grammar in both lines.[19] Qoheleth has recalled (8:10) and reflected (v. 14) to us that the righteous and the wicked receive treatment according to the acts of the other, and this indeed is "absurdity." Moreover, the comparison presents striking similarity to 3:16 and 7:15, even down to similar vocabulary. In all three cases "righteous" and "wicked" appear as comparative categories. In 8:14 the comparison relates to the treatment of the righteous and the wicked; in 7:15 the comparison is about the longevity of the righteous and the wicked; in 3:16 the comparison relates to the expected location (whether literal or metaphorical) of the righteous and the wicked. The comparison of "righteous" and "wicked," repeated throughout the book, emphasizes Qoheleth's concern about the matter of divine justice. The culmination of this pericope, the *carpe diem* in 8:15, provides more of a distraction than a resolution for the injustices and contradictions that Qoheleth has described in 8:11-14.[20] After all, what kind of resolution does eating and drinking provide to injustice if you suffer from poverty and chronic hunger? Qoheleth's privilege is showing.

The underlying sentiment in 8:10-15 is that Qoheleth "knows" retribution theology should work, even if for pragmatic reasons (vv. 11, 12b, 13), but Qoheleth "sees" that it does not (vv. 10, 12a, 14). Qoheleth gives a firsthand example of retribution's failure in 8:10, and in 8:14 moves to state it generally. Each new statement in 8:10-14 undercuts and calls into question Qoheleth's previous remark (8:10-12a, 12b-13, 14). By the end of 8:14, Qoheleth has identified the breakdown of retribution theology as *hevel* three times. Qoheleth's response to this problem is not unusual in Qoheleth, recommending the *carpe diem* in verse 15. Despite the fact that doing evil will neither lengthen nor shorten one's days (12a, 13a), Qoheleth implies that fearing God is still worthwhile (12b, 13b). Qoheleth

---

19. A minimal variation is in the relative pronoun, which varies from אשר to the shortened form שׁ.

20. Qoheleth similarly uses the *carpe diem* after explaining a situation of *hevel* in 2:24; 9:7-10; 11:9-10, and after questioning divine justice in 3:12-13; 9:7-10.

advocates the fear of God seven times throughout the book.[21] This does not appear to arise either out of sarcasm or as a gesture of piety. While Qoheleth undercuts any kind of assurance in what fear of God might provide to a person, Qoheleth advocates it still, if only to "hedge one's bets" by living as though retribution may still work.[22] This unpredictable God demands fear.

Despite Qoheleth's apparent ignorance of the oppressed, and the Sage's privilege, which shows throughout, 8:10-14 can serve as a liberating lament for all who suffer injustice: for women, whose biology means that they inordinately suffer rape and that they endure forced and unwanted pregnancies; for the man sleeping on the couch behind me in a coffee shop as I write, because he apparently has nowhere else to sleep. From dire circumstances to the more mundane injustices of pay inequities, women resonate all too well with the injustices Qoheleth so meticulously articulates. These circumstances are all the more gripping for women of color and for women who live in poverty and slavery. Those "see" too clearly that no one—God included—is ensuring justice. As a chaplain, I was called to a woman in an emergency room. She was cradling her dead baby and crying, "How could God have done this to me? I just started going back to church." She, and we, like Qoheleth, are inclined to hedge our bets, hoping that fear of God will somehow protect us from such episodes. Adding to her burden, that African American woman, who was brought by ambulance from a low-income housing unit, was questioned—more than most?—about her baby's bruised chest. I wondered—and a nurse stated—wasn't that from the paramedics giving CPR? "The righteous are treated according to the acts of the wicked; and the wicked are treated according to the acts of the righteous" (8:14). *Hevel*, indeed.

The unstated outcome of the "dialogue" Qoheleth presents here is to question traditional views on divine justice, without abandoning these beliefs altogether. The Sage does this by riddling the reader with experiences that contradict traditional theology, without offering a viable solution. In the end, Qoheleth retains the traditional beliefs, having severely scrutinized them. Retribution continues to be a central enough

---

21. 3:14; 5:7 [6]; 7:18; 8:12 [2x], 13; 12:13.

22. Crenshaw states, "This [12b-13] reaffirmation of traditional belief indicates a refusal to give up the conviction of an orderly universe. Whether one views this optimism as Qoheleth's inability to abandon dogma altogether or as the religious community's inability to do so, the presence of 8.12b-13 demonstrates the force of the belief that good people fare well and bad people suffer" (*Ecclesiastes*, 156).

principle that Qoheleth debates it over and over again. This ongoing conversation with the tradition indicates that Qoheleth has not fully abandoned the idea.

As I have discussed in the introduction and elsewhere in this commentary, the act of undermining tradition can be viewed as the first step in feminist theology. When it comes to creating a new theology, we will likely have to look beyond Qoheleth for that.

Qoheleth's continued reflections on in/justice and death in 8:16–9:6 continue many of the same points we have seen in 8:10-15. Again, an important practice is to uncover the gendered language: in 8:16, "his eyes see sleep"; in verse 17, "no man may find . . . what a man may toil . . . he will not find . . . even if the wise [masc.] says he knows, he cannot find it out." Note the Hebrew does not read "no one" or "they," as in the NRSV, but אדם, "human" or "man" and "he" throughout. Next, in verses 16-17, Qoheleth will amplify the "not knowing" theme that marks chapter 8 and the whole second half of the book. Qoheleth leaves the reader with one last barrage of the point about "not knowing" through a three-time repetition in 8:17, which explains that no matter how hard one tries, no matter how wise one is, no one is able to find out what is being done under the sun.

We might be tempted to think that Qoheleth is wrapping up the book at the beginning of chapter 9, with the auspicious opening: "For all this I put to my heart." The Sage revisits theodicy in verse 1, reemphasizes *hevel*, and provides a list to delineate "all" in verse 2, ultimately addressing death, though only referring to it as לכל מקרה, "the same fate." In 9:2 we find the disputed thirty-ninth use of *hevel*, which hinges on an emendation of הכל, "everything," to הבל, "*hevel*"—the similarity in looks (the middle letter!) should be apparent. The LXX and other ancient translations support this reading, but the NRSV is an outlier among the translations in accepting it.[23] While it would be nice to know for certain

---

23. See discussions of the text criticism in Schoors, who emends (*Ecclesiastes*, 649, 655–56), and Seow, who does not (*Ecclesiastes*, 299); neither does Krüger, nor does he discuss the issue. Thomas Krüger, *Qoheleth: A Commentary*, ed. Klaus Baltzer, trans. O. C. Dean, Hermeneia (Minneapolis: Fortress, 2004), 166–69. There is room for dispute about whether the script used in Qoheleth's time would have made such a transcription error possible, but the Hebrew script from the Great Isaiah Scroll of Qumran shows great similarity in the two letters at issue here: כ and ב. Eric Christianson even relates a conversation with John Jarick suggesting Qoheleth's frequent use of הכל may be a "visual word play" on הבל. In other words, "everything" even *looks* like *hevel*. Eric S. Christianson, *A Time to Tell: Narrative Strategies in Ecclesiastes*, JSOTSup 280 (Sheffield: Sheffield Academic, 1998), 88 n. 39.

how many times Qoheleth repeats *hevel*, the important point is in the comment מקרה אחד, "same fate." If we had any doubt of that, Qoheleth repeats "same fate" in verse 3. And what is that "same fate"? Death, death, and more death pervades 9:1-6, reminiscent of 7:1-4, though at least in 9:4, as opposed to 7:1-4, Qoheleth seems to slightly privilege life over death: "the living ones know that they will die, but the dead ones know nothing" (9:5). "Living ones" and "dead ones" are both masculine plural, but these are surely universal truths, transcending gender.

Death encompasses 9:1-6. One of the exemplary but apparently meaningless actions that Qoheleth lists in 9:2 includes זבח (*qal* participle), "[he who makes a] sacrifice," which is almost an exclusively male activity. We find the verb used in relation to women in 1 Samuel 28:24, in which the Medium of Endor prepares a *non*-sacrificial meal, and 1 Kings 11:8, in which Solomon's foreign wives prepare sacrificial offerings for their foreign gods. A cultic "swear" or "oath," which would seem to be Qoheleth's meaning, given the context of "sacrifice," has a similar dearth of use by women.[24]

More hope resides in life than in death in 9:4, as opposed to what we read in 7:1-4, though much evil resides even in life (9:3). Qoheleth does not rely on the traditionally meaningful aspect of death, that of being well-remembered;[25] the Sage further undermines even that in 9:5b. Despite Qoheleth's androcentric verbiage and grammar throughout this section, this portion of Qoheleth has much to offer both women and men, as existentialist struggles afflict humans universally. Though perhaps a morbid alternative to perfectionism, that "the same fate comes to everyone" certainly undermines the common female trait of overachieving in the face of an unfair system. Here, Qoheleth would perhaps concede: It's not just the system that is unfair, and it's not just unfair for women! The whole world, and indeed God, is unfair! Similarly, how true it is that life is terminal for all of us, that we must all grapple with our finite existence in the face of a truly unknowable future in which all previous accomplishments and emotions are not only meaningless but forgotten (9:5-6)?

24. While the women in Song call on one another to שבע (*hiphil*), "swear," in regard to a lover (2:7; 3:5; 5:8-9; 8:4), and Rahab made the Israelite spies "swear" not to betray her (in the *niphal* stem, Josh 2:12; in vv. 17 and 20 in the *hiphil* and also as a noun, "oath"), we find a specifically female instance of a cultic swear only in Num 5:19, where a priest makes the woman "swear," thus attesting to her marital fidelity when accused otherwise.

25. Gen 48:15-16; Ruth 4:11, 14; 2 Sam 18:18; Ps 34:16 [17]; cf. Qoh 1:11; 2:16; 9:15.

Qoheleth 9:7-18

Carpe Diem
and Related Imperatives

Qoheleth 9:7-9 importantly follows Qoheleth's reflections on death as the great equalizer that comes to all persons regardless of their behavior or status before God (8:10–9:6). Death ends all happiness; it is the ultimate "absurdity." Yet again, the *carpe diem* seems to be Qoheleth's last best hope for enduring this all-too-unpredictable life with some modicum of happiness. In between the bread and wine, white garments and oil of 9:7 and 8, Qoheleth includes a significant theological comment: "For God already approves what you do" (9:7). This sentiment sounds both pious (much like Ps 104:15) and defeatist—or gluttonous! After all, this comment relates back to 9:2 and 3, in which what you do has no ultimate correspondence to your fate. We all have the same fate: death. Thankfully, we may find some relief for the existential angst of the previous section through Qoheleth's most effusive *carpe diem*, which effectively takes up three verses (9:7-9). In 9:7, Qoheleth actually specifies the food and drink: bread and wine. In 9:8 the Sage goes on to specify a festive dress code: white clothing and well-coiffed hair. In 9:9 Qoheleth adds "a woman whom you love" to the short list of ways to endure the absurdity of life and the futility of toil. In sum: "Eat, and drink, and enjoy your wife."

But what about this woman—or would it be these women—who conclude Qoheleth's list of ways to find enjoyment in one's toil? The Sage refers to her as "a woman whom you love," assuming a male

[7]Go, eat your bread with enjoyment, and drink your wine with a merry heart; for God has long ago approved what you do. [8]Let your garments always be white; do not let oil be lacking on your head. [9]Enjoy life with the wife whom you love, all the days of your vain life that are given you under the sun, because that is your portion in life and in your toil at which you toil under the sun. [10]Whatever your hand finds to do, do with your might; for there is no work or thought or knowledge or wisdom in Sheol, to which you are going.

[11]Again I saw that under the sun the race is not to the swift, nor the battle to the strong, nor bread to the wise, nor riches to the intelligent, nor favor to the skillful; but time and chance happen to them all. [12]For no one can anticipate the time of disaster. Like fish taken in a cruel net, and like birds caught in a snare, so mortals are snared at a time of calamity, when it suddenly falls upon them.

audience, each of whom should find some satisfaction with their woman. In order to imagine this collective, unnamed woman as more of a person, I will refer to "a woman whom you love" by using the transliteration of the Hebrew phrase אשה אשר־אהבת, as if it were her name: 'Ishah-'asher-'ahavta.[1] Most translations refer to her as "the wife whom you love," yet it is pertinent to note that Hebrew does not necessarily specify "wife"; it could just be "woman," אשה, so the translation "wife" would be an interpretive assumption, albeit no major leap.[2] Furthermore, the Hebrew does not include a definite article (ה) here, so it is ultimately possible to translate the phrase in four different ways: (1) "a woman whom you love," (2) "the woman whom you love," (3) "a wife whom you love," or (4) "the wife whom you love."[3] (This last one perhaps is

1. The practice of giving this transliteration as a "name" follows the practice of other feminist interpreters, such as Mieke Bal, who initiated this by calling Jephthah's Daughter in Judges 11 "Bath" ("daughter"). Also see J. Cheryl Exum, who in the same spirit "names" this young woman "Bat-jiftah," and similarly refers to the concubine in Judges 19 as "Bat-shever," "the daughter of breaking." Mieke Bal, *Death and Dissymmetry: The Politics of Coherence in the Book of Judges* (Chicago; London: University of Chicago Press, 1988), 43. J. Cheryl Exum, "Judges: Encoded Messages to Women," in *Feminist Biblical Interpretation: A Compendium of Critical Commentary on the Books of the Bible and Related Literature*, ed. Luise Schottroff, Marie-Theres Wacker, and Martin Rumscheidt (Grand Rapids, MI: Eerdmans, 2012), 119, 123.

2. Choon-Leong Seow, *Ecclesiastes: A New Translation with Introduction and Commentary*, AB 18C (New York: Doubleday, 1997), 303. Normally in Hebrew "wife" appears as "his/my/your woman."

3. See discussion in Tremper Longman, *The Book of Ecclesiastes*, NICOT (Grand Rapids, MI: Eerdmans, 1998), 230. He notes, based on various interpreters' work, that

¹³I have also seen this example of wisdom under the sun, and it seemed great to me. ¹⁴There was a little city with few people in it. A great king came against it and besieged it, building great siegeworks against it. ¹⁵Now there was found in it a poor wise man, and he by his wisdom delivered the city. Yet no one remembered that poor man. ¹⁶So I said, "Wisdom is better than might; yet the poor man's wisdom is despised, and his words are not heeded." ¹⁷The quiet words of the wise are
more to be heeded
than the shouting of a ruler among fools.
¹⁸Wisdom is better than weapons of war,
but one bungler destroys much good.

comparable to Prov 5:18: "Let your fountain be blessed, and rejoice in the wife of your youth.") These translation options could contribute in varying ways to a paraphrase of Qoheleth's *carpe diem* list in 9:7-9: "Eat, drink, and be merry! Dress nicely! Be well groomed! And have sex!" or "Be in love!" or "Appreciate female companionship!" (either with your wife or of some woman whom you love)—or all of those. Some writings relevant to Qoheleth's time provide a bit of helpful context: "Wine and music gladden the heart, but better still sexual love." Also, "Our Rabbis taught: . . . Three things benefit the body without entering it: washing, anointing and sexual intercourse; three are like the world to come: Sabbath, Sun and sexual intercourse."⁴ Sadly, while both of these quotes highlight the extent to which sexual intimacy could have been considered a legitimate part of the *carpe diem*, they do not necessarily clarify the identity of the sexual partner. But perhaps a clue can be found in the Babylonian Talmud, to paraphrase: "Three things increase the pleasure of a man [אדם]: A beautiful dwelling, and a beautiful wife [אשה; could also be translated "woman"] and beautiful clothes."⁵

Regarding the ambiguity over "a woman whom you love," we should admit that our already formed views about Qoheleth will inform our understanding of how best to interpret the comment in 9a. Is this a characterization of Qoheleth being an "old boy," giving a wink and a nod to his buddies over a beer at a "girly bar," or is this something more like a

---

the definite article in Qoheleth is used inconsistently, as is אשה as "wife" vs. "woman" so that we cannot be certain as to which of these is correct.

4. Ṭal Ilan, *Jewish Women in Greco-Roman Palestine* (Peabody, MA: Hendrickson Publishers, 1996), 107 cites Sira 40:20 and the Babylonian Talmud Ber. 57b, respectively.

5. שלשה מרחיבין דעתו של אדם אלו הן דירה נאה ואשה נאה וכלים נאים (Babylonian Talmud Ber. 57b).

somber Sage thinking longingly about a woman who embodies Woman Wisdom? It is possible that Qoheleth's reference fits in the context of the "test of pleasure," which listed "concubines" along with other luxuries (2:8). As usual, our conclusions on those things would partly be decided by our overall understanding of Qoheleth, the ongoing *Catch-22* for Qoheleth interpreters. Accordingly, commentators have produced varying interpretations of this reference. The majority of commentators tend to conclude that Qoheleth, as an ancient sage, would not have been promoting promiscuity.[6] And Michael Fox makes a solid point in stating that "the only woman who would be a life companion is one's wife."[7] Tal Ilan explores literature about marriage in the Greco-Roman period, which unsurprisingly comes from a male perspective and shows the preference for a good wife and the drawbacks of a bad wife. Furthermore, polygamy did continue to be practiced—even if minimally—in Jewish circles during this time.[8] Interestingly, Ilan also highlights a few women who chose husbands for themselves. Nonetheless, I find it helpful to retain the ambiguity in the translation "a woman whom you love." The point is that all of these varying interpretations would agree that the—or a—woman in this instance is an object who is somehow related to Qoheleth's "toil." That topic first surfaced in 1:3 and functions as a theme within the book; the root for "toil" (עָמָל) appears thirty-five times throughout.

This link between 'Ishah-'asher-'ahavta ("a woman [wife] whom you love") and "toil" is worth considering. What does it mean that 'Ishah-'asher-'ahavta appears in such proximity with "toil" in this verse? There is something about a man's toil that relates to his life with "a woman he

---

6. Michael V. Fox, *The JPS Bible Commentary: Ecclesiastes* (Philadelphia: Jewish Publication Society, 2004), 64. Crenshaw concludes, "Would Qoheleth have advocated lasciviousness of the sort that Wisd. Of Sol. 2:9 attacks? Probably not." He also observes that this statement betrays "Qoheleth's audience as exclusively male." James L. Crenshaw, *Ecclesiastes: A Commentary*, OTL (Louisville: Westminster John Knox, 1987), 163. Michael V. Fox states, "The point is that a man should marry a woman he loves, not, say, one who only brings a hefty dowry or family connections" (Michael V. Fox, *A Time to Tear Down and a Time to Build Up: A Rereading of Ecclesiastes* [Grand Rapids, MI: Eerdmans, 1999], 294). Yet Robert Gordis writes, "Koheleth was almost certainly a bachelor, and was certainly no apologist for the marriage institution" (W. Sibley Towner, "Ecclesiastes," in *NIB* [Nashville: Abingdon, 1997], 5:341 cites Gordis, *Koheleth* [1987], 296).

7. Fox, *Ecclesiastes*, 64. Craig Bartholomew similarly states, "Once we realize that the *carpe diem* vision is rooted in a theology of creation, then the case for this woman being one's wife is compelling. Thus v. 9a is a positive affirmation of marriage that is to be fully enjoyed in all its dimensions" (Craig G. Bartholomew, *Ecclesiastes* [Grand Rapids, MI: Baker Academic, 2009], 305).

8. Ilan, *Jewish Women*, 57–60, 60–62, 85–88.

loves," yet the text is unclear about the precise nature of that (or a) relationship (and by "a man" here I refer to Qoheleth's audience). Perhaps his "toil" allows him to spend life with this woman, or it allows him to have this woman as an actual outcome of the toil. Maybe the idea is that, like bread and wine, white clothes and oil, 'Ishah-'asher-'ahavta also tempers the absurdity of death as the ultimate injustice, simultaneously reducing the absurdity of toil. Maybe Qoheleth's mention of "toil" at the end of verse 9 is just a way of limiting the *carpe diem*, lest the audience think that good food, good looks, and good love will truly resolve life's absurdity. After all, *hevel* dominates Qoheleth's rhetoric throughout the book, not *carpe diem*. Notably, 'Ishah-'asher-'ahavta is not referred to as profit but rather as חלקך, "your portion." So she is not necessarily a benefit but more like "what you have coming to you"—an entitlement, perhaps?[9]

To turn the situation a bit on its head, we could allow the themes of "toil" and "profit" in Qoheleth to help us consider how those things might have affected the woman who is loved. Whereas Qoheleth asks, "What advantage is there for a man in all his toil at which he toils under the sun?"[10]—what if we read the underside of the text, as it were, and ask about *her* toil, about her profit? Those questions compel our query precisely because Qoheleth does not overtly consider the loved woman's toil or what might be her "advantage" or "profit." She is merely an object in his lessons to the young men who were presumably Qoheleth's earliest audience (11:9). But today, we are the audience, so I want to raise those unasked questions on behalf of the 'Ishah-'asher-'ahavta who may have wondered about profit and toil much like "her man"—to use the complement of Qoheleth's terminology. What if we compare her to the אשת-חיל, the "strong" or "mighty" woman of Proverbs 31:10-31, who is the very embodiment of "profit," whose "toil" is clearly economically beneficial?[11] Given all of that, I highly suspect that Qoheleth would not have had *her* in mind even as an object on a *carpe diem* list.

It could be illuminating, however, to ask about her "toil" and "profit" by comparing "the woman/wife you love" to today's stay-at-home mom, whose unpaid-for work often remains undercompensated even in the context of divorce proceedings that are specifically supposed to monetarily care for and acknowledge her informal contributions to the economy. We could additionally compare her to today's work-outside-the-home mom,

9. One meaning assigned to the word by Matt Tsevat is "destiny," which could have a more positive connotation. See "חלק," *TDOT*, 4:448.

10. This phrase appears with similar wording in 1:3 and 3:9.

11. See Prov 31:13-14, 16, 18-19, 24.

who, in the United States, will almost certainly receive no paid maternity leave. Could she prompt us to think about the pay inequity that plagues women at all levels of the work force in our own time?

The version of *carpe diem* in 9:7 differs from all others, in that it specifies the menu for how one should enjoy life: bread and wine. Additionally, Qoheleth mentions fashion: oil for one's coiffure and white for one's garments. Not only are food and fashion stereotypical of contemporary women's literature: most of the items in this verse arise from women's work, even in the ancient world. We see biblical examples of women making bread when Abraham asks Sarah to bake bread for their surprise guests (Gen 18:6); in the Medium at Endor baking for Saul (1 Sam 28:24); in Tamar baking for Amnon in an ignorant act of generosity that heightens the evil of his attack (2 Sam 13:8); and in a Widow of Zarephath preparing the last meal for herself and her son, who is prepared to include the prophet Elijah in the meal (1 Kgs 17:12-16). Bread-making was largely women's work in Qoheleth's culture, so to enjoy bread would have involved at least some women's labor.[12] Biblical and ethnographic research suggest that ancient Near Eastern women would have at least participated in viticulture; perhaps their roles were quite prominent (Prov 31:16; Song 1:6).[13] Celebratory white garments, or clothing of any sort for that matter, would also have been produced by women. From spinning to weaving to sewing, and even selling any garments not needed by the family, these jobs were mainly women's work.[14] Proverbs 31:13, 19 offer biblical examples of these jobs in the context of the אשת־חיל, the "Strong Woman."[15] It is important to consider the toil and profit of a "woman you love," 'Ishah-'asher-'ahavta—or of the poor laborers regardless of gender—whose interests Qoheleth ignores. The items in the *carpe diem* of

---

12. See 1 Sam 8:13, and further discussion in Jennie R. Ebeling, *Women's Lives in Biblical Times* (London: T & T Clark, 2010), 48–53. Carol Meyers explains that the development of new milling techniques in the "last centuries B.C.E." probably allowed for bread-making to at least be a less onerous task than it had been in the Iron Age (*Rediscovering Eve: Ancient Israelite Women in Context* [New York: Oxford University Press, 2012], 208). Also see section on 11:1 below, regarding women's role in beer-making. Bread was a key ingredient in beer, so production of the two went hand in hand.

13. Ebeling, *Women's Lives in Biblical Times*, 64–67.

14. Like milling, the work of spinning and weaving benefitted from new inventions in the Hellenistic period, which may have lightened the load of that task, at least for some women. Meyers, *Rediscovering*, 209.

15. Ebeling, *Women's Lives in Biblical Times*, 56–59.

verses 7-8 are all the more reason for Qoheleth to appreciate the "woman," for, without her, would there be bread, wine, white garments, or oil?

Thus מעשה, "work, deed," in verse 10 brings us back to the question, "Whose work allows for the *carpe diem*?" Since the answer seems largely to be "women's work," we should wonder whether and how women are to experience the *carpe diem* as well; who will provide their bread, wine, white garments, oil, and a partner to love? And when will they have a chance to sit or lie down and enjoy those gifts? Of course, this question only lurks, remaining hidden amid Qoheleth's apparently androcentric reflections. Perhaps by bringing this question to the fore we can imagine new ways to seize the day that allow women to joyfully participate rather than setting the stage (and the table) for someone else. Klaas Spronk's observation is relevant here, that "for people in a situation of poverty and oppression, the advice to enjoy life can be heard as a call for protest against their situation and an urge not to give in to resignation."[16] A stance of protest cannot abide much resignation, true; but protest without results does wear one down at some point. Meanwhile, in verse 10 Sheol stands watch as yet another reminder that one's actions have meaning only during one's lifetime. We might wonder whether women could then or can now muster enough כֹּחַ, "might," to make equal impact during our lifetimes as men. History has shown all too often that even a double amount of female "might" (ability) as compared to that of males still leaves us wanting for something as simple as equal pay or recognition.

And just when we might start wallowing in this sad scenario, Qoheleth reminds us that it does not matter anyway. Neither quantity nor quality of effort makes us winners in life; עֵת וָפֶגַע, "time and [mis]chance" (9:11), affect everyone. This statement substantiates my analysis of Qoheleth's "time" poem in 3:1-8—or, rather, what Qoheleth thinks of that poem. That is, while there may well be a "time for everything," the infuriating thing is that we cannot know when that will be, nor can we seem to affect this timing by our own efforts. And while Qoheleth's language in verse 12 is again androcentric ("No אָדָם, *'adam*, knows . . . בְּנֵי הָאָדָם, sons of *ha-'adam*, are snared"), surely the female experience has much to do with this lack of knowing, such as in waiting for menstruation to disprove a suspected pregnancy or waiting for pregnancy to turn into labor.

16. Klaas Spronk, "Dealing with Death: Reading Qoheleth in Different Contexts," in *The Five Scrolls*, ed. Athalya Brenner-Idan, Gale A. Yee, Archie C. C. Lee, Texts@ Contexts 6 (London: Bloomsbury, 2018), 153.

In 9:13-16, Qoheleth tells a story that arguably becomes a parable. At first it seems like it is going to extol wisdom, as one would expect from most sages other than Qoheleth; instead, the commentary on the story undermines wisdom, echoing the theme of the whole section. Wisdom cannot accompany you in death, nor can it necessarily make you memorable after death. This bare-bones story tells of a poor but wise man who saves his small city from a well-equipped army with his wisdom alone. Qoheleth dwells on the fact that the man did not live on in anyone's memory (and deconstructs his own conclusion by remembering and retelling). Furthermore, the Hebrew Bible does contain a similar story about such a hero who was remembered even by King David's General Joab: the nameless woman of Thebez who staved off Abimelech's attack on her town by throwing a millstone down on him from the city tower. Ironically, her memory is preserved in both Judges (9:53-54) and 2 Samuel (11:21), despite the fact that Abimelech went to extreme means to ensure she was forgotten: he had his servant kill him with a sword so that no one could say a woman killed him!

As the chapter closes, Qoheleth illogically continues to extol wisdom (vv. 17-18), having only just undermined it (vv. 15b, 16). Qoheleth similarly undermines wisdom by having cast the shadow of death throughout chapter 9 (as well as in chap. 7 and elsewhere in the book). Yet the effect that Qoheleth's focus on death has on the reader varies widely. Klaas Spronk conducted a reader-response exercise with students, asking for their thoughts about 9:1-12. The notable result was in the diversity of opinion about the passage. From the view that life is, of course, fleeting and one should make the most of it, to the concern that Qoheleth's remarks on death conflict too much with Christian beliefs, the thirty students Spronk surveyed illustrated "the great influence of the context on the way Qoheleth's message is understood and digested."[17] Spronk nuances that statement by pointing out that one's view of death itself varies depending on having either a "community" or "individual" mindset.[18] This finding has much in common with Julie Duncan's analogy that Qoheleth is a "Rorschach Test for the interpreter" and my discussion above about who is at liberty (or not) to *seize the day*. Do wisdom or knowledge or toil or enjoyment matter, over against death? What do we readers think that Qoheleth thinks about these questions? It depends who you ask.

17. Ibid., 148.
18. Ibid., 153.

"You Are Not a Nobody, for 'God Has Accepted Your Deeds' (Qoh 9:7)"

The world is not a safe place, that much we know. Refugees, wars around the globe, increasing tensions between fundamentalists, shootings in schools, earthquakes, viruses—the list could go on and on. Death reigns. "This is an evil in all that happens under the sun" (9:3). How we take awareness of death makes a difference in how we live. Qoheleth urges us to move ahead rather than sit and wait until we die: Go! Eat and drink! Enjoy life with your beloved! Do your best work but do not have any expectations that any of these actions will deliver you from death!

Watching the news one realizes how cheap life is; despite democracy, human rights, advances in medicine and technology, and "progress," we people are "nobodies" at the service of great systems—capitalism, neoliberalism, fundamentalist religious groups, you name them. Annually, thousands die at wars, in slums, in gangs, on the Italian shores or the Mexican–US border trying to enter "paradise"; enslaved, prostituted, environmentally poisoned, lacking medical treatment or food security, or suffering from eating disorders. The vast majority of us are parts in financial, economic, and ideological machines that only look at their own self-preservation. We are nobodies but we suffer in our own bodies these and other marks of corruption, crime, and death—signals of sin, in theological language. These bodies, just as these sins, are gendered; they suffer certain perceptions and treatments and are given a particular use according to how they are perceived to be biologically (or sexually). Just to offer a quick example, the majority of those involved in military conflicts are male, while victims of prostitution are mainly female.

This text offers us good advice to counter those feelings of being nobody to this world. I would stress verse 10: live fully while you live. Why? Because in Sheol there are no deeds, planning, knowledge, or wisdom. A second, very good reason appears in verse 7: "God has accepted your deeds." In a world where our economic value is what we produce; where people's religious value depends on their sacrifices, Qoheleth's assurance is liberating. It is good news! Do what you can while you live, and meanwhile enjoy life's treats (food, drink, oil, clothing, love), knowing that God rejoices with you. In a world ruled by pressure to produce tirelessly, to take seriously this affirmation would mean a humane way of resistance. Being human is much more than working as slaves; being human is being alive, enjoying God's creation (including love), and being no nobody anymore, for God has rejoiced in your deeds. I can hardly imagine a better manner of speaking of God's redeeming love for our time, for the millions of "nobodies" who cannot find a value in themselves because Mammon tells them they do not produce enough, they do not spend enough, they do not count.

Mercedes García Bachmann

Qoheleth 10:1–12:14

Closing Advice and Epilogue

Folly and Wisdom, Kings and Servants (10:1-20)

Chapter 10 contains various proverbs that include imagery ranging from pit digging (v. 8) to wine drinking (vv. 17, 19) and sundry matters in between. Many of these proverbs serve the purpose of illustrating wisdom or folly, but aside from the oft-made connection between the concept of wisdom to the female personified Wisdom, women and women's issues seem to have little place in this chapter. Most contemporary English translations provide the translation "perfumer" or "perfumer's" in 10:1, which likely draws women into a reader's imagination. We should not, however, think of this as the cosmetics section of a department store but rather the workshop of one who mixes scented herbs with oil, most often for cultic purposes.[1] Indeed, Exodus 30:33 and 38 caution against using cultic ointment for secular purposes, though use of noncultic scents by women likely did occur.[2]

Having run through the Hebrew behind many of the distinctive words in the chapter ("perfumer," 1; "slave," 7; "dig," 8; "quarry," "log splitter,"

---

1. As in Exod 30:25, 33, 35; 37:29.
2. Carol Meyers, *Rediscovering Eve: Ancient Israelite Women in Context* (New York: Oxford University Press, 2012), 152; Jennie R. Ebeling, *Women's Lives in Biblical Times* (London: T & T Clark, 2010), 63–64, 71–74. And see, for instance, the list of aromatics and perfumes in Song 4:13-14, associated with a woman.

10:1Dead flies make the perfumer's
ointment give off a foul odor;
so a little folly outweighs wisdom
and honor.
2The heart of the wise inclines to the
right,
but the heart of a fool to the left.
3Even when fools walk on the road,
they lack sense,
and show to everyone that they
are fools.
4If the anger of the ruler rises against
you, do not leave your post,
for calmness will undo great
offenses.
5There is an evil that I have seen
under the sun, as great an error as if it
proceeded from the ruler: 6folly is set
in many high places, and the rich sit
in a low place. 7I have seen slaves on
horseback, and princes walking on foot
like slaves.
8Whoever digs a pit will fall into it;
and whoever breaks through
a wall will be bitten by a
snake.

9; "sharpener," 10; "charmer," 11) while seeking their association with biblical women, the striking result is the notable absence of activities that relate to women. The chapter actually appears to be even more androcentric than we might have assumed, even in a highly androcentric book. The word for עבד, "slave," in verse 7 has masculine connotations; references to female slaves normally use a different word entirely: שפחה (in the plural in Qoh 2:7). The few exceptions to the androcentric vocabulary in chapter 10 include בוקע, "splitting [open]," in 9b, which has only negative associations when applied to females: the "splitting" open ("hatching") of snake eggs in Isaiah 34:15 and 59:5, which appear as metaphorical associations for the day of vengeance on evil ones; horribly, in Hosea 14:1 and Amos 1:13, pregnant women were "split open" as acts of war. The word קלקל, translated "sharpen" or "whet," in verse 10 only has this translation in this place; elsewhere this root basically means "to be light," and may have to do with minimizing or cursing another person. We see this in an interaction between women in Genesis 16:4-5, when Hagar "looks with contempt" as on Sarai in light of Hagar's pregnancy. Finally, the root לחש for "charm" in verse 11 has only to do with women in Isaiah 3:20, which criticizes the Daughters of Zion for their use of "amulets." Thus ancient women may have been hard-pressed to specifically find themselves in or even addressed by the material in chapter 10.

Nonetheless, both ancient and contemporary women can find relevant content in the generic material in chapter 10, finding guidance for living a life of wisdom rather than foolishness, from carefully chosen words

⁹Whoever quarries stones will be hurt by them;
and whoever splits logs will be endangered by them.
¹⁰If the iron is blunt, and one does not whet the edge,
then more strength must be exerted;
but wisdom helps one to succeed.
¹¹If the snake bites before it is charmed, there is no advantage in a charmer.
¹²Words spoken by the wise bring them favor,
but the lips of fools consume them.
¹³The words of their mouths begin in foolishness,
and their talk ends in wicked madness;
¹⁴yet fools talk on and on.
No one knows what is to happen, and who can tell anyone what the future holds?
¹⁵The toil of fools wears them out, for they do not even know the way to town.

(vv. 12-14) to the importance of hard work (v. 18). More specifically, women of all times may find interest in Qoheleth's critique of hierarchy. Wisdom does not necessarily correspond to a high station in society (vv. 5-7). Furthermore, in verses 16-17 Qoheleth seems to extol what we could identify as virtue-led servant leadership, which features a level-headed ruler who presides over serious, sober meals. It is quite possible that Qoheleth sincerely means to extol feasts, wine, and money as reasonable salves or rewards for a ruler, either knowing full well—or completely ignoring—the fact that these luxuries would not be available to most. In contrast to verses 16-17, however, verses 18-19 instead depict laziness and drunkenness. It is possible to imagine a tone of sarcasm between these two sets of verses, particularly if verses 16-17 are stated longingly in the context of a ruler who is best described in verses 18-19.

The chapter ends with a caution that is so foreign to our own time that we have claimed one of its admonitions as a central feature of our current communications: Twitter. The little "bird" identified in verse 20 is the logo of Twitter. This 280-character-limited social media plat-form is so popular with the forty-fifth president of the United States, Donald Trump, that at least one person has identified him as "Tweety."[3] Qoheleth's reference, however, cautions a "speaker" low in society's hierarchy to censure even their thoughts, but especially their words—

3. Christina K. Young, personal communication.

Qoh 10:1–20 (cont.)

¹⁶Alas for you, O land, when your king is a servant,
and your princes feast in the morning!
¹⁷Happy are you, O land, when your king is a nobleman,
and your princes feast at the proper time,
for strength, and not for drunkenness!
¹⁸Through sloth the roof sinks in, and through indolence the house leaks.
¹⁹Feasts are made for laughter; wine gladdens life,
and money meets every need.
²⁰Do not curse the king, even in your thoughts,
or curse the rich, even in your bedroom;
for a bird of the air may carry your voice,
or some winged creature tell the matter.

lest they cause trouble with the regnal leaders. While few in our society heed such warnings, the sentiment is nonetheless apt: students, employees, and other low-power players today risk their stations with their tweets, while higher-ups seem to get away with carelessness in those 280 characters. This close to the chapter draws together additional "watch your mouth" comments in the chapter as well as in the book as a whole (10:12-14; 5:4-6 [3-5]).

Cautionary Proverbs, What You Don't Know (11:1-10)

Qoheleth 11:1-2 has long struck interpreters as obscure in meaning. Does it advocate charity, assuming that sharing one's food with those far away will bring rewards? Is Qoheleth's point here to promote wise investment, with the idea that the investment will go across the waters on a merchant ship and return in the form of profits? Antoon Schoors summarizes the scholarship on these verses and concludes that the meaning is "that one should act both daringly and prudently."[4] In stark contrast to the consensus of interpretations, Michael M. Homan argues that the process of ancient beer-brewing is described in these verses and offers the following translation of them:

> Throw your bread upon the face of the water,
> because in many days you will acquire it.

---

4. Antoon Schoors, *Ecclesiastes* (Leuven: Peeters, 2013), 763–68.

11:1Send out your bread upon the waters,
for after many days you will get it back.
2Divide your means seven ways, or even eight,
for you do not know what disaster may happen on earth.
3When clouds are full,
they empty their rain on the earth;
whether a tree falls to the south or to the north,
in the place where the tree falls,
there it will lie.
4Whoever observes the wind will not sow;
and whoever regards the clouds will not reap.
5Just as you do not know how the breath comes to the bones in the mother's womb, so you do not know the work of God, who makes everything.
6In the morning sow your seed, and at evening do not let your hands be idle; for you do not know which will prosper, this or that, or whether both alike will be good.

Give a serving to seven and also to eight,
because you do not know what evil will be upon the land.[5]

In the ancient Near East, brewing beer basically involved baking loaves of bread out of malted barley, placing the bread in water, and then allowing that mixture to ferment for about five days before drinking it through a perforated straw or pitcher designed to strain out the detritus.[6] If these verses are about brewing and sharing beer, we could thus consider 11:1-2 an eighth instance of the *carpe diem*: "make ale, and share it broadly!" Qoheleth's concluding comment in 11:2b, "for you do not know what disaster may happen on earth," finds parallels in justifications for the *carpe diem* elsewhere in the book.[7]

Of note for our feminist analysis of Qoheleth is the likelihood—argued by Homan, Jennie Ebeling, and a few others—that women were

5. Michael M. Homan, "Beer Production by Throwing Bread into Water: A New Interpretation of Qoh. Xi 1-2," *VT* 52 (2002): 276; Michael M. Homan, "Did the Ancient Israelites Drink Beer?," *BAR* 36 (2010): 48. In note 11 Homan explains that the beverage was more like ale than beer, in the absence of carbonation and hops.

6. Michael M. Homan, "Beer and Its Drinkers: An Ancient Near Eastern Love Story," *Eastern Archaeology* 67 (2004): 84–95, at 91; Homan, "Did the Ancient Israelites Drink Beer?"

7. Homan links it specifically to 9:7. "Beer Production by Throwing Bread into Water," 276. Other justifications for the *carpe diem* are: 2:24b-25; 3:13, 22b; 5:18b-19 [17b-18]; 8:15b; 9:9b; 11:9b.

Qoh 11:1-10 (cont.)

[7]Light is sweet, and it is pleasant for the eyes to see the sun.

[8]Even those who live many years should rejoice in them all; yet let them remember that the days of darkness will be many. All that comes is vanity.

[9]Rejoice, young man, while you are young, and let your heart cheer you in the days of your youth. Follow the inclination of your heart and the desire of your eyes, but know that for all these things God will bring you into judgment.

[10]Banish anxiety from your mind, and put away pain from your body; for youth and the dawn of life are vanity.

the primary brewers and vendors of beer, at least in home settings, but perhaps also in the context of the wider community.[8] The basic logic here is that since in the ancient world beer was made from loaves of bread, and women made the bread, women made the beer too. Beer was a daily dietary staple that supplemented calories and provided something safe to drink, since the alcohol content (albeit low, 2–3 percent) killed the harmful impurities in straight water.[9] Thus women prepared beer along with the other regular foodstuffs of ancient Near Eastern families. In Egyptian artistic depictions of brewing, the women who baked bread were the same ones who then used that bread to brew beer.[10] Allred notes elsewhere that the Sumerian beer deity Ninkasi was a goddess, whereas other deities linked to manufacturing processes were male. He views this as one of many reasons to link ancient beer production to women, who were also often the tavern keepers of the time, perhaps in part due to the linkage of taverns and prostitution.[11] Here readers of Qoheleth

8. Homan, "Did the Ancient Israelites Drink Beer?"; Lance Allred, "Beer and Women in Mesopotamia," unpublished, 2015. Michal Dayagi-Mendels, *Drink and Be Merry: Wine and Beer in Ancient Times* (Jerusalem: The Israel Museum, 2000), 119.

9. Homan, "Beer and Its Drinkers," 85. In contrast, Dayagi-Mendels, *Drink and Be Merry*, cites W. Röllig, *Das Bier im Alten Mesopotamien* (1970) to assert that ancient beer had an alcohol level of 6–8 percent. Since Homan describes his own experiment in ancient beer-making, his conclusion seems well supported, but the alcohol content probably did vary based on who was brewing the ale, and when and how.

10. Homan, "Did the Ancient Israelites Drink Beer?" Michael Homan and Jennie Ebeling, "Baking and Brewing Beer in the Israelite Household," in *The World of Women in the Ancient and Classical Near East*, ed. Beth Alpert Nakhai (Newcastle upon Tyne: Cambridge Scholars, 2008), 49, 62.

11. Lance Allred, "Beer and Women in Mesopotamia," 1–2 *et passim*. Allred's anthropological analysis later in the article supports this point with evidence of female ale-brewers ("often women of ill-repute") from Early Modern England (4–5).

would do well to recall Siduri, the "brewer" in the Gilgamesh Epic, who essentially gave Qoheleth's *carpe diem* advice (9:7-9) to Gilgamesh.[12] Homan explains that "after the Old Babylonian period, when a mass production industry was implemented and males began to dominate the state-run business . . . women continued to produce beer on a smaller scale in their homes."[13] This would likely have affected women of different classes in varying ways.

In the mid-Hellenistic period, when Qoheleth was likely written, most anyone would have some limited familiarity with the brewing process; boys would have at least watched or helped their mothers with the process, and men may have had experience with mass-produced ale. If Qoheleth's comments in 11:1-2 indeed describe beer brewing, it may well have connoted a scene of women brewers. This point could easily be lost on contemporary readers. Furthermore, given the likelihood that women produced the ale to which Qoheleth refers here, this may be another instance of Qoheleth taking for granted the fruits of women's work, as we have observed elsewhere in the book with regard to mourning, the making and serving of other foodstuffs, child bearing and rearing, among other things. The expectation that food and drink will be available for the sake of enjoying life relies on women to produce those things, yet—at least as far as Qoheleth is concerned—does not acknowledge their contribution.

In 11:2-6, Qoheleth again dwells on the matter of "not knowing," recalling prior sections of the book.[14] In three places in chapter 11 Qoheleth actually repeats the phrase "you do not know" (2, 5 [twice], 6). With strikingly feminine imagery, verse 5 explicitly connects this "not knowing" to the mysteries of conception and gestation. The root of the word in verse 5 for "filled" or "full" (belly), בטן מלאה, as in, "the breath/spirit's way in the full belly [e.g., womb]," notably also appears in verse 3 in reference to full clouds (מלא, *niphal*). Thus the quickening of rain clouds and fetus provide imagery for Qoheleth's reflections on both hopefulness and "not knowing" and the futility of trying to know "the work of God, who

12. See Julie Ann Duncan, *Ecclesiastes*, AOTC (Nashville: Abingdon, 2017) for an excellent treatment of the Gilgamesh Epic in comparison to Qoheleth (xxix–xxiv; 134–37).

13. Homan, "Beer and Its Drinkers," 85; Allred, "Beer and Women," 1. This also relates to Meyers's point that new milling technologies were available "in the last centuries B.C.E.," which would have lightened the load for women in terms of bread-making (*Rediscovering*, 208).

14. "Not knowing" appears in 3:11, 21; 2:19, 22; 6:12; 8:1, 7, 17; 9:12.

makes everything" (5b). We could rightly wonder whether this imagery places women closer to knowing or to unknowing! The theological framing of this section has Qoheleth's distinctly unhopeful mark. The point is not "rest assured, God has it handled," but "only God knows; you do not!" The process of planting in verse 6—whether seeds for food crops or semen for procreation—similarly illustrates an unknowable process with an unknowable outcome. The logic of the verse makes life sound a bit like gambling: do as much as you can, as much of the time as you can, because some of what you do might not matter!

Verses 7-10 take on a distinctly positive tone, in contrast to the "not knowing" theme from the earlier verses. Still, Qoheleth finds a way to hold most of these upbeat comments in check by pairing them with cautionary caveats. In 8b "the darkness" (החשך) and *hevel* restrain "the light" (האור) and the joy of life in 7-8a. Divine judgment stands watch over the pleasures of youth in verse 9; verse 10 wraps up the chapter with warnings about "anxiety, anger" (כעס), "pain, suffering" (רעה), and, of course, *hevel*. Verse 9 in particular describes Qoheleth's audience, that of one "young man" (בחור) or more. This reference could easily marginalize female readers—not to mention verse 6, if we sexualize it—yet there is plenty here of use for women, whether Qoheleth intended that or not. This would be a good time to remember the possible "slip" in 7:22, which addressed Qoheleth's listeners with a feminine second-person form.

Closing Poem: "Days of Youth; Days of Trouble" (12:1-8)

Interpreters have assigned this poem two main meanings: one in which the images are viewed as allegorical for physical decay and death; the other in which the poem as a whole describes the eschaton, the end of time.[15] Both meanings are worth considering, for a very logical reason: individual death is the end of time for each of us. We should not be surprised that apocalypticism continually resurfaces in various time periods and social situations, as the end is potentially near for each of us at all times. Perhaps this is the ultimate self-centeredness: When I end, the world ends—at least for me—so what's the difference? Certain events

15. Michael V. Fox provides a helpful discussion of both options in *A Time to Tear Down and a Time to Build Up: A Rereading of Ecclesiastes* (Grand Rapids, MI: Eerdmans, 1999), 347–49. Also see a summary of views in Thomas Krüger, *Qoheleth: A Commentary*, ed. Klaus Baltzer, trans. O. C. Dean, Hermeneia (Minneapolis: Fortress, 2004), 198–201.

Qoh 12:1-8

12:1Remember your creator in the days of your youth, before the days of trouble come, and the years draw near when you will say, "I have no pleasure in them"; 2before the sun and the light and the moon and the stars are darkened and the clouds return with the rain; 3in the day when the guards of the house tremble, and the strong men are bent, and the women who grind cease working because they are few, and those who look through the windows see dimly; 4when the doors on the street are shut, and the sound of the grinding is low, and one rises up at the sound of a bird, and all the daughters of song are brought low; 5when one is afraid of heights, and terrors are in the road; the almond tree blossoms, the grasshopper drags itself along and desire fails; because all must go to their eternal home, and the mourners will go about the streets; 6before the silver cord is broken, and the pitcher is broken at the fountain, and the wheel broken at the cistern, 7and the dust returns to the earth as it was, and the breath returns to God who gave it. 8Vanity of vanities, says the Teacher; all is vanity.

in life intensify this, from cancer to war, but in the end we all know on some level that any of us and any of our loved ones could die at any given moment for any number of reasons. Qoheleth responds to this knowledge with the usual assessment: *hevel* (three times in 12:8, for the final references). We need not let this prevail in our own minds, however. Qoheleth has also suggested the *carpe diem* throughout the book; perhaps some balance of *hevel* and *carpe diem* will allow us to best manage the apocalyptic realities of life.

Qoheleth 12:1 provides an interpretive lens for the section, the main questionable factor being how to understand "days" and "years"—do these refer to one's individual life or to all of time? Qoheleth invokes בוראיך, "your creator," at the beginning of 12:1. Isaiah favors this particular title for God. In the phrase, "remember your creator," we ought also to remember Qoheleth's previous comments about God; this is not necessarily a comforting admonition when we review the number of times Qoheleth stated "fear God."[16] Qoheleth mentions fear of God five additional times, in various ways or "God will judge" (3:17). In 12:1, as well as 11:9-10 and further into chapter 12, Qoheleth expresses concern about aging and leaving behind youth. Given the lower life-expectancy

---

16. "Fear God" appears in 3:14; 5:7 [6]; 7:18; 8:12, 13; 12:13.

of women in the Hellenistic period, these reflections would likely have affected young women differently than young men.[17]

The obscure references of this passage begin in verse 2 with a series of perplexing images, which can be interpreted in a variety of ways. It seems possible that Qoheleth has in mind the end of all creation with the darkening of the heavenly lights; we do find here some typical apocalyptic imagery. The darkening of the sun, light, moon, and stars has some commonality with images of darkness in Joel 2:2 and Amos 5:18, 20. Indeed, the undoing of the heavenly lights reverses creation in Genesis 1:2, where creation begins with "darkness" and the creator inserts "lights" and "stars" in verses 3-5, 14-17 (use אור, "light," and כוכבים, "stars," like Qoh 12:2). An old-age scenario, on the other hand, could refer to one's dimming vision and "clouds" to cataracts.

Many have provided interesting interpretations of the imagery in verse 3, though they vary widely.[18] In an old-age scenario, the house-guards shaking could suggest tremors, while bent strong men could describe compromised posture. An apocalyptic interpretation could read those shaking as earthquakes and their subsequent destruction; other possibilities include mud or rock slides, uprooted trees, or the idea of mountains crumbling in end times. The NRSV of verse 3 appears to provide one of Qoheleth's few specific references to women. What underlies the translation "women who grind," however, is an infrequently used root, which appears as a feminine participle only here. Including "women" in the translation makes for a poetic parallel with "strong men," but the Hebrew actually includes the word אנשי, "men," while "grinders" only has a feminine ending rather than the word "women." In some cases, we see that grinding was women's work, such as in Isaiah 47:2, and that was still likely the case in Qoheleth's time.[19] In one case it refers to women's sexual activity (Job 31:10). Here it may metaphorically indicate the results of aging, whether that be dental loss (for men or women) or decreased or ceased sexual activity. "Those who look through the windows" at the end of verse 3 uses a feminine participle. (It recalls the scene of Sisera's mother looking through the window in Judg 5:28.) Viewed through an

---

17. Ebeling, *Women's Lives in Biblical Times*, 101; Tal Ilan, *Jewish Women in Greco-Roman Palestine* (Peabody, MA: Hendrickson, 1996), 116–19; Tal Ilan, *Integrating Women into Second Temple History*, TSAJ 76 (Peabody, MA: Hendrickson, 2001), 207.

18. For a detailed summary see Schoors, *Ecclesiastes*, 800–802.

19. Ebeling, *Women's Lives in Biblical Times*, 48–51, 59, 137; Meyers, *Rediscovering Eve*, 208.

apocalyptic lens, it could refer to the end of day-to-day food production work. In any case, the opacity of the words as well as the wider metaphor fits perfectly with the poetic genre, though it frustrates those of us who want to know for sure what the poem means.

The imagery in verse 4 similarly perplexes the contemporary reader. Understanding the poem as an extended old-age metaphor, we could imagine "doors shut" as compromised vision, perhaps even cataracts. The reference to "mill" in verse 4 contains the same infrequently used root as "grinders" in verse 3, and here again it could indicate difficulty chewing or even perhaps the gravelly sound of an elderly voice. One who arises at the littlest birdsong could describe the insomnia typical of old age.[20] We find an interesting feminine reference at the end of 12:4, in בנות השיר, "daughters of song." In all likelihood there is no special significance to the use of "daughters" other than to create a poetic metaphor that might indicate the compromised vocal usage of old age. Perhaps "daughters" would have indicated a diminutive, suggesting that once-high voices were now quite low, maybe to parallel the low grinding earlier in the verse. Didymus the Blind, a fourth-century CE Christian theologian, understood the "daughters" reference as a strong caution against women's "false" teaching, adding to our list of historic sexist interpretations of Qoheleth.[21] An apocalyptic interpretation could invite us to read the imagery in verse 4 as the ceasing of human activity and indeed the absence of human habitation. In that scenario, however, it is more difficult to imagine how arising at the sound of a bird would fit.

The redundant mention of "fear" and "terror" in verse 5 seems to suggest a cautious approach to life, perhaps a life riddled with previously unknown physical limitations. The subsequent images may indicate graying hair and a limping gait. Or perhaps "fear" and "terror" bring us back to Qoheleth's oft-repeated admonition to "fear God."[22] The word אביונה, most often translated "desire," creates much uncertainty, as it is a *hapax legomenon*. BDB identifies it as "caper-berry," which is understood as an aphrodisiac. If it fails, then presumably one has lost sexual desire.[23] The end of this verse refers to בית עולמו, "his eternal home," as well as to

---

20. Choon-Leong Seow, *Ecclesiastes: A New Translation with Introduction and Commentary*, AB 18C (New York: Doubleday, 1997), 357–58.

21. Cited in Schoors, *Ecclesiastes*, 805.

22. Schoors favors this interpretation (*Ecclesiastes*, 807). "Fear God" appears in 3:14; 5:7 [6]; 7:18; 8:12, 13; 12:13.

23. BDB, 2.

"mourners who go around," both of which could fit in an end-of-life or end-of-the-world scenario easily enough. Qoheleth's use of the verb סבב (*qal*) for the "going about" of the mourners recalls the opening poem of the book, where the circular pattern of the wind in 1:6 helps illustrate *hevel*, and yet again this imagery should cause us to imagine the women who would likely have been present in such a scene.

Some of the most perplexing imagery of this poem appears in verse 6. Several text-critical issues apply, and a prominent theological rendering of the verse is quite misleading: "Remember him" (NASB, NIV) may seem to invoke the deity, particularly for faith communities that use the masculine pronoun essentially as a name for the deity, but neither word appears in the Hebrew or Greek.[24] The word כסף, "silver," is straightforward enough, but חבל, "cord," has a range of interpretive options. In addition to "cord," the translations "band" (1 Sam 10:5, 10), "portion" (Deut 32:9 and more),[25] and even "region" (Deut 3:4 and elsewhere)[26] are feasible. In the scheme of the poem, "silver" could refer to the whitening hair of age, as we may have previously seen in verse 5, particularly if it were describing "portion" instead of "cord." It is tempting to make something of the sound similarity of חבל, *chevel*, to Qoheleth's theme-word *hevel*, but it would seem an odd usage, being paired with "silver." The verb relating to the "silver portion" raises some questions too. For instance, the *ketiv* has to do with distance, ירחק, while the *qere* indicates being bound, ירתק (with a difference of one, and similar, letter). In either case, it seems to suggest demise or destruction; if the "silver portion" refers to an aged person's head, then death would certainly come to mind.

A logical poetical pairing with "silver" is "gold" (v. 6). Elsewhere silver and gold unsurprisingly refer to great value and appear as a paired illustration of such in Proverbs 22:1, for instance. Destruction also relates to the "golden bowl," though the interpretation of that metaphor is more elusive. One's bladder, perhaps? The use of "bowl" elsewhere for "spring" (Josh 15:19; Judg 1:15) could lead us to the metaphorical interpretation of "golden bowl" as the imagined housing for one's life-force; a life-spring? The "pitcher" or "jug" in 12:6 has feminine connotations elsewhere. First, it appears in the scene between Rebekah and Abraham's servant, who was seeking a wife for his master's son Isaac. The "jug"

24. Krüger, *Qoheleth*, 191.
25. As in 1 Chr 16:18; Ps 105:11; Josh 17:5, 14; 19:9; Ezek 47:13.
26. As in Deut 3:13, 14; 1 Kgs 4:13; Josh 19:29.

in that scene appears with great frequency,[27] clearly highlighted as the characteristic that will identify a divinely appointed sexual partner for Isaac (v. 14), so that we might imagine the object as a sexual referent, womb-shaped as it is. In the scene between the Widow of Zarapeth and Elijah (1 Kgs 17:12), the "jug" repeatedly connotes the widow's last meal, while in 1 Kings 17:14 and 16 it conversely represents her survival. The "spring" where this "jug" breaks in Qoheleth 12:6 only appears elsewhere in Isaiah 35:7 and 49:10, where it metaphorically provides sustenance for returning exiles. "Wheel," גלגל, has theological connotations in several places.[28] Here, as throughout the poem, the wheel is destroyed, נרץ, "crushed" (probably from the root רצץ), at the בור, "[water] well." "Well" elsewhere can indicate the "grave."[29] Like the "jug" earlier in this verse, "well" has definitively female sexual connotations again, like in Genesis 24 as well as Proverbs 5:15 and Isaiah 51:1.[30] Perhaps the vocabulary here, which can be viewed as sexually suggestive of female anatomy, indicates an "M" voice, as we saw above in Athalya Brenner and Fokkelien van Dijk-Hemmes's categories and Brenner's analysis of the poem in 3:1-8.[31] On the other hand, might these references instead indicate a hidden female presence in this passage? Regardless of all the ambiguity surrounding this particular verse, the combined force of all its verbs recommend ultimate destruction and demise, whether personal, communal, or universal. Furthermore, regardless of how we interpret the nouns in this verse, whether as body parts, bodily functions, or crucial aspects of survival, the point is all about their coming to an end.

Verse 7 works with verse 1 to create an interpretive lens for 12:1-8. The return of "dust" to the earth and "breath" to God invokes Genesis 2:7, thus death.[32] The mention of Elohim in verse 7 recalls the opening reference to "your creator" in 12:1. Despite many unclear metaphors in the passage, the overall picture seems more likely to be one of death, rather

27. Gen 24:14, 15, 16, 17, 18, 20, 43, 45, 46.

28. Ezek 10:2, 6, 13; Ps 77:19.

29. Prov 28:17; Isa 14:19; Ps 30:3 [4]; Isa 14:15; Ezek 32:23, among others.

30. Susan Niditch, "Genesis," in *Women's Bible Commentary*, ed. Carol A. Newsom, Sharon H. Ringe, and Jacqueline E. Lapsley, 3rd ed. (Louisville: Westminster John Knox, 2012), 33–34.

31. Athalya Brenner and Fokkelien van Dijk Hemmes, *On Gendering Texts: Female and Male Voices in the Hebrew Bible*, BibInt 1 (Leiden: Brill, 1993).

32. Gen 2:7 contains the same word for "dust" (עפר) as Qoh 12:7, but not the same words for "earth" (Qoheleth has ארץ instead of אדמה) or "breath" (Qoheleth has רוח rather than נשמה).

than an eschatological vision. Indeed, the book as a whole does not seem to recommend an apocalyptic scenario. Qoheleth has had many opportunities to find recourse in apocalypticism and did not do so. Instead, the Sage dwells on death, proclaims *hevel* repeatedly, and recommends the *carpe diem* as a distraction.

This abundant concern about death, particularly as associated with metaphors about old age in 12:1-8, returns us to the question of ageism I raised in the context of 4:13-16. In 12:1-8, Qoheleth's emphasis on the deterioration of the aging body surely detracts from our confidence in the elderly. In 4:13, the "old but foolish king" receives the downside of the better-than proverb introducing that parable. Nonetheless, the difficulties in understanding 4:13-16 as a whole and the absence of Qoheleth's detraction from age other than in its physical effects in 12:1-8 leave us unable to conclude whether the Sage had an ageist agenda or just viewed everything, as usual, as *hevel*. I am more inclined to think that Qoheleth was as skeptical about youth as about age as a whole but found the aging process particularly worthy of lament in terms of physical suffering—perhaps that was due to personal experience.

Epilogue (12:9-14)

If the book was full of contradictions up to this point, Qoheleth—or whoever authored this section (and this part indeed seems an addition from another hand, according to tradition and to many scholars)—does not stop with the epilogue. Verses 9-10, 11-12, then 13-14 alternate between what seems to be pious praise for the Sage, and much more critical, negative assessments of what we have read above. Verses 9-10 extol Qoheleth in typical wisdom language, calling the Sage "wise" and highlighting "knowledge" and the "proverbs" in the preceding book. Qoheleth's work is identified with positive attributes: "pleasing" and "true." Yet in the very next verses, the description changes significantly. What had been "pleasing" in verse 10 is like a "goad" in verse 11. While "goad" is neither a common word in the Hebrew Bible (other than 1 Sam 13:21) nor a word used in common parlance, its parallel in the verse, "nails," helps express the point. The epilogist—or Qoheleth as the epilogist—now compares Qoheleth's words to harsh physical treatment intended to motivate behavior. The view that "much study wearies the flesh" seems quite anathema to the Sages, or at least only something they would mutter to one another rather than commit to writing! Yet we have seen that Qoheleth is no typical Sage but an author who revels in undermining

⁹Besides being wise, the Teacher also taught the people knowledge, weighing and studying and arranging many proverbs. ¹⁰The Teacher sought to find pleasing words, and he wrote words of truth plainly.

¹¹The sayings of the wise are like goads, and like nails firmly fixed are the collected sayings that are given by one shepherd. ¹²Of anything beyond these, my child, beware. Of making many books there is no end, and much study is a weariness of the flesh.

¹³The end of the matter; all has been heard. Fear God, and keep his commandments; for that is the whole duty of everyone. ¹⁴For God will bring every deed into judgment, including every secret thing, whether good or evil.

traditional beliefs. The epilogue presents a similar situation as what we saw in 8:10-14, where Qoheleth's rhetoric goes back and forth between apparently extolling traditional theology and critiquing it in such detail that the audience can never again accept it without serious misgivings. Unlike the NRSV translation, Qoheleth writes to "my son," not "my child," in verse 12. Here the Sage assumes a male audience, which again raises the issues of gender in the book. Again, maybe it is a good time to recall the feminine form in 7:22, which suggests a less androcentric or at least more ambiguously gendered group. In any case, many of us women have decided to listen to Qoheleth anyway and provide our own critiques, whether we were invited or not.

Finally, verses 13-14 wrap up the book and the epilogue, apparently with due piety. While Qoheleth repeats "fear God" throughout the book,[33] as well as "God will judge" (3:17), "commandments" only appears once before this second-to-last verse, in 8:5. Nonetheless, the material in the epilogue has enough in common with the whole book that we need not assign it to a separate author. Qoheleth's references to God, as well as the alternation between apparently pious statements and compelling critiques, strangely tie the book together, including the epilogue. In the end, Qoheleth does not stand in between any of us and God; we can decide for ourselves what the divine judgment in verse 14 will mean for us.

33. Qoh 3:14; 5:7 [6]; 7:18; 8:12, 13.

Afterword

Qoheleth as a Model for Feminist Hermeneutics[1]

Suspicious Bible reading has long been acknowledged as central to feminist methodology. Accompanied by a hermeneutic of suspicion, feminists have been able to approach the biblical text as well as traditional theologies by asking questions that allow for their full inclusion as interpreters and theologians. The book of Qoheleth, while arguably misogynistic in places, stands as a canonized example of a hermeneutic of suspicion.[2] Qoheleth is full of questions about religious tradition and may thus serve as a canonical model for suspicious reading among feminist interpreters. Qoheleth enlists a healthy hermeneutic of suspicion, of which any feminist should be proud. Qoheleth contains perplexing theological reflections that frequently struggle with the issue of divine justice. One of the unique aspects of this book is that, though it is theological, Qoheleth does not take God or religious doctrine as a starting point. Instead, Qoheleth autobiographically analyzes the experience of life and the observable world. Only secondarily does Qoheleth

---

1. Parts of this section are based on Lisa Wolfe, "Ecclesiastes as a Model for Feminist Hermeneutics," paper presented at the Annual Meeting of the Society of Biblical Literature (Philadelphia, PA, November 22, 2005).

2. See, in particular, 7:26-28, and my commentary on it in this volume.

ask how God fits in to the scenario of these experiences. Qoheleth's religious tradition answered these theological questions in ways that often did not coincide with the serious and pressing realities that Qoheleth saw throughout life.

Qoheleth aims not to persuade the audience of one particular idea in the area of divine justice (whether the effectiveness of retribution or "fear God") but rather to undermine our beliefs on the topic. In fact, in places such as 8:10-15, Qoheleth challenges or even taunts the audience by harshly juxtaposing dogma with a conflicting reality in a highly dialogical manner. The stanzas of 8:10-15 highlight this tension with their opening words. We have seen how Qoheleth shifts from reporting experience to asserting tradition: "Then I saw" in verse 10a introduces a *hevel* experience. In verse 12b Qoheleth uses "yet I also know" to move from observations to pointing out how tradition contradicts experience. For another shift, Qoheleth returns to "absurd" experience in verse 14, where *hevel* both begins and ends the chiastic verse. Qoheleth then closes the pericope with "so I recommended" to introduce the *carpe diem* conclusion in verse 15. I count this style as the method through which Qoheleth expresses persuasive intent. Qoheleth does not want us to remain in the illusion that divine justice occurs in a humanly observable way. Qoheleth insists on repeatedly pointing out the rent between tradition and experience in the area of divine justice, thus pushing a hermeneutic of suspicion on the audience.

Qoheleth's experiences so contradict Israelite tradition that the Sage questions it rigorously and ultimately develops a hermeneutic of suspicion about it. As illustrated particularly in 3:16-22; 7:15-18; and 8:10-15, Qoheleth "sees" injustice dramatically played out in the midst of ordinary life. Qoheleth still claims a tradition that taught Israelites to expect that God would rectify injustice by rewarding the righteous and punishing the wicked. Instead, Qoheleth observes the reverse to be true. The righteous and the wicked sometimes receive opposite treatment of what they "deserve" according to the understanding of retribution theology, as we see in these three passages. Through the realization that reality does not always bear out Israelite ideology, Qoheleth encounters a severe challenge to this view of divine justice. For Qoheleth, seeing gives rise to disbelieving. Furthermore, Qoheleth illustrates the reality that *hakkol hevel*, "everything is absurd." Qoheleth shows this by carefully structuring the rhetoric so that "the way things should be" and "the way things are" stand in stark contrast.

One of the most significant contemporary meanings we can glean from Qoheleth concerns this experience-based hermeneutic of suspicion. As

Qoheleth relates the struggle between doctrine and experience, the Sage models the difficult theological act of truth-telling when truth challenges the status quo. Suspicion is not an uncomplicated or automatic hermeneutical response, especially in light of widely held religious doctrines. Sharon Ringe articulates this in regard to feminist hermeneutics. She writes that feminist interpretation "is not easy because of the effort that must be expended to analyze the experience that results from one's reality, and, most of all, because commitment to the vitality of women's lives requires living against the grain (including reading against the texts) of the dominant kyriarchal society."[3] Thus, being rooted in experience that does not conform to doctrine (Scripture and/or tradition) may lead to the difficult task of reading with a hermeneutic of suspicion. This frequently has been true for women, as our experiences are often dissonant with the sacred texts and traditions. Indeed, Valerie Saiving's groundbreaking essay on feminist theology relied on her observation that the standard definition of "sin" in theology was utterly foreign to her experience and, more broadly, to the female experience.[4]

Although women are not the only interpreters who read with a hermeneutic of suspicion, this stance is one that has been appropriately adopted and refined by women hermeneuts. While the job of suspicious reading is difficult because it goes "against the grain" of the text—and indeed against the grain of the faith community—it nonetheless offers women and other oppressed groups a way to "be" in a faith whose sacred texts and religious doctrines frequently conflict with their experiences. Through a hermeneutic of suspicion, women have found the freedom to reject or to reinterpret texts that conflict with their experience. Many of us are familiar with Renita Weems's telling of the story about Howard Thurman's grandmother, for whom this meant rejecting Paul's writings supporting slavery in light of her experience as a slave.[5] For some women, this means rejecting and reinterpreting biblical texts that denounce female church leadership in light of their own experience of a call to ordained ministry. The difficult job of reading texts against the

3. Sharon H. Ringe, "An Approach to a Critical, Feminist, Theological Reading of the Bible," in *A Feminist Companion to Reading the Bible: Approaches, Methods and Strategies*, ed. Athalya Brenner and Carole Fontaine (Sheffield: Sheffield Academic, 1997), 156–57.

4. Valerie C. Saiving, "Where Is the Woman?" *ThTo* 19 (1962): 111–14.

5. Renita J. Weems, "Reading *Her Way* Through the Bible: African American Women and the Bible," in *Stony the Road We Trod: African American Biblical Interpretation*, ed. Cain Hope Felder (Minneapolis: Fortress, 1991), 61–62. Also see my longer discussion of this reference above, in commentary on 7:15-29.

grain of oppressive tradition could be identified as a vital act, especially for women.

The author of this Scroll fervently expresses the androcentric world-view of the time. Nonetheless, Qoheleth, like feminists, uses an experience-prompted hermeneutic of suspicion toward religious doctrine in light of those experiences that discredit tradition. Carole Fontaine also notes this irony in her chapter on "Ecclesiastes" in the second edition of the *Women's Bible Commentary*.[6] In 8:14 we find Qoheleth's provocative comment that the righteous and the wicked are treated according to the acts of the other—a stark challenge to the tradition of retribution theology, which is the standard answer to theodicy in Israelite tradition.

Because Qoheleth reads against the grain of the texts and traditions that would have been lifeblood for an ancient Sage, I believe this book can serve as a scriptural model for a hermeneutic of suspicion and, as such, as a model for feminist hermeneutics. The book has suspicious readings in common with feminists, and, for feminists who claim connection to communities of faith, Qoheleth may be a pattern and a reminder to read the rest of the canon warily, especially when one's experience clashes with tradition.

Qoheleth undoubtedly has limits as a "feminist" hermeneut. Aside from the blatantly misogynistic passages and the inherent androcentrism of the book, Qoheleth's experiences only prompt the suspicious, deconstructive part of the hermeneutical circle. The Sage either cannot or does not offer any adequate hermeneutic of recovery. *Carpe diem* may provide salve for the day, but it does not replace the theology that Qoheleth deconstructs. To employ some of Elisabeth Schüssler Fiorenza's vocabulary, Qoheleth is a good model for the feminist act of "resistance" to dominant texts but does not in my view attain any level of "transformation," which is the final and crucial step.[7] Therefore, in order to help Qoheleth out of the mediocre conclusion to "seize the day," we might place Qoheleth in dialogue with any number of contemporary feminist theologians in order to attain a hermeneutic of recovery—or, to again use Schüssler Fiorenza's words, "a hermeneutics of creative imagination and ritualization"—in response to the same kinds of questions the Sage pondered.[8] Feminist biblicists receive from Qoheleth a canonized model

6. Carole R. Fontaine, "Ecclesiastes," in *Women's Bible Commentary*, ed. Carol A. Newsom and Sharon H. Ringe, 2nd ed. (Louisville: Westminster John Knox, 1998), 162.

7. Elisabeth Schüssler Fiorenza, "Feminist Hermeneutics," *ABD*, 2:786.

8. Ibid., 790.

for reading not only tradition but also the text itself with a similarly suspicious approach.[9] Furthermore, for those who assign authority to the biblical text, Qoheleth's validation of experience-based theology holds significance. It shows that theology as rooted in experience arose long before nontraditional, modern, or postmodern approaches.

9. For example, Lisa M. Wolfe, "Seeing Gives Rise to Disbelieving: Experiences that Prompt a Hermeneutic of Suspicion in Ecclesiastes and Wendy Farley's Theodicy of Compassion" (PhD diss., Northwestern University, 2013); Lisa M. Wolfe, "Ecclesiastes as a Model."

Works Cited

Allred, Lance. "Beer and Women in Mesopotamia." Unpublished, 2015.

Andrews, Susan R. "Ecclesiastes 7:1-19." *Int* 55 (2001): 299–301.

Attridge, Harold W., ed. *The HarperCollins Study Bible: Fully Revised and Updated.* New York: HarperCollins, 2006.

Bal, Mieke. *Death and Dissymmetry: The Politics of Coherence in the Book of Judges.* Chicago and London: University of Chicago Press, 1988.

Bartholomew, Craig G. *Ecclesiastes.* Grand Rapids: Baker Academic, 2009.

Bergant, Dianne. *Israel's Wisdom Literature.* Liberation-Critical Reading of the Old Testament. Minneapolis: Fortress, 1997.

———. *Job, Ecclesiastes.* OTM 18. Wilmington, DE: Glazier, 1982.

Bird, Phyllis A. *Faith, Feminism, and the Forum of Scripture: Essays on Biblical Theology and Hermeneutics.* Eugene, OR: Wipf and Stock, 2015.

———. *Missing Persons and Mistaken Identities: Women and Gender in Ancient Israel.* Philadelphia: Fortress, 1997.

———. "Translating Sexist Language as a Theological and Cultural Problem." *USQR* 42 (1988): 89–95.

Bloom, Harold. *The Book of J.* Translated by David Rosenberg. New York: Grove, 1990.

Botterweck, G. Johannes, and Helmer Ringgren, eds. *Theological Dictionary of the Old Testament.* Translated by John T. Willis. 16 vols. Grand Rapids, MI: Eerdmans, 1975-2018.

Brenner, Athalya, and Fokkelien van Dijk Hemmes. *On Gendering Texts: Female and Male Voices in the Hebrew Bible.* BibInt 1. Leiden: Brill, 1993.

Brenner, Athalya, and Carole Fontaine. *A Feminist Companion to Reading the Bible: Approaches, Methods and Strategies.* London: Routledge, 2013.

Brenner-Idan, Athalya, and Carole Fontaine. *A Feminist Companion to Wisdom and Psalms.* FCB 2nd ser. 2. Sheffield: Sheffield Academic, 1998.

Brothers, Robyn. "Time to Heal, 'Desire Time': The Cyberprophecy of U2's 'Zoo World Order.'" In *Reading Rock and Roll: Authenticity, Appropriation, Aesthetics*, edited by Kevin J. H. Dettmar and William Richey, 237–67. New York: Columbia University Press, 1999.

Brown, William P. *Ecclesiastes*. IBC. Louisville: Westminster John Knox, 2011.

Broyde, Michael J. "Defilement of the Hands, Canonization of the Bible, and the Special Status of Esther, Ecclesiastes, and Song of Songs." *Judaism* 44 (1995): 65–79.

Burkes, Shannon. *Death in Qoheleth and Egyptian Biographies of the Late Period*. Atlanta: Society of Biblical Literature, 1999.

Buttrick, George Arthur, ed. *The Interpreter's Dictionary of the Bible*. 4 vols. New York: Abingdon, 1962.

Camp, Claudia V. *Wisdom and the Feminine in the Book of Proverbs*. BLS 11. Sheffield: Almond, 1985.

———. *Wise, Strange and Holy: The Strange Woman and the Making of the Bible*. JSOTSup 320. Gender, Culture, Theory 9. Sheffield: Sheffield Academic, 2000.

Capra, Frank. *You Can't Take It with You*. DVD. Columbia Pictures, 1938.

Carter, Warren. *Matthew and the Margins*. New York: T & T Clark, 2005.

Chapin, Harry. *Sniper and Other Love Songs*. Audio CD. Wounded Bird Records, 1972.

Christianson, Eric S. *Ecclesiastes through the Centuries*. Blackwell Bible Commentaries. Malden, MA: Blackwell, 2007.

———. "Qoheleth the 'Old Boy' and Qoheleth the 'New Man': Misogynism, the Womb and a Paradox in Ecclesiastes." In *A Feminist Companion to Wisdom and Psalms*, edited by Athalya Brenner-Idan and Carole Fontaine, 109–36. FCB 2d ser. 2. Sheffield: Sheffield Academic, 1998.

———. *A Time to Tell: Narrative Strategies in Ecclesiastes*. JSOTSup 280. Sheffield: Sheffield Academic, 1998.

Clark, Elizabeth A., and Herbert Richardson, eds. *Women and Religion: The Original Sourcebook of Women in Christian Thought*. New York: HarperCollins, 1996.

Claassens, L. Juliana M. *Mourner, Mother, Midwife: Reimagining God's Delivering Presence in the Old Testament*. Louisville: Westminster John Knox, 2012.

Code Pink. "What Is Code Pink?" www.codepink.org/about.

Crenshaw, James L. *Ecclesiastes: A Commentary*. OTL. Louisville: Westminster John Knox, 1987.

———. "Popular Questioning of the Justice of God in Ancient Israel." *ZAW* 82 (1970): 380–95.

———. *Qoheleth: The Ironic Wink*. Studies on Personalities in the Old Testament. Columbia: University of South Carolina Press, 2013.

Daly, Mary. *Gyn/Ecology: The Metaethics of Radical Feminism*. Boston: Beacon, 1978.

Davis, Ellen F. *Proverbs, Ecclesiastes, and the Song of Songs*. Westminster Bible Companion. Louisville: Westminster John Knox, 2000.

Day, Peggy Lynne. *Gender and Difference in Ancient Israel*. Minneapolis: Fortress, 1989.

Dayagi-Mendels, Michal. *Drink and Be Merry: Wine and Beer in Ancient Times.* Jerusalem: The Israel Museum, 2000.

Dell, Katharine J. *Interpreting Ecclesiastes: Readers Old and New.* Critical Studies in the Hebrew Bible 3. Winona Lake, IN: Eisenbrauns, 2013.

Dettmar, Kevin J. H., and William Richey. *Reading Rock and Roll: Authenticity, Appropriation, Aesthetics.* New York: Columbia University Press, 1999.

Duncan, Julie Ann. *Ecclesiastes.* AOTC. Nashville: Abingdon, 2017.

Douglas, Jerome N. *A Polemical Preacher of Joy: An Anti-Apocalpytic Genre for Qoheleth's Message of Joy.* Eugene, OR: Wipf and Stock, 2014.

Ebeling, Jennie R. *Women's Lives in Biblical Times.* London: T & T Clark, 2010.

Erdrich, Louise. "The Preacher." In *Out of the Garden: Women Writers on the Bible,* edited by Christina Büchmann and Celina Spiegel, 234–37. New York: Fawcett Columbine, 1995.

Eskenazi, Tamara Cohn. "Out from the Shadows: Biblical Women in the Postexilic Era." *JSOT* 17 (1992): 25–43.

Even-Shoshan, Abraham. *A New Concordance of the Hebrew Bible.* Tel-Aviv: Kiryat Sefer, 2018.

Exum, J. Cheryl. "Judges: Encoded Messages to Women." In *Feminist Biblical Interpretation: A Compendium of Critical Commentary on the Books of the Bible and Related Literature,* edited by Luise Schottroff, Marie-Theres Wacker, and Martin Rumscheidt, 112–27. Grand Rapids, MI: Eerdmans, 2012.

Farley, Sally D., Diane R. Timme, and Jason W. Hart. "On Coffee Talk and Break-Room Chatter: Perceptions of Women Who Gossip in the Workplace." *Journal of Social Psychology* 150 (2010): 361–68.

Farley, Wendy. *Tragic Vision and Divine Compassion: A Contemporary Theodicy.* Louisville: Westminster John Knox, 1990.

Farmer, Kathleen Anne. *Who Knows What Is Good? A Commentary on the Books of Proverbs and Ecclesiastes.* ITC. Grand Rapids, MI: Eerdmans, 1991.

Feinberg, Leslie. *Trans Liberation: Beyond Pink or Blue.* Boston: Beacon, 1998.

Fontaine, Carole R. "Ecclesiastes." In *Women's Bible Commentary,* edited by Carol A. Newsom and Sharon H. Ringe, 161–63. 2nd ed. Louisville: Westminster John Knox, 1998.

———. " 'Many Devices' (Qoheleth 7:23–8:1): Qoheleth, Misogyny and the *Malleus Maleficarum.*" In *A Feminist Companion to Wisdom and Psalms,* edited by Athalya Brenner and Carole Fontaine, 137–68. FCB 2nd ser. 2. Sheffield: Sheffield Academic, 1998.

Fox, Michael V. "Frame-Narrative and Composition in the Book of Qohelet." *HUCA* 48 (1977): 83–106.

———. *The JPS Bible Commentary: Ecclesiastes.* Philadelphia: Jewish Publication Society, 2004.

———. "The Meaning of *Hebel* for Qohelet." *JBL* 105 (1986): 409–27.

———. *Qoheleth and His Contradictions.* BLS 18. Sheffield: Almond, 1989.

———. *A Time to Tear Down and a Time to Build Up: A Rereading of Ecclesiastes.* Grand Rapids, MI: Eerdmans, 1999.

Frearson, Amy. "Steilneset Memorial by Peter Zumthor and Louise Bourgeois." Dezeen.com. January 3, 2012. http://www.dezeen.com/2012/01/03/steilneset -memorial-by-peter-zumthor-and-louise-bourgeois/.

Fredericks, Daniel C. *Qoheleth's Language: Re-Evaluating Its Nature and Date.* Lewiston, NY: Mellen, 1988.

Froke, Paula, Anna Jo Bratton, Oskar Garcia, Divid Minthorn, Karl Ritter, and Jerry Schwartz, eds. *The Associated Press Stylebook 2017: And Briefing on Media Law.* New York: Basic Books, 2017.

Frymer-Kensky, Tikva. *In the Wake of the Goddesses: Women, Culture, and the Biblical Transformation of Pagan Myth.* Glencoe, IL: Free Press, 1992.

———.*Studies in Bible and Feminist Criticism.* JPS Scholar of Distinction Series. Philadelphia: Jewish Publication Society, 2010.

Funeral Helper. "Bible Reading—Ecclesiastes 3 (Short)." http://www.funeralhelper .org/bible-reading-ecclesiastes-3-short.html.

Funeral Wise. "Religious Funeral Readings, Scripture, and Spiritual Passages." https://www.funeralwise.com/plan/ceremony/read/scriptures/.

Gafney, Wilda. *Womanist Midrash: A Reintroduction to the Women of the Torah and the Throne.* Louisville: Westminster John Knox, 2017.

Garber, Marjorie. *Vested Interests: Cross-Dressing and Cultural Anxiety.* New York; London: Routledge, 2011.

Garrett, Duane A. "Ecclesiastes 7:25-29 and the Feminist Hermeneutic." *CTR* 2 (1988): 309–21.

Gesenius, Wilhelm. *Gesenius' Hebrew Grammar.* Boston: Gould, Kendall, and Lincoln, 1839.

Ginsburg, C. D. *Coheleth (Commonly Called the Book of Ecclesiastes).* 1861. Repr., New York: KTAV, 1970.

Goldman, Ari L. "The Nation: Even for Ordained Women, Church Can Be a Cold Place," *New York Times* (April 9, 1992), 18.

Goldman, Y. A. P. *Biblia Hebraica Quinta, Fascicle 18: General Introduction and Megilloth.* Stuttgart: Deutsche Bibelgesellschaft, 2004.

Gordis, Robert. *Koheleth: The Man and His World.* New York: JTS, 1951; Repr., New York: Bloch, 1962. Rev. ed., New York: Schocken, 1987.

Graves, Robert. *The Greek Myths: Complete and Unabridged Edition in One Volume.* Mount Kisco, NY: Moyer Bell, 1988.

Gregory of Nyssa: Homilies on Ecclesiastes. Edited by S. G. Hall. Berlin: de Gruyter, 1993.

Guiley, Rosemary Ellen. "*Malleus Maleficarum* (The Witch Hammer)." In *The Encyclopedia of Witches, Witchcraft and Wicca.* 3rd ed. New York: Checkmark Books, 2008.

Hachlili, Rachel. *Jewish Funerary Customs, Practices and Rites in the Second Temple Period.* Supplements to the Journal for the Study of Judaism 94. Leiden: Brill, 2005.

"Hall of Remembrance, The." http://www.summerlands.com/crossroads /remembrance/burning.htm.

Harrelson, Walter J. *The New Interpreter's Study Bible: New Revised Standard Version with the Apocrypha.* Nashville: Abingdon, 2003.

Hart, Moss, and George Simon Kaufman. *You Can't Take It with You: Comedy in Three Acts.* Dramatists Play Service, 1937.

Havea, Jione. "'What Gain Have the Workers from Their Toil?' (Con)texting Ecclesiastes 3:9-13 in Pasifika." In *The Five Scrolls,* edited by Athalya Brenner-Idan, Gale A. Yee, and Archie C. C. Lee, 123–33. Texts@Contexts 6. London: Bloomsbury, 2018.

Hengel, Martin. *Judaism and Hellenism: Studies in Their Encounter in Palestine During the Early Hellenistic Period.* Translated by John Bowden. Philadelphia: Fortress, 1974.

Hengstenberg, Ernst Wilhelm. *Commentary on Ecclesiastes: With Other Treatises.* Philadelphia: Smith, English & Co.; New York: Sheldon, 1860.

Hitchcock, Alfred. *The Man Who Knew Too Much.* DVD. The Criterion Collection, 2013.

Holmstedt, Robert D. "אני ולבי: The Syntactic Encoding of the Collaborative Nature of Qohelet's Experiment." *JHebS* 9 (2009). doi:10.5508/jhs.2009.v9.a19.

Homan, Michael M. "Beer and Its Drinkers: An Ancient Near Eastern Love Story." *NEA* 67 (2004): 84–95.

———. "Beer Production by Throwing Bread into Water: A New Interpretation of Qoh. Xi 1-2." *VT* 52 (2002): 275–78.

———. "Did the Ancient Israelites Drink Beer?" *BAR* 36 (2010): 48.

Homan, Michael, and Jennie Ebeling. "Baking and Brewing Beer in the Israelite Household." In *The World of Women in the Ancient and Classical Near East,* edited by Beth Alpert Nakhai. Newcastle upon Tyne: Cambridge Scholars, 2008.

Hopkins, Jamal-Dominic. "Qoheleth." In *The Africana Bible: Reading Israel's Scriptures from Africa and the African Diaspora,* edited by R. Hugh and Randall C. Bailey, 260–65. Minneapolis: Fortress, 2009.

Horst, F. *Biblia Hebraica Stuttgartensia, Fascicle 13: Megilloth.* Stuttgart: Deutsche Bibelgesellschaft, 1990.

Ilan, Tal. *Integrating Women into Second Temple History.* TSAJ 76. Peabody, MA: Hendrickson, 2001.

———. *Jewish Women in Greco-Roman Palestine.* Peabody, MA: Hendrickson, 1996.

John, Elton. *"The Lion King*/Soundtrack Version." Audio CD. Walt Disney Records, 1994.

Karlsen, Carol F. *The Devil in the Shape of a Woman: Witchcraft in Colonial New England.* New York: W. W. Norton, 1998.

Kim, Hea Sun, and Mary Lou Blakeman, with commentaries by Lisa M. Wolfe. *Ecclesiastes: The Meaning of Your Life.* New York: Women's Division General Board of Global Ministries the United Methodist Church, 1995.

Klein, Jacob. "The Book of Qoheleth: Introduction." In *Qoheleth: Olam Hatanach,* edited by Menahem Haran, 162–68. Tel Aviv: Divrei Ha'yamim Publication, 1999. [Hebrew]

Klein, Lillian R. "Hannah." In *Women in Scripture: A Dictionary of Named and Unnamed Women in the Bible, the Apocryphal/Deuterocanonical Books, and the New Testament*, edited by Carol Meyers, Toni Craven, and Ross Shepard Kraemer, 90. Grand Rapids, MI: Eerdmans, 2001.

Koch, Klaus. "Is There a Doctrine of Retribution in the Old Testament?" In *Theodicy in the Old Testament*, edited by James L. Crenshaw, translated by Thomas H. Trapp, 57–87. Philadelphia: Fortress, 1983.

Koosed, Jennifer L. "Ecclesiastes." In *Women's Bible Commentary*, edited by Carol Ann Newsom, Sharon H. Ringe, and Jacqueline E. Lapsley, 243–46. 3rd ed. Louisville: Westminster John Knox, 2012.

———. *(Per)Mutations of Qohelet: Reading the Body in the Book*. T & T Clark Library of Biblical Studies. New York: Bloomsbury, 2006.

Kopf, Sandy, and Doug Kopf. "Salem Remembered." http://www.sacred-texts.com/bos/bos256.htm.

Krüger, Thomas. *Qoheleth: A Commentary*. Edited by Klaus Baltzer. Translated by O. C. Dean. Hermeneia. Minneapolis: Fortress, 2004.

Kushner, Harold S. *When Bad Things Happen to Good People*. New York: Schocken Books, 1981.

Lamott, Anne. *Hallelujah Anyway: Rediscovering Mercy*. New York: Penguin Random House, 2017.

Lang, Bernhard. *Wisdom and the Book of Proverbs: A Hebrew Goddess Redefined*. Cleveland: Pilgrim, 1986.

Lauretis, Teresa de. *Figures of Resistance: Essays in Feminist Theory*. Urbana: University of Illinois Press, 2010.

Levack, Brian P. *The Witch-Hunt in Early Modern Europe*. New York: Routledge, 2013.

Levine, Lee I. "The Nature and Origin of the Palestinian Synagogue Reconsidered." *JBL* 115 (1996): 425–48.

Levinson, Bernard M. "Better That You Should Not Vow Than That You Vow and Not Fulfill: Qoheleth's Use of Textual Allusion and the Transformation of Deuteronomy's Law of Vows." In *Reading Ecclesiastes Intertextually*, edited by Katharine Dell and Will Kynes, 28–41. London: Bloomsbury T & T Clark, 2015.

Longman, Tremper. *The Book of Ecclesiastes*. NICOT. Grand Rapids, MI: Eerdmans, 1998.

Lorde, Audre. "The Master's Tools." In *Sister Outsider: Essays and Speeches by Audre Lorde*, 110–13. Berkley: Crossing, 2007.

Lovelace, Wicasta, and Christie Rice, transcribers. "The *Malleus Maleficarum*: Online Edition." http://www.malleusmaleficarum.org/shop/the-malleus-maleficarum-pdf/. HTML Scripting Copyright 1998–2000 by the Windhaven Network, Inc.

Lutzky, Harriet. "Shadday as Goddess Epithet." *VT* 48 (1998): 15–36.

Madonna. *Like a Virgin*. Audio CD. Sire Records, 1984.

Maine, Margo, and Joe Kelly. *Pursuing Perfection: Eating Disorders, Body Myths, and Women at Midlife and Beyond*. New York: Routledge, 2016.

Mariottini, Claude F. "2 Kings." In *The New Interpreter's Study Bible: New Revised Standard Version with the Apocrypha*, edited by Walter J. Harrelson, 525–69. Nashville: Abingdon, 2003.

McAndrew, Francis T. "The 'Sword of a Woman': Gossip and Female Aggression." *Aggression and Violent Behavior* 19 (2014): 196–99.

Metzger, Bruce, for the Committee. "To The Reader." In *The HarperCollins Study Bible: Fully Revised and Updated*, edited by Harold W. Attridge. New York: HarperCollins, 2006.

Meyers, Carol. *Rediscovering Eve: Ancient Israelite Women in Context*. New York: Oxford University Press, 2012.

Meyers, Carol, Toni Craven, and Ross Shepard Kraemer, eds. *Women in Scripture: A Dictionary of Named and Unnamed Women in the Bible, the Apocryphal/Deuterocanonical Books, and the New Testament*. Grand Rapids, MI: Eerdmans, 2001.

Muraoka, T. *Emphatic Words and Structures in Biblical Hebrew*. Leiden: Brill, 1985.

Murphy, Roland E. *Ecclesiastes*. WBC 23A. Nashville: Thomas Nelson, 2018.

Murphy, Roland E., and Elizabeth Huwiler. *Proverbs, Ecclesiastes, Song of Songs*. Understanding the Bible Commentary Series. Grand Rapids, MI: Baker, 2012.

Nakhai, Beth Alpert. *The World of Women in the Ancient and Classical Near East*. Newcastle: Cambridge Scholars, 2008.

Newsom, Carol Ann, and Sharon H. Ringe, eds. *Women's Bible Commentary*. 2nd ed. Louisville: Westminster John Knox, 1998.

Newsom, Carol Ann, Sharon H. Ringe, and Jacqueline E. Lapsley. *Women's Bible Commentary*. 3rd ed. Louisville: Westminster John Knox, 2012.

Niditch, Susan. "Genesis." In *Women's Bible Commentary*, edited by Carol Ann Newsom, Sharon H. Ringe, and Jacqueline E. Lapsley, 27–45. 3rd ed. Louisville: Westminster John Knox, 2012.

Noonan, Brian B. "Wisdom Literature among the Witchmongers." In *A Feminist Companion to Wisdom and Psalms*, edited by Athalya Brenner and Carole Fontaine, 169–74. FCB 2nd ser. 2. Sheffield: Sheffield Academic, 1998.

Pahk, Johan Yeong-Sik. "A Syntactical and Contextual Consideration of '*šh* in Qoh. Ix 9." *VT* 51 (2001): 370–80.

Parker, Julie Faith. *Valuable and Vulnerable: Children in the Hebrew Bible, Especially the Elisha Cycle*. BJS 355. Providence, RI: Brown Judaic Studies, 2013.

Pauw, Amy Plantinga. *Proverbs and Ecclesiastes*. Belief: A Theological Commentary on the Bible. Louisville: Westminster John Knox, 2015.

Perry, T. Anthony. *Dialogues with Kohelet: The Book of Ecclesiastes; Translation and Commentary*. University Park: Pennsylvania State University Press, 1993.

Peterson, Eugene H. *The Message: The Bible in Contemporary Language*. Colorado Springs: NavPress, 2002.

Pressler, Carolyn. "Deuteronomy." In *Women's Bible Commentary*, edited by Carol Ann Newsom, Sharon H. Ringe, and Jacqueline E. Lapsley, 88–102. 3rd ed. Louisville: Westminster John Knox, 2012.

Quist-Arcton, Ofeibea. "The Lament Of The Boko Haram 'Brides.'" National Public Radio: Weekend Edition Sunday (August 27, 2017). https://www.npr.org/sections/goatsandsoda/2017/08/27/545912049/the-lament-of-the-boko-haram-brides.

Readings for Funeral Services. https://urc.org.uk/images/Free-Ebooks/WB2_Funeral_Readings.pdf.

Reid, Barbara E. *Wisdom's Feast: An Invitation to Feminist Interpretation of the Scriptures.* Grand Rapids, MI: Eerdmans, 2016.

Ringe, Sharon H. "An Approach to a Critical, Feminist, Theological Reading of the Bible." In *A Feminist Companion to Reading the Bible: Approaches, Methods and Strategies,* edited by Athalya Brenner and Carole Fontaine, 156–63. Sheffield: Sheffield Academic, 1997.

———. "When Women Interpret the Bible." In *Women's Bible Commentary,* edited by Carol A. Newsom, Sharon H. Ringe, and Jacqueline E. Lapsley, 1–9. 3rd ed. Louisville: Westminster John Knox, 2012.

Rousseau, Jean-Jacques. *Confessions.* Oxford: Oxford University Press, 2000.

Rudman, Dominic. "Woman as Divine Agent in Ecclesiastes." *JBL* 116 (1997): 411–27.

Ruggieri, Melissa. "Music Notes." *Richmond Times-Dispatch* (December 19, 2000), D.13.

Russell, Letty M. *Feminist Interpretation of the Bible.* Louisville: Westminster John Knox, 1985.

Saiving, Valerie C. "Where Is the Woman?" *ThTo* 19 (1962): 111–14.

Salyer, Gary D. *Vain Rhetoric: Private Insight and Public Debate in Ecclesiastes.* JSOTSup 327. Sheffield: Sheffield Academic, 2001.

Schaberg, Jane D., and Sharon H. Ringe. "Gospel of Luke." In *Women's Bible Commentary,* edited by Carol Ann Newsom, Sharon H. Ringe, and Jacqueline E. Lapsley, 493–511. Louisville: Westminster John Knox, 2012.

Schoors, Antoon. *Ecclesiastes.* Leuven: Peeters, 2013.

———. *The Preacher Sought to Find Pleasing Words: A Study of the Language of Qoheleth.* Leuven: Peeters, 1992.

Schrick, Brittney, Elizabeth Sharp, Anisa Zvonkovic, and Alan Reifman. "Never Let Them See You Sweat: Silencing and Striving to Appear Perfect among U.S. College Women." *Sex Roles* 67 (2012): 591–604.

Schüssler Fiorenza, Elisabeth. "Feminist Hermeneutics." In *Anchor Bible Dictionary,* edited by David Noel Freedman, 2:786. New York: Doubleday, 1992.

Schüssler Fiorenza, Elisabeth, Shelly Matthews, and Ann Graham Brock. *Searching the Scriptures.* Vol. 1: *A Feminist Introduction.* New York: Crossroad, 1993.

Seow, Choon-Leong. *Ecclesiastes: A New Translation with Introduction and Commentary.* AB 18C. New York: Doubleday, 1997.

————. "Linguistic Evidence and the Dating of Qoheleth." *JBL* 115 (1996): 643–66.

Seufert, Matthew. "The Presence of Genesis in Ecclesiastes." *WTJ* 78 (2016): 75–92.

Shakespeare, William. *Hamlet*. Lippincott, 1905.

Shapiro, Fred R. "Who Wrote the Serenity Prayer?" *Yale Alumni Magazine* (July/August 2008) http://archives.yalealumnimagazine.com/issues/2008_07/serenity.html.

Siegfried, Carl. *Prediger und Hoheslied*. Göttingen: Vandenhoeck und Ruprecht, 1898.

Smith, Betty. *A Tree Grows in Brooklyn*, New York: Harper and Brothers, 1943.

Sommer, Benjamin D. "The Source Critic and the Religious Interpreter." *Int* 60 (2006): 9–20.

Spar, Debora L. *Wonder Women: Sex, Power, and the Quest for Perfection*. New York: Farrar, Straus and Giroux, 2013.

Spears, Britney. *In the Zone*. Audio CD. Jive Records 2003.

Spronk, Klaas. "Dealing with Death: Reading Qoheleth in Different Contexts." In *The Five Scrolls*, edited by Athalya Brenner-Idan, Gale A. Yee, and Archie C. C. Lee. Texts@Contexts 6. London: Bloomsbury, 2018.

Stanton, Andrew, and Lee Unkrich. *Finding Nemo*. DVD. Disney Pixar, 2003.

Stanton, Elizabeth Cady. *The Woman's Bible*. 1895. Repr., Boston: Northeastern University Press, 1993.

Steiner, George. *In Bluebeard's Castle: Some Notes Towards the Redefinition of Culture*. New Haven: Yale University Press, 1974.

Steel, Mel. "Mary, Mary, Quite Contrary." *The Guardian*. (August 25, 1999). https://www.theguardian.com/world/1999/aug/26/gender.uk.

Stendahl, Krister. "Biblical Theology, Contemporary." In *The Interpreter's Dictionary of the Bible Supplement*, edited by George Arthur Buttrick, 418–32. New York: Abingdon, 1962.

Strollo, Megan Fullerton. "Initiative and Agency: Towards A Theology of the Megilloth." In *Megilloth Studies: The Shape of Contemporary Scholarship*, edited by Brad Embry, 150–60. Sheffield: Phoenix, 2016.

Swanborough Funerals. "For Everything There Is A Season—Ecclesiastes 3:1-8." https://www.swanboroughfunerals.com.au/funeral-scripture-ecclesiastes/.

Tamez, Elsa. *When the Horizons Close: Rereading Ecclesiastes*. Maryknoll, NY: Orbis Books, 2000.

Taylor, C. C. W. "Doctrine of the Mean." *Oxford Companion to Philosophy*, edited by Ted Honderich. New York: Oxford University Press, 540.

Thoreau, Henry David. *Walden*. 1854. Repr., Edinburgh: Black and White Classics, 2014.

Tickle, Phyllis. *Emergence Christianity: What It Is, Where It Is Going, and Why It Matters*. Grand Rapids, MI: Baker, 2012.

————. *The Great Emergence: How Christianity Is Changing and Why*. Grand Rapids, MI: Baker, 2012.

Towner, W. Sibley. "Ecclesiastes." In *The New Interpreter's Bible*, edited by Leander E. Keck, 5:265–360. Nashville: Abingdon, 1997.

"Transgender | Gender Neutral Pronoun Blog," n.d. https://genderneutral pronoun.wordpress.com/tag/transgender/.

Trevor-Roper, Hugh R. *The European Witch-Craze of the 16th and 17th Centuries.* London: Penguin, 1990.

Trible, Phyllis. "Authority of the Bible." In *New Interpreter's Study Bible New Revised Standard Version with the Apocrypha*, edited by Walter J. Harrelson, 2248–53. Nashville: Abingdon, 2003.

———. *Texts of Terror: Literary-Feminist Readings of Biblical Narratives.* OBT. Philadelphia: Fortress, 1984.

Turner, Marie. *Ecclesiastes: An Earth Bible Commentary; Qoheleth's Eternal Earth.* London: Bloomsbury, 2017.

U2. *Achtung Baby.* Audio CD. Island Records, 1991.

Walker, Alice. *In Search of Our Mothers' Gardens: Womanist Prose.* New York: Harcourt Brace Jovanovich, 1967, 1983. Repr., Wilmington, MA: Mariner Books, 2003.

Waltke, Bruce K., and Michael Patrick O'Connor. *Introduction to Biblical Hebrew Syntax.* Winona Lake, IN: Eisenbrauns, 1990.

Washington, Harold. "The Strange Woman (אשה זרה/נכריה) of Proverbs 1–9 and Post-Exilic Judaean Society." In *Second Temple Studies.* Vol 2: *Temple Community in the Persian Period*, edited by Tamara C. Eskenazi and Kent H. Richards, 217–42. Sheffield: JSOT Press, 1994.

———. *Wealth and Poverty in the Instruction of Amenemope and the Hebrew Proverbs.* SBLDS 142. Atlanta: Scholars Press, 1994.

Weems, Renita J. *Battered Love: Marriage, Sex, and Violence in the Hebrew Prophets.* OBT. Minneapolis: Fortress, 1995.

———. "Reading *Her Way* Through the Bible: African American Women and the Bible." In *Stony the Road We Trod: African American Biblical Interpretation*, edited by Cain Hope Felder, 57–79. Minneapolis: Fortress, 1991.

Wei, Huang. "*Hebel* and *Kong*: A Cross-Textual Reading between Qoheleth and the *Heart Sūtra*." In *The Five Scrolls*, edited by Athalaya Brenner-Idan, Gale A. Yee, and Archie C. C. Lee, 135–44. Texts@Contexts 6. London: Bloomsbury T & T Clark, 2018.

Weinfeld, Moshe. *Social Justice in Ancient Israel and in the Ancient Near East.* Minneapolis: Fortress; Jerusalem: Magnes, 1995.

Whybray, Roger N. *Ecclesiastes.* New Century Bible Commentary. Grand Rapids, MI: Eerdmans, 1989.

———. "Qoheleth, Preacher of Joy." *JSOT* 7 (1982): 87–98.

———. "Qoheleth the Immoralist (Qoh 7:16-17)." In *Israelite Wisdom: Theological and Literary Essays in Honor of Samuel Terrien*, edited by John G. Gammie, 191–204. Missoula, MT: Scholars Press, 1978.

Williams, Paul, and Kenny Ascher, performed by Frank Oz. "I Hope that Something Better Comes Along." *The Muppet Movie Soundtrack*. Audio CD. Atlantic Records, 1979.

Wolfe, Lisa M. "Does Qoheleth Hate Women, a Woman, or Woman Folly?" Paper presented at the Annual Meeting of the Southwest Commission on Religious Studies. Dallas, TX, March 9, 2013.

———. "Man, Woman, or Human? *'Ish, 'Issah,* and *'Adam* in Ecclesiastes." Paper presented at the Annual Meeting of the Southwest Commission on Religious Studies, Dallas, March 14, 2015.

———. "Ecclesiastes as a Model for Feminist Hermeneutics." Paper presented at the Annual Meeting of the Society of Biblical Literature, Philadelphia, PA, November 22, 2005.

———. *Ruth, Esther, Song of Songs, and Judith*. Eugene, OR: Wipf and Stock, 2011.

———. "Seeing Gives Rise to Disbelieving: Experiences That Prompt a Hermeneutic of Suspicion in Ecclesiastes and Wendy Farley's Theodicy of Compassion." PhD diss., Northwestern University, 2003.

Women in Black. "Who Are Women in Black?" womeninblack.org/about-women-in-black.

Yardeni, Ada. *The Book of Hebrew Script: History, Palaeography, Script Styles, Calligraphy and Design*. London; New Castle, DE: The British Library and Oak Knoll Press, 2002.

Index of Scripture References and Other Ancient Writings

Genesis

Genesis	xxv n. 23, 23, 96	4:2	4, 39	24:16	163 n. 27
1	96	4:4	4	24:17	163 n. 27
1–3	96, 96 n. 33	4:8	4	24:18	163 n. 27
		4:9	4	24:20	163 n. 27
		4:25	4	24:43	163 n. 27
1:2	129 n. 2, 160	6:3	129 n. 2	24:45	163 n. 27
		9:25	5	24:46	163 n. 27
1:3-5	160	12:1-9	69	28:3	10
1:4	96 n. 34	15	68	29:13	46 n. 17
1:10	96 n. 34	15:2	68	29:31	53
1:12	96 n. 34	15:10	lviii n. 42	29:33	53
1:14-17	160	16:2	42	30:3	42
1:18	96 n. 34	16:4-5	152	31:47	xxxvii n. 45
1:21	96 n. 34	16:6-16	69		
1:25	96 n. 34	17:17	43	33:4	46 n. 17
1:26-27	lix	18:6	146	34	92
1:27	lvii, 96	18:12	43	35:17	42
1:31	96 n. 34	18:13	43	38:28	42
2–3	96, 97	18:15	43	38:29	42
2:7	lvii, 163, 163 n. 32	21:6	43	39:17	52
		21:9	43	41:38	129 n. 2
2:9	96	21:15	50	48:10	46 n. 17
2:17	96	21:16	42	48:15-16	140 n. 25
3	108 n. 29	24	163		
3:5	97	24:14	163, 163 n. 27	**Exodus**	
3:7	52			1:16	46, 48
4	1	24:15	163 n. 27	1:19	42

3:14	xxxvi	24:3	53	14:16	53
13:8	xix	25:18	10	14:16-17	42
15:8	129 n. 2	32:9	162	15:14	129 n. 2
20:17	lx, 77			16:10	52
21:17	105	**Joshua**		16:13	52
29:7	91	2:1	41	19	142 n. 1
30:25	151 n. 1	2:3	41		
30:33	151 n. 1	2:12	140 n. 24	**1 Samuel**	
30:35	151 n. 1	2:17	140 n. 24	1–2	70
31:3	129 n. 2	2:20	140 n. 24	1:3	72
35:31	129 n. 2	6:17	41	1:4	72
37:29	151 n. 1	6:23	41	1:7	42
		6:25	41	1:8	42
Leviticus		15:19	162	1:10	42
2:1	91	17:5	162 n. 25	1:11	71
20:9	105	17:14	162 n. 25	1:12-13	72
		19:9	162 n. 25	1:13	53
Numbers		19:29	162 n. 26	1:21	72
5:19	140 n. 24			1:23-24	71
5:21	84 n. 4	**Judges**		1:24-25	72
5:22	84 n. 4	1:15	162	2:21	73
11:15	lxvi	3:10	129 n. 2	8:13	146 n. 12
12:1	52	4–5	41	10:1	91
16:22	129 n. 2	4:1-10	69	10:5	162
24:2	129 n. 2	4:1-16	53	10:10	162
27:1-11	xlviii, 79	5:28	160	13:21	164
27:8-11	xlviii	6:34	129 n. 2	16:13	91
27:16	129 n. 2	9:27-28	105	17:43	105
36:1-12	79	9:53	47, 50	18:6	43
36:1-13	xlviii	9:53-54	lix, 148	18:20	53
36:9	xlviii	9:54	47, 50	24:18 [19]	106 n. 20
		11	142 n. 1	25:24	52
Deuteronomy		11:29	72	28:24	52, 140,
3:4	162	11:30	72		146
3:13	162 n. 26	11:31	72		
3:14	162 n. 26	11:35	72	**2 Samuel**	
17:17	25	11:37	42	11:5	lxix
21:13	42	11:39	72	11:21	lix, 47, 50,
21:15-17	53	13:4	51		148
22:13	53	13:13	51	11:26	43
22:16	53	13:14	51	12:18	86
23:21a [22a]	70–71	13:25	129 n. 2	12:24	85
23:22-24	2	14:6	129 n. 2	13:8	146

13:19	52	11:14	52	**Ezekiel**		
14:2	92	20:13	91	8:14	42	
14:7	91 n. 19			10:2	163 n. 28	
17:2	10	**Isaiah**		10:6	163 n. 28	
18:18	91 n. 19,	1:6	91	10:13	163 n. 28	
	140 n. 25	1:10-17	71	13:17	52	
21:1-14	54	3:20	152	13:18	52	
21:8-14	69	14:15	163 n. 29	32:23	163 n. 29	
		14:19	163 n. 29	47:13	162 n. 25	
1 Kings		22:13	33			
1:22	53	30:7	1	**Hosea**		
1:39	91	32:12	43	6:6	71	
2:13	53	34:15	152	14:1	152	
3:9	12	35:7	163			
3:12	12	42:14	52	**Joel**		
3:22	52	47:1-3a	47	2:2	160	
4:13	162	47:2	160			
4:20	12	49:10	163	**Amos**		
4:20-34	xliii, 12,	51:1	163	1:13	152	
	25	56:5	91	5:18	160	
5:2-8	87 n. 10	57:13	1, 4	5:20	160	
10:2	52	59:5	152	5:21-24	71	
10:14-22	87 n. 10					
10:14–		**Jeremiah**		**Micah**		
11:8	77	2:5	1	2:9	23	
11:1-3	25	2:27	46	6:7	91	
11:1-11	115	4:30	52			
11:2-13	25	6:26	92	**Zephaniah**		
11:8	140	8:19	1	2:4	41	
17:12	163	8:21–9:1				
17:12-16	146	[8:23]	94	**Zechariah**		
17:14	163	9:17-20		10:2	1	
17:16	163	[16-19]	40, 92	12:12	43	
21:5	52	10:3	1, 4			
		10:8	1	**Psalms**	9 n. 12	
2 Kings		10:11	xxxvii n.	6:3 [4]	106	
4:16	46 n. 17,		45	30:3 [4]	163 n. 29	
	51	14:22	1	30:11 [12]	43	
4:23	53	16:8	93 n. 25	33:6	129 n. 2	
4:26	53	18:3	48	34:16 [17]	140 n. 25	
5:1-14	42	31:13	92	39	1	
9:31	53	31:15-17	94	39:5 [6]	1	
11:1	51	49:3	43	51:11 [13]	129 n. 2	

58:9	84 n. 4	5:15	163	22:14	110 n. 35,
77:8	9	5:18	143		116
77:19	163 n. 28	5:20	46 n. 18,	23:27	116, 110 n.
78:33	1		92 n. 23,		36
94:11	1		110 n. 35,	24:21	128
102:11 [12]	135 n. 17		110 n. 36	24:33	46
104:15	91, 141	5:22	112	25:6	128
104:35	xxv	6:2	112	28:17	163 n. 29
105:11	162 n. 25	6:10	46	30:15	126
109:23	135 n. 17	6:23-33	92 n. 23	31:10	107
119:90	9	6:24	84 n. 3,	31:10-30	123
133:2	91		110 n. 36	31:10-31	66, 115,
144:4	135 n. 17	7:1-5	lxv		145
146:10	9	7:4-5	116	31:13	146
		7:5	84 n. 3,	31:13-14	145 n. 11
Proverbs	xlvii, liii,		110 n. 35,	31:16	41, 41 n.
	lxxi, 2, 3,		110 n. 36		12, 145 n.
	87, 107–	7:5-23	110		11, 146
	13, 116–17,	7:10-23	92 n. 23	31:18-19	145 n. 11
	120–24	7:26	41	31:19	146
1–9	lxv n. 59,	7:27	112	31:24	145 n. 11
	84 n. 3,	8	123	31:25	43
	107, 109,	8:1-9:6	lxv		
	111–13	8:7	111	**Job**	xlvii, 2, 12
1:20-21	xxiii	8:17	53		n. 20
1:20-33	lxv	8:22-31	xxiii	1:2	79
1:22	111	8:23	61	1:10	106 n. 20
1:23-25	xxiii	8:30	43	1:21	79
1:28	111	9:1-5	xxiii	3:16	84 n. 4
2:16	84 n. 3,	9:1-6	110	5–6	95 n. 30
	110 n. 35,	9:3-5	xxiii	6:26	31
	110 n. 36	9:4	110	8:9	135 n. 17
2:16-17	92 n. 23	9:16	110	9:20-24	100
2:18	112	10:30	70	10:15-16	100
3:13-15	103 n. 9	11:6	112	14:2	135 n. 17
4:5-9	lxv	11:30-31	135	17:7	135 n. 17
4:6	51	12:12	112	18–21	95 n. 30
4:8	46 n. 18	14:1	lxv	21:32-33	134 n. 14
5:3	84 n. 3,	16:16	103 n. 9	24:8	46
	110 n. 35	17:1	66	27:12	1
5:3-4	125	18:22	108 n. 26	28:15-19	103 n. 9
5:4	112	19:10	23	31:9-10	47
5:5	112	22:1a	90	31:10	48, 160
5:8-17	92 n. 23	22:1	162	42:11	lviii n. 41

42:14-15	79	**Lamentations**		1:18	13, 32
		4:5	46, 50	2:1	17, 26, 28
Song of Songs				2:1-3	17
	1, 3	**Qoheleth**		2:1-10	18, 32
1:1	5	1:1	xliii, lxi,	2:1-11	xlvii, lix,
1:3	53, 91		lxii, lxiii,		17, 18, 23,
1:6	146		1–7, 25		28, 63, 91
1:7	53	1:2	li, lxi, lxii,		n. 20
2:6	46 n. 18,		lxii n. 47,	2:1-12	xliii
	50		lxiii, lxv,	2:1-16	30
2:7	140 n. 24		4–6, 8, 10,	2:1-26	17
3:1	51		17, 114	2:2	17
3:1-4	53	1:3	lx, 6–8,	2:3	lx n. 44,
3:2	51		10, 12, 29		17, 28
3:5	140 n. 24		n. 28, 31	2:4a	17
4:4	113 n. 43		n. 30, 53,	2:4b-6	17
4:13-14	151 n. 2		59, 87, 91,	2:4	20, 22
5:6	51		144	2:4-6	25
5:8-9	140 n. 24	1:3-8	11	2:4-8	17, 30, 34
6:1	51	1:3-11	6–8, 11	2:4-9	25
6:10	113 n. 43	1:4	6–11, 60	2:5	22, 23
7:5-6 [6-7]	113 n. 43	1:5	7, 8	2:7	8, 17, 22,
7:6 [7]	24	1:6	3, 7, 8, 31,		23, 26, 77,
8:3	46 n. 18,		162		123, 152
	50	1:7	7–8	2:7-8	17, 23, 25
8:4	140 n. 24	1:8	lviii, lxi, 8,	2:7-9	25
8:10	53		10	2:8b	23, 24
		1:9	11	2:8	liii, lix, 8,
Ruth	xxxi n. 23,	1:9-11	11		19, 22, 26,
	xxxv, xliii,	1:10	10		95 n. 29,
	69	1:10-14	4		123, 144
1:9	42	1:11	8, 10, 11,	2:9-10	17
1:14	42		140 n. 25	2:11	l n. 26, 17,
1:21	10	1:12	lxiii, 12,		26, 28, 29
2	41		19		n. 28, 31 n.
3:1	51	1:12-18	12, 14, 91		30, 59, 95,
3:15	lxix		n. 20		95 n. 29,
4:3	xlviii	1:13	12–14, 31		129 n. 2
4:3-9	79 n. 21	1:14	l n. 26, 12,	2:12	lix, 13, 25,
4:10-11	91		13, 129 n.		28, 29
4:11	42, 91, 140		30	2:12-16	28, 30
	n. 25	1:15	13, 14, 95	2:13	29
4:14	140 n. 25	1:16	21	2:16	29, 35, 140
4:15	53	1:17	13, 28, 29		n. 25

2:17   30, 31, 31
       n. 30, 32,
       33, 33 n.
       32, 33 n.
       33, 33 n.
       35, 34, 96
2:17-23   31, 34
2:17-26   30
2:18   lix, 31, 33
       n. 35
2:18-19   xliv, 95 n.
          29
2:18-22   31
2:19   33, 34, 157
       n. 14
2:20   31, 32
2:21   lix, 33, 67,
       76, 78
2:22   lx n. 45
2:23   31, 32
2:24   xliv, liii,
       liv, lx, 8,
       11, 12 n.
       22, 32–34,
       96 n. 32,
       137 n. 20
2:24b-25   155 n. 7
2:24-25   liii n. 35
2:24-26   33, 34
2:25   34
2:26   12, 31, 33,
       34
3:1   38, 44, 129
3:1-8   xlviii, lxiii,
        lxvii n. 66,
        37, 37 n. 1,
        38, 39, 43,
        54, 128,
        129, 147,
        163
3:1-9   44
3:1-13   37 n. 1
3:2b   41, 50
3:2   38–42, 45,
      65 n. 1,

3:2-8   128
3:3   41, 42, 45
3:4   41, 43, 45
3:5   38, 44–46,
      48–50, 54
      n. 22, 97
3:6   46, 51, 54
      n. 22
3:7b   52
3:7   45, 52
3:8   31 n. 30,
      39, 44, 46
3:9   12, 29 n.
      28, 44, 58
      n. 28, 145
      n. 10
3:9-22   54, 55
3:10   lx n. 44,
       12, 47, 55
3:11   lii, lx n. 44,
       58, 60, 61,
       157 n. 14
3:11-15   59
3:11-21   58
3:12   liv, 12, 55,
       58, 147
3:12-13   xliv, lx, 56,
          96 n. 32,
          137 n. 20
3:13   lx n. 44,
       58, 58 n.
       28, 155
3:14   55, 60, 138
       n. 21, 159
       n. 16, 161
       n. 22, 165
       n. 33
3:16   31 n. 30,
       55, 56 n.
       25, 57, 58,
       59 n. 30,
       137

130, 134 n.
15
3:16-17   56
3:16-22   100, 168
3:17   55, 57–59,
       159, 165
3:18   lx n. 44, 55
3:19   li, lx n. 44,
       57, 58
3:20   57 n. 26
3:21   lx n. 44
3:22   xliv, liii n.
       35, liv, lx,
       lx n. 44,
       55, 56, 57
       n. 26, 58
4:1   xlvii, 31 n.
      30, 59 n.
      30, 63–65,
      73, 74
4:1-3   64
4:1-4   57 n. 26
4:1-16   63
4:1–5:20
[19]   63
4:2   liv, 64
4:2-3   liv, 64, 65
4:3   liv, 31 n.
      30
4:4   l n. 26,
      lviii, lxi n.
      46, 66, 129
      n. 2
4:4-6   66
4:5   46, 66, 70
4:5-6   57 n. 26,
        67
4:5-9   lxv
4:6   l n. 26, liv,
      66, 86
4:7-8   57 n. 26
4:7-12   69
4:8   12, 67, 68
4:9   liv, 68
4:9-12   68
4:9-14   57 n. 26

4:10	68			16, 76, 77,	6:1–7:14	83
4:10-12	68			86	6:2	lviii, lviii
4:11	68	5:12-16				n. 43, 83,
4:12	68, 69	[11-15]	83 n. 1			83 n. 3, 84
4:13	liv, 6, 69,	5:13 [12]	59 n. 30,			n. 3, 86, 86
	70, 164		77, 78, 81			n. 8, 87, 88
4:13-16	69, 164	5:13-14			6:2-3	90
4:14	69, 70	[12-13]	xliv		6:2-6	83
4:15	70	5:13-17			6:2-8	86, 87
4:15-16	57 n. 26	[12-16]	80, 81		6:3	liv, lv, 66,
4:16	70	5:14 [13]	78			83–88, 95
5:1 [4:17]	lv, 70	5:14-17				n. 29, 134
5:1-7 [4:17–		[13-16]	78			n. 14
5:6]	70, 72	5:14-18			6:3-8	4
5:2 [1]	71, 72	[13-17]	4		6:4	86 n. 7, 90
5:2-7 [1-6]	71	5:15 [14]	75 n. 16,		6:4-5	86
5:3 [2]	12		79, 123		6:5	66, 86, 86
5:4 [3]	70, 71	5:16 [15]	75 n. 16,			n. 7
5:4-5 [3-4]	2		77, 81, 88		6:6	87, 88, 95
5:4-6 [3-5]	154	5:17 [16]	79, 80			n. 29
5:5 [4]	lv, 71, 72	5:17-18			6:7	lx n. 45, 87
5:6 [5]	72, 73	[16-17]	lx, 79		6:8	87
5:7a [6a]	73	5:18 [17]	75 n. 16,		6:9	l n. 26, liv,
5:7b [6b]	73		79, 80			lv, 87, 88,
5:7 [6]	138 n. 21,	5:18b-19				129 n. 2
	159 n. 16,	[17b-18]	155		6:9-12	94
	161 n. 22,	5:18-19			6:10	lx n. 45, 87
	165 n. 33	[17-18]	xliv, liii n.		6:11	lx n. 45, 88
5:8 [7]	xlvii, 73,		35, 80, 81,		6:12	lx n. 45,
	74		96			88, 96, 135
5:8-20 [7-19]	73	5:18-20				n. 17, 157
5:9 [8]	29, 75,	[17-19]	80			n. 14
	76	5:19 [18]	lx, 75 n.		7	55, 107, 111
5:10 [9]	75, 75 n.		16, 77, 81,		7:1	xxvi, liv,
	16, 76, 77,		83 n. 2			lv, 40, 89,
	95 n. 29	5:20 [19]	63			89 n. 14,
5:10-11		6:1	lx n. 45, 4,			89 n. 15,
[9-10]	76		31 n. 30,			92, 93
5:10-12			59 n. 30,		7:1-3	88, 107
[9-11]	78		87, 90		7:1-4	92, 94, 140
5:11 [10]	75 n. 16,	6:1-2	57 n. 26		7:1-6	89 n. 16
	76	6:1-5	66		7:1-10	4
5:12 [11]	24, 31 n.	6:1-8	83		7:1-14	88, 95–97
	30, 75 n.	6:1-12	83		7:1-20	104

7:2	liv, lv, lix, lxi, lxi n. 46, 90, 93, 93 n. 25		16, 161 n. 22, 165 n. 33		106 n. 21, 112, 114, 115 n. 49, 116, 119
7:2-4	130, 134 n. 15	7:19	xlvii, 103, 107	7:27-29	114
		7:19-20	4	7:28b	115
7:3	liv, lv, 31 n. 30, 90, 93, 93 n. 25	7:20	lx, 103–5	7:28	lvi, lix, lxi, 6, 108, 115, 116, 122, 123
		7:21	24, 105		
		7:21-22	105, 106		
7:4	92–94, 104	7:22	lxiv, lxv, 105, 106, 106 n. 21, 115, 158, 165	7:29	lx n. 44, 113, 116
7:4-12	107			8:1a	127
7:5	liv, lv, lviii, lxi n. 46, 90, 94	7:23	107, 110, 116	8:1	lx n. 45, 127, 129–31, 157 n. 14
7:5-14	94				
7:6	li, 94, 95	7:23-24	107, 111		
7:7	94, 104	7:23-29	110–12	8:1-9	127
7:8	liv, lv, 90, 94	7:25	29, 107, 110, 111	8:1-10	134
				8:1–9:6	127
7:9	94, 95	7:25-29	113	8:2	129 n. 4
7:10	lv	7:26a	113, 113 n. 43, 118	8:2-4	127, 128, 130
7:11	xliv, 95				
7:12	29 n. 28, 95	7:26	lvi, lxi, lxvi, 6, 107, 108, 108 n. 26, 109, 109 n. 31, 111, 112, 112 n. 41, 113, 114, 116–18, 120, 122, 123	8:3	31 n. 30
7:12-26	xxxvii			8:4b	128
7:13	12, 95, 116			8:4	136
7:13-14	95			8:5	31 n. 30, 128, 129, 165
7:14	lx n. 44, 83				
7:15	li, 56 n. 25, 100, 101, 137			8:6b	129
				8:6	129
				8:7	129, 131
7:15-18	66, 94, 100, 102, 168			8:8	127, 129
				8:9	xlvii, 31 n. 30, 57 n. 26, 59 n. 30, 129, 130
7:15-29	lxv, 84, 87, 99, 122, 169 n. 5	7:26-28	87, 103, 121, 167		
		7:26-29	8, 105, 116		
7:16b	101	7:27	lxi, lxii, lxii n. 47, lxiii, lxiv, lxv, lxv n. 58, lxvi n. 61, 106,	8:10a	133, 135
7:16	101			8:10b	134, 135
7:16-17	101			8:10	li, 56 n. 25, 57 n. 26, 131, 132, 132
7:17	101, 107				
7:18	102, 138 n. 21, 159 n.				

	n. 7, 132		161 n. 22,		n. 32, 141,
	n. 8, 133,		165 n. 33		143, 157
	133 n. 9,	8:14a	137	9:7-10	137 n. 20
	134, 135,	8:14b	134	9:7-18	141
	137	8:14	lii, 6, 131,	9:8	141
8:10-11	135		132, 132	9:9a	143, 144 n.
8:10-12a	131		n. 7, 132		7
8:10-14	131, 138,		n. 8, 134,	9:9b	155 n. 7
	165		136–38,	9:9	lvi, lxi,
8:10-15	100, 127,		168, 170		6, 8, 121,
	129–32,	8:14-15	122		123, 124,
	137, 139,	8:15a	131		141, 145
	168	8:15b	155 n. 7		147, 149
8:10–9:6	130, 141	8:15	xliv, liii	9:10	
8:11a	132 n. 8,		n. 35, liv,	9:11	147
	136		lv, lx, lx	9:12	157 n. 14
8:11b	132 n. 8		n. 44, 96	9:13	110
8:11	lx n. 44, 31		n. 32, 131,	9:13-15	57 n. 26
	n. 30, 132,		132, 136,	9:13-16	148
	132 n. 7,		137, 168	9:14	lviii, lxi n.
	134	8:16	12, 139		46
8:11-12a	135	8:16-17	139	9:15b	148
8:11-13	136	8:16–9:6	139	9:15	lviii, lviii
8:11-14	137	8:17	lx n. 44,		n. 43, lx,
8:12a	135		129, 139		lxi n. 46,
8:12b	131, 135	9:1	lx n. 44,		140 n. 25
8:12	31 n. 30,		139	9:16	57 n. 26,
	132, 132 n.	9:1-6	140		148
	7, 132 n. 8,	9:1-12	148	9:17	66, 86
	135, 138 n.	9:2	xlix n. 25,	9:17-18	148
	21, 159 n.		139–41	9:18	lv
	16, 161 n.	9:3	29, 31 n.	10:1	151
	22, 165 n.		30, 59 n.	10:1-20	151
	33		30, 140,	10:1–12:14	151
8:12b-13	131, 135,		149	10:5	31 n. 30,
	138 n. 22	9:4	lv, 140		59 n. 30
8:12-13	lii, 129,	9:5b	140	10:5-7	57 n. 26
	135	9:5	140	10:7	xlvii, 24,
8:13a	135	9:5-6	140		151, 152
8:13b	135	9:7	141, 146,	10:8	151
8:13	88 n. 11,		149, 155 n.	10:9b	152
	132, 135,		7	10:9	152
	138 n. 21,	9:7-9	xliv, liii n.	10:10	29 n. 28,
	159 n. 16,		35, lx, 96		152
				10:11	152

10:12-14	154	12:3	lix, 160,	9:10	41 n. 13
10:13	29, 31 n. 30		161	9:12	41, 41 n. 13
10:14	lx n. 44	12:4	161	9:15	41 n. 13
10:15-16	100	12:5	lix, lxi, lxi	9:16	41 n. 13
10:16-17	xlvii, 153		n. 46, 161,		
10:17	151		162	**Ezra**	113
10:18	153	12:6	162, 163	2:55	lxiv n. 54
10:18-19	153	12:7	129 n. 2,	2:57	lxiv n. 54
10:19	151		163, 163 n.	3:3	84 n. 3
10:20	xlvii, 153		32	4:1	84 n. 3
11:1	liii, 146 n.	12:8	lxi, lxii,	4:7–6:18	xxxvii n.
	12		lxii n. 47,		45
11:1-2	154, 155,		lxv, 6, 114,	6:16	84 n. 3
	157		159	7:12-26	xxxvii n.
11:1-10	154	12:8-14	lxiii		45
11:2b	155	12:9	lxi	9:1-2	84 n. 3
11:2	157	12:9-10	lxii, 164		
11:2-6	157	12:9-14	164	**Nehemiah**	113
11:3	157	12:10	lxi, lxv,	7:57	lxiv n. 54
11:4-5	129 n. 2		114, 164	7:59	lxiv n. 54
11:5b	158	12:11	164	9:6	106 n. 20
11:5	157	12:11-12	164	9:20	129 n. 2
11:6	157, 158	12:12	165	9:24	84 n. 3
11:7-8a	158	12:13	lx, 138 n.	9:30	84 n. 3
11:7-10	158		21, 159 n.	10:30-31	84 n. 3
11:8b	158		16, 161 n.	13:25-26	115
11:8	lx n. 45		22		
11:8-9	xliv, liii n.	12:13-14	164	**1 Chronicles**	
	35, 96 n.	12:14	31 n. 30,	16:3	lviii n. 41
	32		165	16:18	162 n. 25
11:9b	155 n. 7			29:15	135 n. 17
11:9	lviii, 145,	**Esther**	3, 41, 69,		
	158		93	**2 Chronicles**	
11:9-10	lx, 18 n. 1,	1:20	134	1:14-16	87 n. 10
	137 n. 20,	4	128	9:1	52
	159	4:8	51	9:13-26	87 n. 10
11:10	158	7:4	51	16:12	42
12:1	159, 163	8:3	52	22:10	52
12:1-8	158, 163,	8:5	51	23:13	52
	164	8:11	41 n. 13		
12:2	160	9:6	41 n. 13	**Tobit**	xxii

Judith   xxii
8:7   79 n. 21
8:32-34   41
9:7   53
11:1–14:4   41
14:7   91
16:2   53
16:5   53
16:12   53

Additions to Esther
                           xxii

Wisdom of Solomon
                           xxii
2:9   144 n. 6

Sirach (Ben Sira)
                           xxii, 12 n.
                           20, 108
6:24-31   112–13,
                           112 n. 42,
                           113 n. 43
15:6   91 n. 19
15:7-8   xxiii
24:23-34   xxiii
25:24   108, 108 n.
                           29
37:26   91 n. 19
39:9   91 n. 19
39:11   91 n. 19

40:19   91 n. 19
40:20   143 n. 4
41:11   90
41:11-13   91 n. 19
42:13-14   108
51:26   xxiii

Baruch   xxii
3:9–4:4   xxiii
3:12   xxiii
38:2   xxiii
46:4-5   xxiii

Letter of Jeremiah
                           xxii

Additions to Daniel
                           xxii

1 Maccabees
                           xxii

2 Maccabees
                           xxii

1 Enoch
42   xxiii

4 Ezra
5:9-10   xxiii
13:55   xxiii

14:40   xxiii

2 Baruch
48:33   xxiii
48:36   xxiii

Matthew
3:9   46
5:1-12   90
5:3   90
11:19   xxiii
11:29   xxiii
19:16-24   77
22:1-14   xxiii

Mark
8:31   xxiii
14:1-9   91

Luke
6:17-38   90
6:20   77, 90
7:35   xxiii
10:38-42   66
10:40-42   67
14:15-24   xxiii

John
1:1-18   xxiii
1:10-11   xxiii

Index of Subjects

Abel, l, 4

abortion, 55

absurd/absurdity, l, lii, lii n. 34, lviii, 4, 6 n. 9, 66, 77, 81, 129 n. 2, 131, 134–37, 141, 145, 168

Adam, lvi, lvi n. 37, 24, 57, 68, 80, 97, 103, 109, 118, 125, 131, 147

advantage, 7, 29, 30, 57, 74–76, 81, 85, 87, 90, 95, 145, 153

agricultural, 41, 41 n. 12

Ahiqar, 128, 128 n. 1

Allred, Lance, 156, 156 n. 8, 156 n. 11, 157 n. 13

Amidah, 9

androcentric, xxx, xxxvii, xlix, lxix, 33, 58, 82, 104, 115–16, 124, 130, 140, 147, 152, 165, 170

anoint, 91, 143

Anthony, Susan B., lxviii

apocalyptic/apocalypse, 158–61, 164

Bachmann, Mercedes Garcia, xv, 150

baking, 81, 146, 155, 156 n. 10

beer, liii, 143, 146 n. 12, 154, 155, 155 n. 5, 155 n. 6, 155 n. 7, 156, 156 n. 8, 156 n. 9, 156 n. 10, 156 n. 11, 157, 157 n. 13

Bergant, Dianne, lxix, lxix n. 72

Bird, Phyllis, xxxi n. 20, xxxi n. 23, xliv, xliv n. 12, lxxi, 7 n. 10, 10 n. 15, 40 n. 8, 60 n. 32, 74 n. 13, 96, 96 n. 35, 110 n. 38

birth, lv, 9, 10, 38–40, 41 n. 10, 42, 48, 49, 79, 89–92

Brenner [-Idan], Athalya, vii, x, xv, xvii, xxviii, xxx n. 18, xxxix, li n. 29, lxiii, lxiii n. 51, lxiii n. 52, lxvii, lxvii n. 66, lxix, lxix n. 72, lxx n. 72, 6 n. 9, 38, 38 n. 2, 38 n. 3, 50, 50 n. 19, 58 n. 28, 58 n. 32, 106 n. 21, 108 n. 24, 117 n. 58, 147 n. 16, 163, 163 n. 31, 169 n. 3

Brison, Ora, xv, xliii n. 8, 4

Byrds, 37

Camp, Claudia, lxxi, lxxi n. 74, 113, 113 n. 46

Camus, lii, 4

canon, x, xxvii, lxxi, 2–4, 85, 109, 121, 170

canonicity, xxxvii, xliii, 1, 3

canonization, 1, 2 n. 3

carpe diem, vii, viii, xlii, xliv, liii, liii
n. 35, liv, lv, lx, 8, 11, 12, 30, 32, 33,
33 n. 34, 34, 55, 56, 58, 63, 73, 75,
80, 83, 94, 95, 130–32, 136–37, 137
n. 20, 141, 143, 144 n. 7, 145–47,
155, 155 n. 7, 157, 159, 164, 168,
170
child/children, x, xiii, xv, xxiv, xxxvi
n. 43, xlii, xlii n. 5, xlix, lv, 8, 9, 30,
32, 41 n. 10, 42, 51, 66, 67, 74, 78,
81, 82, 84–86, 86 n. 6, 88, 88 n. 13,
90, 92, 157, 165
childbirth/child bearing, 8, 41, 51–52,
88
childist, 86
Choate, Laura, xv, 30 n. 29, 35
Christianson, Eric, 6 n. 9, 18 n. 1, 19 n.
2, 26 n. 22, 107 n. 23, 108 n. 24, 108
n. 28, 121 n. 71, 139 n. 23
Claassens, L. Juliana, 41, 41 n. 11, 42
n. 14, 94, 94 n. 27
classism, xlii
commandments, lx, 3, 51, 165
concubine, 22, 24–26, 30, 34, 142 n.
1, 144
cultic, 70–72, 140, 140 n. 24, 151

Daly, Mary, xxxvi n. 41, xli, xli n. 2,
lxviii, lxviii n. 70
daughter, vii, xvii, xix, xlviii, 42, 47,
48, 51, 72, 73, 78, 79, 124, 142 n. 1,
152, 159, 161
David, xxxv, xliii, lxii, lxiii, 2, 3, 53,
55, 85, 86, 148
Dead Sea Scrolls/Qumran, xliv, lxiv, 4
death, viii, xlviii, liv, lv, lx, 9, 18 n.
1, 29, 30, 32, 33 n. 34, 40, 42, 43,
49, 50, 53, 55, 56, 58, 63, 64–66, 79,
86, 88, 88 n. 13, 89, 90–97, 99, 101,
107, 108, 108 n. 29, 112, 113, 115,
117–19 n. 67, 124–30, 134, 139–41,
142 n. 1, 145, 147 n. 16, 148, 149,
158, 162–64
deuteronomistic, xlvi, 2, 136

divine justice, lii, 2, 130–32, 134, 137,
137 n. 20, 138, 167, 168
divorce, lxxi, 26, 145
drink, xliv, liii, lx, lxi, 8, 11, 31, 33, 56,
58, 75, 80, 81, 88, 93, 93 n. 25, 110,
131, 137, 141–43, 149, 151, 155, 155
n. 5, 155 n. 6, 156, 156 n. 8, 156 n. 9,
156 n. 10, 157
Duncan, Julie, li, li n. 31, lxix, lxx n.
72, lxxi, 94 n. 26, 103, 103 n. 9, 112
n. 41, 112 n. 42, 113, 113 n. 45, 148,
157 n. 12

Ebeling, Jennie, xliv, xliv n. 12, 40 n.
8, 41 n. 10, 41 n. 12, 77 n. 19, 88 n.
12, 146 n. 12, 146 n. 13, 146 n. 15,
151 n. 2, 155, 156 n. 10, 160 n. 17,
160 n. 19
Ecclesiastes (other than in citations or
quotes), lxi
ecology/ecological, xxxv n. 40, xxxvi
n. 44, lxviii, lxviii n. 70, 60–61
economic, xxxi, xlv, xlvii, lxxi, 68, 103,
145, 149
El Shaddai, 10, 10 n. 16
Eskenazi, Tamara Cohn, xxii, xxv n.
4, xliv, xliv n. 12, lxiv, lxiv n. 55
Eve, xxxiv n. 33, xlv n. 12, xlv n. 13,
xlvii n. 16, xlix n. 23, 39, 77 n. 18,
80 n. 23, 81 n. 25, 97, 108, 109, 118,
125, 146 n. 12, 151 n. 2, 160 n. 19
existential/existentialism, 27, 58,
63–65, 136, 140, 141
experience, xix, xxiii, xxiv, xxv, xxxiv,
xlviii, liii, lvi, lxviii, lxxi, 9, 10, 13,
14, 14 n. 24, 18, 21, 39, 40, 43, 49,
54, 56, 57 n. 26, 58, 59, 61, 63–65,
78, 80, 81, 85, 87, 100, 100 n. 2, 104,
108, 109, 111, 133, 136, 138, 147,
157, 164, 168–71, 171 n. 9

Farmer, Kathleen, xi, li, li n. 30, lxvi n.
62, lxix, lxxi, 18 n. 1, 66, 66 n. 2, 112
n. 41, 130 n. 6

father, xxv, xxxvi n. 41, xlviii, 20, 78, 79, 84, 85, 90, 125

feminist/feminism (other than in citations), xviii, xxi, xxii, xxiii, xxiv, xxiv n. 8, xxv, xxvii, xxviii, xxix, xxix n. 16, xxx, xxxi, xxxi n. 21, xxxi n. 23, xxxii, xxxiii, xxxiv, xxxvi, xxxvii, xxxviii, xli, xlii, xlii n. 5, xliv, xlvii, lvi, lix, lxii, lxiii, lxviii, lxviii n. 71, lxix, lxx, lxxi, 11, 14, 14 n. 24, 18–19, 23, 38, 39, 58, 59, 60 n. 32, 66, 73, 96, 104–6, 108 n. 24, 115, 122, 127, 130, 139, 142 n. 1, 155, 167, 169, 170

first person, xxvii, 4, 19–23, 28, 33, 34, 56, 63, 70, 77, 84, 99

folly, 13, 17, 18, 28, 29, 63, 101, 102, 107 n. 22, 110, 111, 113, 114, 121, 151, 152

Fontaine, Carole, lxix, lxx n. 72, 60 n. 32, 108 n. 24, 117 n. 58, 118 n. 60, 169 n. 3, 170, 170 n. 6

food/eat, xxix, xliv, liii, lxi, 8, 10, 58, 77, 80, 93, 93 n. 25, 110, 141, 145, 149, 154, 157, 158, 161

fool/foolish, l, liv, lv, lviii, 18, 29–31, 34, 35, 64, 65, 69–73, 85, 87, 89, 90, 93, 94, 95, 100, 101, 107, 110, 111, 112 n. 41, 120, 143, 152, 153, 164

foreign/foreigner, lxv n. 58, 1, 26, 42, 94, 110, 113, 114, 117, 120, 140, 153, 169

Frymer-Kensky, Tikva, xxx n. 17, 10 n. 15, 60 n. 32, 123, 123 n. 76

funeral, 10, 37, 37 n. 1, 92–93, 132, 133, 135

Gafney, Wilda, lxiv, lxiv n. 55, lxviii n. 71, 7 n. 10, 60 n. 32

garden, xxxiv n. 35, lxviii n. 71, 9, 10, 18, 22, 34, 81, 97, 121 n. 72

gender/gendered (other than in citations), xv, xxi, xxiv, xxvi, xxviii, xxxiii, xxxiv, xxxv, xxxvi, xxxvii, xlv, xlvi, xlvii, xlix, lvi, lvii, lviii, lix, lx, lxii, lxiii, lxiv, lxv, lxvi, lxvi n. 61, lxvii, lxviii, lxix, 1, 7, 20, 28, 38–40, 43, 46–49, 51, 57–58, 66–67, 72, 78, 81, 86, 96, 99, 103, 104, 106, 107, 114, 115, 121, 139, 140, 146, 149, 165

genderqueer, lxvi

generation, xix, xxii, 6–9, 60, 61, 120

Gilgamesh, 157

goddess/goddesses, 10, 10 n. 15, 10 n. 16, 123, 123 n. 75, 123 n. 76, 156

gossip, 105, 105 n. 17, 106, 106 n. 18

Great Emergence, 15, 15 n. 25

Greco-Roman, xlv, xlv n. 12, xlvi, xlvii n. 16, xlviii, 41 n. 10, 68 n. 5, 85 n. 5, 143 n. 4, 144

Greek, xxvi, xxxvii, xxxviii, xlvi, lxi, 9 n. 13, 14, 67 n. 3, 102, 124, 162

grind/grinding, xlv, lix, 11, 46, 47, 159, 160, 161

Hachlili, Rachel, xliv, xliv n. 12, 40 n. 8, 40 n. 9, 91 n. 21, 92, 92 n. 24

Havea, Jione, 58 n. 28

heart, liv, lv, 12, 14, 19, 20, 21, 25, 31, 47, 53, 55–57, 67, 71, 72, 75, 89, 93, 94, 100, 101, 107, 118, 125, 126, 129, 131, 132, 139, 142, 143, 152, 156

Heart Sūtra, li, li n. 29, lii n. 34, 6 n. 9

heaven, 13, 17, 18, 38, 71, 72, 160

hegemony, xviii, 40, 54

Hellenistic, xliii, xliii n. 7, xlviii, lxii, 40, 43, 77, 108, 146 n. 14, 157, 160

hermeneutic/hermeneutics, viii, xxxiii, xxxv n. 39, xxxv n. 40, xlii, lxix, lxxi, 14, 39, 56, 60 n. 32, 66

heteronormative, 24, 69

hevel, vii, xlix, l, l n. 26, li, lii, lii n. 34, liii, liv, lv, lviii, lxi, 4, 4 n. 5, 5–8, 10, 12, 12 n. 23, 13, 14, 17, 18, 26–28, 31–34, 63, 66, 70, 73, 76, 86, 88, 99, 127, 130–32, 134–37, 137 n. 20, 138,

139, 139 n. 23, 140, 145, 158, 159,
   162, 164, 168
hierarchy, xviii, xxxvii, xlii, xlvii, liv,
   lxviii, 23–25, 28, 54, 64, 73, 74, 87,
   103, 105, 106, 130, 153
hir, lxvi
Homan, Michael, 154, 155, 155 n. 5,
   155 n. 6, 155 n. 7, 156 n. 8, 156 n. 9,
   156 n. 10
homophobia, xlii
husband, ix, xxv, xlviii, 48, 52, 53, 55,
   71, 78, 110, 144

Ilan, Tal, xliv, xliv n. 12, xlviii, xlviii n.
   20, 41 n. 10, 68 n. 5, 79 n. 21, 85 n.
   5, 88 n. 12, 92 n. 22, 143 n. 4, 144,
   144 n. 8, 160 n. 17
inherit/inheritance, xliv, xlv, xlvi,
   xlvii, xlviii, xlix, 32, 35, 51, 68 n. 5,
   78, 79, 79 n. 21, 90, 95

Jerusalem, xii, xlv, xlvii, lxii, lxiii, 2, 3,
   12, 13, 19, 51, 74 n. 11, 156 n. 8
Jewish (other than in citations), xii,
   xv, xviii, xxiii, xxv, xxvii, xxviii,
   xxx, xxxvi, xxxvii, xlviii, lxi, 2, 3,
   5, 46, 144

Kedusha, 9
ketiv, 106, 106 n. 19, 162
ketubbot, xlviii
king, xii, xliii, xliv, liv, lix, lxii, lxiii, 2,
   3, 9, 9 n. 14, 12, 13, 22, 24–26, 28,
   29, 43, 48, 52, 53, 55, 65, 69, 70, 74,
   75, 85, 91, 128, 129, 129 n. 4, 130,
   143, 148, 154, 164
kong, li, li n. 29, lii n. 34, 6 n. 9
Koosed, Jennifer, xlii, xlii n. 4, lvi, lvi
   n. 38, lxv, lxvi n. 60, lxix, lxx n. 72,
   58, 58 n. 27, 68, 69 n. 6, 115, 115 n.
   50

Lorde, Audre, xviii, xviii n. 1, xli n. 1,
   xlii, xlii n. 5, lxviii n. 70, lxxi

"M" voice, lxiii, 50, 54, 163
Malleus Maleficarum, lxvii, lxx n. 72,
   14, 67 n. 3, 117, 117 n. 58, 118, 124,
   126 n. 78
Megilloth, lxii n. 47, 2, 2 n. 3, 29 n. 26
metaphor/metaphorical, 4, 46–48,
   81, 85, 88, 109, 110 n. 38, 111, 116,
   120, 161
Meyers, Carol, xxx n. 17, xxxiv n. 33,
   xliv, xlv, xlv n. 12, xlv n. 13, xlvii,
   xlvii, xlvii n. 16, xlix, xlix n. 23, 71
   n. 9, 77 n. 18, 80 n. 23, 81, 81 n. 25,
   146 n. 12, 146 n. 14, 151 n. 2, 160
   n. 19
midwife/midwives, 41 n. 11, 42, 42 n.
   14, 48, 94 n. 27
millstone, 47, 50, 148
miscarriage, 85, 85 n. 4
Mishnah/Mishnaic, xii, xliii, xlviii, 3,
   106 n. 21, 108
misogyny/misogynist/misogynistic,
   xxvi, xli, xlii, xlvii n. 16, lvi, lxvi,
   lxvii, lxx n. 72, 87, 100, 103, 105,
   107, 108, 108 n. 24, 109 n. 30, 111,
   114, 116, 117, 117 n. 58, 119–21, 123,
   167, 170
money, xxxiv, 58, 74, 75, 75 n. 16, 90,
   95, 153, 154
mortality, 2, 40, 92, 130
mourning/mourn/mourners, lv, 38,
   40, 40 n. 8, 41, 41 n. 11, 42, 43, 52,
   55, 89, 90, 92, 93, 93 n. 25, 94, 94
   n. 27, 96, 130, 133, 134, 157, 159,
   162

Ninkasi, 156
Noonan, Brian, 117 n. 58

oil, 90, 91, 125, 141, 142, 145–47, 149,
   151
Olojede, Funlola, xv, 124
omnipotence, 9, 95
oppression, xxxiv, xxxvi, xlii n. 5, 25,
   27, 63–65, 73–75, 89, 104, 127, 147

parable, lviii, lx, 67, 69, 70, 148, 164

Parker, Julie Faith, 86 n. 6, 88 n. 13

patriarchy, xxxvi, xlii, xlvii, xlix, 39, 54, 100

Pentateuch, xxxvii, xlvi, xlvii, lx, lxv, 115

perfection/perfectionism, 104, 104 n. 12, 104 n. 14, 105, 140

Persian, xliii, xlv n. 12, xlvi, xlviii, 84 n. 3

persona, xlvi, lxi, lxiii, lxv n. 59, lxvii, 1, 4, 11 n. 18, 27, 32, 115 n. 48

pleasure, vii, xliii, xlvii, liii, lix, 13, 17, 18–19, 22–28, 30, 30 n. 29, 32–35, 56, 65, 67, 71, 143, 144, 159

pleonasm, 19, 21

poverty, 27, 70, 137, 138, 147

pregnancy/pregnancies, 10, 41, 138, 147, 152

prophets, xxxvii, xli n. 2, xlvii, 28, 60 n. 32, 71

proverb/proverbs (other than in citations), xlvii, liii, liv, lviii, lxii, lxv, lxxi, 2, 3, 14, 23, 41, 43, 51, 53, 66, 67, 70, 72–73, 79, 82, 84 n. 3, 86–88, 90, 92, 94, 103, 105, 107–12, 113, 115, 116, 120–23, 124–28, 135, 145, 146, 151, 154, 162–65

Ptolemaic, xliii, 75

qere, lxv, 106, 106 n. 19, 162

Qoheleth: Date, xliii; Etymology, lxiii; Gender, lxiii

Qumran, xliv, 4, 139 n. 23

racism, xxxiv, xli

reformation, 15, 118

retribution/retributive, 56, 74 n. 11, 77, 85, 94, 95, 100, 101, 134–38, 168, 170

Ringe, Sharon, xxvii, xlii n. 4, 51 n. 20, 58 n. 27, 60 n. 32, 67 n. 3, 69 n. 6, 95, 108 n. 24, 115 n. 50, 163 n. 30, 169, 169 n. 3, 170 n. 6

ritual, xvii, 43, 52, 71, 77, 170

Roman, xxi, xxxiii n. 31, xxxvii, xlii n. 3, xlv, xlv n. 12, xlvi, xlvii, xlvii n. 16, xlviii, 41 n. 10, 68 n. 5, 77, 85 n. 5, 143 n. 4, 144, 160 n. 17

Rorschach, li, lii, 21 n. 10, 148

Ruether, Rosemary, Radford, xxxvi, xxxvi n. 42

s/he, lxvi

satire, lxvii, lxvii n. 68, 20, 22, 23, 28

Seeger, Pete, 37, 40

Seow, Choon-Leong, xliii, xliii n. 9, lxiv n. 54, 22 n. 13, 23, 23 n. 16, 24 n. 19, 70 n. 8, 128 n. 1, 129, 129 n. 3, 133 n. 10, 133 n. 11, 134 n. 12, 135 n. 17, 139 n. 23, 142 n. 2, 161 n. 20

Septuagint/LXX, lxi, lxii n. 47, lxv, 39, 76, 114, 133, 134 n. 13, 139

servant, 8, 50, 76, 77, 100, 105, 106, 110, 123, 148, 151, 153, 154, 162

sex, xviii n. 1, xxiv, xxxv, xxxv n. 39, xli n. 2, lvi, lix, lx, lxi, lxi n. 46, lxiii, lxiv, lxvii, lxviii, 19, 26, 42, 46, 49, 60 n. 32, 74, 78, 96, 104, 104 n. 11, 104 n. 14, 105, 119, 121, 126, 130, 143

sexual, xxii, xxiv, xxxv, lix, 8, 24–26, 38, 46, 47, 49, 50, 92, 143, 160, 161, 163

sexualized, 24, 39, 92

Siduri, 157

Sisyphus, 9, 10, 14, 81

slave, xxvi, 5, 24, 26, 42, 47, 76, 76 n. 17, 77, 122, 151, 152, 169

social location, 26, 66

Solomon, xxii, xliii, lxiii, lxviii, 3, 12–13, 25, 28, 52, 53, 87, 108, 115, 140

son, xix, xliii, lxiii, lxiv n. 53, 1–3, 20, 43, 48, 50, 53, 67, 69, 71, 78, 86, 146, 162, 165

sovereignty, 2

Spronk, Klaas, 147, 147 n. 16, 148

stained-glass ceiling, xlii
Stanton, Elizabeth Cady, xxvii, xxviii,
    xxxv, lxviii, 20 n. 5, 108, 109 n. 30
stillborn/stillbirth, lv, 66, 84–86, 90
Strange Woman, xlv n. 12, xlvi n.
    15, xlviii n. 18, 41, 84 n. 3, 87, 92,
    109–12, 112 n. 41, 113, 113 n. 46,
    114, 116, 117, 120–22
Sukkot, 2, 3
sun, liv, 7, 8, 13, 17–19, 31, 31 n. 30,
    32, 33, 56, 57, 59, 59 n. 30, 64, 65,
    74, 75, 80, 84, 85, 86 n. 7, 90, 108 n.
    24, 128, 130, 131, 132, 139, 142, 143,
    145, 149, 152, 156, 159, 160

Tabernacles, 2
Talmud, xxii, xxv, xlviii, 3, 108, 143,
    143 n. 4, 143 n. 5
Tamez, Elsa, lxix, lxx n. 72
temple, ix, xxii, xxv n. 4, xliv n. 12,
    xlv, xlv n. 12, xlvi, xlvii, xlviii,
    lxviii n. 69, 40, 40 n. 8, 71, 79 n. 21,
    82 n. 27, 84 n. 3, 88 n. 12, 91 n. 21,
    92, 133, 133 n. 11, 160 n. 17
test, vii, xliii, xlvii, li, lii, lix, 13, 17–19,
    21 n. 10, 22–28, 30, 30 n. 29, 32–35,
    67, 107, 144, 148
tetragrammaton, xxxvi, 2
theodicy, 14 n. 24, 74 n. 11, 99, 100 n.
    2, 139, 170, 171 n. 9
Thurman, Howard, 122, 169
toil, liv, lviii, lx, lxi, 7, 8, 10–12, 19, 22,
    30–34, 56, 58, 58 n. 28, 63–68, 73,
    75, 75 n. 16, 79, 80, 81, 85, 131, 132,
    139, 141, 142, 144–46, 148, 153
Torah, xxii, xxiii, xxv n. 4, xxvii n. 13,
    xxviii n. 15, xxxvii, lxviii n. 71, 7 n.
    10, 60 n. 32, 70–72
transgender, xxxv, lxvi, lxvi n. 63
Trible, Phyllis, xxxi n. 23, 25, 25 n. 21,
    60 n. 32
Turner, Marie, xv, lxix, lxx n. 72, 11 n.
    19, 61

Twitter/tweet, 30, 153, 154

unclean, 3, 40, 132

Van Dijk-Hemmes, Fokkelien, lxiii,
    lxiii n. 51, lxvii n. 66, lxix n. 72, 38,
    38 n. 2, 163, 163 n. 31
vow, lv, 2 n. 2, 51, 71–73
Vulgate, 1

Washington, Harold, ix, xliv, xlv, xlv
    n. 12, xlvi n. 15, xlviii n. 18, lxxi, 84
    n. 3, 95 n. 31
wealth, xlii, lviii, 12, 27, 28, 30, 32,
    34, 35, 66, 68–70, 73–75, 75 n. 16,
    76–78, 80, 81, 83, 83 n. 2, 84, 91, 103
Weems, Renita, xxxiv n. 35, xli, xli n.
    2, 60 n. 32, 122, 122 n. 74, 169, 169
    n. 5
Wei, Huang, li n. 29, lii n. 34, 6 n. 9
widow, 53, 67, 146, 163
wife, xlviii, lx, 47–53, 81, 84 n. 4, 115,
    121, 141, 142, 142 n. 2, 143, 143 n.
    3, 144, 144 n. 7, 145, 162
wind, l, liv, 7, 8, 12–14, 19, 31, 58,
    64–66, 70, 75, 85, 126, 128, 129, 129
    n. 2, 155, 162
wine, 17, 18, 141–43, 145–47, 151, 153,
    154, 156 n. 8
witch/witches, 117, 117 n. 58, 118, 118
    n. 59, 118 n. 61, 119, 119 n. 64, 119
    n. 65, 119 n. 66, 119 n. 67, 120 n. 67,
    124–26
Woman Wisdom, vii, xxii, xxiii, lxv,
    84 n. 3, 87, 94, 99, 107, 109, 111–14,
    116–17, 122, 144
womanist/womanism, xxxiv, xxxiv
    n. 35, lxviii, lxviii n. 71, 7 n. 10, 60
    n. 32
womb, 42, 74, 79, 81, 108 n. 24, 126,
    155, 157, 163

Zeus, 9

Author

Lisa M. Wolfe is Professor of Hebrew Bible, Endowed Chair, at Oklahoma City University, and also teaches for Saint Paul School of Theology, OCU campus. Lisa is ordained in the United Church of Christ, and preaches and teaches regularly in the community and across the country. Her Bible study DVDs "Uppity Women of the Bible," and companion commentary *Ruth, Esther, Song of Songs and Judith*, were published in 2010 and 2011, respectively. In 2018 she received the Distinguished Faculty Award for the OCU Honors Program, and the University Outstanding Faculty Award.

Volume Editor

Athalya Brenner-Idan is professor emerita of the Hebrew Bible/Old Testament Chair, Universiteit van Amsterdam, The Netherlands, formerly at the Bible Department, Tel Aviv University, Israel; and now research associate at the Free State University, South Africa.

Series Editor

Barbara E. Reid, OP, is a Dominican Sister of Grand Rapids, Michigan. She holds a PhD in biblical studies from The Catholic University of America and is professor of New Testament studies at Catholic Theological Union, Chicago. Her most recent publications are *Wisdom's Feast: An Invitation to Feminist Interpretation of the Scriptures* (2016) and *Abiding Word: Sunday Reflections on Year A, B, C* (3 vols.; 2011, 2012, 2013). She served as vice president and academic dean at CTU from 2009 to 2018 and as president of the Catholic Biblical Association in 2014–2015.